Globalization and the African Experience

Carolina Academic Press
African World Series
Toyin Falola, Series Editor

Africa, Empire and Globalization:
Essays in Honor of A. G. Hopkins
Toyin Falola, editor, and Emily Brownell, editor

African Entrepreneurship in Jos, Central Nigeria, 1902–1985
S.U. Fwatshak

An African Music and Dance Curriculum Model:
Performing Arts in Education
Modesto Amegago

Authority Stealing:
Anti-Corruption War and Democratic Politics
in Post-Military Nigeria
Wale Adebanwi

The Bukusu of Kenya:
Folktales, Culture and Social Identities
Namulundah Florence

Contemporary African Literature: New Approaches
Tanure Ojaide

Contesting Islam in Africa:
Homegrown Wahhabism and Muslim Identity in Northern Ghana, 1920–2010
Abdulai Iddrisu

Democracy in Africa:
Political Changes and Challenges
Saliba Sarsar, editor, and Julius O. Adekunle, editor

Diaspora and Imagined Nationality:
USA-Africa Dialogue *and Cyberframing Nigerian Nationhood*
Koleade Odutola

Food Crop Production, Hunger, and Rural Poverty in Nigeria's Benue Area, 1920–1995
Mike Odugbo Odey

Globalization: The Politics of Global Economic Relations and International Business
N. Oluwafemi Mimiko

In Search of African Diasporas: Testimonies and Encounters
Paul Tiyambe Zeleza

Intercourse and Crosscurrents in the Atlantic World: Calabar-British Experience, 17th–20th Centuries
David Lishilinimle Imbua

Pioneer, Patriot, and Nigerian Nationalist: A Biography of the Reverend M. D. Opara, 1915–1965
Felix Ekechi

The Tiv and Their Southern Neighbours, 1890–1990
Emmanuel Chiahemba Ayangaôr

The Women's War of 1929: A History of Anti-Colonial Resistance in Eastern Nigeria
Toyin Falola and Adam Paddock

The Yoruba Frontier: A Regional History of Community Formation, Experience, and Changes in West Africa
Aribidesi Usman

Globalization and the African Experience

Edited by

Emmanuel M. Mbah

and

Steven J. Salm

CAROLINA ACADEMIC PRESS

Durham, North Carolina

Library of Congress Cataloging-in-Publication Data

Mbah, Emmanuel M.
Globalization and the African experience / [edited by] Emmanuel M. Mbah and Steven J. Salm.
p. cm. -- (African world series)
Includes bibliographical references and index.
ISBN 978-1-61163-158-6 (alk. paper)
1. Globalization--Africa. 2. Africa--Economic conditions--1960- 3. Africa--Social conditions--1960- I. Salm, Steven J., 1966- II. Title. III. Series: Carolina Academic Press African world series.

HC800.M35677 2012
338.96--dc23

2012001333

Carolina Academic Press
700 Kent Street
Durham, North Carolina 27701
Telephone (919) 489-7486
Fax (919) 493-5668
www.cap-press.com

Printed in the United States of America

To Albertina Sisulu and
freedom fighters everywhere

Contents

List of Figures

Series Editor's Preface

The *Carolina Academic Press African World Series*, inaugurated in 2010, offers significant new works in the field of African and Black World studies. The series provides scholarly and educational texts that can serve both as reference works and as readers in college classes.

Studies in the series are anchored in the existing humanistic and the social scientific traditions. Their goal, however, is the identification and elaboration of the strategic place of Africa and its Diaspora in a shifting global world. More specifically, the studies will address gaps and larger needs in the developing scholarship on Africa and the Black World.

The series intends to fill gaps in areas such as African politics, history, law, religion, culture, sociology, literature, philosophy, visual arts, art history, geography, language, health, and social welfare. Given the complex nature of Africa and its Diaspora, and the constantly shifting perspectives prompted by globalization, the series also meets a vital need for scholarship connecting knowledge with events and practices. Reflecting the fact that life in Africa continues to change, especially in the political arena, the series explores issues emanating from racial and ethnic identities, particularly those connected with the ongoing mobilization of ethnic minorities for inclusion and representation.

Toyin Falola
University of Texas at Austin

Acknowledgments

This book was originally conceived in the mind of Emmanuel but it began to take shape during a discussion we had in a van on an early morning trip to the airport in Austin, Texas. We had both dealt with issues of globalization in our research and in the classroom, and we had just wrapped up a dynamic three-day conference full of ideas and now had the energy to push them forward. Authors responded to our call for papers and the project continued to mature. Along the way, babies, books, more babies, and academic duties served as speed bumps on the road but also kept us focused and pointed in the right direction. What you see before you today is the culmination of those efforts. No fruit is ever complete before its time and this one is now ripe for the picking.

We hope that this book does more than simply provide another chapter in the growing library on globalization in Africa. The term globalization has been buzzing around academic and media circles for more than two decades now, yet the more we read the less we seem to know. Perhaps, the following chapters will only add to this confusion but we look forward to the questions that arise and trust that they will add new ideas to the discussion. These chapters not only shine light on the larger subject of globalization but they draw evidence from individual experiences and research areas throughout the continent of Africa to provide new and unique perspectives on significant issues.

This volume owes its greatest thanks to the contributors who not only produced insightful and provocative chapters but who remained most patient while the publishing process moved forward. For them, we hope that this volume meets their expectations and we look forward to collaborative projects in the near future. To CUNY Staten Island and Xavier University of Louisiana, institutions that provided us with the space and resources to bring this to fruition, we express our thanks. Steve owes the utmost gratitude to his best friend and spouse, Susan Ranheim, and his two young sons, Sebastian and Dominic, who continue to provide new insights into life, love and happiness each and every new day. Emmanuel would like to thank his wife Ndah Njohjam, his two children, Ryan and Therese Eves, and all the wonderful colleagues and staff at CUNY/College of Staten Island, especially Mr. Aziz Mohamed, who made this project a complete success.

Emmanuel M. Mbah and Steven J. Salm
Staten Island and New Orleans
June 2011

Contributors

Julius O. Adekunle holds a Ph.D. in African History from Dalhousie University, Halifax, Canada. He is Professor of African History in the Department of History and Anthropology, Monmouth University, New Jersey. His research interests include culture, ethnicity, religion, and politics in Africa. He is the author of *Culture and Customs of Rwanda* (Greenwood Press, 2007); and co-editor of *Color Struck: Essays on Race and Ethnicity in Global Perspective* (University Press of America, 2010).

Maurice Amutabi is an Associate Professor in Social Sciences at the Catholic University of Eastern Africa. He has previously taught at Central Washington University, USA (2005–2010). Amutabi holds a PhD in History (Africa) from the University of Illinois at Urbana-Champaign, USA. He received his B.A (Hons) and M.A degrees from the University of Nairobi, Kenya. Amutabi is the author of *The NGO Factor in Africa: The Case of Arrested Development in Kenya* (New York: Routledge, 2006). Amutabi is co-author of *Nationalism and Democracy for People-Centered Development in Africa* (Moi University Press, 2000). He has also co-authored *Foundations of Adult Education in Africa* (Cape Town/Hamburg: Pearson/UNESCO, 2005). He has written two novels, *Because of Honor* (a novel on Islam in Africa) and *These Good People* (a novel on corruption in Africa). He is also the author of *Nakhamuma Stories* (a collection of short stories from the Abaluyia community of western Kenya). Amutabi's book *Islam and Underdevelopment of Africa* is forthcoming). His chapters have appeared in over two dozen books. His articles have appeared in several refereed and reputable journals such as *African Studies Review*, *Canadian Journal of African Studies*, *International Journal of Educational Development*, and *Jenda: A Journal of Culture and African Women Studies*. Amutabi has made presentations at over one hundred national and international conferences. He has served as the Vice-President of the Kenya Studies and Scholars' Association (KESSA), Kenya's premier research and academic organization.

Seth N. Asumah is SUNY Distinguished Teaching Professor, Professor of Political Science and Chairperson of the Africana Studies Department. Asumah is the author and co-editor of seven books and over 102 scholarly articles, book chapters, reviews and essays. He is President Emeritus of the New York African Studies Association. Asumah is Co-Director of the Summer Institute for Infusing Diversity into the Curriculum and has completed diversity, multicultural and teaching institutes at the National Multicultural Institute, Washington D.C. (2009); University of Michigan, Ann Arbor, MI (1998); Williams College, MA (1994); MIT, Cambridge, MA (1991); and Fisk University, Nashville, TN (1991). In 2006, he was a Scholar-in-Residence at the University of Oxford, England, United Kingdom. Asumah received the Outstanding Teaching in Political Science Award (American Political Science Association), 2008; the Rozanne Brooks Dedicated and Excellence in Teaching Award in 1999, and SUNY Cortland Excellence in Teaching Award in 2003. In 2007, Professor Asumah received the honor and rank of SUNY Distinguished Teaching Professor.

Toyin Falola is the Frances Higginbotham Nalle Centennial Professor in History and a Distinguished Teaching Professor at the University of Texas at Austin. He has published and edited more than 100 books.

Karen Flint is an Associate Professor of History at University of North Carolina, Charlotte. She is the author of several articles and chapters on health and healing in Southern Africa as well as *Healing Traditions: African Medicine, Cultural Exchange, and Competition in South Africa, 1820–1948* (Ohio University Press, 2008) which was a finalist for the 2009 Herskovits Award. Her research and teaching interests include: Southern Africa; science, technology and medicine; cultural studies; gender and sexuality; public history; and globalization.

Roshen Hendrickson is Assistant Professor of Political Science at the College of Staten Island (CUNY). Her research is on US relations with sub-Saharan Africa and the economic and political conditions structuring African countries' options in the global economy.

Emmanuel M. Mbah is Assistant Professor of History at the City University of New York, College of Staten Island. His research focuses on conflict, ethnicity, and socio-economic and political life of Africans in colonial and postcolonial Africa. He is the author of *Land/Boundary Conflict in Africa: The Case of Former British Colonial Bamenda, Present-Day North-West Province of the Republic of Cameroon, 1916–1996* (The Edwin Mellen Press, 2008); "Disruptive Colonial Boundaries and Attempts to Resolve Land/Boundary Disputes in the Grasslands of Bamenda, Cameroon," (*African Journal on Conflict Resolution*, Vol. 9, # 3, November 2009); and about a dozen chapters in edited volumes.

Shadrack Wanjala Nasong'o is Associate Professor of International Studies at Rhodes College in Memphis. He has previously taught at the University of Tennessee, Knoxville, and at the University of Nairobi, Kenya; in addition to serving as a visiting scholar in political science at Kenyatta University, Kenya, and as adjunct professor at Northeastern University, Boston, where he obtained his Ph.D. in public and international affairs. Nasong'o is author of *Contending Political Paradigms in Africa: Rationality and the Politics of Democratization in Kenya and Zambia* (Routledge, 2005), *The Human Rights Sector in Kenya: Key Issues and Challenges* (Kenya Human Rights Institute, 2009), editor of *The African Search for Stable Forms of Statehood: Essays in Political Criticism* (Edwin Mellen, 2008), and co-editor of *Kenya: The Struggle for Democracy* (Zed Books, 2007). His scholarly works have appeared in *African Studies Review, African and Asian Studies; Journal of Contemporary African Studies, Canadian Review of Studies in Nationalism, Estudios de Asia y Africa*, as well as in *Taiwan Journal of Democracy*.

Steven J. Salm is Associate Professor and Chair of the Department of History at Xavier University of Louisiana where he was named 2005 History Teacher of the Year. He received his Ph.D. from the University of Texas at Austin. He has conducted fieldwork in several West African countries and has received a number of awards and fellowships for his work, including a Boren and William S. Livingston Fellowship, an NEH grant, and several Mellon grants for collaborative research. He has published *Culture and Customs of Ghana* as well as many chapters and articles on topics as diverse as gender, youth, music, literature, religion, urbanization and popular culture. His writings have appeared in numerous academic journals and edited books, including *African Historical Research: Sources and Methods* and *Urbanization and African Cultures*, among others. He has published four edited volumes on urbanization in Africa, the most prominent being *African Urban Spaces in Historical Perspective* (Rochester, 2005). His forthcoming work investigates the development of youth culture in Accra, Ghana during the 1950s and 60s.

Bridget A. Teboh is Associate Professor of History at the University of Massachusetts-Dartmouth. She holds a Ph.D. in African History from the University of California Los Angeles. She specializes in African History, African-American Women's History, Women's and Gender Studies, and oral history. Her research interests are colonialism, post-coloniality, historical biography, women's *ikah* [power], African Diaspora, and historical ethnography. She has contributed scholarly articles and book chapters on African history, culture, and gender dynamics, the latest titled, "Science, Technology and the African Woman during (British) Colonization: 1916–1960: the Case of Bamenda Province," in Toyin Falola and Emily Brownell (eds.) *Landscape and Environment in Colonial and Post Colonial in Africa.* (London and New York: Routledge, 2010), "Reproducing African Communities in the US: Settlement Patterns and Social Organization," in Emmanuel Yewah and Dimeji Togunde (eds.), *Across the Atlantic: African Immigrants in the United States Diaspora* (Champaign, Illinois: The University Press/Common Ground, 2010). Dr. Teboh presently is working on two book projects, *Unruly Mothers, Combative Wives: Rituals, Women and Change in the Cameroon Grassfields c. 1889–1960* and *Her-story: The Life and Times of "Madame Maternity"*.

Globalization and the African Experience

Introduction: African Perspectives on Globalization

Emmanuel M. Mbah & Steven J. Salm

Introduction

Scholars have taken an increased interest in globalization since at least 1989. When capitalism seemed to score its victory over communism and the United States of America emerged as the lone superpower after decades of ideological conflict with the former Soviet Union, the pace of globalization grew more rapid while riding on the coattails of capitalism. Growing interest and scholarly research has brought increased debates, as globalization has come to mean many things to diverse intellectual groups who employ disparate theories to advance their arguments. The numerous theories surrounding the globalization debate are reflected in the difficulty in defining it. Many in the business community and those with economic interests, for example, have used the post-Cold War victory of capitalism to define globalization solely in economic terms. Others such as Jim Hite see it as, "an ongoing process by which markets grow and expand into a network that reaches around the world."[1]

This volume embraces a more inclusive definition of globalization. It begins with the assumption that it is not new; it is a process that goes way back in history and involves much more than just economics. Just as the quest for economic pursuits in distant geographical confines has been a preoccupation of mankind for several centuries, the spread of global political, religious, and socio-cultural systems and ideas has also been at work for centuries. Undoubtedly, the onset of the Modern Age in the late-fifteenth and sixteenth centuries marked the rapid expansion of the process, and this was brought about by new technological innovations that aimed to enhance the flow of people, resources, and ideas around the globe. This enhanced flow, together with changes in market conditions, brought societies together to a degree not seen previously in history. Still, one cannot gainsay that these changes became even more extreme in the post-Second World War era and have been exacerbated by the unfettered post-Cold War capitalism that has reinforced global connectivity and has reduced our world to the mighty global village that it is today.

The picture of the pros and cons of today's global village is not difficult to discern. The availability of nuclear energy for the supply of power far and near, air travel that makes it possible to move from one continent to another in a single day, and instantaneous high speed internet, fax, and telephone networks that instantly connect people in the most remote corners of the globe are some of the many advantages of globalization. But these benefits come with repercussions. The implications of the March 2011 earthquake and tsunami in Japan reflect the vulnerability of humans to nuclear annihilation, and the not so recent tragic terrorist events in the city of New York in September 11, 2001 have inspired a new awareness to the realities and full meaning and repercussions of globalization. This, however, comes decades after similar events such as the Lockerbie bombing in Scotland, the Chernobyl nuclear accident in the former Soviet Union, and the embassy bombings in East Africa had served as pointers to the realities of living in a world that has been transformed, virtually and practically, into a connected village. How best, then, can we define the concept of globalization without leaving out all its disparate parts? The best way to do this is to begin by reexamining some of the definitions of globalization that have been presented by scholars and professionals thus far.

Mapping the Scholastic Frontiers of Globalization

As a result of the numerous interpretations of globalization, the editors of this volume have decided to parse them under two sub categories. The first category utilizes the use of basic economic indicators such as capital flows as the basis for defining globalization. In his definition of globalization, for example, business magnate George Soros refers to it as the unhampered global mobility of capital under the control of giant multinational corporations that have used such power to dominate and control national companies. Expanding on this definition, Soros writes:

> Above all, globalization refers to the emergence of a world economy in which international financial transactions: stock, bond and futures market exchanges; and currency mobility are supplemented by a worldwide labor market and global production facilities. The integration of politics, technology, information, and capital has created a global marketplace that is characterized not just by global free trade but more specifically by the free movement of capital.[2]

From this definition, it is clear that Soros perceives globalization as a phenomenon that commenced in the aftermath of the Second World War with the emergence of truly global multinational corporations that had an unprecedented and significant impact on capital flow. Thomas Friedman of *The New York Times* also sees globalization from this same narrow economic lens, defining it as "the central organizing principle of post-Cold War society, an international order that has replaced the Cold War system so as to develop transparency and improve the efficiencies of economies worldwide."[3] Accepting Friedman's definition of globalization, Peter Schwab and Adamantia Pollis are not hesitant to add that "its distinctive feature [is] the contraction of time and space enabling [instantaneous] financial and communications transactions throughout the world." While Schwab and Pollis rightly argue that globalization reflects the existence of a global economy that goes beyond, and in some cases diminishes, the power of a state to the advantage of large Western financial and technological corporations, nothing seems to indicate in their argument that globalization is a phenomenon that transcends the narrow economic perspective of the post-Second World War period. This is evident in Schwab's definition of globalization as "a far more sophisticated and assertive contemporary economic development in which global production facilities are incorporated into a worldwide network where lightning-fast international financial transactions are the sine qua non of commerce."[4]

Gary Teeple's definition of globalization also falls in line with others in this first category. To him, globalization is more about the influence of capitalism in the spread of neo-liberal policies that espoused the uninhibited might of private property at the expense of social democracy, trade unionism, and the welfare state, a process that began at the close of the 1980s and was characterized in part by corporate demands to lessen restrictions on global capital flows that were part of the system before that date. This ushered in a process that changed the nature of production by placing more emphasis on internationalization as opposed to previous notions that hinged on national growth. The globalization of capital, together with those institutions that oversee its internationalization, has become, Teeple contends, the mantra of neo-liberalism whereby economics, not politics, is now the benchmark for societal decisions. As a result, Teeple posits, "semi-automated processes" have been replaced with electronics and computer applications in the production of goods and services. Political institutions are consequently undergoing transformation to meet these changes, which in individual states is eroding nationalized economic development as states are gradually being replaced by multinational organizations in overseeing socio-economic productivity.[5]

All four points of view, as well as countless others not discussed here, examine globalization from a narrow economic perspective. They examine economic globalization as a process that began principally only after the Second World War, negating earlier examples from past centuries. They also fail to consider other non-economic aspects of globalization. No one doubts how recent technologies such as the Internet, cell phones, and satellites, as well as recent transformations in the banking and capital flow operations of corporations, have transformed the lives of people living in Western and non-Western societies, especially those in Africa previously cut-off from such innovations. But to restrict the definition of globalization to these innovations negates a more encompassing view that sheds light on the impact of complex global exchanges on all aspects of societies.

In the second and final category are scholars who view globalization as a phenomenon that started a long time ago and is not exclusive to contemporary economic trends. Schaebler and Stenberg, for example, examine globalization as a process that encompasses "the ever faster and ever denser streams of people, images, consumer goods, money markets, and communication networks around the world."[6] Stanley Fischer of the International Monetary Fund (IMF) succinctly sums up this perspective by defining globalization as a phenomenon that is:

> multi-faceted, with many important dimensions—economic and social, political and environmental, cultural and religious—which affect everyone in some way. Its implications range from the trade and investment flows that interest economists, to changes that we see in our everyday lives: the ease with which we can talk to people all over the world; the ease and speed with which data can be transmitted around the world; the ease of travel; the ease with which we can see and hear news and cultural events around the world; and most extraordinarily, the internet, which gives us the ability to access the stores of knowledge in virtually all the world's computer.[7]

In his remarks at the France-Africa Summit of 2001 Fischer pointed out that while internet technology is increasingly less costly, necessitating reduced capital input, it has equally become more "human capital intensive," portraying severe socio-economic policy implications in all discussions involving globalization and internet technology.[8] The second category of definitions of globalization is more in line with the approach that this volume takes. The contributors of this volume view globalization as a historical process grounded in time and space; this includes the notion that the world has shrunk, and continues to shrink, due to scientific and technological innovations that have influenced many aspects of the human experience for more than half a century.

How Does Africa Fit in Our Narrative on Globalization?

Africa's experience at connecting with the rest of the world has been at worst pernicious, and at best contradictory and questionable. The culture of violence attendant to internal conflict, lack of infrastructure, and the poor performances of African economies have been blamed for the lack of connectivity between Africa and the rest of the world, especially during the last five decades. Questions arise, however, when scholars present globalization as a hegemonic concept of the West that is unconscionably applied to Africa and other developing areas, particularly in the realm of economics. We must go further than this to gain a complete and African-centered understanding of the continent's place within a complex globalizing world. This edited volume puts Africa at the center of globalization networks and expands the scope of globalization to include a variety of connected topics that influence everyday life in and out of Africa. It presents the complex nature of globalization by incorporating an historical perspective that explains current trends and inherent contradictions while revealing how Africans have perceived and interpreted the processes. In short, it accounts for the macro processes of globalization but it also shows how the micro processes affect individuals at every level of society.

This volume brings together ten chapters that focus on economic, political, and socio-cultural aspects of globalization and address the history of Africa, especially since the Second World War, from a variety of African perspectives. There is no shortage of scholarly works on globalization on and about Africa, but too often the topic is approached with a narrow focus on economic structures alone. Even then, scholars often portray Africa solely as a victim of the hegemonic and exploitative forces of world trade whose strings have been and are continuously pulled by Western puppet masters. The perspective is unquestionably that of scholars versed in economic principles grounded in Western societies, thus ignoring the impact of globalization on people throughout sub-Saharan Africa. Those that do make an attempt to analyze the concept more deeply have focused on a specific society or country and give only a nod to non-economic matters. James Maruba's edited work, *Globalization and Africa*, acknowledges in the preface that globalization is a combination of economic, technological, socio-cultural, and political forces, and yet the book focuses almost exclusively on the economic flows that characterize globalization.[9] One book that does address many of the important aspects of globalization is George Klay Kieh Jr.'s *Africa and the New Globalization*.[10] Although touching on issues of economics, human rights, development, government, and health, it is restricted by its definition of "new globalization" as the processes that began after the Cold War ended, thus narrowing its practical use to readers interested in a deeper historical analysis. This book, in contrast, focuses on the history of globalization in traditional, colonial, and independent African societies.

One of the earliest works on globalization to proffer another perspective is Paul Zeleza's *Rethinking Africa's Globalization*.[11] It moves away from the strict economic interpretation of globalization and addresses the macro theories and constructs behind globalization and Africa's place within it. It lacks, however, deeper political and socio-cultural analysis at the level of individuals and society. African intellectuals, universities, and academic exchanges all come into play in the context of post-colonialism and the place of African Studies. One recent project remains within the economic realm while another holds some hope for a more holistic approach, signifying that the issue of globalization is growing more and more significant within academic and non-academic circles alike. Pádraig Carmody's *Globalization in Africa: Re-colonization or Renaissance*? focuses largely on economic globalization and draws especially on the geographic areas of Chad, Sudan and Zambia, as well as the thematic areas of the commodity boom, the scramble for oil, lack of resources, and the increase in mobile phones.[12] The narrow thematic approach significantly reduces the potential readership and limits its use in the classroom. The themes also do not reflect the increasingly diverse perspectives of globalization as a multifarious force affecting African societies at all levels. Malinda Smith's *Globalizing Africa* represents a much more comprehensive approach to the subject, depicting the representation of Africa, the struggle for democracy and good governance, conflict resolution, human rights, economic challenges in post-colonial Africa, and intellectual and cultural knowledge on the continent today.[13] Although the topics are more diverse than previous works, it is still lacking a clearly defined focus on globalization from a variety of African perspectives.

In addition to presenting significant issues in the context of globalization from multiple African perspectives, this book is also unique because it is a suitable text for teaching a Modern Africa course. In the realm of textbooks on modern African history, there are a few but they do not successfully deal with the issues of a modernizing and globalizing world, that is, Africa's connections with the rest of the world. Frederick Cooper's *Africa Since 1940: the Past and the Present* portrays the history of decolonization and the independence period in Africa.[14] It is unique in that it provides connections that span the Second World War to the early twenty-first century but it takes a largely political view and fails to provide any meaningful portrayal of the lives of everyday people. Paul Nugent's *Africa Since Independence: A Comparative History* is an excellent source on the various colonial legacies of independent African countries but it does a less than stellar job of tackling issues of globalization.[15] One of the finest textbooks on contemporary Africa is Toyin Falola's edited volume, *Africa, Vol. 5*, but with its 38 chapters it may be too lengthy for instructors looking to dedicate only a segment of a semester's class to post-Second World War Africa.[16]

This volume's strength lies in its ability to approach post-Second World War African history with a twenty-first century definition of globalization while also presenting salient issues from various African perspectives, past and present. Unlike, for example, the pessimistic emphasis on corruption and conflict contained within the 768 pages of Martin Meredith's *The Fate of Africa: A History of Fifty Years of Independence*, this book presents a more balanced view of African agency, both positive and negative, in the face of global pressures.[17] Overall, this edited volume offers unique insights into African history since the Second World War with a particular focus on Africa's place within the processes of globalization.

How the Book is Partitioned

Our goal in designing this book is to produce a resource that would be used both as a scholarly guide to everyone interested in African perspectives on globalization and as a textbook for modern-era African history courses. The bulk of the chapters are penned by Africans and written by scholars from many different academic areas. The ten chapters are presented in two sections. The respective themes in each chapter are woven through individual chapter analysis to reinforce our central arguments about the age-old and multi-faceted nature of globalization. Individual contributors have focused on specific aspects of this multi-faceted phenomenon and how they affect Africa and Africans.

Part A, "Economic and Political Globalization," presents five different views of globalization in the economic and political realm: 1) an overview of precolonial activities; 2) African trade and monetary relations with the West; 3)

Africa's dealings with developing world economies; 4) the relationship between conflict and globalization; and 5) the negotiations between NGOs, the state, the market and civil society. In Chapter 1, "Globalization in the Pre-Contemporary Period," Julius Adekunle discusses the various ways that people from different parts of the world related to one another in the past. He posits that the concept of globalization in pre-colonial Africa was premature despite numerous inter-regional and inter-group contacts and relations. Although Africa had contact with Europeans, it was only North Africa that experienced significant political, economic, and social relations with the Arabs, Greeks, and Romans before the fifteenth century. The Swahili states on the coast of East Africa also had early contact with the Arabs, Chinese, and Indians. The rest of sub-Saharan Africa engaged in more significant contacts with Europeans only in the first half of the fifteenth-century when the Portuguese were trying to find a sea route to Asia. In the process, the Portuguese established commercial and religious relations with the rulers of the Kingdoms of Benin, Warri, Kongo, and others. Of course, the trans-Atlantic slave trade provided profound evidence of African-New World-European relations for a period of approximately four hundred years. But the process of lasting relations with Europeans, leading to contemporary globalization, began only in the second half of the nineteenth century, when the era of new imperialism commenced. The chapter ends with a survey of the various inter-group and inter-regional relations that existed in the African continent in pre-colonial time, as well as how the continent has adjusted to the concept of globalization since the end of the Second World War.

Despite their historical integration into the global economy, African states account for such a small proportion of global flows of trade and finance that they play a marginal role in decision-making within most powerful international economic organizations. In Chapter 2, "Global Economies: Africa and the West," Roshen Hendrickson describes Africa's position in the web of global economic relations, addressing both historical economic trends and critical debates about free trade and foreign investment. On trade and financial policy, African states have increasingly challenged the imposition of economic ideas originating in the United States and Europe, though their bargaining power is limited. Domestic African economic decision-making has been constrained by the necessity to implement neo-liberal reforms in exchange for access to trade and financial opportunities. The failures of externally-imposed structural adjustment programs and international development assistance to instigate significant reductions in poverty have highlighted the need for alternative economic approaches. Hendrickson comments on recent developments as both state and sub-state actors have sought adjustments in traditional power relations, and have offered new ideas about economic possibilities. At the state level, there are renewed efforts to increase regional economic cooperation, form a united front in multi-national negotiations, and insist on more development oriented investment deals. At the sub-state level, domestic Non-Governmental Organizations (NGOs) and social entrepreneurs are challenging both centralized state control and the controlling influence of foreign financiers. In this chapter, Hendrickson makes it clear that African economies provide interesting opportunities for experimenting with alternatives to the neo-liberal policies encouraged by Western powers and the global economic institutions they dominate.

Chapter 3 in this section examines Africa's relations with other developing nations. Shadrack Nasong'o starts the chapter by positing that prior to the twenty-first century, the global economy was dominated by the industrial countries of the Global North (GN) with countries of the Global South (GS), especially African countries, dependent on them for economic aid, markets for their primary products, as well as moral and ideological political support. Since then, especially at the beginning of the twenty-first century, global economic relationships seem to have flipped toward self-reliance with increasing South-South economic partnership. The most positive attribute of South-South cooperation is that such partnership is less bureaucratic, less politically and strategically conditional and more in touch with the realities on the ground than economic cooperation between GN and GS countries. Nasong'o, therefore, argues that relations between African countries and other GS nations constitute an effort to break free from the economic conditions imposed by Western powers and shield themselves from the fragile economies of the industrial world. The chapter concludes that given the emerging South-South economic partnership, GN countries can no longer count on ready access to raw materials and consumer markets in GS countries where strategic GS rivals, particularly China, are gaining greater influence facilitated largely by the South-South cooperation framework.

In Chapter 4, "Globalization and African Conflict," Emmanuel M. Mbah unveils the historical context that led to heightened levels of conflict in Africa and ties it to increasing levels of globalization. It is an incontrovertible axiom that the technological advancements in travel that ushered in the fourteenth and early fifteenth-century European intrusion in the African continent opened it up to global forces in a new way. For the next three hundred years Europe would turn to Africa for human capital through the transatlantic slave trade in order to sustain a global economy that was increasingly perched on the products of the plantation-industrial complex. There is no denial that the heightened level of conflict in Africa during this period was a product of global labor demands. Then came the agricultural and industrial revolutions of the eighteenth and nineteenth centuries, during which period the quest for global sources of raw materials and markets, as well as the zeal to spread European ideals, led to a second European intrusion in the continent. The result was conflict throughout Africa as Africans attempted to repulse European occupation. The negative impact bequeathed by European colonial rule in Africa such as arbitrary boundaries, ethnic dysfunction, and ideological confusion have conspired with the new global forces of resource accumulation, arms proliferation, religious fundamentalism, terrorism, and piracy, amongst others, to establish a permanent relationship between conflict and globalization in the African continent.

Development reinforces globalization and vice versa. Since the 1960s there has been growing evidence of the inability of the African state to deliver its development promise, making it "weak" or "soft"—in other words, it is unable to fulfill its development objectives. In the last chapter of Part A (Chapter 5), "NGOs, Civil Societies, and Development in Africa," Maurice Amutabi examines the role of NGOs in development, especially how these organizations have negotiated with three competing and sometimes oppositional forces: the state, the market and the civil society (so-called stakeholders in development). Examining case studies from mainly Anglophone Africa, Amutabi argues that the withdrawal of the state has allowed market forces and NGOs to move more effectively into areas of service provision in many African countries. He contends that the decline of the state and the emergence of the neo-liberal hegemony of the Washington consensus such as the World Bank and the International Monetary Fund (IMF) and donor preference for the "Third Sector" have transformed NGOs from autonomous agents of "alternative development" into Public Service Contractors (PSCs). As PSCs, their aim is to fulfill contractual obligations, such as road-building, construction of bridges, delivery of piped water, provision of health services, and running private schools and colleges. When NGOs present themselves as PSCs, they become profit driven, acting as business enterprises and cease to be philanthropic. This chapter demonstrates that the neo-liberal logic of the donor-led welfare system privileges market forces, which are often detrimental to civil societies. Amutabi interrogates the new emphasis on neo-liberal-type projects such as privatization of land, ecotourism, health, water, education, and whose concern with economic material improvement does not benefit so much the very poor, but the relatively wealthier elements in Africa. He also examines the development of the dualistic pattern of provision of services, in which the economically active segment of the population must seek services in the market place directly, by paying for them, where market forces are fully unleashed whereas the remaining section of the population, often the so-called underclass or lower class, receive assistance by way of a "safety net" put in place through contractual relations between local authorities and voluntary agencies.

Part B, "Socio-Cultural and Intellectual Globalization," also offers five chapters: 1) globalization's impact on women and gender relations; 2) health and Africa's place within globalizing medical and biomedical industries; 3) western influences on African traditional culture and development; 4) the influence of global cultures on African urban youth and popular culture; and 5) Africa's role in the intellectual globalization of Blackness. Central to the dialectical relationship between Africa and globalization is the imbalance within the dogma of profit maximization, ethical values and gender equality. In Chapter 6, "Gender and Globalization in Africa," Bridget Teboh examines one of the most contentious issues of our time—globalization and its impact on women, and by extension on gender relations, during the twentieth and twenty-first centuries. Teboh argues that far from being a disembodied force, globalization takes place through people and institutions that together determine its direction. While debates about the advantages or disadvantages of globalization rage on, it is no secret that following African colonization and its differential gender impact, poverty has been feminized while gender discrimination and a disregard for basic human rights have been institutionalized in most African economic and political spheres. Of the 1.3 billion people living in poverty today, 70 percent are women, and most of them live in Africa. How, therefore, have global interactions affected women in Africa? Using gender as a category of analysis this chapter explores the ways in which African women have protested their positions and navigated multiple roads to globalization, a process that links them to the West. It also analyzes women's responses to global economic, political, and socio-cultural processes using self-help thrifts and loan schemes, transnational pursuits, and political ideas of democracy. Teboh posits that although globalization may offer hope, its concrete benefits have not been equitably distributed between genders and between nations of the world. Thus like the continent of Africa, women have benefitted the least from globalization and remain disadvantaged in many areas of life, despite significant efforts by actors in global processes.

On a macro level, the health of Africans has been held hostage by global agricultural and medical policies that enhance the power of the dominant economies but exacerbate food and health crises within the continent. Divided into four parts, Chapter 7, "Impact of Globalization on Health, Food Security, and Biomedicine in Africa," by Karen Flint and Bridget Teboh, examines the historical precedents behind some of today's major issues regarding public health and biomedicine in African societies. The first part focuses on the spread of tropical and communicable diseases; it examines this topic from early global trade routes that exposed Africans to Afro-Eurasian diseases, to the Columbian exchange and more recent migration patterns inside and out of Africa. The second part turns to issues of international trade and agriculture and their impact on food insecurity in African societies. It also looks at the history and future prospects for a Green Revolution in African states. The third part assesses the role of Africa as a laboratory for experiments; a phenomenon that began during the colonial period, but has persisted to this day, as witnessed by more recent actions undertaken by pharmaceutical companies and NGOs in Africa. The final part of the chapter examines the rise of the HIV/AIDS pandemic and argues that Africans' perceptions of globalization have played an important role in their responses to this health crisis.

Culture is an important component of globalization. The analyses of issues that affect African cultures and the process of development cannot be fully comprehended and appreciated without a critical evaluation and meta-cognition of the African world and the entities that reside outside the boundaries of Africa. Globalization makes cultural and development issues in Africa inescapable in understanding the totality of the global human condition. African history, cultural studies, and development research must, therefore, consider cross-cultural dynamics, structural and systemic variables that contribute to sustainable development in order for the continent to thrive. Yet, within the processes of modernization and development, the convergence theory maintains that once African cultures are exposed to the forces of modernization and development, the marginal propensity of abandoning African cultures in the interest of Western ones is very high, hence dependency, Coca-colization, McCulturalization and Chinanization. The development of underdevelopment of Africa, some argue, is attributable to cultural values and histories that tend to impede the process of modernization and development. Eminent scholars such as Talcott Parsons, Samuel Huntington, David Apter and Lucian Pye have suggested that the transformation of African cultures is "the most crucial step in the modernization process"[18]

The third and fourth chapters of this section focus on globalization and African cultures but they take very different approaches. In Chapter 8, "African Cultures, Modernization and Development: Reexamining the Effects of Globalization," Seth Asumah argues that the global forces of modernization, development, and Chinanization contribute to the bastardization and gradual extinction of African histories and cultures, and that unless Africans are able to navigate the dynamics of cultural imperialism from the United States, Europe and China to become true development partners of the West and China, and not just exotic "cultural objects" for the global village, African histories and cultures could become extinct. Asumah also posits that Africa's underdevelopment will continue to be irrepressible because complex development issues, problems, and questions are likely to be relegated to the hegemonic powers of the global village with little reference to the historical and cultural contexts of Africans.

In Chapter 9, "Africanizing the West: Changing Expressions of Popular Culture among Urban Youth," Steve Salm takes quite a different approach in exploring the impact of seemingly hegemonic western cultural forms by taking the perspective of African urban youth. He argues that, rather than always painting Africans as victims in the global cultural wars, we must acknowledge that they have also exercised a high degree of agency. African youth not only adopted foreign influences but they also actively adapted them and reimagined them to suit their particular physical and cultural environments, thus creating new forms that in some instances became part of what was considered traditional culture. For years scholars have emphasized the development of creolized cultural forms in the many communities of the African diaspora. Yet, too often, many of these same individuals want to preserve the idea or ideal of a "traditional" Africa that exists only on the pages of *National Geographic.* Simply portraying the spread of sounds and images from around the world into Africa as cultural imperialism is not enough; we must also emphasize Africans as cultural brokers who play a lead role in deciding what can be *retained* from the past and present and what can be *obtained* for the future.

Writing about "The Centralization of Africa and the Intellectualization of Blackness," (Chapter 10), Toyin Falola examines the process of knowledge creation as it is generated around the black community. His analysis centers on how knowledge is constituted around the black experience (epistemology), how this knowledge is gathered and presented (methodology), and how it is put to use (activism). Aspects of this knowledge constitute a political manifesto—the use of knowledge to ensure the survival of the race, its emancipation from all forms of domination, and the generation of a proud future that must face the precipitous spread of global ideas and initiatives. Falola identifies a history to all these issues (process of knowledge production), a focus on the historical specificity of the black experience (focalization), as well as academic attacks on studies around blackness (hegemonic opposition) in this intellectually rich chapter.

As a whole, the ten chapters in this volume reinforce our central argument about the age-old and multi-faceted nature of globalization and the need to take a local and global approach in assessing its impact. While we certainly do not assume that this work has touched on every aspect of globalization, nor that it has expounded on the differences among all African societies, it offers an African-focused approach to significant issues, an approach that will prove most useful within the classroom. It also presents more detailed scholarship that those with a keen interest in globalization and African history will find extremely useful.

Bibliography

Carmody, Pádraig. *Globalization in Africa: Re-colonization or Renaissance?* Boulder, CO: Lynne Rienner, 2010.

Cooper, Frederick. *Africa Since 1940: the Past and the Present.* Cambridge: Cambridge University Press, 2002.

Edi, Eric M. *Globalization and Politics in the Economic Community of West African States.* Durham, N.C.: Carolina Academic Press, 2007.

Falola, Toyin (ed.), *Africa, Vol. 5.* Durham, NC: Carolina Academic Press, 2003.

Fischer, Stanley. "The Challenge of Globalization in Africa." Remarks Presented at the France-Africa Summit, Yaoundé, Cameroon, January 19, 2001. Stanley Fischer held the post of First Deputy Managing Director of the International Monetary Fund.

Grant, Richard. *Globalizing City: The Urban and Economic Transformation of Accra, Ghana.* New York: Syracuse University Press, 2009.

Handelman, Howard. *Challenges of Third World Development.* 6th Edition. New York, N.Y.: Longman, 2011.

Herbst, Jeffrey. "Africa and the Challenge of Globalization." Paper Presented at the Conference on Globalization and Economic Success: Policy Options for Africa. Singapore, November 7–8, 2005.

Hite, Jim. "Land Use Conflicts on the Urban Fringe: Causes and Potential Resolution." Presented at the Strom Thurmond Institute of Clemson University, SC, 1998.

Kieh Jr., George Klay ed. *Africa and the New Globalization.* Surrey: Ashgate Publishers, 2008.

Maruba, James L. *Globalization and Africa.* New York: Nova Science Publishers, 2008.

Meredith, Martin. *The Fate of Africa: A history of Fifty Years of Independence.* New York: Public Affairs, 2006.

Nugent, Paul. *Africa Since Independence: A Comprehensive History.* Hampshire: Palgrave, 2004.

Schaebler, Birgit and Stenberg, Leif eds. *Globalization and the Muslim World: Culture, Religion, and Modernity.* First Edition. New York: Syracuse University Press, 2004.

Schwab, Peter. *Africa: A Continent Self-Destructs.* New York: Palgrave, 2001.

Smith, Malinda. *Globalizing Africa.* Trenton, NJ: Africa World Press, 2010.

Teeple, Gary. *Globalization and the Decline of Social Reform: Into the Twenty-First Century*. 2nd Ed. Ontario: Garamond Press, 2000.

Zeleza, Paul Tiyambe. *Rethinking Africa's Globalization*. Trenton, NJ: Africa World Press, 2003.

Part A

Economic and Political Globalization

Chapter 1

Globalization in the Pre-Contemporary Period

Julius O. Adekunle

Introduction

Emmanuel Mbah and Steven Salm noted in the general introduction that globalization in Africa is not new; it has been in existence for centuries and today constitutes an essential part of interdisciplinary study. Because many factors bring out the interconnectedness of the world, it is pertinent to consider the various ways in which people from different parts of the world related to each other in the past. This chapter, therefore, elaborates further on the concept of globalization in Africa as it existed in the form of inter-regional and inter-group contacts and relationships. Although all of Africa had contact with non-Africans at different times, North Africa, a strategic region that connected Europe to Asia, experienced significant political, economic, and social relationships with the Arabs, Greeks, and Romans before the fifteenth century. Later, the Swahili states on the coast of East Africa had frequent contact with Arabs, Chinese, and Indians within the context of the sprawling Indian Ocean trade. The rest of sub-Saharan Africa came in contact with Europeans in the first half of the fifteenth-century when the Portuguese were on exploration to find a sea route to Asia. In the process, they established commercial and religious relationships with the rulers of Benin, Warri, the Kongo kingdoms, and others.

The trans-Atlantic slave trade provided profound evidence of a tragic African-European relationship for a period of approximately four hundred years. The abolition of the slave trade by the middle of the nineteenth century produced a new dimension to global connectedness through the rise of a new era of European imperialism. The introduction of this new interaction, which included the scramble for and partition of Africa into European colonies and spheres of influence, was part of a continuing process of globalization. As noted earlier, this chapter will attempt a survey of inter-group and inter-regional relationships and how Africa fit into the concept of globalization during this pre-contemporary period.

Africa and the World

Historical evidence, supported by science and archaeological discoveries, indicates that Africa is the cradle of humankind. From several parts of eastern and southern Africa, early humans dispersed to various parts of the world marking the beginning of global connectedness. The early civilization of Egypt provides a means to assess the advanced socio-political and economic culture that Africans developed, which further served to gain them exposure to the outside world. Biblical traditions indicate that the Hebrews served Egyptians as slaves for many centuries. Kush, an African ancient kingdom with its capital at Meroe, exchanged cultural, diplomatic, and economic relations with Europe and Asia Minor. With the birth of Christianity and its subsequent expansion, St. Mark introduced the religion to Egypt in the first century. Alexandria emerged as a cultural and religious center, where Hellenism, Judaism, and Christianity flourished.[1]

Egypt's proximity to Europe strengthens the argument on global connections. Separated only by the Mediterranean Sea, Egypt and the whole of North Africa engaged in multi-dimensional relations with Europe. Through cultural, economic, and diplomatic relations, Egypt's influence spread to the north. For example, North African peoples related closely with the Greeks, Phoenicians (modern day Lebanese), and Romans. The Phoenicians even established Carthage (modern Tunis) as a colony through which they benefitted from the North African economy. During the expansion of the Roman Empire, northern Africa became a target because of the political and economic rivalry between the Phoenicians and Romans. After defeating the Phoenicians in the Punic Wars, the Romans took over political control of North Africa simply to prevent the domination of another power in Africa. The Roman Empire was in control of North Africa until the Germanic migrations that took place in the fifth century A.D.

North Africa's connection to the east was partly the result of trade and religion. The founding and spread of Islam in the seventh century brought Arabs to northern Africa. Through this contact, Africans were exposed to Arabic and Islamic civilization as well as oriental trade. As in North Africa, West Africa experienced contacts with Arab merchants, missionaries, and scholars as early as the eleventh century. Arab scholars such as Al-Yaqubi, Al-Idris, Al-Bakri, Ibn Batuta, Ibn Fatua, and Ibn Sa'id not only visited West Africa, but also wrote on the culture and history of the region. Similarly, Portuguese travelers such as Joao de Barros, Duarte Pacheco Pereira, Duarte Pires, Olfert Dapper, and A. Dalzel had records of their visit to West Africa. On the east African coast, city states such as Kilwa, Malindi, Mogadishu, Mombasa, Pate, Pemba, and Sofala established trading and cultural connections with Indians, Chinese, and Arabs. The extensive and long interaction with foreigners led to the emergence of the Swahili culture and language.

Pre-Colonial Inter-Group Relations

Without gainsaying, Africa is a continent of ethnic, socio-cultural, and linguistic diversity. As numerous as the ethnic groups were, a number of similar practices indicated their cultural, social, and political interconnectedness. The multi-dimensional relations proved that African societies did not exist in isolation of each other. Diversity did not necessarily prompt ethnic violence or warfare but sometimes did. While each group maintained its ethnic and cultural identities, political expansion and economic domination were partly responsible for the internecine warfare that took place. For example, the Kuba kingdom in Central Africa comprised eighteen different ethnic groups under the Bushongo. As a result of migration and political expansion, the Twa were integrated into the Kuba kingdom. The Bushongo, however, permitted each ethnic unit to remain independent and maintain their cultural characteristics. The Kuba kingdom expanded and reached the zenith of its power by the mid-nineteenth century by warring against its neighbors.[2] In the kingdoms of Mwata Yamvo and Monomotapa, the multiplicity of ethnic groups brought about untold rivalries and frequent warfare. The rise of the Zulu to power in southern Africa brought several ethnic groups together. That diversity and interconnectedness still exists today in spite of the long pre-colonial history, colonial experience, and Western influence. Toyin Falola rightly put it that, "No African community could be treated as an island, removed from other communities."[3] This suggests that as there were regional connections within Africa, Africans also related with the outside world through different and various agencies.

Within each of the pre-colonial kingdoms, numerous ethnic groups interacted and intermarried thus providing the basis for the argument that ethnic identity was fluid. The emergence of Swahili society was the result of profound inter-group relations between the indigenous Africans and the Arabs. Also, the case of Rwanda with the extensive Hutu-Tutsi interaction and intermarriage makes distinction between the two groups, especially in physical appearance, sometimes difficult. Mobility and migration were possible from one region to the other, thus providing the genesis for economic and political inter-group relations. Pre-colonial inter-group relations were therefore established strongly on a political, economic, and social basis. African political philosophy involved the extension of power by stronger communities over the weaker ones. In all the kingdoms, expansionist policy dominated political thought and practice of the rulers. Wars were fought; captives were taken; kingdoms were dominated.

In the preface to his edited book, *Africa and the New Globalization*, George Klay Kieh, Jr. opined that globalization is not a new phenomenon, but "the various phases of globalization have had divergent scope, actors, dimensions and dynamics—that is, each of the phases of globalization can be differentiated according to these terms."[4] This viewpoint supports the argument that Africa was not an isolated geographical expression, but an integral part of the global system; it also reinforces the narrative of a globalized past raised in the introduction to this volume.

Pre-Colonial Inter-Regional Relations

Africans, like other societies of the world, developed the concept of state formation with the growth of urbanized, sophisticated, and orderly political structures. In these structures, there were socio-cultural, economic, and diplomatic relations. Trans-border trade was established; the most popular being the trans-Saharan trade, primarily between North and West Africa. Dominated by Arab and Berber merchants from the North and ubiquitous Wangara merchants in West Africa, the trans-Saharan trade served the purpose of moving goods across the regions.

Articles of trade included ivory, ornaments, agricultural produce, and slaves but the two most important were gold and salt. While gold was mined in the Bambuk and Wangara regions of West Africa, salt was produced in the desert in North Africa. Arab, Berber, and Wangara merchants settled in trading cities such as Gao, Ghat, Jenne, Sijilmasa, Taghaza, Timbuktu, and Walata. El Fazari, an Arab traveler, described the Ghana Empire in West Africa as the land of gold. A twelfth-century Arabic source also mentioned that, "in the sands of the country [Ghana] is gold, treasure inexpressible. They have much gold and merchants trade with salt for it, taking the salt on camels from the salt mines.

They start from a town called Sijilmasa ... and travel in the desert as it were upon sea, having guides to pilot them by the stars or rocks in the deserts."[5] Merchants often traveled in large caravans of between five to 1000 camels and the Tuareg people served as professional guides in the desert. Ibn Battuta, a fourteenth-century Arab scholar and traveler, referred to Taghaza as a prosperous trading city where merchants enjoyed the easy life. Mansa Musa (1312–1337), the King of Mali, went on an ostentatious pilgrimage to Mecca in 1324 and displayed the wealth of West Africa by generously giving out gold. By 1591 when the Moroccan invasion on the Songhay Empire occurred, the trans-Saharan trade had begun to decline. Although the Moroccans destroyed the trans-Saharan trade, the Portuguese succeeded in redirecting the trade in the interior of West Africa to the coast in their favor.

The Atlantic Slave Trade and Economic Globalization

Slavery was an ancient and universal institution and it represented the global connections that occurred in pre-contemporary times. It was practiced not only as an integral part of the economic system, but also as part of life in Greek and Roman civilizations. In Biblical times the Hebrews became slaves in Egypt where they performed hard labor. Everywhere slavery was practiced, slaves performed hard domestic and industrial labor. Herbert Klein argues that:

> While slavery was an institution known to many complex societies, slavery as a system of industrial or market production was a much more restricted phenomenon. Most scholars now date its origins for Western society in the centuries immediately prior to the Christian era in the Greek city-states and the emerging Roman empire of the period and argue that, for slavery to become a dominant factor in the society, it was essential that an important market economy at the local international level be developed, that a significant share of the agricultural production for that market come from non-peasant producers, and that slave labor become the major factor in that production.[6]

Outside Europe, slavery was practiced in the Indian and Chinese civilizations. Tomb burial in China became a popular phenomenon during the Eastern Zhou Dynasty (770–221 B.C.) when slaves and other items were buried along with rulers as sacrifices. In both ancient Europe and Asia, captives of wars became slaves and so were the children born of slave parents. This shows that slavery was an important ingredient of the global economy whether in the pre-industrial or industrial times.

Slavery also constituted an important part of the African economic system in pre-colonial times. Since many African societies were agriculturally based, the use of slave labor in the production system became a crucial factor. For example, the early empires of Western Sudan used slave labor in their agricultural production; the economy of the Oyo Empire was largely dependent on slave labor; and as Klein pointed out, "several of the Wolof states had agricultural slaves who produced for local consumption as well as for export."[7] Slaves were taken, sold, and bought from many parts of Africa and they traveled from one region to the other. In the trans-Saharan trade between North and West Africa, slaves constituted one of the primary articles of trade. The Swahili states in East Africa also used slaves for agricultural purposes.

Early written documents on East Africa indicated that slaves were procured from East Africa and exported to Arabia, Persia, and India in exchange for glass, beads, clothes, spices, and cowries. Black slaves were transported to the modern day Middle East, "across the Red Sea and Indian Ocean to Arabia, Iraq, and Iran, down the Nile to Egypt, and across the Sahara to the slave markets of north and northwest Africa."[8] Bernard Lewis, a prolific historian on Islam and Islamic civilization, pointed out that slaves were part of tribute payment, but they were also frequently purchased. The need for slaves according to Lewis, "led to a great expansion of slave raiding and slave trading on the frontiers of Islam, in Europe, in Asia, and above all in Africa."[9] Slaves in the Middle East were used as either palace guards or as warriors to expand the frontiers of Islam. Between A.D 868 and 883, there were numerous slave revolts which seriously threatened the Baghdad Caliphate.

Africans from East Africa were also shipped to India where some of them became successful as palace guards. Some even rose to the position of prime minister. For example, an African king of slave origin led Jaunpur to gain independence from Delhi in 1394. Similarly, an African army commander overthrew the civilian government until he in turn was overthrown by the leader of the palace guard, also of African and slave origins. Other individuals of slave ancestry included Mahmud Gavan, who became the African prime minister of the United Bahmani Kingdom, which flowered briefly under his rule, but fragmented after his death in 1481. Aside from numerous African military commanders who became famous in Gujarat, mention should be made of Sayeed al-Habshi, a wealthy noble who performed the pilgrimage to Mecca and generously fed approximately 1,000 people daily.[10] Evidence of the early African presence in the Middle East and Asia explains the role played by economics as an important factor in globalization. The slave trade in particular constituted a primary factor that linked Africa to other parts of the world before the commencement of the trans-Atlantic slave trade.

The fifteenth century marked the beginning of European expansion to sub-Saharan Africa. Led by the Portuguese in the Age of Discovery, Europeans penetrated Africa for economic, political, and religious reasons. The Portuguese intended to find a sea route to India for spices and to participate in the gold trade in Africa. In the process, they not only established commercial relations with African rulers, but they also introduced Christianity and Western culture in parts of the continent. According to Klein:

> The arrival of the Portuguese explorers and traders on the sub-Saharan African coast in the early 1400s would ultimately represent a major new development in the history of the slave trade in Africa in terms of the intensity of its development, the sources of its slaves, and the uses to which these slaves would be put.[11]

With the opening up of Africa, a period of intense economic relations with Europe had been inaugurated. When the Portuguese arrived in West Africa, they established plantations and employed Africans. It was then they conceived the idea of transporting Africans to Portugal for labor. Thus the voyages of discovery opened up Africa to European interaction and led to the beginning of the Atlantic slave trade. As the trade became lucrative and firmly established, explorers and slave dealers received political support from their home governments. Prince Henry the Navigator of Portugal, King Ferdinand of Spain, and Queen Elizabeth I of England in different ways supported and participated in the Atlantic slave trade. By the sixteenth century, sub-Saharan Africa had emerged as the principal source of slave labor that supplied the growing European economic system.

By the mid-fifteenth century, the Portuguese had reached the coast of West Africa and by the end of the century, they had arrived in South and East Africa. Although the Portuguese focused on participation in gold trade, they were also responsible for beginning the Atlantic slave trade. The first group of Africans transported to Portugal in 1441 became slaves. Portugal's monopoly of the slave trade was broken in the sixteenth century when other European nations began to participate in it. For example, the Spaniards joined in 1510, the English in 1562, the Dutch in 1620, and the French in 1640. To establish strong trade relations, the Europeans built forty-three fortified stations in West Africa with thirty-one of them located in the Gold Coast. The first and largest European station, Elmina Castle, was built by the Portuguese in the Gold Coast. The Portuguese also established fortified stations in Senegambia, Upper Guinea, and Angola, their three most important sources of the Atlantic slave trade. The trading stations served the purposes of expanding European economic and political influence and interests to the interior and the growth of the Atlantic slave trade between the sixteenth and seventeenth centuries. In turn, European-African relations increased substantially.

The Portuguese founded trading stations in East and Central Africa as well. From their stations in Mombasa and Kilwa in East Africa they tried to control the gold trade that originated from Sofala, but their economic and cultural relations did not last, except in Mozambique. Before the Portuguese arrived, the Arabs, Indians, and Persians, had established a network of commercial relations with the people of East Africa. Arab and Persian cultures and languages as well as Islam had been widespread. Confining their interactions to the coast, the Portuguese did not penetrate inland either for gold or slaves and because they could not compete with the Arabs and Persians in trade and were unable to convert Africans to Christianity, they shifted their commercial focus to Central Africa. Significantly changing and strengthening their trade in the Kongo and Angola, the Portuguese expanded to Luanda and the Loango coast between 1610 and 1650. Eventually, Angola became the principal source for slaves for the Portuguese market in Brazil.

In 1602 Holland (the Netherlands) founded the East India Company to compete with Portugal in the spice trade in Asia. The Dutch also formed the West India Company, which was granted a monopoly of trade in the Atlantic slave trade in 1621. Initially, Dutch and Portuguese merchants traded in beads, cloth, gold, and slaves in West Africa but the Dutch later controlled the sources and supply of slaves and restricted Portuguese commercial relations. They captured the Portuguese fort of Elmina in the Gold Coast in 1638. Seizing control from the Portuguese in Asia and Africa, the Dutch became a dominant power in the Atlantic slave trade system. The exportation of slaves from Africa soon assumed a wider dimension with the Dutch establishing sugar plantations and mines in the New World. According to Klein, "the Dutch West India Company was initially the most successful of [the] early monopoly companies, the one most involved in delivering slaves to colonies of other European powers, and the one that shipped the most slaves to America."[12]

Denied the ability to expand in West Africa, the Portuguese turned their attention to Angola and Central Africa. In Central Africa, Nzinga Mbande (1582–1663), the female ruler of the Ndongo Kingdom converted to Christianity and allied with the Portuguese in order to control the slave trade. When the alliance collapsed, Nzinga denounced Christianity, and ordered Portuguese trading stations attacked. She then turned to the Dutch who supported and assisted her in fighting the Portuguese and later forced them to sign a peace treaty in 1656 that included sharing of the slave trade. The Dutch took Luanda and most of Angola from the Portuguese in 1641 and their merchants were active in Central Africa as cloth suppliers in exchange for copper, ivory, and slaves. By the mid-seventeenth century, the Dutch slave trade developed a capacity for transporting 2,500 slaves per year.

The Dutch dominance in the African trade was most apparent in southern Africa. After rounding the Cape of Good Hope in 1497, Vasco da Gama succeeded in crossing the Indian Ocean to Calcutta in India. Because the interior of the Cape did not offer any immediate economic potential, the Portuguese bypassed it to settle in Mozambique for its lucrative gold trade. This explains why Portuguese influence in southern Africa remained minimal. Under the leadership of Jan van Riebeeck, the Dutch East India Company established the Cape as a refreshing station for sailors in 1652 and introduced slave labor. The company bought slaves from West Africa, Angola, and southeast Africa and sold them to private farmers in the Cape. As the Dutch population increased in the Cape, they dominated the trade, annexed the land, and began to employ Africans for slave labor. The company created a slave society in the Cape for surplus production and greater profit.

British merchants and investors intended to control the exportation of Africans to the New World when they began to participate in the Atlantic slave trade in 1562. Before that period, British merchants who visited West Africa traded in gold and sometimes took Africans back to England. In 1555, Richard Eden, an adventurer to Africa published his report in which he described Africans as a people of beastly living, without law or religion. This report triggered more voyages to West Africa. But a serious interest in the slave trade began when John Hawkins, a privateer and slave merchant from Plymouth, made three successful and rewarding voyages to West Africa in the 1560s. Because the trade in slaves was very lucrative, Queen Elizabeth I also participated in it and provided political support for Hawkins. James Rawley, a scholar of the slave trade, affirmed that the crown encouraged commerce with Africa and bestowed privileges upon merchants and companies. According to West Indian historian, Walter Rodney, Hawkins went to West Africa and:

> stole Africans whom he sold to the Spanish in America. On returning to England after the first trip, his profit was so handsome that Queen Elizabeth I became interested in directly participating in his next venture; and she provided for that purpose a ship named the Jesus. Hawkins left with the *Jesus* to steal some more Africans, and returned to England with such dividends that Queen Elizabeth made him a knight. Hawkins chose as his coat of arms the representation of an African in chains.[13]

Hawkins himself explained his exploits and experiences of raids for slaves in West Africa. He indicated how European slave merchants assisted African chiefs to fight wars in order to capture slaves. He stated:

> ... there came to us a Negro, sent from a king, oppressed by other kings, his neighbors, desiring our aid, with [the] promise that as many Negroes as by these wars might be obtained, as well of his part as of ours. Should be our pleasure; whereupon we concluded to give aid, and sent 120 of our men, which the 15 of January [1568], assaulted a town of the Negroes of our ally's adversaries, which had in it 8,000 inhabitants ... [We] obtained the town, put the inhabitants to flight, where we took 250 persons, men, women, and children, and by our friend king of our side, there were taken 600 prisoners, whereof we hoped to have our choice: but the Negro (in whose nation is seldom or never found truth) meant nothing less: for that night he removed his camp and prisoners, so that we were fain to content us with those few which we had gotten ourselves.[14]

Hawkins, in this report, presented a situation where an un-named African king invited him to offer military assistance against his neighbors. The unmentioned fact was the deliberate desire to take captives of war as slaves. Victory in war was to the advantage of both Hawkins and the African king. Even if not directly invited, Hawkins would have found other ways of procuring slaves, since that was his mission to Africa. The un-named African king only became the means through which Hawkins' mission was achieved.

The British built their first fort in West Africa in the Gold Coast in the 1630s and in spite of the competition with the Spanish in the Caribbean, their economy expanded and their quest for slaves increased. The slaves from West Africa provided labor for the large-scale sugar plantations of the British in the Caribbean. As the value of sugar rose and the production of tobacco in the Chesapeake colonies of North America grew, the demand for African slaves also increased. By the end of the seventeenth century, the British had become the leading exporters of slaves from the West African coast through the Royal African Company, which they established in 1660 for a trade monopoly. The British gained ascendancy of the slave trade because they received strong support from a government that promoted national commercial interest. In addition, there existed a powerful merchant class and an industrial base, which made possible the production of goods that were exchanged for slaves.

British merchants also dominated trade in North Africa. They controlled the trade in gold, ostrich feathers, indigo, and slaves. In Morocco, they established sugar plantations where they used slave labor. They exported slaves from Morocco to England through English merchants, who controlled the trade in North Africa for a long time without any regulation. Before the trade monopoly came to an end in 1597, Queen Elizabeth and King Mulai Ahmad al-Mansur of Morocco had kept secret their agreement on arms supplies from England to Morocco for the purposes of slave procurement.[15]

Although French private companies began to participate in the Atlantic slave trade in the early sixteenth century, France's strong interest and active involvement took place only in 1642 as a result of European companies monopolizing the trade. To compete with others, the French formed the *Compagnie des Indes Occidentales* (French West Indies Company) in 1664 and granted it trading rights in Africa and America. As French interest in the slave trade increased, the French government supported the taking over of Dutch stations in West Africa, and set up another company known as the *Compagnie du Sénégal* (Senegal Company). With two monopoly companies, the French like the British, transported slaves from West Africa to their sugar plantations in the West Indies.

Thus, the expansion and globalization of the slave trade underscored the importance of Africa as the primary source of slave supply. Global economy flourished because Africans provided cheap human labor not only in Europe, the Middle East, and Asia, but also in the Americas. The slave trade inflicted many negative impacts on Africa, but it also emphasized African role in the global economy between the fifteenth and nineteenth centuries.

The New Imperialism and Globalization

The end of the slave trade was the beginning of another form of global connection between Africa and the rest of the world. Based on the curiosity of what existed in the interior of Africa, Western associations and countries sponsored explorations to Africa. Explorers such as Mungo Park (made two explorations to Africa, 1795 and 1805), Major A. G. Laing (arrived at the source of the Niger River, 1822), and Hugh Clapperton and Major Dixon Denham (joined Walter Oudney in Tripoli to cross the Sahara to Lake Chad) reported that the interior of Africa presented great opportunities for European resources, markets, and investments. With subsequent explorations and an influx of European merchants and companies, Africa became a lucrative market for European goods.

Following the explorers were the European Christian missionaries who penetrated the interior of Africa in the nineteenth century. The spread of Christianity to Africa has been closely linked with the abolition of the slave trade. Thomas Buxton, a humanitarian and member of the Aborigines Protection Society, popularized the concept of "legitimate commerce" in order to shift the focus of African slave merchants to other acceptable trade relations with Europeans. Missionary societies saw the collaboration between Christianity and commerce as a means to salvaging Africans from slavery. Many Christians felt it was their responsibility to share Christianity and Western civilization with the "less fortunate" non-European peoples of the world. Thus, they sought to prove that Africans and Asians were capable of accepting and adopting Western civilization by providing Western education and Western forms of medical care. Christianity and legitimate commerce became avenues of integrating Africa into the social and economic global system.

The Church Missionary Society (CMS) and the Wesleyan Methodist began work in Sierra Leone in 1806 and 1811 respectively. By 1842 the Wesleyans had extended to the Gold Coast while the CMS established churches in Nigeria in 1844. In East Africa, the CMS established a station at Mombasa under two German missionaries, Johann Krapf and Johann Rebmann. Scottish missions and the Roman Catholic White Fathers were also active in East Africa. Missionaries from the Barmen Rhine Society operated in southern Africa under the auspices of the London Missionary Society (LMS). For example, Robert Moffat (1795–1883), a Scottish pioneer missionary to South Africa, arrived in Cape Town in 1817. He opened mission stations and translated the Bible into the language of the Bechuana people. Following him was David Livingstone, a Scottish missionary, doctor, and explorer whose time in southern Africa was filled with inter-ethnic warfare and conflict with the Boers (White settlers in South Africa) who were expanding from the coast to the interior. Livingstone not only received a strong support from Robert Moffat, but he also married Moffat's daughter, Mary, in 1844.

Missionary activities supported not only the imperialistic ambitions of the Europeans in Africa, but also the globalization of Christianity. As a universalizing religion, Christianity became a force to connect Europe to Africa. Christianity also became a vehicle of introducing Western civilization to Africa. Thus the Europeans used economic, political, and religious relations to expand their influence to Africa.

By the mid-nineteenth century, the slave trade had been outlawed in Europe and the Industrial Revolution allowed the use of machines to replace human labor in production. Many arguments were made for the abolition of the slave trade, but Eric Williams, in his *Capitalism and Slavery*, argued that since the slave trade was used to develop European economy and capitalism, it was more expedient for the Europeans to stop utilizing human slaves and resort to the use of machines.[16] Simply, the abolition of the slave trade was driven more by economics than by any other factor.

In Europe, there was the urge for the acquisition of overseas colonies for economic purposes. For example, in Britain, entrepreneurs, such as George Taubman Goldie and Cecil Rhodes provided the necessary inspiration that influenced policy-makers to consider colonial acquisition. Similarly in France, Paul

Leroy-Beaulieu, an economist, urged French investors to stake their money in colonies because overseas investments would be protected from domestic political upheavals that were affecting the economy. Leroy-Beaulieu's economic idea inspired Cecil Rhodes to engage in overseas investment through his British South Africa Company. The new imperialism thus became associated with the age of capitalist expansion for economic control. It was an indirect strategy of establishing a global economy. As a result of commercial competition, European countries erected tariff barriers to protect their young industries. The policy of protectionism made overseas investment a viable option for merchants and industrialists.

The competitive and technologically advancing European industries depended largely on raw materials such as beeswax, cocoa, cotton, groundnuts, palm products, rubber, and sisal, which were available in Africa. Because these raw materials were bought at cheap prices, Europeans derived tremendous benefits from the trade. The manufactured finished products that came from Europe were sold to Africans at high prices, which explained the exploitative nature of legitimate trade. Apparently, the new imperialism was based on economic power and exploitation. However, legitimate trade not only provided a shift from the Atlantic slave trade, it also served as the continuity of economic globalization. In many respects, legitimate trade mirrored several of the issues of economic globalization, which are discussed as part of international trade in contemporary times.

Africa provided a market for European manufactured goods since it did not develop an industrial economy on the Western model. Before the 1860s British and French trade along the coasts of western and eastern Africa was going well through companies and merchants but by the 1870s, when economic depression hit Europe, it became necessary to give serious consideration to the reports of the explorers about the vast, fertile, and empty lands of tropical Africa where markets could be established.

For other reasons such as the creation of spheres of influence, national prestige, and nationalism, seven European countries dominated Africa. By 1914 almost all of Africa had been colonized. In modern Africa, only two countries (Ethiopia and Liberia) did not experience European colonization. This does not mean that they were not influenced by Europeans, because they also became part of the globalization that took place during and after colonialism.

Africa and Globalization Since 1945

The end of the Second World War in 1945 brought considerable changes in the status of colonialism in Africa. One of the major factors that sparked the change was the opposition to continued colonization as indicated in the Atlantic Charter Article Three of August 1941 on self-determination, which respects "the right of all people to choose the form of government under which they will live."[17] In effect, the process of decolonization, which culminated in the gaining of independence, launched Africa into world affairs in a different but significant way. Hitherto "relegated to the fringes of international politics," according to J. Gus Liebenow, African states became participants in world politics.[18]

By the early 1960s, independent African states faced many challenges in both domestic and foreign affairs. One of the legacies of colonialism was the arbitrary demarcation of boundaries, discussed in Chapter Four of this book. Hence domestically, African states faced the challenge of national identity and nation building, given their multi-ethnic, multi-cultural, and multi-religious compositions. For the new states to survive and thrive, leaders had to provide political and economic stability. The leaders, having no prior experience in the parliamentary system, struggled with determining a form of realistic political ideology to adopt. They needed to embark on and promote development programs that would help economic growth and provide social services as well as job opportunities for the people. In matters of foreign affairs, the immediate problem was the Cold War, the ideological conflict between the United States of America and the former Soviet Union. The Cold War was a global issue and Africa became part of the phenomenon because African leaders were faced with the question of which side to align with. For example, Egypt in 1972 and Somalia in 1975 switched their support from the Soviet to the United States while Ethiopia changed from the United States to the Soviet Union in 1974. Unsure of which side to favor, some African states played the politics of neutrality. Apollos Nwauwa states that:

> At the height of the Cold War, domestic and international relations in post-independence Africa were often subject to the vagaries of the ideological competition between the superpowers. Although many African states opted for neutrality in the ensuing conflict with the formation of the Non-Aligned Movement in the 1950s, Africa did not escape the contagion of the Cold War rivalry and polarization as both the United States and the Soviet Union carved out for themselves spheres of influence by virtue of their predominant positions ideologically and militarily in Africa.[19]

The depth of the impact of the Cold War on emerging Africa states cannot be ignored. Without a doubt, the Cold War demonstrated the centrality of Africa in global affairs as the two super powers strove to gain foothold in the continent. The politics of containment and domination by the super powers became intense in Africa, and in some cases led to catastrophic end as in the case of the Congo. As Nwauwa concludes, "the politics of the Cold War wrecked havoc on Africa."[20] While globally connected, Africans and their leaders struggled to find their place on the international political stage.

It is important to note that globalization is strongly supported by economic growth. As technology advances and many governments adopt free-market economic systems, the world becomes more closely connected through international trade. Africa has become a new frontier of the global economy by possessing many of the economic resources needed by the world market. Paradoxically, African states do not possess the industrial and technological base to support a virile economy and make them competitive with developed countries. This goes back to the colonial period when the Europeans deliberately decided not to establish major industries in order to make Africans primary consumers of their manufactured goods. In other words, Europeans did not teach Africans how to fish; they merely gave them fish to consume. It should be noted that African indigenous technology did not support the new economic and industrial dispensation as dictated and dominated by the Western world. Claude Ake, a political economist, argued that "colonial Africa depended on the capitalist West for virtually all her technology. This put the colonial economy in a position analogous to that of a producer who has no instruments of labour."[21] Ake points out further that "technological dependence underlies the exploitation of the colonial economies by the metropolitan economies."[22] This argument has proven to be right given the deplorable economic condition of modern African countries.

Following the end of colonialism, the economies of African countries remained closely tied to those of their former colonial masters. With a lack of industries to support exportation, African states remain essentially as importers thus weakening their economy. A skill shortage, lack of capital, and insufficient entrepreneurial experience partly accounted for the deficiency in industrialization. Partnering with the developed and industrialized countries of Europe became a viable option to change the state of industrialization and economies of Africa. The economies of African states continued to worsen in the 1970s as industrialization was static, external debts increased, and foreign aid rose. At the Second Conference of Ministers of Industry held in Cairo in 1973, it was observed that the rate of industrialization in Africa was slow. Noted with concern, the ministers declared that:

> Industrialization has so far failed in many African countries to provide a major impetus to development, structural change and employment and that although the range of industries established had widened in the last decade, African countries continue to import a higher pro-

portion of most of their requirements of consumer, intermediate and capital goods than other regions.[23]

The predicament of Africa in terms of poor industrialization should be considered *vis a vis* the global economy. Africa cannot afford to remain backward and unconnected to the global economy. The economies of African countries have been largely state controlled and leaders realized that without a strong connection to international trade, their economic situation would continue to get worse. A way to rectify and revamp their economies was to take international loans from either the World Bank or the International Monetary Fund (IMF). In the 1980s, the IMF increased its activities in Africa, but the stringent conditions attached to the loans made it extremely difficult for African states to service the interest and the principal.[24]

Economic infrastructure in Africa, especially in sub-Saharan Africa, has not changed much since independence. The transformation of the Organization for African Unity (OAU) to the African Union (AU) was a step not only to strengthen political ties, but also to promote economic relations by linking Africa to the economy of the rest of the world. Addressing the African Union in 2008, John A. Simon, U.S. ambassador to the African Union emphasized the need for Africa to be fully and strongly integrated into the global economy. According to Simon, "Connecting to the global economy is fundamental to Africa's future," and for that to happen requires "investing in entrepreneurship from all sources, the development of larger markets along regional lines, and the retention of its most gifted people."[25] To move away from economic neo-colonialism, African nations have to develop all sectors of their economy, become exporters, and take their rightful place in the international market.

Conclusion

The concept of globalization has been an integral part of African politics and economics. It existed in pre-historic times and it is a continuing practice in contemporary times. It did not originate from the slave trade nor was it solely a practice between Africans, Europeans, Arabs, and Asians. From then to now and in various ways, Africa has been part of global affairs. Globalization relates to the concept of give and take and it deals with the interdependence of nations. Hence Africa has given to the global world and has received as well. Although the tragic events of the slave trade and the new imperialism were exploitative and retarded Africa's progress, they both served as historic facts that Africa had been and will continue to be an important part of w economy and politics. The history of the world is not complete without adequate reference to Africa.

Globalization is a useful tool not only for economic reasons (international trade), but also for the sustenance of political stability, for the maintenance of fundamental human rights, and for collective security in the world. African countries belong to world organizations such as the United Nations, Africa provides human resources for the world, and Africa takes part in global peacekeeping. As the unstable politics and economy of African countries suggest, global connections are a means of changing the conditions. Especially in economic consideration, globalization is a useful strategy for providing assistance for needy countries.

Bibliography

Ake, Claude. *A Political Economy of Africa*. Ibadan, Nigeria: Longman, 1981.

Bovill, E. W. *The Golden Trade of the Moors: West African Kingdoms in the Fourteenth Century*. 2nd edition. Princeton, NJ: Markus Wiener Publishers, 1995.

Bozeman, Adda B. *Conflict in Africa: Concepts and Realities*. Surrey: Princeton University Press, 1976.

Corey, Charles W. "Africa Is New Frontier of Global Economy." *www.america.gov/st/econ ... /20081010111004WCyeroC0.1286432.html*, October 10, 2008, (accessed April 9, 2010).

Falola, Toyin. "Intergroup Relations." In Falola, Toyin, (ed.), *Africa: African Cultures and Societies Before 1885*. Vol. 2. Durham, NC: Carolina Academic Press, 2000.

Harris, E. *The African Presence in Asia: Consequences of the East African Slave Trade* Evanston, IL: Northwestern University Press, 1971.

Hawkins, M. John. "The Third Troublesome Voyage ... to the Parts of Guinea, and the West Indies, in the Yeeres 1567 and 1568." In Richard Hakluyt, *The Principal Navigations, Voyages, Traffiques and Discoveries of the English Nation*. New York: 1928. Cited in Northrup, David, (ed.), *The Atlantic Slave Trade*. Boston: Houghton Mifflin Company, 2002.

Kieh, George Klay ed. *Africa and the New Globalization*. Surrey: Ashgate Publishing, Ltd., 2007.

Klein, Herbert S. *The Atlantic Slave Trade*. Cambridge: Cambridge University Press, 1999.

Lewis, Bernard. *Race and Slavery in the Middle East*. Oxford: Oxford University Press, 1990.

Lewis, Bernard. *The Arabs in History*. Oxford: Oxford University Press, first published 1950 reprinted 1993.

Liebenow, J. Gus. *African Politics: Crises and Challenges*. Bloomington, IN: Indiana University Press, 1986.

Nwauwa, Apollos O. "The Legacies of Colonialism and the Politics of the Cold War." In Toyin Falola ed. *Africa: Contemporary Africa*, Vol. 5. Durham, NC: Carolina Academic Press, 2003.

Rodney, Walter. *How Europe Underdeveloped Africa*. Washington, D.C.: Howard University Press, 1982.

Roosevelt, Franklin D. and Roseman, Samuel I. *The Public Papers and Addresses of Franklin D. Roosevelt*. Vol. 10. New York: The Harper Brothers, 1950.

Ungerer, Gustav. "Portia and the Prince of Morocco." *Shakespeare Studies*, January 1, 2003. Online version, goliath.ecnext.com/coms2/gi_0199-3181225/Portia-and-the-Prince-of.html (accessed April 14, 2010).

United Nations Industrial Development Organization. *Industrialization in Africa: Principles and Guidelines for Co-operation and Development*. Second Conference of Ministers of Industries, Cairo, 1973.

Vrettos, Theodore. *Alexandria: City of the Western Mind*. New York: Free Press, 2001.

Williams, Eric. *Capitalism and Slavery*. Chapel Hill, NC: The University of North Carolina Press, 1944.

Chapter 2

Global Economies: Africa and the West

Roshen Hendrickson

Introduction

David Held describes globalization as "a shift or transformation in the scale of human organization that links distant communities and expands the reach of power relations across the world's regions."[1] In the last couple decades, scholars have explored these linkages in the spheres of economics, politics, culture, and technology and debated the degree to which the intensity of current linkages is new and unprecedented.[2] Globalization is associated in the popular consciousness not only with transformation in every sphere of life but also with global capitalism and the backlash against it, as well as global economic growth and global inequality. In this chapter I describe historical patterns of trade and capital flows between sub-Saharan Africa and the West, comment on recent developments and debates, and point to some of the responses from African states and civil society.

In the general introduction as well as in chapter one of this volume, the authors posited that African economies have been integrated into global flows of trade and capital for centuries; but many of the people of Africa have been excluded from the economic and technological transformations of the last century. The way in which they are currently integrated into global economic networks has been determined in large part by the nature of their historical interactions with Western nations. Although the influence of Western powers is gradually diminishing, in relation to the growing power of China and other large developing countries, the rules and institutions that govern trade and financial relations are informed by liberal economic ideas that have been most fully explored in the West. These rules and institutions have primarily served Western interests.

Sub-Saharan Africa has about twelve percent of the world's population but produces around two percent of the world GDP.[3] Despite its historical integration into the global economy, the region accounts for only a small proportion of global flows of trade and capital. From 1981 to 2005, while global poverty fell from 40 percent to 28 percent, poverty increased in Africa. Using a poverty line measure of $1.25 day, a 2008 World Bank study estimated that 50 percent of the people of sub-Saharan Africa lived below the poverty line in 2005.[4]

Despite the great variations between African countries, in terms of both their histories and the structure of their economies, it is possible to generalize about the way in which they are integrated into the global economy. For both domestic and international reasons, African economies have gained less from their economic integration than other developing regions and yet their integration makes them profoundly vulnerable to shocks in the global economy.

Julius Adekunle notes in Chapter One that the late fifteenth to the seventeenth century was the period when European sailors first explored the coasts of Africa. First the Portuguese and then the French and Dutch set up trading posts. By the eighteenth century, European explorers started venturing inland. American traders from New England also sold goods along the coasts, though they withdrew during the American Civil War, leaving the region to European dominance for the next century.[5] Although African slaves had been sold via the trans-Saharan trade routes for centuries, during the trans-Atlantic slave trade, more than ten million Africans were sold to Western countries between the fifteenth and nineteenth centuries. The impact of the slave trade on African economies is impossible to measure; however one analysis suggests that the slave trade explains much of the current income gap between Africa and the rest of the world. According to this argument, the loss of so many people undermined political institutions and fragmented societies.[6]

Britain, France, Belgium, Portugal, Italy, and Spain all colonized parts of Africa. From 1884 to 1885, fourteen European nations met in Berlin to negotiate control of much of the African continent, leading to the eventual European control of the entire continent. The United States also sent a representative to try to protect US commercial interests by calling for free trade in the Congo Basin.[7] Most African countries were independent by the 1960s, but freedom for those under Portuguese rule and minority white settler rule came much later.

The way in which African economies were integrated into the global economy during the colonial period set up economic patterns that persist to this day. Although there was significant variation between the colonial powers, most imposed taxes on their subjects to finance colonial administrations. Both export crops and wage labor were introduced as sources of tax revenue, although forced labor was also common.[8] The colonial administrators invested in infrastructure that would enable the transport of both minerals and agricultural goods from the colonies to the metropoles. In addition to the exploitation of economic resources, the impact of colonial rule on African societies was radically transformative, in many cases destroying or undermining traditional social systems and replacing them with new political entities that attempted to unite distinct peoples and in many cases divided peoples across arbitrarily drawn borders.

Economic growth was quite rapid in the first decade after independence but the regional rate of growth started to decline in the mid-1970s. The development strategies of the 1960s and 1970s focused on state-owned enterprises, channeled resources from the agricultural sector to the industrial sector, heavily regulated foreign investment, and protected trade. While oil exporting countries gained from OPEC's increase of oil prices in 1973 and the price increase of 1979, most economies that were dependent on oil imports suffered. By 1979, increased interest rates, in combination with falling commodity prices triggered by global economic recession, culminated in an economic crisis for African nations. Most African countries were forced to turn to the International Monetary Fund (IMF) and World Bank for loans and by the 1980s for debt rescheduling. The terms of debt rescheduling required a set of policy prescriptions which came to be known as the Washington Consensus, because it originated in the international financial institutions (IFIs) based in Washington, under the ideological leadership of the US government; although the European powers went along with this agenda.

Structural Adjustment programs (SAPs) included deficit reduction, tax reform, interest rate and exchange rate adjustments, trade and financial liberalization, privatization and deregulation. Flaws in the policy recommendations and in the governments' implementation undermined the effectiveness of the reforms and SAPs came to be seen as part of the cause of the economic malaise, rather than part of the solution.[9] Economic conditions continued to worsen through the 1980s and 1990s.

Sub-Saharan Africa averaged a record 6.5 percent growth rate during the period of 2004 to 2008. Although the growth rate dipped down to 2.7 percent in 2009, it returned to above 5 percent in the following two years. Growth has been boosted by high global commodity prices; however some countries have been adversely affected by high food and fuel prices as well as natural disasters.[10]

There is an intense debate over the relative contributions of domestic and international factors to the causes of the long economic crisis in the African region. Liberal analysts associated with the IFIs have focused on the failures of domestic politics while critics of the Washington Consensus point to historical power relations and structural inequalities. Specifically, they point to factors such as declining terms of trade, high interest rates, unsustainable debt, and trade protectionism in wealthy countries.[11] Giovanni Arrighi points to the world systemic context after the 1970s, when the US had begun to compete for global capital to finance its own growing trade and budget deficits. Capital-poor Africa was unable to compete with the newly industrialized countries of Southeast Asia and later China that began manufacturing and exporting their way to rapid growth.[12]

African countries have a limited voice in the institutions that govern flows of trade and capital, such as the World Trade Organizations (WTO), the World Bank and the IMF. Their dependence on external sources of capital has constrained their ability to determine their own economic policies. Poor economic conditions and persistent patterns of economic interaction have triggered a wide range of responses, both inside Africa and globally. The fairness of international institutions, the efficacy of structural adjustment programs and the impact of development aid have all been questioned. At the same time, other aspects of globalization have challenged existing power relations in complicated ways. International travel and migration as well as linkages through modern telecommunications infrastructure have sped up and deepened the exchange of ideas about political economy and provided new opportunities for political organization and activism. These new linkages as well as shifts in global power relations are gradually altering global patterns, but deeper changes are needed. The African region has the potential to be an interesting site for new developments in political economy, but this will require interacting transformations in both domestic and international institutions.

Trade

For many centuries, African peoples have been integrated into the global trading networks that extended along the Nile River, across the Saharan desert and along the coasts. It was not until the sixteenth and seventeenth centuries that Europeans played a big role in controlling trade between Africa and the rest of the world, but trade patterns that developed during the colonial period have proven difficult to change. British colonial trade policy, for example, ensured that the colonies produced primary goods that were not produced in England, and bought manufactured goods from England. Most African countries are still dependent on the export of commodities such as agricultural products, oil, and minerals and most rely on only a few commodities for their export revenue. Reliance on these primary products is a problem because commodity prices tend to fluctuate dramatically while prices for manufactured goods tend to be higher and steadier partially because they are not vulnerable to natural disasters and other climate conditions. Economic studies have shown that the share of manufactured goods as a percentage of total exports is linked to economic success because developing the manufacturing sector encourages various technological developments and stimulates innovation.[13] According to a 2008 United Nations Conference on Trade and Development (UNCTAD) report, only six sub-Saharan African nations had manufactured exports accounting for more than a tenth of their GDP.[14] The potential for long-term economic diversification and industrialization is also undermined by the fact that although Africa has all the raw materials necessary for industrial development, it is currently supplying these to the industrial north.

Sub-Saharan Africa accounts for less than 2 percent of world trade. Despite this small share of global trade, the proportion of the regional economy that is accounted for by trade is greater than 50 percent, a proportion similar to China's and twice that of India.[15] Between 1990 and 2010, the proportion of sub-Saharan Africa's trade that went to Europe and the United States declined rapidly as trade with other developing countries increased to almost half of all trade with the region. Trade with Brazil reached 3 percent, with India 6 percent, and China 17 percent. Trade within the African region also increased from 7 percent in 1990 to 14 percent in 2010.[16]

Central to the SAPs of the 1980s was the effort to liberalize African economies by reducing barriers to trade. Although most African countries have carried out extensive trade liberalization since then, the extent to which the region benefits from free trade is intensely contested. According to UNCTAD, the increase in export growth that occurred after the trade liberalization of the 1990s has been much lower than expected, and the increase may simply have been a result of higher commodity prices in those years. Even taking advantage of traditional market opportunities has been a challenge. Due to insufficiently trained workforces, unreliable electricity supply, poor banking services, inadequate transportation networks, and inadequate investment in agriculture, African exporters are unable to compete with exporters from other developing regions. Over the last few decades, the lack of domestic investment in agriculture, combined with a drop in donor assistance for the agricultural sector contributed to a shift from exporting food to becoming the largest recipient of external food aid.[17]

Post-colonial trade relations with the West, governed through a series of bilateral, regional, and multilateral trade agreements, have played a significant role by structuring trade opportunities. As French colonies became independent, preferential access to European markets that they had received under the 1957 Treaty of Rome which established the European Economic Community, were extended under the 1963 and 1969 Yaoundé Conventions. In 1971 the European Union's Generalized System of Preferences extended this benefit to all developing countries. After Great Britain joined the EU, preferential access for African products was established under the Lomé Conventions which governed trade relations between the EU and the African, Caribbean and Pacific states from 1975 to 2000. The first Lomé agreement was negotiated at a time when commodity prices were high and the EU was eager to secure its access to these commodities so the agreement allowed for non-reciprocity (although Europe lowered barriers to African goods, African countries did not have to do the same). Lomé also included the STABEX and SYSMIN mechanisms to guarantee prices for raw materials and minerals. Although the agreements were intended to promote economic development and integrate these economies into the global economy, the European Commission argued by 1997 that Lomé had failed to improve many African countries' export performance.[18]

By the time the fourth Lomé Convention was negotiated, the global context had changed. Africa was of less strategic importance to European countries as trade within the EU increased. Some EU member states challenged the European Commission's Africa agenda, demanding reduced aid to Africa.[19] The trend towards global trade liberalization, embodied in the Uruguay Round creation of the WTO, reduced the value of these regional preferences, but also strengthened enforcement of the rules, ultimately leading to the end of this exception to the Most Favored Nation Principle (that trade advantages extended to one member of the group must be extended to all the other members). Not only did the Cotonou Agreement of 2000 strengthen the political and economic conditions under which benefits were granted, but it also eliminated the support for raw materials that had been provided through STABEX and SYSMIN.[20]

After the Cotonou Agreement expired in 2007, the least developed countries (LDCs) were still eligible for duty-free and quota-free access under the Everything But Arms (EBA) initiative. Countries that weren't classified as LDCs were to sign Economic Partnership Agreements (EPAs) that would be negotiated regionally; otherwise they would only have the access given to all developing countries through the Generalized System of Preferences. These EPAs would provide virtually free access to the EU market in exchange for gradual reduction of African trade barriers. The EPAs have proven very controversial however, as some political leaders and many analysts questioned the benefits of liberalization, arguing that the agreements would reduce tariff revenue for states and undermine local industry with competition from low cost European imports.

Although China is now Africa's largest trading partner, the United States is still the largest market for African goods. In 2010 crude oil constituted 81 percent of total US imports from SSA and most of the trade was with only a few African countries: 80 percent of US exports went to South Africa, Nigeria and Angola, while 83 percent of imports came from Nigeria, Angola, South Africa and the Republic of Congo.[21] The US Generalized System of Preferences (GSP), initiated in 1976, historically provided duty-free entry to goods from developing countries although some developing countries were excluded and there were still barriers to certain politically sensitive goods.

The African Growth and Opportunity Act guided through Congress by the Clinton administration and passed in 2000 extended GSP benefits in combination with other efforts to promote trade and investment in Africa. It was central to the Clinton administration's efforts to shift economic relations from a focus on aid to a focus on trade. The AGOA was reauthorized with enhancements three times during the Bush administration and in the 2006 version benefits were extended until 2015. At the latest AGOA ministerial meeting in Kenya, Secretary of State Clinton called for greater intra-Africa trade, better utilization of the AGOA, as well as efforts to improve food security and empower women; while African activists called on the United States to open up its own markets further and increase the number of products eligible under the AGOA. Eligibility for access to AGOA benefits is reviewed each year and is based on progress towards various liberal economic goals such as the development of a market economy and elimination of barriers to US trade and investment, as well as efforts to reduce poverty, implement the rule of law, protect worker rights, and reduce corruption.

The actual effects of AGOA have been less consequential than projected. Imports under AGOA rose steadily and the goods that were able to enter the US market diversified, but petroleum products still made up 91 percent of all AGOA imports in 2010. Although the AGOA does offer duty-free access to almost all categories of products, its impact is still limited because many of the products African countries actually can produce are excluded. On top of this, African countries face many non-tariff barriers to trade with the US such as stringent regulations and reporting requirements. Even the sector targeted for trade boosting, textiles, is governed by an immensely complex system of regulations although the current rules of origin are favorable to African countries.[23] Unfortunately, the African textile industry has suffered from the elimination of the Multi-Fiber Arrangement in 2005 which has allowed competitive Asian producers to increase their market share. The African textile industry has also been undermined by the massive market in second-handing clothing exported from the West.

By 2008, most African nations were members of the WTO, but their interests are still not well represented in the decision-making process. They have little influence on the choice of the issues to prioritize on the agenda, and inadequate resources to ensure the legal capacity to represent their interests. The United States and Europe still have massive agricultural subsidies that lower the prices of Western agricultural exports making it difficult for African agricultural producers to compete domestically and globally. In addition to this, African exports face significant barriers in the form of regulatory requirements such as quality standards, reporting rules, as well as packaging and labeling rules.[24] The priorities of Western states, such as protection of intellectual property rights, liberalization of the services sector and liberalization of investment are seen as threatening to developing countries.

The Doha Round of WTO trade negotiations, begun in 2001, was supposed to be focused on development, but talks have broken down several times, most recently in July of 2008 after disagreements between the US, China, and India over a special safeguard mechanism. The Africa Group is part of an alliance of one hundred developing countries that support this mechanism which would allow developing countries to raise tariffs in special cases, when the price of agricultural imports fell suddenly or the volume rose suddenly. In addition to this, the Africa Group continues to demand deeper cuts in American subsidies of cotton, at a rate faster than for the rest of agriculture, because of the loss of an estimated $450 million in earnings for cotton farmers.[25] The US was reluctant to even discuss cotton because although it had agreed to cut cotton subsidies beyond the seventy percent reduction of overall farm subsidies; it was already bound by the 2008 US Farm Bill to continue the high levels of cotton subsidies.[26]

The United States and Europe continue to take a hard line in trade talks, requiring further trade opening in exchange for lowering agricultural subsidies.[27] In the midst of the economic recession, in early 2009, there were calls for a resolution to the current trade impasse so that a new trade deal could send positive signals of economic cooperation in the midst of the global economic downturn, but the impact of a trade agreement would have a variable impact on African states according to their particular export and import needs. Vyborny argues that a conclusion that included "full preferential trade treatment" that would include politically sensitive products and aid to build competitive advantage could provide net gains for African countries. One way the Doha Round may actually be harmful for Africa is that an agreement would erode the preferences African countries have through the AGOA and EU agreements by reducing tariffs for all countries.[28]

Liberalization of trade in Africa was carried out largely because of external pressures, in a way that served the interests of Western powers; although African consumers have benefitted from access to cheaper goods and some producers from access to Western markets. The global policies could have been calibrated more precisely to respond to African needs, if concerns about global poverty had been elevated over protectionist demands from Western producers. Most African economies are small and face great barriers to diversification and yet efforts to develop manufacturing have been stymied by trade policies. OECD trade policies have constrained Africa's integration into the global economy through the mechanisms of tariff escalation (imposing higher tariffs on more processed goods), tariff peaks (imposing higher tariffs on sensitive products), and agricultural protectionism.[29] A recent study shows that trade liberalization has exacerbated the excessive demand for imported goods, rather than boosting exports.[30] Because of this terrible failure to boost economic growth, many analysts argue that African governments need more flexible trade rules to protect their public services, regulate foreign investment, and enable local producers to become more competitive.[31]

Capital Flows

Sub-Saharan Africa has long been integrated into global flows of capital but it was not until 2006 that private capital flows (foreign direct investment and portfolio investment) overtook official aid flows (bilateral and multilateral).[32] During the colonial period and in the first decades of independence, European states were the primary sources of external capital for most states in Africa. By the late nineties, the United States was the primary source of foreign direct investment, followed by France and the UK.[33] This dominance by Western sources is changing as Asian countries such as China, Singapore, South Korea, India, and Malaysia increase their investments in Africa. Intra-regional investment has also grown, especially from South Africa.[34]

Due to both global economic conditions and changing domestic policies, Africa's share of global flows of Foreign Direct Investment (FDI) increased during the first decade of this century. In 2010, Africa received 4.5 percent of global flows of FDI, accounting for 10 percent of inflows to developing countries. Inflows reached a height of $72 billion in 2008 but declined to $55 billion in 2010. Most FDI still targets the extractive sectors, petroleum and mining, so the FDI that does reach Africa is still concentrated in South Africa and oil producers such as Nigeria and Angola.[35] Portfolio flows which had multiplied from $1.5 billion in 2005 to $6.5 billion in 2007 slowed down in 2008.[36] Remittances (funds transferred from migrant workers to their home countries) also became a significant new source of capital, rising from $13 billion in 2006 to an estimated $20 billion in 2008.[37]

Africa now has more than twenty stock exchanges, a majority of which are very new and in very small economies. According to a study by Moss, shares are not traded frequently and the rate of return fluctuates significantly so this has limited interest from major Western funds.[38] In recent years, however, more private equity funds have been targeting the region. Despite these new flows of private funds, it is believed that Africa actually loses more than $50 billion in capital flight each year.[39]

After World War II, the United States and its European allies set up the international financial institutions (IFIs) that still form the core of the international financial regime. Since the 1970s, the United States and the UK have played a leading role in reducing the barriers to capital flows.[40] The executive boards of the IMF and the World Bank are dominated by the United States and European nations, with the most powerful role reserved for the United States. Voting is structured in such a way that Africa has limited representation in the decision-making process.[41]

The management of African debt, through the imposition of structural adjustment programs exacerbated the economic crisis experienced by most countries in Africa in the 1980s and 1990s. Structural adjustment programs required a reduction in budget deficits and thus decreased government spending on programs in education, and health as well as critical subsidies, leading to an immediate decline in welfare in many countries.

Thomas Callaghy points out that until the 1980s, the members of the Paris Club—an informal institution of wealthy nations' financial officials that meets regularly in France to organize the response to heavily indebted nations—took it for granted that debtor countries were bound to repay all their debt.[42] Despite this, African debt became a significant issue among political activists in the late 1990s. A coalition of NGOs organized under the name Jubilee 2000 called for the cancellation of the debt of the poorest nations. Callaghy argues that while these actors played a significant role, the transformation of the debt regime was a result of their interaction with an epistemic community focused on development issues as well as creditor and debtor governments and institutions responding to a structural dilemma—the insolvency of the weakest economies in the global system.[43] In response to these interacting pressures, the Heavily Indebted Poor Countries Initiative (HIPC) to reduce debt payments was developed in 1996, followed by the Enhanced HIPC Debt Initiative in 1999. At the G-8 summit in 2005, the G-8 pledged to completely cancel the debt owed by 14 African Heavily Indebted Countries to the World Bank and IMF. The United States promised total debt forgiveness for all qualifying HIPC countries, on debt accumulated before 1999.[44]

The Multilateral Debt Relief Initiative (MDRI) was set up in 2005 when HIPC I and II failed to significantly reduce levels of debt. For all countries that complete the HIPC process, the MDRI promises 100 percent debt cancellation on obligations to the IMF, the International Development Association and the African Development Fund. By 2008, nineteen African countries had achieved this and eight were on their way. Although the burden of debt is still very significant, sub-Saharan Africa's external debt has decreased in the last few years, down to 25 percent of GDP.[45]

The US Congress is considering legislation that would increase the number of countries eligible for full debt cancellation, end harmful conditionalities, and require greater transparency from the lenders. It would also set up new rules to stem the negative effects of "vulture funds" which buy up poor country debt at low prices, then seek payment of the full value of the debt, thus undermining debt relief programs. Another initiative would investigate debts considered to be odious or illegitimate because they were incurred by despots from willing lenders for purposes other than those in the interests of their societies.[46]

The sub-Saharan African region has received more development assistance (consisting of both grants and concessional loans) than any other region of the world, according to one estimate, more than $1 trillion over the last 60 years.[47] While OECD countries have been the main source of development assistance in the last few decades, aid flows from other countries have been increasing since 2000, possibly exceeding $5 billions in 2006.[48]

For the United States as well as European powers, development assistance always served political goals such as assisting in the transition to independence in the 1960s, countering the spread of Communism during the Cold War, securing access to raw materials, and strengthening relations with African states, though there was a great deal of variation in policies within Europe. US development assistance started after World War II, increased steadily during the Cold War then declined significantly in the 1990s. During the 1960s, much development assistance spending focused on infrastructure building, education support, and the health sector. In the 1970s, there was a shift to focusing on the basic human needs of the poorest, which included projects in primary health care, education, clean water and agriculture. By the 1980s development assistance was geared towards economic policy reform and the development of the private sector. In the 1990s a significant proportion of aid was used to promote democracy and stability.[49] Each shift was a response to perceptions that development assistance was not achieving its mandated goals.

As early as the 1960s, the United Nations set a target of .7 percent of gross national income (GNI) for development aid from the wealthiest countries. By 2007 only the small northern European countries, Denmark, Luxembourg, the Netherlands, Norway and Sweden surpassed this goal; while the average was .45 percent of GNI.[50] Continued high levels of global poverty stimulated multilateral efforts to focus on the issue. In 2000, 189 countries signed the

Millennium Declaration to set up the Millennium Development Goals for economic development and poverty reduction.

Ever since the 2002 UN Conference in Monterrey, there has been a big push to increase aid to Africa. In 2005, the G8 countries pledged to increase aid by $28.3 billion by 2010, but by 2009, they had delivered only $9.4 billion of this promised increase.[51] This effort to push out more aid coincides with a profound and heated debate over the legacy and efficacy of aid. The fact that half of Africa's population still lives on less than $1.25 a day would indicate that development assistance has not been very successful in its goal of promoting economic development and reducing poverty. Although development assistance is credited with reducing the suffering from disease, and providing goods such as schools, roads, and clinics, it has been less successful at stimulating sustainable economic development. African governments, international donors, and global economic conditions have all been implicated in the failure of development assistance.

Many politicians, grassroots groups and some scholars such as Jeffrey Sachs, who headed the advisory body that helped develop the UN Millennium Project, continue to advocate for a significant increase in aid to Africa to pull African states out of their "poverty trap". This is the idea that countries remain extremely poor because they suffer from insufficient capital, therefore an influx of investment in education, health, infrastructure, clean water, scientific research, and public administration would enable these countries to break out of their negative economic cycle.[52]

Others, such as William Easterly, a major critic of World Bank lending, caution that it is necessary to move away from grand plans and focus on development efforts that have been shown to work. He advocates support for clearly defined projects that have been proven to have positive results and embraces market solutions to the challenges of development assistance.[53] Rimmer argues that development assistance has failed in Africa because of the scarcity of productive uses for capital. He suggests that free trade and free migration would do more to decrease poverty in Africa.[54]

Some African intellectuals are calling for an end to development assistance. Dambisa Moyo, for example, argues that the "aid-based development model" has not succeeded and should be ended (Moyo's position is examined in greater detail by Maurice Amutabi in Chapter 5). She suggests that aid flows be gradually ended and replaced with trade, direct investment, capital markets, remittances, micro-finance and domestic savings. This would stimulate African entrepreneurialism as well as enable Africans to hold their governments more accountable.[55] In a 2009 editorial, President Kagame of Rwanda argued that aid had never addressed the underlying conditions for poverty; instead it encouraged dependence, so aid should be targeted more effectively with the ultimate goal of ending development aid.[56]

On the left, African intellectuals argue that development aid is structured by the capitalist system to perpetuate institutional power relations and provide markets for Western exporters and jobs for Western advisors. Manji and O'Coill argue that the development regime fails to address historical and structural causes of poverty.[57] Rasna Warah argues that development aid has done little more than benefit the elite while poverty and inequality have increased and traditional institutions have been destroyed.[58]

Western ideological influence over the type of development pathway that African countries should pursue is being challenged by democratization at the national and multilateral levels. There is practically unanimous support for the improvement of governance and leadership, but great debate over the way in which to integrate into the global economy and how to define "development". Criticism of the capitalist development model has been heightened recently by the financial crisis originating in the U.S. African intellectuals continue to call for greater self-reliance and regional integration, but because of limited domestic savings and capital flight, foreign sources of capital and technology are still necessary to build infrastructure, transform agriculture and finance manufacturing as well as the extraction of raw materials.

African countries have carried out significant economic policy reforms to make their economies more attractive to foreign investors. Forty African countries instituted substantial liberal reform measures including allowing greater foreign investment in the telecom sector, reforming banking sectors, allowing foreign ownership of land, easing registration and taxation requirements, and creating special investment zones.[59] African stock markets were developed as part of country strategies to reform their financial sectors, attract foreign capital and carry out privatization.[60] The Economic Commission for Africa credits these reforms and developments with stimulating the latest interest in investment in Africa though it is difficult to separate the effects of these reforms from the global market conditions.[61] Wade argues that the liberal trends within the world financial system have had a negative impact on many developing countries by increasing the volatility of exchange rates, capital flows, interest rates and prices.[62]

Toward the end of 2007, one of the early responses to the United States' subprime crisis and the falling value of the dollar was an increased flow of funds to developing countries and especially "frontier markets." This growth was driven primarily by a commodities boom as well as the fact that sub-Saharan Africa was experiencing the strongest growth and lowest inflation in thirty years; also investors were hoping that a slowdown in the West would not affect growth in developing countries.[63] Africa was thought to be less vulnerable to the financial crisis because most capital flows are public, most private investment is FDI, rather than the more volatile portfolio investment, and African financial markets had little exposure to sub-prime mortgages; but as financiers rushed to raise money to cover bad debts, stocks in Africa were sold.[64] By 2009, the global credit crisis had started to affect all emerging markets' stocks, bonds and currencies, as global credit contracted. Although economic slowdowns can bring the benefit of lower fuel and food costs, the impact of reduced foreign trade, repatriation of finances, and the stress on banking is likely to outweigh the benefits.[65] If private sector lending decreases then African countries will need to lean more heavily on development finance.

African economies are vulnerable to global recession. By 2009 there were indications that remittance flows had slowed dramatically as migrant workers lost jobs in developed countries.[66] But by October of 2011, the IMF projected that economic growth in sub-Saharan Africa would rise to close to 6 percent if the global economic growth rate remained at least 4 percent.[67]

African Responses

In recent years there have been a plethora of responses to these trends in trade and capital integration. In this section I address some efforts to alter current patterns of trade and capital flows at the levels of the state, civil society and global civil society. In response to the widespread criticisms that policies promoting rapid market reforms have benefitted external actors and local elites at the expense of African societies, political actors are proposing alternatives to prevailing economic institutions.

At the state level, there are ongoing efforts to strengthen regional economic cooperation and form a united front in multilateral negotiations over economic issues. More than 100 organizations from 30 African countries signed the Accra Declaration during the African Union Summit of 2007 calling for quickened economic integration through progress towards an African Union Government as well as continued strengthening of the Regional Economic Communities.[68]

At the sub-state level, domestic nongovernmental organizations (NGOs) and social entrepreneurs are challenging ineffective and non-transparent centralized state control as well as the dominating influence of foreign instruments of economic governance. Members of civil society are making some progress in their efforts to play a bigger role in decision-making. In 2005, the Economic, Social and Cultural Council of the African Union (ECOSOCC) was launched as an effort to enable interactions between governments and grassroots organizations, deepen democracy and improve efforts to govern external economic interventions in African economies. The council includes trade unions, NGOs, members of the African diaspora, women's groups, human rights and anti-poverty activists, and representatives from business. Participating NGOs are prohibited from receiving more than half of their funding from foreign sources.[69]

At the WTO, efforts to form a united front and obstruct trade deals that have inadequate provisions have the potential to make a material difference to African opportunities in global trade. Although forty-one African nations are members of the African Group at the WTO, the effect of lower tariffs on African economies varies tremendously, depending on whether the nation exports or imports manufactured goods or agricultural goods. This variation in interests can undermine the ability of the Africa Group to unite to lobby for policy positions; nevertheless, grassroots organizations such as labor unions have played a big role in lobbying for a positive outcome on cotton and the right to protection in the manufacturing sector.[70] As of 2011, no sub-Saharan African country had used the Dispute Resolution Mechanism as a primary complainant, but countries acting on behalf of the developing countries, such as Brazil, have challenged Western dominance. In 2007, in a case brought by Brazil, the WTO ruled against US government subsidies for cotton farmers.

Grassroots efforts have also played a big role in altering international policies on intellectual property rights. Starting in 1998 in South Africa, the grassroots movement, the Treatment Action Campaign, fought for the rights of HIV-positive South Africans to access affordable treatment. In 2001, an international petition also bolstered the South African government's fight to defeat pharmaceutical company efforts to prevent it from maintaining a law that allowed the government to produce and import generic AIDS treatment drugs. After a groundswell of international pressure, in 2007, the WTO made permanent a waiver to allow member states that did not have the capacity to produce pharmaceuticals and were in the midst of a health crisis to import generics from other countries.[71]

Although enforcement of intellectual property rights can be detrimental for developing countries because of the high costs of license payments and the consequent limitation on access to technology, there is also potential for African producers to take advantage of these trade rules. For example, in 2007 Ethiopian coffee producers signed an agreement with Starbucks to protect their rights to determine the use of their brands of specialty coffees.[72]

Another development establishing progressive trade links between Western and African people is the fair trade movement. The concept, developed at a

1985 conference in London, was to establish direct trade between consumers and producers that would enable purchasing from democratically organized cooperatives. It originally sought to address specific countries that were excluded from trade for political reasons but also sought to address the problem of the negative terms of trade experienced by developing countries. The originating organizations, Third World Information Network and Twin Trading, were soon followed by others across Europe and the United States. Fair trade came to refer to the marketing of products that had achieved criteria such as wages at the International Labor Organization's standard, producers' prices set at least above a tenth of the world price, and direct supply. In various countries in Africa, cooperatives were set up to sell fair trade products such as coffee, cocoa, nuts, and tropical fruit. These efforts have improved the living standards of workers, and provided opportunities for education.[73]

The most significant state level effort to attract more capital to Africa was the creation of the New Partnership for Africa's Development (NEPAD) in 2001, to set up a new framework for development. While many African leaders and the African business elite are heavily invested in this liberal agenda because it is seen as the best means to attract capital; critics see NEPAD as an endorsement of the Western agenda to integrate Africa into the global economy through liberalization of trade and investment, rather than the result of a democratic process. These critics associate liberal policies with the exacerbation of poverty in Africa and call instead for development plans that address needs like debt cancellation, investment in social services, and changes in the financial and trade rules.[74]

Increasingly, African countries are insisting on more development-oriented investment deals, calling for greater investment in power, manufacturing and other aspects of domestic production, rather than just in the export sectors. This need for investment in basic infrastructure is behind the multiple deals signed between China and African countries.

There are also new grassroots institutions to monitor the efficacy of development assistance, such as African Monitor. Conferences in Paris in 2005 and Accra in 2008 have attempted to address issues like greater coordination between donors, efforts to ensure that aid programs are determined by the national interests of the recipient states, and elimination of the practice of tying aid to purchases of goods and services from the donor.

Starting with widespread protests against structural adjustment programs in the 1980s, civil society groups have organized to express opposition to the role of IFIs in the formation of domestic economic policy. Critics are still concerned about the undemocratic nature of the Poverty Reduction and Growth Facility that replaced the Enhanced Structural Adjustment Facility, arguing that IFI policies still prevent domestic control over policy formation and undermine the accountability of African governments.[75] They call for deeper changes ranging from more substantial reform of IFI rules to the closing of the IFIs.[76]

There have also been well-organized violent responses to perceived government complicity with external investors. In Nigeria, for example, the Movement for the Emancipation of the Niger Delta (MEND) has been fighting against the collaboration between the federal government and Western oil companies to extract oil from the Niger Delta. They seek both greater local control over oil resources and reparations for the high levels of pollution that have occurred during the many years of extraction. Militants associated with this group carry out attacks on oil facilities and kidnap oil workers.

Both nonviolent and violent responses to foreign investment have contributed to an understanding that in many cases resource extraction is profoundly detrimental for local communities. The AU Commission's African Mining Vision 2050 is a collaboration between states and civil society to develop a framework to help improve local benefits from resources exploitation. It aims to improve the governance of mining companies, alter the apportionment of profits and integrate the mining sector into more sustainable economic development.

Across Africa there has been a resurgence in attention to agriculture and food security, exemplified by Claude Ake's call for an agricultural development strategy focusing on smallholder farmers and rural industrialization;[77] but there is a profound debate over the course that should be taken. In September of 2010, African leaders meeting at the first African Green Revolution Forum agreed on a plan of action to achieve food security through policies such as investment support for farmers and agribusiness, agricultural research, greater access to "improved" seed and fertilizers.[78] This market-oriented idea of a green revolution characterized by foreign investment, a major role for agribusiness, and harmonization of donor policy is supported by a $20 billion pledge from the G8, the United States "Feed the Future" initiative, various investment funds and development projects. While these efforts promise attention to small scale farmers and locally controlled planning and research, some international critics argue that the focus on industrial farming threatens the role and potential contribution of small farmers to bio-diversity and more sustainable low-tech methods.[79]

New international financial trends also have the potential to empower local entrepreneurs. Microfinance, offering banking services to the poor who have previously been excluded, has steadily expanded in Africa, as major commercial banks enter the market. New organizations like Kiva.org, microplace.com and MyC4.com allow investors anywhere in the world to make small loans to entrepreneurs in Africa. Unlike remittances, the necessity to pay back the loan may encourage careful targeting of productive investment rather than consumption.

Conclusion

The countries of sub-Saharan Africa are integrated into global flows of trade and capital, but they have little power in the forums where the rules that govern these flows are designed. In addition to this, because of dependence on foreign capital and commodity exports, they are especially vulnerable to financial crises and economic recessions. To some extent, economic globalization has undermined African opportunities for economic development; but globalization can provide opportunities, in the form of new markets, new sources of capital, new skills and technology. The question is how to access the opportunities without exposing economies to unacceptable costs. The trade-off in Africa has been determined by political actors that rarely act in the interests of the majority of people.

Global capitalism is constantly evolving. The latest financial crisis and ongoing political crises could point the way towards global reforms such as universal financial regulations, a slow-down and rethinking of trade liberalization, a re-evaluation of the role of the state in the development process, and a new conceptualization of development aid. New green technologies as well as efforts to preserve natural environments will be necessary to sustain economic growth in Africa, but may not be implemented fast enough to counter the negative effects of global warming. Grassroots campaigns, such as that of Wangari Maathai's Green Belt Movement can be integrated into regional and global efforts to protect the environment.

African economies are deeply affected by the brain drain. Increasing economic opportunities in Africa could go a long way towards attracting the educated diaspora and their capital back home. Certainly the debates over the definition of development and the best path towards economic growth will continue, but the policy formation must be controlled by Africans. There is a tension between the eagerness of some in the West to get involved in reducing poverty in Africa and the need for Africans to have greater local control over their economic institutions and policies; but Africa and the West are linked, through trade, capital and a diaspora that is constantly on the move. While the response to that tension may lie in greater South-South partnership, the topic of the next chapter of this book, democratization of both domestic and international institutions has the potential to change historical patterns in a way that contributes to more sustainable economic growth.

Bibliography

"Accra Declaration." July 2007, http://www.pambazuka.org/aumonitor/images/uploads/ACCRAJuly2007AUSummitDECLARATION.pdf.

"Africa: Trade Unions Speak Out on Trade." *AfricaFocus Bulletin* (070317), Mar 17, 2007. www.AfricaFocus.org.

Ake, Claude. *Democracy and Development in Africa.* Washington D.C: Brookings, 1996.

Alliance for a Green Revolution in Africa. "Concrete Actions to Accelerate Africa's Green Revolution." Sept 7, 2010, http://allafrica.com/stories/201009120003.html.

Arrighi, Giovanni. "The African Crisis." *New Left Review* 15 (2002).

Bond, Patrick. "Strategies for Social Movements from Southern Africa to the United States." *Foreign Policy in Focus* (January 20, 2005).

Bretton Woods Project. "Civil Society letter on IMF review of lending instruments, facilities and policies." September 30, 2008, www.brettonwoodsproject.org.

Brown, Michael Barratt. "'Fair Trade' with Africa." *Review of African Political Economy.* 112 (2007).

Callaghy, Thomas M. "Networks and governance in Africa: innovation in the debt regime." In Callaghy, Thomas M.; Latham, Robert; Kassimir, Ronald, (eds.). *Intervention and Transnationalism in Africa: Global-Local Networks of* Power. Cambridge, 2001.

Chazan, Naomi; Lewis, Peter; Mortimer, Robert; and Rothchild, Donald, (eds.). *Politics and Society in Contemporary Africa.* Boulder, CO: Lynne Rienner, 1992.

Chen, Shaohua and Ravallion, Martin. "The Developing World Is Poorer Than We Thought, But No Less Successful in the Fight against Poverty." *Policy Research Working Paper* 4703 (August 2008).

"Civil Society Gains Strength at African Union ECOSOCC Meeting." Africafiles, 9-10-2008, http://www.africafiles.org/article.asp?ID=18975.

"Cotton Producers celebrate WTO ruling against US subsidies." www.irinnews.org, October 16, 2007.

DATA. "The DATA Report 2009: Monitoring the G8 Promise to Africa Executive Summary." http://www.one.org/international/datareport2009/.

Delechat, Corinne; Kovanen, Arto; and Wakeman-Linn, John. "Sub-Saharan Africa: Private Capital Fueling Growth." *IMF Survey Magazine,* May 22, 2008, http://www.imf.org.

Duignan, Peter and Gann, Lewis. *The United States and Africa: A History.* New York: Cambridge: Cambridge University Press, 1984.

Easterly, William. *The White Man's Burden: Why the West's Efforts to Aid the Rest Have Done so Much Ill and So Little Good*. New York: Penguin, 2007.

Economic Commission for Africa. "Economic Report on Africa 2004: Unlocking Africa's Trade Potential." (2004), http://www.uneca.org/era2004/.

Gibb, Richard. "Post-Lomé: the European Union and the South." *Third World Quarterly*, Vol 21, No 3 (2000), 463.

Harsch, Ernest. "Africa braces for global shockwaves." *Africa Renewal* 22 4 (2009). *http://www.un.org/ecosocdev/geninfo/afrec/vol22no4/224-shockwaves.html.*

Held, David. *Global Covenant: The Social Democratic Alternative to the Washington Consensus*. Cambridge: Polity Press, 2004.

Held, David; McGrew, Anthony; Goldblatt, David; and Perraton, Jonathan. *Global Transformations: Politics, Economics and Culture*. Stanford: Stanford University Press, 1999.

Helleiner, Eric. *States and the Reemergence of Global Finance: From Bretton Woods to the 1990s*. Ithaca: Cornell University Press, 1994.

Hurt, Stephen R. "The European Union's External Relations with Africa after the Cold War: Aspects of Continuity and Change." In Taylor, Ian and Williams, Paul (eds.). *Africa in International Politics: External Involvement on the Continent*. New York: Routledge, 2005.

"In for the long haul? Why a boom is under way in emerging markets." *Financial Times*, October 18, 2007.

International Monetary Fund. "Battered by Crisis, African Growth to Fall Sharply." *Survey Magazine* (April 24, 2009), http://www.imf.org/external/pubs/ft/survey/so/2009/CAR042409A.htm.

International Monetary Fund. "World Economic and Financial Surveys: Regional Economic Outlook: Sub-Saharan Africa." (October 2011), http://www.imf.org.

"Investors' enthusiasm grows for the new frontiers." *Financial Times*, November 20, 2007.

Jonasse, Richard. "Africans Face Competing Visions of Agricultural Development at a Critical Juncture." May 20, 2010, www.foodfirst.org.

Kagame, Paul "Africa has to find its own road to prosperity." *Financial Times*, May 7, 2009.

Khor, Martin. "Trade: Africans played pivotal role at turning point of WTO talks." *Third World Network Info Service on Trade and WTO Issues* (Aug 08/06), http://www.twnside.org.sg/title2/wto.info/twninfo20080806.htm.

Lancaster, Carol and Dusen, Ann Van. *Organizing U.S. Foreign Aid: Confronting the Challenges of the Twenty-first Century*. Washington D.C.: Brookings, 2005.

Lavelle, Kathryn C. "Architecture of Equity Markets: The Abidjan Regional Bourse." *International Organization* 55, 3 (Summer 2001).

Manji, Firoze and O'Coill, Carl. "The missionary position: NGOs and development in Africa." *International Affairs* 78 3 (2002) 567–83.

Melamed, Claire. "Briefing: Wrong Questions, Wrong Answers—Trade, Trade Talks and Africa." *African Affairs* 105/420 (2006), 451–460.

Mistry, Percy S. "Reasons for Sub-Saharan Africa's Development Deficit that the Commission for Africa Did Not Consider." *African Affairs*, 104/417 (2005).

Moss, Todd. *Adventure Capitalism: globalization and the political economy of stock markets in Africa*. Palgrave Macmillan, 2003.

Moyo, Dambisa. *Dead Aid: Why Aid is Not Working and How There is a Better Way for Africa*. New York: Farrar, Straus and Giroux, 2009.

Moyo, Dambisa. "Why Foreign Aid Is Hurting Africa." *Wall Street Journal*, April 16, 2009.

Naumann, Eckart. "AGOA at nine: some reflections on the Act's impact on Africa-US trade." January 2009, http://www.agoa.info/?view=about&story=details.

Nunn, Nathan. "The Historical Origins of Africa's Underdevelopment." Nov 8, 2007, http://www.voxeu.org/index.php?q=node/779.

Nyang'oro, Julius E. and Shaw, Timothy M. "The African State in the Global Economic Context." In *The African State at a Critical Juncture: Between Disintegration and Reconfiguration*. Boulder, CO: Lynne Rienner, 1997.

OECD. "Private Equity: An Eye for Investment under African Skies?" *Policy Insight* #60 (April 2008), 1, www.oecd.org/dev/insights.

Office of the United States Trade Representative. "2008 Comprehensive Report on U.S. Trade and Investment Policy Toward Sub-Saharan Africa and Implementation of the African Growth and Opportunity Act." (May 2008), http://www.ustr.gov, 30.

Olsen, Gorm Rye. "The European Union: 'European Interests', Bureaucratic Interests and International Options." In Engel, Ulf and Olsen, Gorm Rye, (eds.). *Africa and the North: between Globalization and Marginalization*. New York: Routledge, 2005.

Oxfam. "Oxfam Celebrates Win-Win Outcome for Ethiopian Coffee Farmers and Starbucks." June 20, 2007, www.oxfam.org.

Prempeh, E. Osei Kwadwo. *Against Global Capitalism: African Social Movements Confront Neoliberal Globalization*. Surrey: Ashgate, 2006.

Ratha, Dilip; Mohapatra, Sanket; and Xu1, Zhimei. "Outlook for Remittance Flows 2008–2010: Growth expected to moderate significantly, but flows to remain resilient." *Migration and Development Brief* 8 (The world Bank, November 11, 2008), http://siteresources.worldbank.org/INTPROSPECTS/Resources/334934-1110315015165/MD_Brief8.pdf.

Reisen, Helmut. "The Fallout form the Financial Crisis: Emerging Markets under Stress." *Policy Insights* #83 (December 2008), www.oecd.org/dev/insights.

Rimmer, Douglas. "Learning About Economic Development From Africa." *African Affairs* 102, (2003).

Sachs, Jeffrey. *The End of Poverty: Economic Possibilities for Our Time*. New York: Penguin, 2006.

Santos-Paulino, A.U. and Thirlwall, A.P. "The Effects of trade liberalization on imports in selected developing countries." *The Economic Journal* 114 (2004).

Shatz, Sayre. "Structural Adjustment." In Bond, George C. and Gibson, Nigel C. eds. *Contested Terrains and Constructed Categories: Contemporary Africa in Focus*. Boulder, CO: Westview Press, 2002.

Thomas, Caroline. "The International Financial Institutions' relations with Africa: Insights from the issue of representation and voice." In Taylor, Ian and Williams, Paul eds. *African in International Politics: external involvement on the continent*. New York: Routledge, 2005.

United Nations Conference on Trade and Development. "Economic Development in Africa: Export Performance following Trade Liberalization: Some Patterns and Policy Perspectives." (July 29, 2008), http://www.unctad.org.

United Nations Conference on Trade and Development. "World Investment Report 2011." http://www.unctad.org.

United Nations. "Millennium Development Goal 8: Delivering on Global Partnership for Achieving the Millennium Development Goals." MDG Gap Task Force Report 2008, http://www.un.org/esa/policy/mdggap/mdg8report_engw.pdf.

United States Department of Commerce International Trade Administration. "U.S.-African Trade Profile." USDC Market Access and Compliance Office of Africa (2008).

United States Department of Commerce International Trade Administration. "U.S.-African Trade Profile." USDC Market Access and Compliance Office of Africa (March 2003).

United States Department of Commerce International Trade Administration. "U.S.-African Trade Profile." USDC Market Access and Compliance Office of Africa (July 2009).

United States Department of Commerce International Trade Administration. "U.S.-African Trade Profile." USDC Market Access and Compliance Office of Africa (July 2010).

Vyborny, Katherine. "What Could the Doha Round Mean for Africa?" *Carnegie Endowment for International Peace* Web Commentary, June 12, 2007, http://www.carnegieendowment.org/files/vyborny_wc1.pdf.

Wade, Robert. "Choking the South." *New Left Review* 38 (2006).
Walle, Nicolas van de. *African Economies and the Politics of Permanent Crisis, 1979–1999.* Cambridge: Cambridge University Press, 2001.
Warah, Rasna. "The Development Myth," May 12, 2009, http://www.zmag.org/znet/viewArticle/21438.
World Bank's 2008 World Development Indicators.
Young, Crawford. *The African Colonial State in Comparative Perspective.* New Haven: Yale University Press, 1994.

Chapter 3

Reshaping the Global Economy: The South-South Economic Partnership

Shadrack Wanjala Nasong'o

"South-South cooperation is less bureaucratic and more in touch with the realities of recipient countries than conventional cooperation, as well as being unconditional and not interfering in the domestic affairs of states ... South-South cooperation [means] ownership" (FRIDE 2009).

Introduction

The global recession of the second decade of the twenty-first century shook the foundations of the global political economy rooted in the mantra of free market capitalism. Arguably, this development marked the turning point when the industrial world began to lose its monopoly control over the world economy. As the world's strongest economies slipped into recession, many developing non-Western economies continued to grow partly on account of the strength of their interactions with other developing countries in the global South. South-South relations, both formal and informal ties between Africa and other non-Western nations, especially Brazil, China, and India, have grown over the last 40 years as African trade turned more and more toward their developing world neighbors, Asian Tigers, and a surging China.[1] African countries are at the center of this South-South economic renaissance, averaging a seven percent annual increase in exports between 1995 and 2007. This chapter focuses on these developments in South-South economic relations with a view to evaluating their implications for the global economy.

In particular, the chapter aims to demonstrate that Africa's economic relations with other countries of the South constitute an effort to break free from the economic conditions imposed by Western powers (examined by Hendrickson in the preceding chapter) and shield themselves from the fragile economies of the industrial world. The chapter proceeds by examining the historical development of South-South economic development, evaluating the emerging solidarity of South countries within the rubric of the World Trade Organization (WTO), and finally focuses on the dynamics of trade among countries of the global South with particular emphasis on Sino-African trade. The main thesis of the chapter is that whereas the economic crises of the 1980s and subsequent economic cycles of boom and bust derailed efforts by global South countries to reshape the international economic order embodied in the 1978 Buenos Aires Plan of Action for Technical Cooperation among Developing Countries, a number of countries have emerged with strong and diverse economies within the South-South cooperation rubric that can stand as cornerstones for the future.

South-South Economic Partnership: An Overview

One of the most common denominators undergirding the emerging close economic relations between countries of the global South is their shared sense of domination and exploitation by global North economies. From the Opium Wars and the Boxer Rebellion in China through the Gandhian motif of peaceful anti-colonial resistance to the dynamics of anti-colonial nationalism in Africa and decolonization in Latin America, countries in the global South share the experience of having been collectively exploited by the Western world. Following the end of formal colonialism, the solidarity of these countries manifested itself in a number of developments at the international level. First was the Afro-Asian Bandung Conference of 1955 that brought together 29 mostly newly independent African and Asian countries in Bandung, Indonesia between April 18 and 24. Organized by Indonesia, Burma (now Myanmar), Pakistan, and Ceylon (now Sri Lanka), and coordinated by Ruslan Abdulgani, the secretary of the Indonesian Foreign Affairs ministry, the Bandung Conference represented nearly one fourth of the Earth's land surface and a total population of 1.5 billion people.[2] The conference aimed to promote Afro-Asian economic and cultural cooperation and to oppose colonialism and neocolonialism both by the United States and the Soviet Union, as well as imperialistic tendencies by other industrial nations.

The Bandung Conference was closely followed by the Belgrade Conference in Yugoslavia in 1961. This marked the second major development in South-South relations as it led to the formation of the Non-Aligned Movement (NAM). The crystallization of the NAM was a consequence of the perception by the Belgrade Conference organizers (Yugoslavia's Josip Broz Tito, India's Jawaharlal Nehru, Egypt's Gamal Abdel Nasser, and Indonesia's Sukarno) that Western powers were unwilling to consult them on decisions affecting them within the context of the Cold War. They were also concerned about the tensions between China and the United States and fueled by their opposition to colonialism, especially French influence in North Africa, as well as the desire by Indonesia to promote its case in its dispute with the Netherlands over Western New Guinea.[3] Indonesia's Sukarno dubbed the NAM 'Newly Emerging Forces' (NEFOS) and portrayed himself as its leader.[4]

The overall aim of NAM was to chart a middle course for developing states between the contending Cold War ideological forces of the East and the West. The concrete objectives of the NAM were elaborated in the 1979 Havana Declaration as to "ensure the national independence, sovereignty, territorial integrity and security of non-aligned countries in their struggle against imperialism, colonialism, neo-colonialism, racism, and all forms of foreign aggression, occupation, domination, interference or hegemony as well as against great power and bloc politics."[5] At this point in time, the NAM represented close to two thirds of members of the United Nations (UN) and about 55 percent of the world's population, largely located in the global South.[6]

The third major development at the international level with consequences for South-South relations was the establishment of the United Nations Conference on Trade and Development (UNCTAD) in 1964 with a view to promoting development-friendly integration of developing countries into the world economy. Over time, UNCTAD has progressively evolved into an authoritative knowledge-based institution whose work aims to help shape current policy debates and thinking on development with a particular focus on ensuring that domestic policies and international action are mutually supportive in bringing about sustainable development. In particular, UNCTAD seeks to accomplish its mandate by performing three critical functions: (1) serving as a forum for intergovernmental deliberations in consultation with experts and exchange of experience geared toward building consensus; (2) undertaking research, policy analysis and data collection for the deliberation of government representatives and experts; and (3) providing technical assistance tailored to the specific needs of global South countries with particular focus on the needs of the least developed countries as well as economies in transition.[7]

The fourth major development in the South-South economic relations was the establishment of the Group of 77 in June 1964 by the Joint Declaration of the Seventy-Seven Countries issued at the UNCTAD Conference of the same year. The G-77's first major meeting was in Algiers in 1967, where the *Charter of Algiers* was adopted and the basis for permanent institutional structures was established. The G-77 has since expanded to 131 member countries. It is the largest inter-governmental organization of countries of the global South that operates within the United Nations system. It provides a forum for member countries to articulate and promote their collective economic interests and enhance their joint negotiating capacity on all major international economic issues within the rubric of the UN system. In addition, the G-77 promotes South-South cooperation for development.[8] The supreme decision making organ of the organization is the South Summit, which convened for the first time in Havana, Cuba in April 2000; then in Doha, Qatar in June 2005; and in Nairobi, Kenya in September 2009.

According to Jarle Møen, it was with the establishment of the NAM, UNCTAD, and the G-77 in the 1960s that South-South co-operation on a global scale was put on the international agenda.[9] Partly inspired by the success of the Organization of Petroleum Exporting Countries (OPEC) in the early 1970s, the G-77 focused on pushing for a New International Economic Order within the framework of the United Nations. With their large voting majority in the General Assembly global South countries could, in principle, push through any proposal they wanted. However, as Møen rightly observes, a voting majority and a morally superior position, were not enough.[10] By the early 1980s it became clear that the notion of "commodity power" was not rooted in reality, and Southern demands did not correspond to Southern strengths. Furthermore, global North countries continuously moved international economic negotiations away from UN organizations to the Bretton Woods institutions—the World Bank and International Monetary Fund (IMF). These disappointing experiences resulted in little interest in South-South issues for several years. Nevertheless, in the early 1990s, the subject seemed to gain some renewed interest as demonstrated by the establishment of the South Commission.[11]

The establishment of the South Commission in 1987 following the 1986 Harare NAM summit meeting marked the fifth major development in the evolution of South-South economic partnership. The South Commission, chaired by Tanzania's former president, Julius Nyerere, operated as an independent organization with its officials serving in their personal capacities though it was financed by contributions from developing countries. Its secretariat was set up in Geneva, Switzerland. The Commission was formed against the NAM realization that the 1980s was a lost decade with regard to economic development in the global South as evidenced by the debt crises, high interest rates, low world prices for commodities, and ongoing Northern protectionism.[12] In the first three years of its existence, the South Commission focused on two critical issues—the South's external debt burden and the Uruguay Round of Trade Negotiations on which it released a report in 1990, *The Challenge to the South*. In the Report, the Commission evaluated the South's achievements and failures in economic development and proposed remedial measures.[13]

According to Adam Sneyd, although the Commission carried out its work in the final years of a decade that devastated many economies in the South, the Commission's Report struck a positive note of hope and made a strong case for self-reliant, people-centered development strategies. It demonstrated how developing countries could gain strength and bargaining power through mutual co-operation in international organizations.[14] Describing how the global arrangements for trade, finance, and technology handicap the South, the Report impressed upon countries of the global South to act in solidarity in the multitude of North-South economic negotiations. The Report further contended that growing global interdependence makes it beneficial to all peoples that countries of the global South are afforded a fairer chance to escape poverty and attain sustainable development.

Building upon the Report's recommendations and the work of the South Commission's follow-up office, forty-six developing countries agreed to establish a permanent center on South-South cooperation in July 1995. The South Center was tasked with promoting South-South solidarity, knowledge sharing, and cooperation, as well as coordinating common development policy positions on the world economy. To meet the goal of functioning as a think tank and a policy support organization for the global South, the South Center was mandated to disseminate its research output widely. Overall, the Centre seeks more policy space or autonomy for Southern countries interacting with the global economy, and a more equitable distribution of global income. Members meet at least every three years as the Council of Representatives to set the direction of the Board, which is charged with day-to-day oversight and fundraising. The South Center typically produces news and policy reports on topics that the G-77 suggests. Its principal research focuses on intellectual property and trade. On the latter, the Center helps to coordinate developing countries' policy positions within the framework of WTO's trade negotiations. The Center's output helped to facilitate the South's united front evident at the WTO Ministerial Conference in Cancun in 2003.[15]

South-South Solidarity within the WTO

As mentioned above, despite the existence of the G-77 and the NAM, the interests of global South countries were not given much attention especially within the UN system in spite of the fact that these countries were the majority in the UN General Assembly. Their interests were circumvented by industrial countries through shifting negotiations on critical economic and development issues to the Bretton Woods institutions as well as to the World Trade Organization (WTO) within which the industrial states held sway. However, by the turn of the 1990s, South countries established solidarity in pursuit of their common objectives within these international forums, partly as a result of the work of the South-South Commission and its think tank, the South Center. South-South solidarity was particularly demonstrated in the Doha Round of Trade Talks under the aegis of the WTO that began in 2001 in the city of Doha in Qatar. The Doha Round followed the successful completion of the Uruguay Round of Talks that began in 1986 in Puntadel, Uruguay under the General Agreement on Tariffs and Trade, the precursor to WTO, and ended in Marrakesh, Morocco, in 1994. The Uruguay Round culminated in a daunting list of about 60 agreements, annexes and decisions. The agreements, which are legally binding, gave birth to the WTO in 1995.[16]

Even before the Doha Round began in 2001, African countries together with other countries of the global South blocked the launch of a new 'round' at the WTO's ministerial meeting, in Seattle, United States, in December 1999. This was on the basis that the continent had not seen any benefits from the agreements it had signed as part of the 1994 Uruguay Round. Some 70 percent of gains registered went to industrial nations of the global North with the remainder going mostly to a few large export-oriented, developing countries. Iddi Simba, Tanzania's trade minister and chief negotiator for Africa at the 1999 WTO meeting, noted: "Many developing countries would prefer to solve the implementation issues remaining from the Uruguay Round agreement before advancing to the next stage of multilateral negotiations."[17] In the run-up to the Doha Round, African countries met in Addis Ababa, Ethiopia, in June 2001 to prepare for the WTO meeting. African trade ministers concluded that they should continue to push for the effective implementation of WTO obligations by developed countries. They noted that they had expected that a number of trade-related issues of importance to Africa and other developing countries such as trade and commodities, trade and finance, and transfer of technology would be taken up in the WTO work program, which had not materialized.

The Doha Round is the current WTO trade negotiation round that began at ministerial level in Doha, Qatar in November 2001. Subsequent ministerial meetings were held in Cancun, Mexico in 2003 and in Hong Kong in 2005. Related negotiations were also held in France in 2005, Geneva, Switzerland in 2004, 2006, and 2008, as well as in Potsdam in Germany in 2007. The Doha Round collapsed, most spectacularly in Cancun in 2003 and in Geneva in 2008. The most significant differences are between global North countries including the European Union (EU), the United States, Canada, and Japan—so-called Quad countries—and a newly robust and united bloc of major countries of the global South led mainly by Brazil, China, India, South Korea, and South Africa. Industrial countries pushed for newer issues that mostly they themselves would have benefited from—especially the need to expand free trade and economic liberalization. In particular, they sought to liberalize rules for investment, competition policy, government procurement, trade facilitation and electronic commerce, all designed to open domestic markets to foreign companies. Industrial countries, home to most of the world's multinational firms, want to limit the ability of governments to favor domestic companies over foreign firms for instance by reserving import or distribution rights for local businesses or national government agencies. They further want the removal of barriers to investment, such as government policies that compel foreign corporations to form partnerships with local firms or to recruit and train local professionals. The same countries would like the WTO to allow members to restrict trade with countries that fail to meet certain levels of environmental protection, do not guarantee the right to unionize and permit the employment of children.

For their part, global South countries pushed the case for completing older issues mostly on agriculture that affected them the most, especially the impact of European and U.S. subsidies on their own agriculture and the South's lack of access to Northern markets—a reality that is inconsistent with the free trade mantra, which these two regions promote. Specifically, developing countries demanded implementation of all Uruguay Round commitments including delivery of promised financial and technical resources and assistance to the poorest net food importing countries; increased access to Northern markets through removal of domestic support measures such as agricultural subsidies, which, despite pledges by industrial nations to reduce them, have continued to grow and, by the time of the Cancun talks, averaged $300 billion annually—more than five times greater than official development assistance to poor countries; exemption of South countries from trade-related investment measures (TRIMs) such as protecting local businesses and industry from open competition with foreign companies; formal interpretation of trade-related aspects of intellectual property rights (TRIPs) that acknowledges the right of developing countries to affordably obtain medicines to combat HIV/AIDS, tuberculosis, and malaria among other deadly diseases; assurance that TRIPs will not be interpreted in a way that endangers food security and that grants patents to life forms and biological processes; as well as extension of trade in services negotiations to allow easier movement of workers from the global South to the global North. In addition, South countries opposed introduction of new issues into the negotiations including new rules on trade facilitation. They contended that international trade could be improved by extending more financial and technical assistance to narrow the gap between the rich and poor countries in technical knowledge and human resources.[18] Countries that took a strong position on these issues included larger ones such as China, India, Brazil, and South Africa but also included blocs such as the African, Caribbean and Pacific (ACP) group, the African Union, the Least Developed Countries (LDCs) and Asian countries such as Malaysia.

The impasse between the global North and global South led to the collapse of the Doha Round of trade negotiations. This has left rich countries blaming poor countries for the failed talks. However, depending on one's identity and location in the global scheme of things, the collapse of the Doha Round can be viewed as a sort of success for countries of the global South insofar as their failure meant their economic lot was not worsened. Additionally, the Doha Round galvanized, for the first time, a united and bold stand by poor countries against their rich counterparts who had previously applied non-democratic pressures to get their interests advanced in the WTO system often at the expense of poor countries. The counter-position to global North countries was spearheaded by a grouping of 21 countries (G-21), including Egypt, Nigeria, South Africa, Argentina, Bolivia, Brazil, Chile, China, Colombia, Costa Rica, Cuba, Ecuador, Guatemala, India, Indonesia, Mexico, Pakistan, Paraguay, Peru, Philippines, Thailand and Venezuela—collectively home to more than 50 percent of the world's population and more than 60 per cent of its farmers, and producing roughly one quarter of global farm exports. In spite of application of divide-and-rule tactics by industrial powers to disorganize the G-21, including seeking to divide the group on the basis of those included and excluded in trade preferences, on the basis of those more developed and less developed, and on the basis of their continental origin, the group remained intact and acted in solidarity with other countries of the global South during the Doha Round.

Against the foregoing, Carlos Aguilar argues that South-South relations are becoming increasingly relevant because of the role countries like South Africa, Brazil, India and China play both at the global and at the regional levels in sub-Saharan Africa, Latin America and Asia.[19] The debate and progress that might eventually take place within the WTO, according to Aguilar, will be key to understanding how international power arrangements unfold. He contends that any structural and urgent solution to the problems we are facing needs to address both the meaning of change in current relations among these South countries, and how it might influence the creation of an alternate power structure in international relations. Indeed, according to UNCTAD Secretary-General Rubens Ricupero, the emergence of the G-21 is an important factor for future WTO negotiations, as the major trading nations will be forced to take the new power reality into account. It is arguable, further, that African countries seem to have come of age within the context of international trade negotiations and will no longer be taken for granted. As Mauritian minister and head of the Africa Group at the 2003 Cancun talks asserted,

> the call from Africa for a fair and just global trading system has been construed in some quarters to be indicative of a growing radicalization of the African position on international trade issues ... Nothing could be further from the truth ... the continent is merely responding to its weakening trade position, growing poverty and realization that it will fail to meet the Global Millennium Development Goals—including cutting global poverty in half by 2015—in the present climate.[20]

Partnering for Development: South-South Trade

The decade of the 1980s saw reductions in foreign aid to the global South, especially to Africa, from industrial countries and the imposition of stringent conditionality on aid and loans from multilateral institutions such as the World Bank and IMF. This was manifested in structural adjustment programs whose implementation wrought pernicious effects on the economies of developing countries. This reality engendered increased awareness among countries of the South of the need to obviate economic dependence on global North countries and instead enhance mutual cooperation between South countries. Since then, global South countries have increasingly turned to each other for economic cooperation including trade, investment, and development assistance. South-South Cooperation is seen as an alternative to North-South aid with its overtones of economic and cultural hegemony. The objective of this South-South cooperation, according to Global Envision, is to promote self-sufficiency among countries of the global South and to strengthen economic ties among states whose market power is more equally matched than the asymmetric North-South economic relationships.[21] This reality has seen concerted efforts to broaden and intensify regional integration schemes in Africa and elsewhere in the global South.

Available literature indicates that that South-South cooperation is important and advantageous for countries of the southern hemisphere on account of several factors: (1) it immensely contributes to economic growth and development of these countries; (2) it is devoid of the overtones of cultural, political, and economic hegemony associated with traditional North-South economic relations; (3) by trading more with each other global South countries increasingly become less dependent on Northern markets and the fluctuations therein; (4) South-South trade is more technology intensive than South-North trade and thus helps the industrialization and differentiation of Southern economies; (5) on account of Southern countries' closer proximity, shared marketing and distribution of goods and services may facilitate easier and quicker availing of commodities to the final customers, thereby increasing profit.[22]

Against the backdrop of increased economic partnership between countries of the global South, UNCTAD observes that the 1990s and 2000s have witnessed the emergence of a new geography of trade that is reshaping the global economic landscape with the South gradually moving from the periphery of global trade to the center.[23] According to UNCTAD, a similar pattern is emerging in international investment flows, suggesting the possible emergence of a new geography of international investment relations. UNCTAD suggests that a South-South cooperation strategy focused on a number of key thrust areas could consolidate and expand the transformation that is taking place in South-South trade, investment and economic cooperation: "This would enable the South to play the role of a genuine locomotive for sustained economic growth, diversification, employment and poverty reduction in the South itself and in the rest of the world."[24]

Two crucial attributes of this transformation, which is facilitating new opportunities for development gains from international trade and trade negotiations for global South countries, are apparent. The first relates to the emerging significance of the South as a producer, trader, and consumer within the global markets. Accordingly, the South represents a future engine of growth and dynamism for the global economy. This is manifested in the steady growth of the South's share of global trade from 20 percent in the mid 1980s to 30 percent in the mid 2000s. The second attribute of the transformation relates to the new dynamism and momentum in trade in commodities, manufactures, and services between and among countries of the global South. Over 40 percent of exports from South countries are headed to other South countries—and this South-South trade is increasing at an annual rate of 11 percent, nearly twice the growth rate of total global exports.[25] This "silent revolution" as UNCTAD refers to this emergent trade geography, is further underlined by increased

South-South investment, transfer of technology, and enterprise-level interactions at the intraregional and regional levels. A number of factors account for this eventuality: (1) increasing complementarities in production and trade among developing countries; (2) a growing number of supporting bilateral, regional and interregional trade, investment, and economic cooperation agreements; and (3) the difficulties and high cost of entry in Northern markets, hence the commitment to South-South interdependence.[26]

In particular, Africa's trade with the new emerging economies—which include Brazil, China, India, Malaysia, as well as Russia and Turkey—grew rapidly, from a combined export and import total of US$ 8.8 billion in 1990 to US$ 148 billion in 2007. The growth in Africa-emerging economies trade was particularly evident beginning the second half of the 1990s and this included improvement in the terms of trade for Africa. As a result, the balance of trade between the two blocs improved for Africa from a deficit of US$ 1.7 billion in 1995 to a surplus of 1.9 billion in 2000 and a surplus of US$ 2.8 billion in 2006.[27] The significance of this development is that whereas traditionally, the bulk of Africa's exports has been destined to the European Union, this is declining significantly as South-South trade relationships grow more intense. Between 2001 and 2007, Africa's exports to China, Malaysia, and Brazil grew by 42 percent, 37 percent, and 24 percent annually respectively. Conversely, Africa's exports to the European Union declined by 20 percent between 1990 and 2007—from 60 percent of all exports in 1990 to 40 percent in 2007.[28]

Among the major emerging economies or newly industrializing economies in the global South with significantly improving economic partnership with Africa are Brazil, China, and India. Between 1998 and 2006, Africa's share of the Brazilian import market tripled from 3 percent in 1998 to 9 percent in 2006. Conversely, Africa's share of Brazilian exports grew from 3.2 percent in 1998 to 5.5 percent in 2006. During the same period, Africa's total exports to Brazil—mainly oil, calcium, platinum, phosphates, and fertilizer—increased by over 300 percent from a total of approximately US$ 2.0 billion in 1998 to US$ 8.1 billion in 2006 (see Figure 3.1).

Similarly, Africa's imports from Brazil—mainly sugar, beef, iron ores, and poultry meat—grew by 316 percent from US$ 1.8 billion in 1998 to US$ 7.5 billion in 2006 (see Figure 3.1). As of 2006 therefore, the balance of trade between Africa and Brazil was US$ 600 million in favor of Africa. Brazil's main sources of imports in Africa are Nigeria, Algeria, and Angola.[29]

With regard to India, trade with Africa has also improved though it seems to have fluctuated more in the 2000s than Afro-Brazil trade. Available sources indicate a dramatic increase in both imports and exports between Africa and India since 2003. In 2006, India's imports from Africa—mainly oil, gold, phos-

Figure 3.1 Africa-Brazil Trade, 1998–2006, US$ Billion

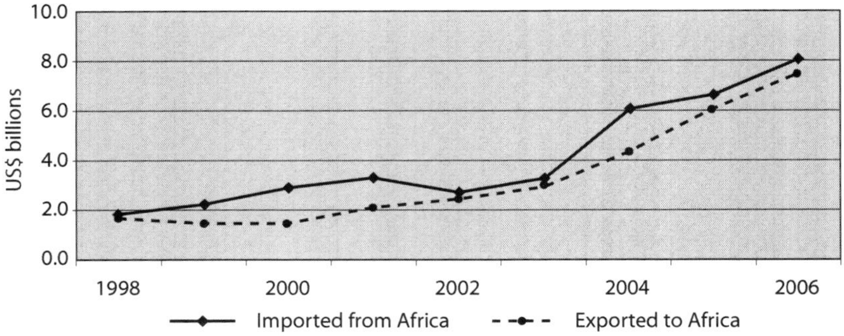

Source: Trade Law Center of Southern Africa, 2007a

phates, nuts, and copper—totaled US$ 12.6 billion, a growth of over 100 percent from US$ 6 billion in 1999.[30] On the other hand, India's exports to Africa—mainly oil (not crude), pharmaceuticals, rice, and automobiles—grew by over 450 percent from US$ 2.0 billion in 1999 to US$ 9.5 billion (see Figure 3.2). India's main trading partners in Africa are Nigeria, South Africa, Egypt, Algeria, and Morocco. The fluctuation in Africa-India trade is manifested in the shifts in Africa's share of the Indian import market, which was 12 percent in 1999 but dropped to 3.4 percent in 2005 before rising to 7.3 percent in 2006. The main factor accounting for the fluctuation is India's sourcing of oil supplies from elsewhere other than Africa during the material timeframe.

Figure 3.2 Africa-India Trade, 1999–2006, US$ Billion

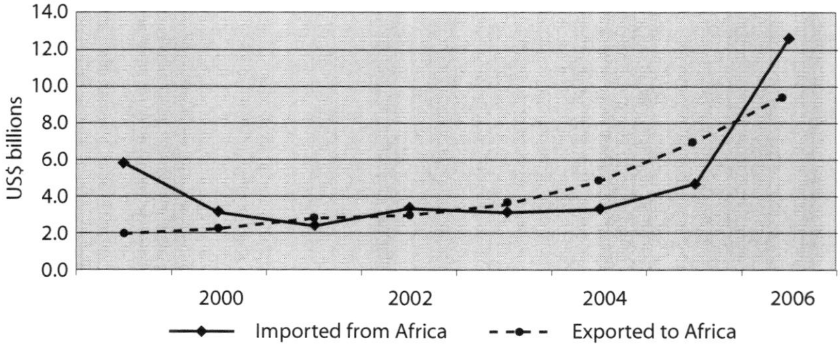

Source: Trade Law Center of Southern Africa, 2007b

Nevertheless, Africa-India trade is likely to grow tremendously following the signing of a comprehensive Framework for Cooperation in Delhi in April 2008 between African Heads of State and Government and a delegation representing the African Union and its institutions on one hand and the Indian Prime Minister on the other. These leaders were driven by their recognition of the rich history of Africa-India relations; their satisfaction with the then existing close, deep and multi-layered relations between the two sides; and realization of the imperative need to give new impetus and dimension to this cooperation, hence the adoption of the Framework for Cooperation between them covering a whole gamut of developmental issues from the economic through the political and social to the cultural and environmental.

Of the three emerging economies mentioned above, China has emerged as the most prominent economic partner with African countries so much so that the U.S. is worried about China's fast advances in Africa in general and in Kenya in particular.[31] Whereas Africa and China have traded with each other for centuries, the level and intensity of their economic partnership grew dramatically in the first decade of the twenty-first century. Writing for the IMF's *Finance and Development Quarterly*, Wang and Bio-Tchané note that at the turn of the 1990s, official development aid and government ministries dominated Africa-China relations.[32] However, since then, with the relationship developing to focus on markets for each region's exports and Africa's demand for infrastructure, government agencies have been replaced by the Chinese corporate sector and joint ventures. "In other words, for Africa, China is now a major market, financier, investor, and builder—as well as donor."[33] This transformation of Africa-China economic partnership has been marked by improved terms of trade for Africa (see Figure 3.3). Africa's export prices relative to the price of imports from China improved by 80–90 percent between 2001 and 2006. This was a consequence of rising world prices for oil and raw materials, Africa's main exports. The price increases have been driven partly by strong demand for these products from China. As of 2008, China's top four trading partners in Africa included South Africa, Sudan, Nigeria and Egypt. Indeed, China has become South Africa's top export market.

Trade flows between Africa and China grew rapidly between 2001 and 2006. During this period, Africa's imports from China—mainly machinery, transport equipment, footwear, textiles, and plastic products—rose by more than 40 percent while the continent's exports to China—oil, gas, mineral products, precious stones, base metals, and wood products—rose by 35 percent. According to Wang and Bio-Tchané, these increases are significantly higher than the growth rate of world trade at 14 percent as well as commodities prices at 18 percent during the same period: "In dollar terms, for both imports and ex-

Figure 3.3 Improving Africa-China Terms of Trade

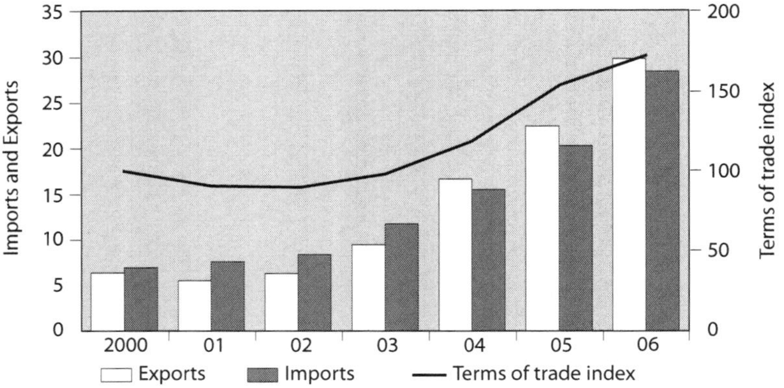

Source: Wang and Bio-Tchané 2008:44

ports, the increase in that period was from about US$ 10 billion to more than US$55 billion."[34] Notably, the value of Africa's exports to China rose from US$ 21 billion in 2005 to peak at US$ 57 billion in 2008 before dropping to US$ 42 billion in 2009 (see Figure 3.4). Consequently, in 2005 China overtook the UK as Africa's third most important trading partner after the US and France.[35] There are a number of economically positive things about this development. First, the bilateral trade between Africa and China has been fairly balanced with Africa maintaining a small surplus between 2004 and 2008. Second, as

Figure 3.4 Africa-China Trade, 1995–2009, US$ Billion

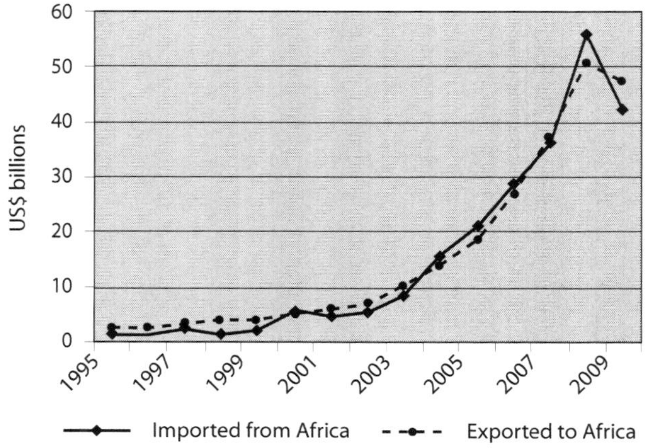

Source: Trade Law Center of Southern Africa, 2009

Figure 3.5 Chinese Aid to Global South Countries, 2003–2007

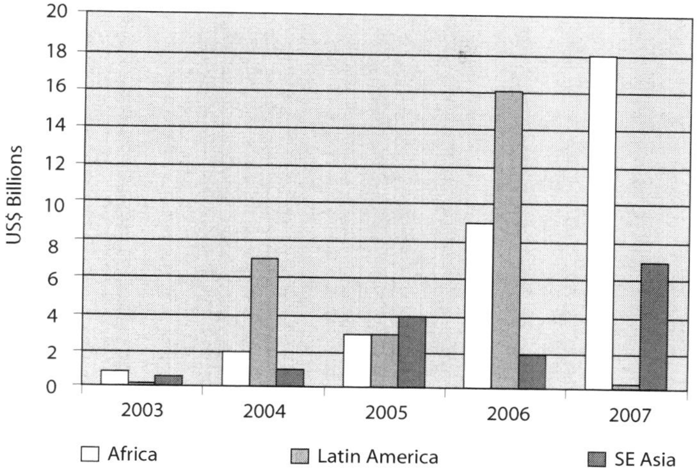

Source: Lum et al. 2009:6

Wang and Bio-Tchané (2008) point out, the composition of goods traded between Africa and China is similar to the one between Africa and her other major trading partners, a pointer to the fact that "the recent surge in Africa-China trade largely reflects the comparative advantages of each partner, given their stage of economic development, rather than any unilateral interest by China in exploiting [Africa's] natural resources."[36]

Not only has trade between Africa and China grown and intensified, China has also emerged as an increasingly important aid donor and investor in Africa as well as in many other countries of the global South. For instance, in 2002 some 44 percent—US$ 1.8 billion—of China's overall aid to global South countries went to Africa.[37] A 2009 US Congressional Report demonstrates that Africa received less aid from China than Latin America and Southeast Asia in the first half of the decade of the 2000s, but by the second half of the said decade, Africa was receiving more aid from China than the two other regions. Whereas Chinese aid to Latin America increased from US$2.6 billion in 2004 to US$ 16 billion 2007 and that for Southeast increased from US$ 1 billion to US$ 6 billion, Chinese aid to Africa increased tremendously from US$ 2 billion in 2004 to US$ 18 billion in 2007 (see Figure 3.5). A key attribute of Chinese aid to developing countries is that it is disbursed with very few if any conditionalities. Tull notes that "The Chinese government and its African counterparts frequently stress that Beijing's aid comes with few political strings attached. Contrary to Western donors, China's cooperation with or support of

African governments does not hinge on conditionalities pertaining to specific political objectives or standards ..."[38] Furthermore, in December 2004, China cancelled the bilateral debts of 31 African countries, amounting to US$ 1.27 billion—a large amount relative to the country's GDP per capita of US$ 911 at the time.[39] According to Leslie Feinberg, this show of solidarity provided African leaders greater leverage to demand that the International Monetary Fund, the World Bank, and the wealthy finance capitalists in the global North bastions of imperialism do the same for the least developed countries of the world.[40]

China's active promotion of economic ties with African countries has been underscored by the establishment of institutions to facilitate and coordinate interaction between the parties. Perhaps of critical significance in this regard is the Forum on China-Africa Cooperation, (FCAC) formed in 2000. Four ministerial summits of the Forum have since been held—in Beijing in 2000, in Addis Ababa in 2003, Beijing in 2006, and the latest one in November 2009 in the Egyptian resort city of Sharm el-Sheikh. In November 2006, the China Council for the Promotion of International Trade in conjunction with the Union of African Chambers of Commerce, Industry, Agriculture, and Professions established the China-Africa Joint Chamber of Commerce. The purpose of the Chamber is to develop, promote, and coordinate cooperation between Chinese and African entrepreneurs, especially given the fact that by 2006, 700 Chinese enterprises were operating in Africa with a total investment of US$ 1.5 billion. In line with the effort to institutionalize Sino-Africa cooperation, by 2005, China had signed bilateral trade and investment agreements with 75 percent of all African countries, and has since signaled its willingness to negotiate the setting up of a free trade zone with Southern African countries within the rubric of the Southern African Development Community.[41]

Against the foregoing, it is arguable that Sino-African economic cooperation will continue to broaden and deepen. The cooperation is driven by China's increasing demand for strategic natural resources to sustain its economic boom and the African quest for foreign investment and access to the vast Chinese market as well as concessional loans that Beijing is willing to advance.

Conclusion: Shifting Global Economic Power?

According to Global Envision, South-South Cooperation is altering the global balance of power. Industrial countries of the global North can no longer count on ready access to raw materials and consumer markets in countries of the global South where strategic rivals, particularly China, are gaining greater influence facilitated largely by the South-South cooperation framework.[42] Arguably, the collapse of the post-war rigidly bipolar political-economic system at the end of the 1980s is what facilitated the dispersion of power towards regions containing emerging economies. Aguilar notes that these emerging economies have two new and important features in the global system: first, they have significant reserves of strategic resources and second, they show high economic growth rates, new investment partnerships, large growing domestic markets, greater fiscal and macroeconomic stability, and a lower debt burden.[43] This regionalization of economic power, in Aguilar's view, is what accounts for the emergence of new countries from the global South that are strategically positioning themselves on the international stage in the contest for power—including the quest to expand UN Security Council membership and to liberalize decision making in the IMF and World Bank. Given that this competition takes place within a scenario of energy and economic constraints, resource-abundant areas become the center of this new global geopolitics. Hence Africa, Asia and Latin America have regained attention in a scenario of regionalization and new patterns of accumulation.[44]

Within the context of the burgeoning South-South Cooperation, the African continent seems to have recorded the most gains compared to other global South regions including Latin America and Asia (excluding the giant economies of China and India). According to *The Economist*, much has been written about the rise of the BRICs—Brazil, Russia, India, and China—and the shift in economic power eastward as Asia outruns the rest of the world in economic growth.[45] However, according to the newsmagazine, the surprising success story of the decade ending 2010 lies in Africa, even as the economies of industrial countries dithered on the brink of financial collapse. Quoting figures from the IMF, *The Economist* notes that during the said decade, no fewer than six of the world's 10 fastest-growing economies were in sub-Saharan Africa. These included Angola, Nigeria, Ethiopia, Chad, Mozambique, and Rwanda, all with annual growth rates of around 8 percent or more. Interestingly, during the previous two decades—1980–2000—only one African economy, Uganda, made the top ten. Overall, in the decade ending 2010, sub-Saharan Africa's real GDP growth rate jumped to an annual average of 5.7 percent, up from only 2.4 percent over the previous two decades. For the half-decade 2011–2015, forecasts indicate that the average African economy will likely outpace its Asian counterpart and grow at the rate of 7 percent annually (slightly faster than China's) over the next two decades (see Figure 3.6).

A number of factors are said to account for Africa's changing economic fortunes. These include China's surging demand for raw materials, higher commodity prices, big inflows of foreign direct investment into Africa especially from

Figure 3.6 African and Asian GDP Growth Rates (Unweighted Annual Average, %)

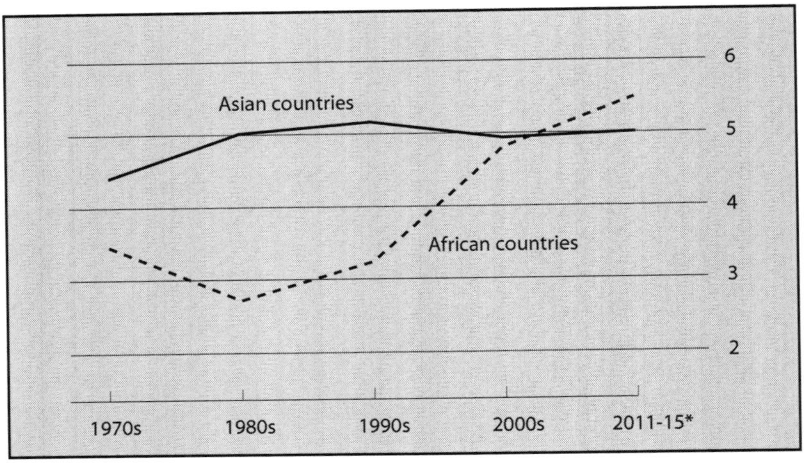

* Forecast. *Source:* The Economist, January 6, 2011

China, foreign aid and debt relief, improved economic management on the continent, as well as urbanization and rising incomes, which have fueled faster growth in domestic demand. Furthermore, many governments, notably Tanzania and Mozambique, have learnt to put aside government revenue to cushion their economies during periods of downturn instead of embarking on a spending spree given bolstered revenues from improved commodity prices. It is against this background that *The Economist* observes that the "lion economies" of Africa are earning their place alongside Asia's tigers in the global economic scheme of things.[46]

Bibliography

Abdel-Malek, Talaat. "South-South Co-operation and Capacity Development: Some Issues and Questions," A Discussion Paper for the High Level Event, Bogota, March 24–26, 2010.

Agliatello, Oscar. "Is South-South Trade the Answer to Bringing the Poor into the Export Process?" In *International Trade Centre Executive Forum*, Berlin, Sept. 27–30, 2006.

Aguilar, Carlos G. "South-South Relations in the New International Geopolitics." *Global Studies Review*, vol. 6, no. 3 (2010.

Andrade, Melissa. "South-South Cooperation: The same old game or a new paradigm?" Brasilia: International Policy Centre for Inclusive Growth, Paper no. 20, 2010.

Bartels, Frank L. and Jebamalai Vinanchiarachi. "South-South Cooperation, Economic and Industrial Development of Developing Countries: Dynamics, Opportunities and Challenges." Vienna: UNIDO, 2009.

Choucri, Nazli. "The Nonalignment of Afro-Asian States: Policy, Perception, and Behavior." *Canadian Journal of Political Science*, Vol. 2, No. 1 (1969) 1–17.

Corbin, Gary. "South-South Cooperation Defies the North." in *Global Envision: The Confluence of Global Markets and Poverty Alleviation.* December 6. 2006.

Cowie, Hamilton Russell. *Australia and Asia: A Changing Relationship*. South Melbourne: Thomas Nelson, 1993.

Feinberg, Leslie. "China Cancels Africa's Debt" (2005) http://www.odiousdebts.org/odiousdebts/index.cfm?DSP=content&ContentID=9341.

Flemes, Daniel. "IBSA: South-South Cooperation or Trilateral Diplomacy in World Affairs?" Brasilia: International Policy Centre for Inclusive Growth, 2010.

Folke, Steen, Niels Fold and Thyge Enevoldsen. *South-South Trade and Development.* New York: St. Martins Press, 1992.

FRIDE. "South-South Cooperation: Regionalizing the Development Agenda in Latin America and the Caribbean." Bogota, Activity Brief, March 6, 2009.

Global Envision. "South-South Cooperation Defies the North," 2006. http://www.globalenvision.org/library/3/1371.

Grant, Cedric. "Equity in Third World Relations: A Third World Perspective." *International Affairs*, vol. 71, no. 3 (1995) 567–587.

Hellström, Jerker. "China's Emerging Role in Africa: A Strategic Overview," *FOI Studies in African Security.* (2009) www.foi.security/africa.

Lum, Thomas, Hannah Fischer, J. Gomez-Granger and Anne Leland. "China's Aid Activities to Africa, Latin America, and Southeast Asia." *Congressional Research Service Report* (February, 2009).

Møen, Jarle. "Trade and Development: Is South-South Co-operation a Feasible Strategy?" Forum for Development Studies, 2 (1998) 245–270.

Mukherjee, Shri Pranab. "South-South Cooperation: For Shared Prosperity & Inclusive Globalization." INSouth—Intellectual Network for the South, 2008.

Mutume, Gumisai. "Hope Seen in the Ashes of Cancun: WTO Trade Talks Collapse as Africa and Allies Stand Firm." *Africa Recovery*, United Nations, vol. 17, no. 3 (2003).

Mutume, Gumisai. "Africa Opposes New Round of Trade Talks." *Africa Recovery*, United Nations, vol. 15, no. 3 (2001).

Okonjo-Iweala, Ngozi. "Promoting South-South Cooperation—Framing a New Development Landscape." In South-South Cooperation and Capacity Development Meeting, Bogota, March 24–25, 2010.

Rosenbaum, H. Jon and William G. Tyler. "South-South Relations: The Economic and Political Content of Interactions among Developing Countries." *International Organization*, 29, 1, (1975) 243–274.

Sabolo, Yves. "Trade between Developing Countries, Technology Transfers and Employment." *International Labor Review*, vol. 122, no.5 (1983).

Singh, Jaspal. "South-South Cooperation or Trilateral Diplomacy?" Sydney: Australia News, April 6, 2010.

Sneyd, Adam. "South Commission/South Center." Globalization and Autonomy Online Compendium, 2005. http://www.globalautonomy.ca/global1/glossary_entry.jsp?id=OR.0045.

South Commission. *The Challenge to the South.* Oxford: Oxford University Press, 1990.

Southern Leaders' Roundtable, "South-South Development Cooperation." Discussion Paper, Shanghai, China. October 17–18, 2006.

The Economist. "Africa is One of the World's Fastest-Growing Regions." January 6, 2011. http://www.economist.com/node/17853324.

Trade Law Center of Southern Africa. "African Trading Relationship with China," 2009. http://www.tralac.org/cause_data/images/1694/china09.pdf.

Trade Law Center of Southern Africa. "African Trading Relationship with Brazil." (2007a). http://www.tralac.org/unique/tralac/pdf/20071023.

Trade Law Center of Southern Africa. "African Trading Relationship with India." (2007b). http://www.tralac.org/cgi-bin/giga.cgi?cmd=cause_dir_news&cat=1044&cause_id=1694#india.

Tull, Denis M. "China's Engagement in Africa: Scope, Significance and Consequences." *Journal of Modern African Studies*, vol. 44, no. 33 (2006) 459–479.

UNCTAD. "The New Geography of International Economic Relations." Background Paper No.1, Doha High Level Forum for Trade and Investment. December 5–6, 2004.

United Nations. *Africa's Cooperation with New and Emerging Development Partners: Options for Africa's Development.* New York: Office of the Special Advisor on Africa, 2010.

United Nations. Trends in South-South and Triangular Development Cooperation. New York:UN Dept. of Economic and Social Affairs, Development Cooperation Forum (2008).

Wang, Jian-Ye and Bio-Tchané, Abdoulaye. "Africa's Burgeoning Ties with China," *Finance and Development*, Quarterly Magazine of the IMF, vol. 45, no. 1 (2008) 44–47.

Warnapala, Wiswa. "Bandung Conference of 1955 and the Resurgence of Asia and Africa" in *Daily News*, Sri Lanka (1955 [2005]) http://www.dailynews.lk/2005/04/21/fea01.htm.

Chapter 4

Globalization and African Conflict

Emmanuel M. Mbah

Introduction

Globalization has been the cause of numerous conflicts in Africa, especially during the past two decades. Some scholars have linked such conflict to the dysfunctional nature of free market economies, especially where corporations continue to seek profits from markets without considering the effects on African economies. Others have gone even further to argue that where governments in developing nations pursue nationalistic policies as against those of the West, conflict is often the end result especially when Western corporations rush to undermine these governments, many of them in Africa. Globalization then becomes virulent, introducing conflict where resistance to capitalism is met with responses that seek to promote Western interests. For example, French military assistance to rebels led by former President of the Republic of Congo, Denis Sassou Nguesso, against the democratically elected government of President Pascal Lissouba, was done to protect French interests. According to Eric Edi,

> Because globalization, as it is practiced, entails Western values, empire, modernity, colonialism and neo-colonialism, it goes without saying that it necessitates the subjugation of non-western realities. In other words, the forces and agents of globalization utilize all means necessary including international diplomatic pressures and military actions in other to annihilate individual or collective attempts that threaten their

> hegemony. When the forces of globalization fear the rise of ideas, philosophies, and actions, which challenge the foundations of the global market, violence under the forms of ideology, racism, class, culture, knowledge, and military becomes the rescuing weapon.[1]

Globalization has also introduced conflict in Africa when states' economic strategies are not reconciled with political goals. Thus while free markets have been economically beneficial to minority groups, Western democracy has instead attracted and benefited impoverished majority groups more, putting them in a strong position to resist autocratic regimes. Simply put, because free market and democratic institutions serve different interests, conflict is unavoidable. It is, therefore, not surprising that both forces are responsible for many recent ethnic, religious, and political violence in parts of Africa. Thus while Western societies continue to reap positive rewards from globalization, the results in Africa are at best contradictory, especially with the realization that the evil hand of globalization was partly responsible for wars of the 1990s in Guinea-Bissau, Sierra Leone, Liberia, Cote d'Ivoire, Guinea, Mali, the Republic of Congo, the Democratic Republic of Congo, Sudan, and others.[2] Ali Mazrui has argued that these wars simply reflect the multitude of problems faced by neo-colonial African states.[3]

Because globalization entails control and dominance from wealthy nations, it has introduced negative reactions and/or conflict from less developed countries that detest such ideals. The responses from the less developed world have ranged from overt hatred against Western interests to open terrorism. But the West has always found ways at striking back because, according to Mazrui, wealthy nations have a greater potential for violence to protect what they already have than do poorer ones.[4] The results, as we all know, have been global insecurity and an unending cycle of conflict.

In this chapter I examine the role played by globalization on African conflict. Composed of four parts, the first takes a brief look at conflict and globalization from the transatlantic slave trade era to the period of European colonial rule. In part two, I analyze the connections between globalization and arms build-up/proliferation. The third part dwells on the link between global ideologies and African conflict. In the last part, the chapter takes a look at how international African boundary disputes respond to the forces of economic globalization. Throughout the chapter, I have established direct connections between the burgeoning forces of globalization and conflict in the continent. Understanding such connections contributes significantly to how economic policies are applied in the continent as well as how conflict management, reduction, and resolution strategies are conceptualization and strategized.

From the Transatlantic Slave Trade to European Colonial Rule

The transatlantic slave trade constitutes a meaningful starting point for our study on globalization and African conflict. Adekunle argued in Chapter One that it was during this period, particularly from the sixteenth century, that Africa came into serious trade contacts in commodities but most importantly in slaves with the West. The need for cheap human capital to feed the sugar plantations of the New World, the need to satisfy other European labor requirements, as well as African greed for wealth and power resulted in many forms of conflict on the African continent. It was not unheard of for young African men and women to be kidnapped by African, European, and Arab slavers who initially roamed communities for slaves. Later, Arabs and Europeans bought African slaves from African warlords and/or ruling elites, who remained the only ones capable of maintaining brigands, criminal gangs, or the type of militias that could effectively raid for slaves.[5] Before long, the greed for slaves eventually transformed African polities into conflict-ridden slave enterprises by a process that has been aptly referred to as the gun-slave cycle. Because the most feasible way of acquiring arms in Africa was through the sale of slaves, the European sale of firearms to African polities "created conflict and undermined the authority of African rulers" as well as mandated African "participation in the slave trade ... even if the ultimate goal was simply to acquire firearms to defend yourself against conquest and potential enslavement."[6]

In the nineteenth century, Europeans no longer needed African labor in New World plantations; African labor was now needed onsite for mineral extraction and the production of raw materials for European industries and global markets. This marked the beginning of European colonization of Africa. It was an extension of European greed geared toward the continuous exploitation of African resources and human capital, and was precipitated by global economic forces spiraled from nineteenth-century industrial capitalism. European invasions to forcefully occupy the continent were marred by recurrent and bloody conflicts such as what happened during the 1898 Anglo-Egyptian battle against the Sudanese at Omdurman. Once occupation was completed European powers set out to impose rules under which exploitation and colonization would be pursued. The methods used in achieving these goals led to further conflict with Africans where many lives were lost. Belgian atrocities in the Congo and the German mayhem in Southwest Africa against the Herero and Nama are potent examples of European brutality during the colonial period.[7]

Conflict was also a major component of decolonization, or the African struggle for independence. Afraid of losing the benefits of an emerging global economy, European powers were unwilling to leave Africa, hence the numerous conflicts over decolonization. Portugal, for example, fought ferociously in Angola and Mozambique to preserve those benefits. Besides introducing conflict between states, decolonization also introduced power struggles between African factions, backed by Western forces before and after 1960. The struggle for independence was a complex process involving factions who sometimes worked together, but in most cases separately. The presence of many such groups transformed the struggle into fierce competition as each group worked desperately to gain control of the process. In Angola, for example, the National Union for the Total Independence of Angola (UNITA) was one of those political factions struggling with the National Liberation Front of Angola (FLNA) and the Popular Movement for the Liberation of Angola (MPLA) for the country's independence. When independence came in 1975 it was accompanied with disunity. The three political factions became rivals, pitting the FLNA and UNITA against the MPLA. This conflict became ideological when it was taken into the battle field of the super-powers. Angola thus remains a good example of how the globalization of ideas got enmeshed into power struggles between factions to produce violent conflict. African conflicts would escalate just after independence when belligerents began buying or receiving shipments of ammunition from foreign powers.

Arms Build-Up and Proliferation

Innovations in weapons technology have led to the mass production and global sale of sophisticated arms. The proliferation of arms is a major impediment to world security and peace because the potential for conflict amongst nations increases when governments stockpile arms. Proliferation is difficult to curtail because the sale of arms is a very lucrative business for Western and other developed economies.[8] It is, therefore, not out of place to attribute the heightened incidence of conflict in postcolonial Africa to the sophisticated nature of armaments that have made their way into the hands of governments, militias/warlords, and private individuals in many parts of the continent.

Throughout its postcolonial history, but most especially before the collapse of the Cold War, African states continued to seek external military support and alliances to enable them to pursue conflict. This explains the vast quantity of ammunition that filtered into the continent from foreign, most often former communist or capitalist donors. Foreign military aid was either linked directly to a particular conflict such as Soviet assistance to Ethiopia in 1977 during the Ogaden war, or not directly connected to any conflict—usually in anticipation of future problems—such as massive Russian military aid to Somalia from 1963.[9] Interestingly, many of these weapons have remained to this day to fuel recurrent conflict in the Horn of Africa, especially in Somalia which has been transformed into one of the most insecure nations on planet Earth.

Arms sales generate money to industrialized nations and remain a potent fixture in global economic transactions. African states stockpile arms in anticipation of conflict because seeds of discord are embedded in their colonial and post-colonial relations. Frequently, the negotiation and purchase of arms by one state is an indication to a rival or neighboring state to do same. As a result, ammunition stockpiles have, therefore, precipitated military growth in many African states since independence. In East Africa between 1970 and the end of the Cold War, for example, there was a symbiotic relationship between interstate armed conflict and growth in military capabilities. This was not the situation in the 1960s when African armies were limited both in numbers and skill, a limitation which was positive in that the conflicts that ensued between 1963 and 1967, particularly in the Horn, were not as intense as those that came after this period.[10] Thus, while the global proliferation of weapons has strengthened African armies, it has also inspired and intensified conflict between states. Arms donors, many of whom are external to the continent, pretend to aid their African partners as stipulated by bilateral alliances or pacts; their actions only intensify an arms race.

Somalia in the 1970s offers a unique perspective on how external military aid introduced an arms race in the Horn of Africa in particular and in East Africa in general. With aid from the former Soviet Union, Somalia (with a population of barely 4 million people) increased its military from approximately 2,500 men in 1969 to about 22,000 men in the early 1970s. Meanwhile, Kenya had a military of about 20,000 men, while Ethiopia's military was estimated at 43,000 men. By the mid 1970s, state armies in East Africa changed drastically as the entire region witnessed an arms race, the magnitude of which has been succinctly expressed by Ojo et al. in the following quote:

> Kenya joined the race immediately after Amin's claim on its territory in 1976. By the time of the Ethiopian-Somali War of 1977 and Tanzanian-Ugandan War of 1978–9, the regional balance of power appeared altered. Each of the countries in the region had an army of not less than 20,000 men. Each had an air force, the smallest of which, the Kenyan air force, was equipped with 12 United States F5E and F5F fighter aircraft and employed some 700 men. All the ground forces in the region were armed with advanced battle tanks, armored cars, heavy

> artillery and long-range field guns, among other military material. Somali forces were the most heavily armed. Its ground forces could field 250 T-34, T-54 and T-55 Soviet made battle tanks and more than 300 BTR-152 armored cars. Its air force of 2,700 men boasted 66 combat aircraft including Mig-15s, Mig-17s and Mig-21s. At the time of its war with Ethiopia the Somali army had reached an estimated 53,000 men.[11]

The competitive quest for arms as well as its proliferation also contributed to the recent conflicts in Liberia, Sierra Leone, Sudan, the DRC, and others. In failed African states, individual warlords or groups, frequently in armed conflict with rivals or with organized authority, have controlled and continue to control private militias who use foreign arms to terrorize subjects and pillage economic resources in areas they occupy. It is not uncommon for Western powers, including France and Britain, to modernize ethnic warfare in Africa with lethal weapons just for the profits that accrue from their sale.[12]

The pillaging of resources enables warlords to create sustainable economic and political links with the outside world as well as with criminal networks.[13] This happened in Liberia and Sierra Leone during the civil wars that started there in the 1990s; it has been going on in Sudan (where the Chinese have both benefitted from the purchase of oil, and the sale of arms to the Sudanese Government, which in turn delivers them to janjaweed militias for the pursuit of conflict), the Democratic Republic of Congo, as well as in Somalia (a classic example of a failed African state) for quite some time. In a continent increasingly deprived of the benefits of economic globalization, it is, therefore, not a tall order to argue that the stockpile of arms coupled with the precipitous rise in the most contumacious form of global Islamic radicalism (discussed below) might well transform Africa into a continent of unending conflict, with the possibility of more violent wars as well as continuous intervention from outside. When this happens, the vicious cycle of foreign arms and African conflict would only spiral out of order.

Global Ideologies and African Conflict

The 2001 terrorist attacks on the World Trade Center could be seen as a reflection of the rejection of American ideological extremism, or what Islamic radicals consider as an attempt by the United States to impose its ideals on others. Edi has posited that "those who attacked the Wall Street center wanted to avenge the humiliation that neo-liberalism and globalization have bestowed upon their respective countries and on their social and political cultures."[14] Globalization's quest for free markets and the spread of Western democratic ideals the world over have reinforced these anti-American sentiments and rejections by those who consider globalization and neo-liberalism as ploys to reinforce US wealth and hegemonic dominance. President George Bush's declaration in the aftermath of the 2001 attacks, labeling countries that did not condemn such terrorist acts as enemies of the US, went a long way to convince some nation-states, including those with anti-American sentiments, that the US was trying to standardize its ideals the world over. The statement by the Italian Premier, Silvo Berlusconi, at the G-8 meeting in Italy in 2002 that "the war in Afghanistan was the manifestation of the clash of two civilizations: the Western and Christian world on the one hand and the Arab world on the other," is a simple re-iteration of how far the conflict of global ideas can go.[15]

In discussing global ideologies in Africa my focus is on those that have been directly responsible for conflict between and within African states. In the first section, I evaluate the role of pre-1990 ideologies on African conflict; in the second, the focus is on post-1990 democracy; the last section interrogates the spread of Islamic radicalism/terror and its impact on Africa.

Africa and Pre-1990 Global Ideologies

The two forms of global ideological discourses that introduced conflict in Africa before 1990 include disagreements over the racist regime in South Africa (apartheid) and nonalignment/superpower (Cold War) politics. With regard to the first, African states disagreed over what policy to implement against the former racist apartheid regime of the Republic of South Africa (RSA), despite the fact that the now defunct Organization of African Unity (OAU) had taken a stand against diplomatic and economic dealings with that regime. Disagreements on how to treat RSA brought into conflict states whose economies relied essentially on it (Malawi, Lesotho, Swaziland, and Botswana) with all other African states. In the same vein, Kenya's strong links with the West restrained her from prohibiting Western planes flying to and from RSA from refueling in its capital, Nairobi, while Mozambique, which could not afford to lose the gains brought home by its emigrant workers, persistently maintained its citizens' rights to work in RSA.[16] These are but a few examples of how a pre-1990 ideology, smeared with enlightened state-interests, introduced conflict between African states.

On the issue of whether or not to dialogue with the former racist South African regime, African states were equally divided. While many, through the Lusaka Declaration of April 1969, vehemently condemned such dialogue Chad, Côte d'Ivoire, Benin, Gabon, Ghana, and Malagasy refused to abide by the declaration, arguing that it could serve as a bridge for moderate whites and business groups to pressure the South African minority government to carry out meaningful reforms and introduce humane policies toward the black majority group. Led by Julius Nyerere and General Gowan, presidents of Tanzania and Nigeria respectively, the issue over dialogue was brought to the June 1971 OAU Heads of States summit at Accra, Ghana where a majority of heads of states voted against dialogue with RSA.[17] This division introduced a conflict in the OAU between those for dialogue and those against, and the organization almost split.

The issue of non-alignment also introduced ideological discord between African states when some disagreed on its concept and application. Two varying views discerned at the time were those of Houphoüt Boigny and Leopold Sedar Senghor, presidents of Côte d'Ivoire and Senegal respectively, and those of presidents Sékou Touré of Guinea and Julius Nyerere of Tanzania. While the former perceived non-alignment as a pact with communism, the latter viewed it more as a step toward bridging the gap between capitalism and communism. A majority of African states sided with the latter view, interpreting non-alignment as a preemptive measure of not being dragged into the ideological conflict between the West and the East, believing that African states could reap benefits in the form of aid packages from both ideological worlds. This conflict of ideas was marred by heightened suspicion over the respective agendas of the socialist and non-socialist-inclined African states. Before long, disagreements over non-alignment were infused into Cold War conflict theatres. The conflict between Kenya and Tanzania that emanated from Cold War ideology, stemmed from the different modes of economic, social, and political organizations of these states; ideology was, in part, responsible for Kenya's assumption that Tanzania was jealous of its gains from the free market system because it had failed in its socialist ambitions. On its part, the Tanzanian government did not hesitate to refer to the Kenyan system as that of survival of the fittest, or a "man-eat-man society."[18]

Differences on the perception of Cold war ideology also contributed to the power struggle that ensued between Ghana and Nigeria in the early 1960s. While rejecting the appeal made by Kwame Nkrumah (former Ghanaian leader), on re-organizing and re-unifying Africa based on socialist principles, Nigeria officially declared that Nkrumah was attempting to build a system in Africa which centered essentially on his ideas of what African unity should entail. During the same period, Sékou Touré of Guinea fell out with a host of former French colonies who associated him with communism.[19]

Ideological differences were also partly responsible for the conflict between Angola and the Democratic Republic of Congo (former Zaire) between 1975 and 1979. Opposition at home convinced then Zairian President Mobutu Sesse

Seko that neighboring socialist-inclined Angola had deliberately let its territory to be used as a safe haven from where Zairian rebels could launch attacks on the homeland. This resulted in Zaire's apparently hostile dispensation towards Angola, although it is equally true that Mobutu had his eyes on the oil and natural gas resources of the Angolan town of Cabinda.[20]

Some pre-1990 ideological conflicts were transformed into serious crisis as Africa progressively became the testing ground for Cold War battles. Today, Africa has become the battlefield of another form of ideology—the spread of Western-style democracy.

Post-1990 Democracy

When the Cold War came to an end in 1991 a new round of conflict, heightened by the unwillingness of dictatorial regimes to permit alternative voices demanding Western-style democracy, commenced in Africa. Richard Joseph rightly observed in 1997 that multiparty politics in Africa "tended to take the form of competition among communities rather than individuals, parties, and administrative subunits."[21] This led to conflicts that were hardened by poverty and ethnic competition, and fueled by charges of exclusion and corruption leveled at political opposites; competition intensified where precious minerals or valuable resources were available, or where incumbents and political elites, many of them groomed during the colonial era, struggled to hang on to power. The result was a break down in peace, severe human rights abuses, and an increase in the number of displaced persons/refugees. Not all African states were afflicted with these problems; for those affected, including Sierra Leone, Liberia, Côte d'Ivoire, the DRC, and others, the problems came in multiple facets. Because these conflicts were usually preceded by demands for multiparty politics, democracy, and transparency, they should be appropriately considered as conflicts introduced by the global spread of ideas, more so because this period came on the heels of the wind of change following the fall of the Berlin Wall and the collapse of the Soviet Union.

The civil wars in Liberia that started in 1989 could be traced back to 1980 when the forces that led to the conflict started coalescing; chief amongst these was the quest for democratic transparency. In April 1980 Master Sergeant Samuel K. Doe assassinated President William R. Tolbert and became the first Liberian outside the Americo-Liberian group to lead the nation. Doe quickly became unpopular, and from 1984 there was general outrage against him and the Liberian military for stifling democracy and contravening the constitution. Amos Sawyer and other advocates for constitutional democracy were charged with treason and detained. Doe declared himself winner in the 1986 rigged election, undermined the constitution, and from 1986–89 opponents of his administration were detained and tortured. There were widespread demands for constitutional and democratic reforms in Liberia just before 1990 and that atmosphere boosted Charles Taylor's rebel forces to invade Liberia from neighboring Guinea, unleashing unthinkable carnage on citizens.[22]

In Sierra Leone, general frustration about poverty, dissatisfaction over the democratic process, and corruption by officials who swindle public funds including those generated by diamond mining, whipped-up popular sentiments. The war started in 1991 when Liberian backed Sierra Leonean rebels occupied the diamond-rich region of Kailahun. By 1992 President Joseph Momoh had been overthrown in a military coup and government troops were engaged in an atrocious battle with rebels of Foday Sankoh's Revolutionary United Front (RUF). Sankoh's control over diamond, bauxite, and titanium, all globally tradable minerals enabled him to wage one of the most brutal assaults on the citizens of Sierra Leone.[23]

In a 1996 presidential election organized by the new military leaders, Ahmad Tejan Kabbah of Sierra Leone's People's Party (SLPP) won and became president. He immediately reached out to Sankoh in an effort to end the civil war; as part of the deal, Sankoh was promised an important government post. Before finalizing the deal, Kabbah was overthrown by another military coup and he fled to Guinea. The organizer of the coup, Major Johnny Paul Koromah became the new Sierra Leonean leader, and by 1997 the nation plunged into yet another civil war as subjects rose in support of the democratically elected leader, Ahmad Tejan Kabbah. By 1999 the belligerents agreed on ending hostilities and Sankoh was given a ministerial post that gave him control over the diamond mines; he later resumed guerrilla war to gain complete control of the state but was captured by troops backing President Kabbah.[24]

In the Sierra Leonean civil war, we see how a crisis that developed out of the quest for democratic ideals got enmeshed in a struggle to control globally marketable resources. The impact of diamonds on the conflict was identified by the United Nations (UN), which declared a ban on diamond exports from Sierra Leone for a period of three months. But because diamonds did not only fund the war but were also a source of the conflict, it became extremely difficult to enforce any regulation that restricted their sale.[25] The recent civil war in Libya that led to the capture and killing of President Gaddafi resulted from a quest for democracy by the Libyan people.

In African nations where civil wars have been averted, clashes between governments and pro-democracy groups, sometimes fought over the new media, continue to threaten the peace in Cameroon, Zimbabwe, Sudan, Burkina Faso and many others.

The Globalization of Islamic Radicalism/Terror

A significant number of the one billion Muslims worldwide live in Africa. There is a connection between the growth of Islam, especially Wahhabism, which espouses (in the words of Judy Duncker), "the spread of the faith with missionary zeal; political jihad and jihad; the commitment to use violence to preserve Islamic rule and the global community of believers (umma) from the infidel enemy"[26] and instability in the Horn of Africa as well as in other parts of the continent. Wahhabism is the form of Islam practiced by the Saudi Arabian ruling family that has been known to promote its spread with the use of oil revenues; Osama bin Laden, mastermind of the September 11, 2001 attacks in the USA, is a member of that family. The Saudis have constructed Islamic centers and mosques throughout Africa, and continue to offer much charitable assistance including funding for educational exchanges, in hopes of spreading the faith.[27]

But the globalization of Islamic terror and its potential to propel the African continent close to the center of conflict dates back to 1998. On August 7 of that year, Islamic terrorists bombed the US Embassy in Nairobi, Kenya killing 291 people including 12 US citizens, and wounding 5,000 including 6 Americans. The US Embassy in Dar Es Salaam, Tanzania was also seriously hit. Both events were turning points on how the African continent was perceived in relation to global terrorism. The attacks of September 11, 2001 only convinced the international community that religious globalization via Islamic fundamentalism had given birth to the globalization of terror.[28] Africa has since figured prominently as a major hub in that network.

Africa's marginalization in the global economic network is partly responsible for why some have sought solace in radical Islam or Islamic fundamentalism, a movement that has been facilitated by the rapid spread of information technology. Al Qaeda-sponsored terrorism has spread from the Middle East to Kenya, Ethiopia, Djibouti, Somalia, Algeria, Eritrea, and Sudan, and the presence of its networks in these countries have been growing steadily. In West Africa, in addition to Nigeria and Niger Republic, al Qaeda has financial networks in Sierra Leone and Liberia, while in Central Africa, international terrorism has profited from the diamond trade in the DRC to finance terrorist activities worldwide. As a result, much of the US effort on the global war on terror is manifested in these regions, particularly in the vicinity of the Horn of Africa, which arguably has become the most unstable region in the continent. Instability, state collapse, and conflict in the Horn and its surroundings are the result of the acute absence of the rule of law, spiraling into state inability to control borders and protect local and foreign interests.[29] But this thinking negates the United States' role (through direct or indirect military and financial assistance), in the region through its global war on terror.

Of course, the African prominence in the globalization of terror and the various attempts pursued by the US and its allies to combat its spread, including financial and military assistance to particular Africa countries, have in some ways heightened the state of conflict in parts of the continent, but most especially in Islamic communities. For example, US troops have been actively engaged in military maneuvers in Algeria to prevent al Qaeda terrorists who flock in and out of the territory (in view of its unprotected borders), from planning and masterminding terrorist plots there. The US has also been involved in Kenya, Uganda, and Tanzania in hopes of flushing out al Qaeda operatives. In fact, the African continent from West to East remains a major theatre in the global war on terror, and the US spends millions of dollars each year on the African front of the war, redirecting development cooperation and military assistance to suit its global security agenda, and persuading nations of the continent to enforce anti-terrorism legislation.[30]

But just as the US invests financially in the war on terror on the African front, so too do Islamic radicals, and they have stepped-up financial aid to Islamic communities marginalized by economic globalization. And as mentioned earlier, Islamic communities in Africa also receive financial aid from Saudi Arabia, much of which, as Judy Ducker posits, "is accompanied by an alternative religious, cultural and ideological base (Wahhabism), whose ideology attributes blames the West for the increasing decadence and declining economic base and one that calls for their destruction."[31] For lack of an appropriate profile, many in the West, led by the US, have identified the enemy to be Islam; this is daunting for Africa, which is home to many Muslims. This is, according to Ali Mazrui and others, a big problem for Africa in view of the US doctrine of defending the heartland by fighting the enemy abroad.[32] Because the enemy (as perceived) lives in Africa, the continent will remain a significant battle ground for the war on terror; and the vicious cycle of terrorist attacks and western responses will continue.

Globalization and Interstate Boundaries in Africa

There are two main sources of the international boundary conflicts in Africa. The first involves artificiality resulting from the nineteenth and early-twentieth century European partition of the continent and the sometimes vague treaties signed between these colonial powers, dividing African territories with little or no consultation with its rulers. This resulted from European greed to control specific territories endowed with human and agro-extracting resources required for a global economy structured by industrial capitalism. The second, which became a problem only after independence, involves the issues of national interest and resource exploitation between African states over disputed boundaries. The resource requirements of today's global economy have heightened African conflict over richly endowed territories. Both sources of interstate boundary conflict are interrelated, with the second feeding on the first.

Artificiality and Vague Treaties

International African boundaries, as defined by European colonial powers, were supposed to separate territorial possessions from each other as sanctioned by the Berlin West Africa Conference of 1884–85. The German intention for calling the conference was to subject the scramble for territories in Africa to some form of international control, and to limit continuous British territorial expansion in the continent. Despite the differences in outlook and objectives between European powers, their willingness to jointly exploit opportunities offered by the global economy, at the expense of Africa, compelled them to agree to joint economic exploitation of the continent.[33] African boundaries, the result of European greed for global resources and markets, have changed very little since the end of colonial rule, and have remained a source of recurrent conflict between states.

Greed, resulting from global economic need, was largely responsible for how African boundaries were surveyed and demarcated. European powers surveyed and demarcated only those portions of the frontier that had economic potential. The Benin-Nigeria boundary, established by the 1889 Anglo-French Agreement, for example, was supposed to have been surveyed from the Atlantic coast to the River Niger. Unfortunately, both colonial powers concentrated only on the strategically and economically significant sections of the boundary. The unmarked portions of the boundary, comprising approximately 53 percent of the entire 800-kilometer boundary, have not been surveyed or delineated, and there is increasing uncertainty regarding the fate of those living along the border enclave, especially because no one knows for certain which state actually owns some of the villages located along the unmarked border.[34] The future discovery of mineral resources along those unmarked sections may well serve as a wakeup call for Benin and Nigeria to survey and demarcate the entire stretch of the boundary; when that happens, the possibility of conflict cannot be ruled out.

Greed for human resources was also an underlying factor in the struggle by colonial powers to regroup under their territorial confines particular groups of

Africans whom they believed would bestow an added economic and/or political advantage to their economic pursuits in the continent. During the Anglo-French negotiations to amend their boundary over Togo, for example, a colonial official observed that the French were eager to include the Konkomba group on their side of the boundary because they would constitute a veritable fighting force.[35] Thus the urge for economic gains from Africa, became the force behind the drawing of arbitrary boundaries, and remains the reason for many interstate African conflicts today.

Arbitrariness, impreciseness, and vagueness of colonially-imposed boundaries, characterized by a dysfunctional split of ethnicities, resulted in the grouping of people who had no business being together. These boundaries cut through or divided close to 177 ethno-cultural, economic, or social groups, and have created severe obstacles to unity and development in many socio-cultural areas. They have also introduced conflict within local communities. The boundary between Cameroon and Nigeria, for example, cuts through 14 ethno-cultural groups, while those of Burkina Faso splits 21.[36] By turning a blind eye on colonial boundaries during the process of negotiating independence, the new African statesmen, who at the time were more interested in assuming political power, blundered.[37] Independence was followed closely on its heels by a wave of boundary conflicts. Today, the propensity for interstate boundary disputes in Africa is so high that almost all modern African states have at least one boundary conflict with its neighbor. This has happened because post-Cold War African boundary conflicts have, to a large extent, been heavily defined by economic resources.

Resources/National Interest

While the ethnic card is often invoked in boundary conflict between modern African states, I agree with Ieuan Griffiths that "it is unlikely that there will be any major redrawing of African boundaries, particularly to take account of divided culture areas."[38] With the exception of the Somali situation, international boundary disputes in Africa today are less the result of the disruption caused to homogenous ethno-cultural groups, and increasingly more about exploitable economic resources.

The quest for economic resources to guarantee state survival in today's globalized world is a major source of boundary conflicts between modern African states. The problem has been exacerbated by poverty. Frequently, the disruptive colonial boundary and the argument of divided ethnic communities are used to bolster boundary claims. Moroccan claims over parts of the Algerian desert in the Tindouf frontier, for example, were sparked off more by the presence of large quantities of oil reserves than by any colonial disruption in the boundary. Similarly, the presence of large deposits of Uranium was in part responsible for Libyan claims over the Aouzou strip of land in northern Chad;[39] before long, both states were engaged in a protracted war over these mineral deposits.

Access to the sea is also a very important economic concern for many African states. Presently, there are fourteen landlocked states in continental Africa, the greatest number so far in any continent. Originating from the lack of foresight in drawing boundaries, landlocked states in Africa have a high propensity for boundary-related conflict.[40] Access to the sea for trade and other economic transactions that have been amplified by economic globalization were the underlying causes of a May 1998 border conflict when Eritrea invaded the Yirga-triangle, claimed by Ethiopia as part of its territory.

As a land-locked country, Ethiopia relies heavily on ports in Eritrea for much of its shipments and other transactions. The Eritrean port of Assab, with its huge oil refinery, had served as a free port for Ethiopia before the 1998 crises. In contrast to Ethiopia, Eritrea had benefited immensely from its coastline including this port, in developing profitable trade relations with the Arab world. The leaders of both countries, Meles Zenawi of Ethiopia and Isayas Afewerki of Eritrea, were personal friends and former rebel leaders who had previously helped each other in their respective conflicts against the Mengistu regime in Ethiopia. Eventually, the former took over power in Ethiopia while the latter became president of a new sovereign state of Eritrea. But personal friendship meant little to the political and economic aspirations of their respective countries, as was tested in 1997. In that year, economic tension overshadowed that friendship when Eritrea decided to introduce a new currency for its state, the nacfa, to replace the Ethiopian birr, which had before then served as a common currency for both countries.[41]

From the Ethiopian perspective, there were negative economic implications of the introduction of the nacfa. Jos van Beurden has observed that "the new currency came to be seen as an expression of Eritrea's sovereignty and an indication of economic differences between the two countries."[42] Trade between both countries suffered and relations deteriorated when the border was closed, preventing Ethiopian migrant workers and traders from doing business in Eritrea. Ethiopia considered the Eritrean action an attempt to economically strangulate the Ethiopian economy.[43] The Yirga-triangle (a piece of land 160-square miles in size) over which the war was fought, was of little economic value to either Eritrea or Ethiopia.[44] This conflict was more about national interest concerns in a rapidly globalized world, and less about the ethnic groups inhabiting the triangle.

Meanwhile in Nigeria, the conflicts in the Niger Delta region are arguably more about the equitable distribution of resources of the global market. In fact, there are various forms of violent conflict between communities in the region, as well as between these communities and major oil companies. Located to the South of Nigeria, on the shores of the Niger and its tributaries, the region provides much of Nigeria's crude oil. Conflict in this region commenced in 1965 when Isaac Boro led a group of secessionist demanding autonomy from Nigeria. The conflict became more violent in the 1990s when elites and youths raised the issues of exploitation and marginalization by both the Nigerian state and the big oil companies. The pursuit of conflict in this region has been globalized with the use of internet communication, a medium where the aspirations of the respective communities are vociferously defended. Competition between individual communities for access to the resources of the region and other developmental concerns has left them disunited and unable to pursue a common front on issues such as pollution by major oil companies.[45]

Because globalization has introduced negative competition in Africa, especially among marginalized states, survival of the fittest has become part of a new reckoning. African boundaries with all their ambiguities will remain sources of conflict in the continent especially where economic resources are anticipated or have been discovered along the ambiguous boundary enclaves, for as long as the forces of economic globalization continue to unleash havoc on the continent.

Conclusion

Globalization has resulted in mixed results in Africa; because it has failed to positively impact many parts of the continent, competition and conflict to grab its crumbs have been the norm in recent years. Ironically, the industrial world has chosen not to integrate those parts of the continent afflicted by conflict or those exhibiting extremely harsh political and socio-economic conditions into global economies. Multinational giants, many of them based in the US and Europe, are worried about investing technology and capital in the conflict-prone and unpredictable parts of the continent, especially in sub-Saharan African states where economies are in very bad shapes.

Even the few economically sound African states not embroiled in conflict, but sharing borders with one or more conflict-prone states, have also been marginalized economically. The ongoing political crisis/chaos in Zimbabwe, for example, has severely impeded the RSA's currency, the rand, and has prevented it from enjoying the full benefits of economic globalization because of cutbacks by foreign investors who worry that the chaos in Zimbabwe might extend to the RSA. As Peter Schwab succinctly observed in 2001 "globalized investor confidence has undeniably been called into question, even by normally astute investors, because they tend to hear Africa as a whole note rather than as separate quarter notes."[46]

Even in areas where industrial giants have chosen to risk their capital, they have found it difficult to introduce or expand their technological base because of conflict in the continent. Oil or petroleum has been one of those key areas where these giants have chosen to risk finance capital. For example, the 800,000 barrels of crude oil a day produced off the coast of Cabinda in Angola has taken place in spite of the conflict that has been brewing there for close to five decades. But such drillings are only feasible because there is adequate protection for personnel and investment capital at the offshore locations, away from the loci of conflict.[47] The industrial giants have preferred to steer clear of conflict zones; and as Maurice Amutabi writes in the next chapter, developmental concerns in such areas, as well as in the rest of the continent have increasingly become the preoccupation of NGOs and civil society. Simply put, Africa's marginalization in the global economy is a major source of conflict in the continent; conflict prevents its nation states from reaping meaningful benefits from globalization.

Bibliography

Adetoun, Bolande Akande. "The role and function of research in a divided society: A case study of the Niger-Delta region of Nigeria." In Porter, Elizabeth; Robinson, Gillian; Smyth, Marie; Schnabel, Albrecht; and Osaghae, Eghosa (eds.). *Researching Conflict in Africa: Insights and Experiences.* New York: United Nations University Press, 2005.

Allot, Anthony. "Boundaries and the Law in Africa." In Widstrand, Carl Gosta (ed.). *African Boundary Problems.* Uppsala: Scandinavian Institute of African Studies, 1969.

Beurden, Jos van. "Eritrea vs Ethiopia: A Devastating War Between Former Friends." In Mekenkamp, Monique; Tongeren, Paul van and; Veen, Hans van de (eds.). *Searching for Peace in Africa: An Overview of Conflict Prevention and Management Activities.* Utrecht, the Netherlands: European Platform for Conflict Prevention and Transformation, 1999.

Boahen, A. Adu. *African Perspectives on Colonialism.* Baltimore, MD: The Johns Hopkins University Press, 1987.

Duncker, Judy. "Globalization and Its Impact on the War on Terror." In Davis, John (ed.). *Africa and the War on Terrorism.* Burlington, VT: Ashgate Publishing Company, 2007.

Edi, Eric M. *Globalization and Politics in the Economic Community of West African States*. Durham, NC: Carolina Academic Press, 2007.

Gilbert, Erik and Reynolds, Jonathan T. *Africa in World History: From Prehistory to the Present*. Upper Saddle River, NJ: Pearson Education, Inc., 2004.

Griffiths, Ieuan. "Permeable Boundaries in Africa." In Nugent, Paul and Asiwaju, A. I. (eds.). *African Boundaries: Barriers, Conduits and Opportunities*. Edinburgh: Center of African Studies, University of Edinburgh, 1996.

Herbst, Jeffrey. "Africa and the Challenge of Globalization." Paper Presented at the Conference on Globalization and Economic Success: Policy Options for Africa." Singapore, November 7–8, 2005.

Joseph, Richard. "Democratization in Africa after 1989: Comparative and Theoretical Perspectives." In *Comparative Politics*, Vol. 29, No. 3. *Transitions to Democracy: A Special Issue in Memory of Dankwart A. Rustow*. April 1997, 363–382.

Katzenellenbogen, Simon. "It Didn't Happen at Berlin: Politics, Economics and Ignorance in the Setting of Africa's Colonial Boundaries." In Nugent, Paul and Asiwaju, A. I. (eds.). *African Boundaries: Barriers, Conduits and Opportunities*. Edinburgh: Center of African Studies, University of Edinburgh, 1996.

Kieh, Jr., George Klay. "Introduction: From The Old to the New Globalization." In Kieh, Jr., George Klay (ed.). *Africa and the New Globalization*. Surrey, England: Ashgate Publishing Limited, 2009.

Kieh, Jr., George Klay. "The New Globalization: Scope, Nature and Dimensions." In Kieh, Jr., George Klay (ed.). *Africa and the New Globalization*. Surrey, England: Ashgate Publishing Limited, 2009.

Lantis, Jeffrey S. "Weapons Proliferation and Conflict." In Snarr, Michael T. and Snarr, D. Neil, (eds.). *Introducing Global Issues*. Fourth Edition. Boulder, Co.: Lynne Rienner Publishers, 2008.

Mazrui, Ali A. "Between Global Governance and Global War: Africa before and after September 11." In Adem, Seifudein and Bemath, Abdul S. (eds.). *The Politics of War and the Culture of Violence: North-South-Essays by Ali A. Mazrui*. Trenton, NJ: Africa World Press, Inc., 2008.

Mazrui, Ali A. "Numerical Strength and Nuclear Status in the Politics of the Third World." In Adem, Seifudein and Bemath, Abdul S. (eds.). *The Politics of War and the Culture of Violence: North-South-Essays by Ali A. Mazrui*. Trenton, NJ: Africa World Press, Inc., 2008.

Mazrui, Ali A. "The Barrel of the Gun and the Barrel of Oil in North-South Equation." In Adem, Seifudein and Bemath, Abdul S. (eds.). *The Politics of War and the Culture of Violence: North-South-Essays by Ali A. Mazrui*. Trenton, NJ: Africa World Press, Inc., 2008.

Mbah, Emmanuel M. *Land/Boundary Conflict in Africa: The case of Former British Colonial Bamenda, Present-Day North-West Province of the Republic of Cameroon, 1916–1996.* Lewiston: The Edwin Mellen Press, 2008.

Nugent, Paul. "Arbitrary Lines and the People's Minds: A Dissenting View on Colonial Boundaries in West Africa." In Nugent, Paul and Asiwaju, A. I. (eds.). *African Boundaries: Barriers, Conduits and Opportunities.* Edinburgh: Center of African Studies, University of Edinburgh, 1996.

Nugent, Paul and Asiwaju, A. I. "The Paradox of African Boundaries." In Nugent, Paul and Asiwaju, A. I. (eds.). *African Boundaries: Barriers, Conduits and Opportunities.* Edinburgh: Center of African Studies, University of Edinburgh, 1996.

Ojo, Olatunde J. C. B.; Orwa, D. K.; Utete, C. M. B. *African International Relations.* London, New York, Lagos: Longman Group Ltd., 1985.

Reader, John. *Africa: A Biography of the Continent.* New York: Alfred A. Knopf, Inc., 1997.

Schwab, Peter. *Africa: A Continent Self-Destructs.* New York: Palgrave, 2001.

Chapter 5

NGOs, Civil Societies, and Development in Africa: The Case of Kenya

Maurice N. Amutabi

Introduction

For quite some time now, some development activists in Africa have looked up to nongovernmental organizations (NGOs) and civil societies as the panacea to Africa's development problems.[1] The grassroots programs and their appeal to accountability and transparency gave these organizations immense advantages compared to bloated, inefficient and corrupt civil service structures and institutions in Africa. These are perhaps the reasons why NGOs and civil society groups are thriving in Africa. They are thriving largely as a result of the failure of many African states to deliver reliable and quality services to their citizens. Many observers believe that many African states are "failed states" not because they do not have functioning governments, but because they have not been effective in adjudicating in matters of delivery of basic needs—food, water, shelter, clothing, security. Many African governments continue to perform poorly on the human rights index, because they do not adequately protect the rights of vulnerable groups such as women and children and minority groups. Many of these governments are corrupt and perform badly on transparency and accountability indices as well. The poor performance of African states is not new. Since the 1960s there has been growing evidence of the inability of the African state to deliver on its development promise, making it "weak" or "soft"—in other words, it is unable to fulfill its development objectives. These weaknesses have made it possible for NGOs to take up new roles as public service contractors (PSC) because previous contractors have not done a good job. I argue that the decline of the African state, particularly its involuntary withdrawal from provision of quality services and capital development has allowed global market forces and NGOs to move more effectively into areas of service provision in many African countries.

In this chapter, I examine the role of NGOs in development in Africa, using their development projects as indicators as well as their role as PSCs.[2] I describe how they have negotiated with three competing and sometimes oppositional forces—the state, the private sector and the civil society (so-called stakeholders in development). Using information acquired through archival research, interviews and observations, I explain how the work of Oxfam in Kenya, demonstrates how NGOs are replacing governments in development and service-provision.[3] Due to the declining state and the ascendance of neoliberalism and market forces, civil society has been at the receiving end, often suffering the impact of neo-liberal policies such as structural adjustment programs. My contention is that the decline of the state and emergence of the neoliberal hegemony of the Washington consensus such as the World Bank and the International Monetary Fund (IMF), and donor preference for the "Third Sector" have transformed NGOs from autonomous agents of "alternative development" into PSCs. As PSCs, their aim is to fulfill contractual obligations, such as road-building, construction of bridges, and delivery of piped water, provision of health services and running private schools and colleges. Since PSCs are market-driven and profit-driven and usually implement components of official aid programs, this is a new role for NGOs which is not only creating confusion but raises questions of conflict of interest. When NGOs present themselves as PSCs, they become profit driven, acting as business enterprises and cease to be philanthropic. Many scholars have been questioning whether NGOs can continue to enjoy non-profit status while taking on new responsibilities as contractors.[4]

Thus, this chapter demonstrates that the neo-liberal logic of the donor-led, globalized welfare system privileges market forces, which are often detrimental to civil societies. I interrogate the new emphasis on neoliberal-type projects such as privatization of land, eco-tourism, health, water, education, and whose concern with economic material improvement does not benefit so much the very poor, but the relatively wealthier elements in Africa. This examines the development of the dualistic pattern of provision of services, in which the economically active segment of the population must seek services in the market place directly, by paying for them, where market forces are fully unleashed whereas the remaining section of the population, often the so-called underclass or lower class, receive assistance by way of a "safety net" put in place through contractual relations between local authorities and voluntary agencies.

Outsourcing: NGOs as Public Service Contractors (PSCs)

Outsourcing attracted public interest in the 1990s as a result of Western manufacturing companies moving their labor-intensive production lines to developing countries in order to maximize on cheap labor in those countries. China, India, Mexico and other Asian and Latin American countries were the major beneficiaries of this relocation of labor-intensive jobs. Some African countries such as Kenya and South Africa have benefitted from this as well. There has been a lot of political and public outrage over outsourcing, because it has led to significant job loss in many Western countries. There has also been hue and cry over the manner in which the outsourcing is carried out in the developing countries, especially in regard to the use of child labor in many of the manufacturing plants (sweat shops) in the South. Of course the rapid growth and massive profits earned by such American retail giants like Wal-Mart and K-Mart are largely attributed to this cheap labor. Outsourcing in the Voluntary or Third Sector or the NGO's world has created similar tensions.

Many governments in Africa feel threatened by the involvement of NGOs in direct development. Some NGOs that have not been contracted as PSCs have also expressed outrage and displeasure with the new arrangements; they have argued that this has compromised their independence and neutrality. Some private enterprises that were usually contracted to perform such functions have complained about conflict of interest and pointed out how this new role is compromising the NGOs' position as non-profit organizations. All these are legitimate concerns, because outsourcing has the potential to upset the status quo. It not only brings new actors into play, but it also creates new rules and increased competition. Since NGOs pride themselves as being efficient, transparent and accountable, their business enterprises have raised new ways of conducting business.

Looking at the new role of NGOs in development as PSCs, I opine that NGOs will remain in Africa for many years to come. They have continued to find new ways of remaining relevant. Clearly, there appears to be an NGO dilemma in dealing with these three stakeholders in the development of Kenya. I argue that the weakness and withdrawal of the state from its core roles has allowed market forces and NGOs to replace it in the provision of development infrastructure. This has allowed them to move more effectively into areas of service provision. Due to the decline of the state and the ascendance of neo-liberalism and market forces, the grassroots has been at the receiving end, often suffering the impact of neo-liberal policies such as structural adjustment programs.

My research findings affirm those of scholars such as Robert Jackson, Carl Rosberg, and Joel Migdal who argue that NGOs replaced governments in developing or providing social services, as African governments have systematically become weak.[5] As for the Kenyan situation, the main basis for its withdrawal in subsidizing social services has been due to declining fiscal fortunes caused by mounting foreign debt, decline of producer prices for coffee, tea, cotton, sisal, among others, and the 1970s decade that shattered any hope for recovery. The 1970s decade saw the oil crunch in 1973/4 and drought and famine in 1974/5.

The decline of the state allowed NGOs to move more effectively into areas of service provision. Looking at how NGOs have embraced these new roles as PSCs, it is obvious that they are endorsing the neo-liberal logic of the donor-led welfare system that privileges market forces, which are often detrimental to the local communities in Africa. NGOs are made to develop dual and paradoxical apparatuses; focusing on areas that can reproduce results and which are economically viable on one hand, but also work towards evening the social and economic fabric on the other, where they intervene among the poorest of the poor without expecting much in return. This chapter will show how Oxfam has immersed itself into the development problems of nomadic pastoralists in northern Kenya. By comparing what Oxfam has accomplished in its projects in northern Kenya to government ones, I seek to demonstrate the substantial differences in quality as revealed through interviews, observations and interaction with project beneficiaries.

The development of the dualistic pattern of provision of services by the government and Oxfam in Kenya is one case for concern. Also, there is concern for the capitalist overture where a significant segment of the population must seek services in the market place directly, by paying for them, where market forces are fully unleashed. There is a contradiction where a section of the population, often referred to as the underclass or lower class, receive their due by way of a "safety net" put in place through contractual relations between local authorities and voluntary agencies as a form of welfare. My contention is that whereas NGOs are supposed to be helping the government in its development endeavor, they are in fact reversing the development gains by pursuing "welfarism" and dependency instead of encouraging self-reliance and sustainability.

There are some features of NGOs that make them inappropriate avenues of development, especially their emphasis on neoliberal-type projects such as privatization of veterinary services and focus on privatization and market forces. The development and famine relief projects of Oxfam threaten the long-term development ability of pastoralists to survive and feed themselves in these arid lands. This is the same argument Dambisa Moyo advances in her book *Dead Aid*, examined briefly by Hendrickson in chapter two. *Dead Aid* has received a lot of attention largely as a result of what she claims rather than the real role that foreign aid does or does not play in Africa.[6] Listening to her when she appeared on various talk shows in the United States, and as one of the historians who have studied the history of foreign aid in Africa, I was surprised to see how uninformed Moyo was in regard to the history of aid in Africa.

At the core of Moyo's argument is the claim that aid is the fundamental cause of poverty in Africa. This is a watered down argument of the dependency and underdevelopment theories that was advanced by the likes of Andre Gunder Frank, Samir Amin, Walter Rodney and others.[7] She posits that aid is responsible for poverty in Africa and eliminating aid is critical in stimulating growth for struggling African economies. Her position is that aid is the illness that afflicts Africa; an illness that the continent needs to take care of in order to experience economic recovery. Her position can only be applauded for its courage rather than any scholarly substance and economic sense because it flies in the face of what is taking place in Africa today.

Moyo's position is inconsistent with my interviews with regular people in many parts of rural and urban Africa who are alive today largely as a result of aid. Her arguments do not have any answers as to why aid still remains an important part of the development of many rural communities in Africa nor does her book give credit to the incredible work that NGOs and civil societies have played in the development of many parts of Africa. Moyo's claims are so simplistic and a bit naïve for such a complicated subject as aid. I sympathize with her claims, especially when I realize that her book is an armchair, theoretical project devoid of any empirical field research. To be sure, the rate at which states in Africa are joining the ranks of "failed states" is alarming and many observers think this is creating a lot of agency for non-state actors on the continent, and many of the reasons have nothing to do with foreign aid. If anything, Africa needs more aid now than before. This might partly account for the increasing role and research interest in the work of NGOs and civil societies. It is not my view that "development is bad," or that pastoralists in northern Kenya lived in a pristine unblemished state before the arrival of Oxfam; rather my argument is that Oxfam has mishandled development in its attempts to perform development in northern Kenya. There is need for a middle group where NGOs such as Oxfam recognize local inputs in their development agenda rather than pushing an entirely Northern Agenda, especially neoliberalism.

In many African countries NGOs have become too powerful since the 1990s (largely after the Cold War) and play a leading role in defining the development agenda on the continent. NGOs are leading actors in service sectors—education, health and water. They have also taken on new roles as spokespeople for the poor. Because of the increasing influence of NGOs, many governments are extremely distrustful of them. The suspicion is exacerbated by the fact that NGOs work with civil societies (grassroots or community based organizations) on many of their projects, creating tensions with governments. African governments are very suspicious of these relations between NGOs and Community Based Organizations (CBOs) because NGOs criticize government programs, thereby suggesting that governments have failed. NGOs also emphasize transparency and accountability, indices on which African governments do not perform well. The power of NGOs has translated into an emboldened civil society in Africa, increasing suspicion by African governments.

Billions of dollars have been channeled through NGOs through such programs as the U.S President's Emergency Plan for AIDS Relief (PEPFAR), and the U.S President's Malaria Initiative (PMI) which has given them a lot of power over government departments. Apart from describing the characteristics of the new role and increasing influence NGOs have in Africa, this chapter also examines their activism, lobbying and participation in direct economic development. It describes how the roles of NGOs in Africa have been changing; starting with traditional NGO activity that concentrated on the "service side of development": emergency relief, provision of basic social services and assisting governments to intervene in vulnerable groups and regions. Much of the literature and pioneering work of service NGOs now concentrates on what could be called the capital or economic side of development: initiating capital-intensive development projects, helping communities establish capital bases as well as articulating their concerns and preferences. There are also additional roles for NGOs, regarded generally as enhancing democracy where issues of equity and egalitarianism are taken up through activism and lobbying, in order to create free space and empowerment of the marginalized and the voiceless, through networking and collective action. NGOs have become significant agents of civil society.[8] Thus, the entrance into PSC is likely to raise the NGO influence in Africa even more.

Oxfam's Intervention in Northern Kenya: Bridging the Development Gap

Northern Kenya is unquestionably Kenya's development backwater, inhabited by nomadic pastoralist ethnic groups in a very unforgiving environment that is arid, hot and dry. Three major problems afflict the region: scarcity of water, insecurity, and livestock-related problems such as cattle diseases and lack of proper markets. Conflict over water, among people, and between people and wild animals is a common occurrence. Oxfam has worked in northern Kenya for over fifty years dealing with these three problems. Oxfam has been assisting victims of drought and famine.[9] I do not want to appear uncritical and sound like an NGO operative, but Oxfam has helped the internally displaced, mainly as a result of livestock raids. For victims of raiding, Oxfam has often assisted in replacing lost animals, knowing that victims of livestock raids cannot hope for life without a new supply of cattle. It also assists farmers that lose their livestock to drought. During drought, some livestock keepers do not own enough livestock for the off-take necessary in the wet season and Oxfam's intervention has often been indispensable. Through direct intervention, Oxfam has helped victims of economic destitution and political marginalization. The NGO has set up food distribution points and operates emergency feeding centers during periods of severe famines.

Therefore, to reduce conflict over resources Oxfam has over the years deployed poverty eradication programs such as restocking (replacement of cattle), drilling of water boreholes, building of dams and tanks for rainwater harvesting projects, improvement of roads and empowerment of women through income-generating programs. Many individuals with whom Oxfam works are desperate; they have lost their herds; are destitute; have been abused; have been injured; or have recently moved to urban slums. Others are impoverished orphans and refugees. Still others are rescued from exploitation in low paying jobs as night guards or watchmen, herdspersons, or laborers in private homes or ranches owned by white ranchers and rich Africans. Restocking puts the pastoralists back to normalcy. There is nothing sinister and wrong about this type of intervention, and saying it does not make one uncritical.

Conversations with development experts have revealed that restocking is increasingly viewed as the primary method of rehabilitating the small-scale pastoral sector in Kenya. In the last decade, Oxfam spent approximately US $5 million on this program.[10] Since the 1970s restocking projects were implemented in response to disaster and were undertaken by the government in collaboration with NGOs compared to the period after 1990s when NGOs have taken over the entire program. In the past, restocking was seen as a way of rehabilitating the impoverished into the social and economic fabric, a form of restoration. In the ensuing decades, the focus of programs has subtly shifted. At present restocking projects are being implemented not only as relief and rehabilitation but as a means of long-term development as well. Oxfam often justifies restocking as a means of improving household food security and sustainability, although little evidence exists to show that these programs fulfill these goals.[11]

The aim of Oxfam's focus on cattle in northern Kenya and rationale for cattle-restocking program have been to hasten pastoralists' return to self-sufficiency after the long spells of drought or armed cattle raids that are frequent in the region. In some cases Oxfam has done this secondarily to ensure the maintenance of suitable local breeds against haphazard restocking with weaker breeds. In this context, livestock is seen as a bridge linking post-disaster relief and rehabilitation with sustainable development. Lessons learned by Oxfam indicate that such effort must be based on community participation in order to be sustainable.

Oxfam has facilitated and encouraged pastoralists to sell livestock early in the drought cycle and this has been working very well since the 1990s. Many Oxfam beneficiaries confirm this. One said, "In the past we lost our animals with no hope of recovering them at all. Buyers who came during the onset of drought exploited us. They bought our animals cheaply. But this thing [Oxfam] has helped us to 'live like people again' [to live decently]."[12] By allowing them to sell livestock and to buy others after drought, Oxfam has ensured that the pastoralists are better equipped to survive drought without heavy losses. This has guaranteed that the terms of trade remain favorable to pastoralists and has prevented the absolute wastage of livestock that occurred in the past, where the herds "lost condition", could not be sold and died in pastoralists' hands.[13] This affected pastoralists' economies, increasing their poverty and vulnerability.

By helping pastoralists to restock, Oxfam has earned the right and legitimacy to facilitate destocking. So when Oxfam argues that overloading of grazing and holding areas has been the cause of environmental degradation in the region, the herders listen to it due to the promise of post-drought restocking that has achieved tremendous success and effectiveness among pastoralists. However, many studies have revealed that destocking has a direct, but marginal, positive environmental impact in these arid and semi arid areas (ASALs) of northern Kenya, because a small proportion of stock being taken off reduces pressure on the range only temporarily.[14] Oxfam's position has been that an integrated policy of assisted restocking and destocking avoids weakening the traditional pastoral economy.[15] However, this is not consistent with the fact that restocking has led to increases in livestock mortality, less resistance in the new breeds that have been developed and abundance of diseases. Pastoralist systems, for a combination of reasons including expropriation or modern individuation of grazing resources, are now more vulnerable to drought and less able to recover post-drought stock numbers. Nevertheless, through its international position and strong lobbying capacity, Oxfam has cultivated interest in this cultural pattern, first at the project level and at the policy level in interventions that do assist timely destocking and subsequent restocking.[16]

Evidently, Oxfam recognizes the fact that the pastoralist production system in northern Kenya can be used in self-correction, as an intervention in its own disorder. It declares that, "the production system has always been based on a 'tracking' strategy of matching animal numbers to grazing resources, allowing itself to suffer losses during dry seasons and during drought and replenishing or rebuilding herds during wet seasons."[17] In the past this was an area of conflict as many NGOs and even the government did not understand this pattern and just gave animals only for them to "die unexpectedly." As one beneficiary from Oxfam projects observed,

> Government officers would just come and tell us to sell our animals because they thought the animals were too many. At other times they would come and tell us to sell our animals because drought was approaching. Many people would hide their livestock in the bush and lie that they had sold them. None of us sold because we knew not all of them [livestock] would die anyway, and some actually did survive droughts. But these people [Oxfam] explain to us and help us to sell, and in replacing our animals during and after drought. We now sell and buy voluntarily whenever the situation demands.[18]

Also, careful consideration has been given to the participation of the beneficiaries in stock selection and distribution and project monitoring and training in animal husbandry and the use of equipment and the development of service organizations. It was very clear from the interviews that Oxfam programs were working. The ecological and environmental balance seems to be working as well. These are environmental issues that the government of Kenya ignored before it suddenly realized in the 1990s that they were getting out of hand and which Oxfam is correcting.

Oxfam has ensured improved marketing for livestock and livestock products from northern Kenya as a whole, especially access to external markets, which has led to a greater demand for pastoralist livestock and livestock products. It has enabled many pastoralists to send their animals to local auctions and markets outside the region. Oxfam has done a good job in targeted subsidies within the existing private livestock marketing systems, as it has organized livestock owners in useful economic groups. They know about collective bargaining and such trading and business strategies. This is clearly visible at the livestock auctions such as the Isiolo Livestock Holding Center, where livestock owners' associations that have been created by NGOs sell animals on behalf of their members and spread the benefits to their respective constituents collectively. On this an NGO beneficiary Chafano Tari said,

> In the past, we would not even reach here [Isiolo], as we did not have enough money to hire lorries [trucks] to bring our livestock here. They [middlemen] would buy an animal at 1,000 shillings and come and sell it here at 5,000 and benefit from our sweat. Nowadays they have stopped coming to our place and when we meet here (Isiolo), they just look away as they know what they have done to us in the past, and they know that now we know the truth. So this thing [Oxfam] has helped us very much.[19]

However, this development has also led to the emergence of cartels and belligerent middlemen in livestock trading. These cartels and middlemen organize and sponsor their own raids by hiring mercenaries and bandits to execute their schemes. Thus traditional raiding has been replaced by merciless raids by private militias where whole families or clans are often wiped out in a single attack. These militias engage in bandit activities when not raiding for livestock and the result has been an escalation of insecurity in northern Kenya.[20] Security of the region is always in great danger of getting out of hand, but Oxfam and other NGOs have been calling and lobbying for government intervention. Peace builders and conflict resolution experts are teaching many groups about respect for the law, respect for private property and sanctity of human life. To check rustling and stock theft, Oxfam and other NGOs in northern Kenya have also initiated programs for the branding, labeling, tagging and identification of animals, programs that the Kenya government abandoned decades ago, in the 1960s. Experts have recommended that microcomputer chips with electronic code numbers for each animal as is currently done in Britain, Denmark, New Zealand, Australia and the United States should be implanted in pastoralist animals through incisions on ears, necks, etc. Experts believe that this will help in tracking down stolen animals across national borders. They believe that this will help in making identification of stolen animals easy, rendering stock theft a futile endeavor. In this case, veterinary officers can be used to vet the identity of every animal slaughtered or exported by verifying information from the microchips. There have been programs by Oxfam that provide support to thousands of smallholders to reconstitute the cattle lost during ethnic skirmishes in the region.

As part of its strategy in stabilizing and making northern Kenya attractive to investors, Oxfam has been involved in peace building and mediation. However, like everybody else Oxfam holds the notion that power has slipped from the hands of elders since many people now have access to instruments of power—weapons. On the contrary, there is still some residual power in the hands of the elders. Because combatants are mainly pastoralist youth, elders are still powerful. Even with the emergence of banditry and commercial raiding, elders are still useful as they control clan herds and lands. Clan herds often build from internal fining. Fines are acquired from infringements of clan taboos and rules. Elders control clan lands and sanction settlement pattern such as the building of a new *manyatta* (dwelling). Clan lands also include the surrounding free-range areas and any resources therein. Elders are also still involved in marriage, dowry negotiations, and in clan rituals and other ceremonies. They are therefore, still powerful in some ways.

Veterinary services are scarce and lacking in many parts of Kenya. Oxfam has played an important role in the sustainable delivery of veterinary services to the poor in northern Kenya. It has initiated cost-sharing and communal services. This is achieved through several instruments, including the training of village pre-vets (vaccinators and auxiliaries), improving livestock-keepers' awareness of the benefits and hazards of drug treatment, the creation of revolving funds administered by herders' associations, the training of village extension workers in the treatment and provision of basic health services, and empowering local communities by giving them the right to manage drug purchases and distribution. In Samburu District for example, Oxfam supports adaptive research to enhance the control of endemic diseases through technical assistance, for example, trypanosomiasis control technologies, testing the efficacy and economics of East Coast Fever vaccine, and integrated internal-parasite control in neighboring districts.

Livestock breeding has had advantages in Kenya in the past. Oxfam has been active in promoting breed improvement programs in northern Kenya, where the Borana cattle and other local zebu cattle have been improved. The emphasis has been on developing disease-resistant, quality breeds that produce better milk and beef. Oxfam projects help provide communities with cross-breeds, or crossing of exotic breeds with the indigenous ones. The interventions also include training on improved husbandry skills.

The economy of northern Kenya has been closed for a long time. Oxfam played a leading role in opening up the economy of the region to the outside world. This has allowed pastoralists to engage in economic enterprises beyond the traditional pastoralist boundaries, by taking their herds to markets in Nairobi and even abroad. Oxfam has encouraged the creation of marketing associations and even cooperatives that have made this possible. With increased auctions, sells and turnover of herds, the consumption patterns of pastoralists have changed since the 1990s to include tastes beyond their fringe, even global tastes.

Oxfam has also been involved in drought monitoring, successfully using data collected for intervention in the plight of pastoralists. This differs sharply with a similar program developed by the government of Kenya since 1974 whose results have never been used successfully in intervention. The major problem with government monitoring was that the data were never used during the time of need, compared to the Oxfam strategy where results are used and situations attended to. An Oxfam beneficiary reported this:

> These people [Oxfam] are better than what we have witnessed in the past. Long ago before they [Oxfam] came, we would starve before government representatives would come. By the time the government officials arrived bones would have started to show on our bodies. But these people [Oxfam] know our needs very fast. They just come, ask you questions every week and before you know it, you see them bringing food. We had planned to go away from this area ten years ago but they are helping us now, we can keep our animals in our ancestral land. Look at me. Where can I go at this age? I do not even know how to cultivate or work in an office.[21]

There were many positive appraisals for Oxfam's work similar to this one. This means that drought monitoring by Oxfam is an effective intervention in the plight of pastoralists. Therefore, although I know that some of the work of NGOs has created dependency, I would not recommend the end of aid to Africa based on the fact that aid has created economic dependence. Contrary to scholars like Dambisa Moyo who have argued that aid keeps Africa in a beggar's role, I argue that African governments need to be made more accountable and transparent. African governments need not be bunched together, for some have done quite well. The underperforming ones need to create structures of self-reliance and sufficiency. Even if the doors of aid were shut for Africa, there will still be some regimes that will remain corrupt, because corruption has to do with bad leadership and nothing to do with aid. Dambisa Moyo's suggestion that foreign aid to Africa be stopped within 10 years misses the bigger picture. One of my interviewees in Northern Kenya pointed out that without aid, she would have died. To such an interviewee, aid is life. Moyo says that "Aid engenders laziness on the part of the African policymakers," seeing it as obstructive and ineffectual.

The government of Kenya has been accused of lacking appropriate development models. To overcome this, Oxfam has adopted a new model of development, known as 'embedding' where program coordinators "work with the people and not among the people." The "embedding" by Oxfam is not really a new model of development (rather just another NGO jargon for the bottom-up approach). Nevertheless, it has been more effective than the government approach, which is top-down.[22] Most of the Oxfam projects, using bottom-up models support restocking, provision of credit (soft loans), as well as training. In the case of livestock, the aim is to improve existing animal production systems, and provide sustainable access to services, markets and inputs. The predominant approach for Oxfam is to design user-based systems for resource management such as livestock owners associations, pastoral and rangeland users' associations.[23]

Oxfam as Public Service Contractor (PSC): A Development Balance Sheet

From many years of working in northern Kenya, Oxfam has increasingly become a PSC. It is more and more being contracted by foreign donor agencies to perform roles that were previously performed by the state in Kenya. Such tasks as provision of water and veterinary services were for a long time a preserve of the state in Kenya. Oxfam has ably moved in and replaced the state, sometimes being used by the British department of international development as an implementing agency. An Oxfam employee revealed that this is only a recent development. He said:

> We [Oxfam] have recently been contracted to provide consultancy services by bi-lateral and multi-lateral donors. We have undertaken projects in many sectors such as water, health, education, etc and implemented many veterinary services, just like a private company would.... I cannot give you figures of the amount involved but it is substantial, similar to what would be given to any development partner or government ministry.[24]

Public service contracting has increased due to the prevalence of corruption in government departments, coupled with inefficiency observable in poor project management. Government projects in Kenya tend to be concentrated in southern Kenya leaving pastoralist-inhabited northern Kenya isolated and without development programs. The public sector is becoming less effective in providing health, water and veterinary services particularly to herders in northern Kenya. The deficiencies of the public systems mainly affect the poorest among the pastoralists. One approach the government has used and which was never effective was the privatization of veterinary services. This has reduced access to services by those that cannot afford them. From the 1990s, cost sharing in service-provision as demanded by donor agencies has weakened the capability of the Kenyan state to take development to the larger part of its constituency. Due to these reasons Northern donors prefer to deal with NGOs in disbursement of development funds, as they are believed to be more transparent, accountable, and impartial. Thus, because of the need to push through with reform policies in water, health, education and agriculture, donors have made NGOs such as Oxfam take the responsibility for social sector management. Therefore, Oxfam has designed projects that are capable of enabling and empowering local communities to manage resources and services.

As Oxfam willingly assumes this role, its usefulness so far as the objective of institution building in Kenya becomes contested terrain, as two camps are discernible: those for and those against NGOs in Kenya. There is a negative feeling that creeps into bureaucrats when an NGO assumes the role of a PSC and takes over their role. Many bureaucrats feel threatened by this shifting power dynamics. Oxfam is equipped with more efficient development models and approaches that have given it advantages in northern Kenya. From interviews with its project managers and beneficiaries, Oxfam has a hands-on approach and a very efficient response team. Its program officers are well equipped in dealing with pastoral economies and this has led to improvements in animal husbandry, veterinary care, and range conservation. Its decision-making process is faster and more efficient. It also has adequate finances. Time and experience have enabled Oxfam to establish and use consultative and proactive approaches for pre-project design and post-appraisal surveys and models such as Rapid Rural Appraisal (RRA), Participatory Rural Appraisal (PRA) and Socio-Economic and Production Systems Surveys.[25]

These approaches are popular and are widely embraced by Northern NGOs all over Kenya, sometimes uncritically. The approaches have provided Oxfam project managers with the ability to ascertain the needs of pastoralist communities, solicit the direct involvement of communities in problem identification and problem solving, and use the results to develop sustainable projects. Oxfam has used this to intervene in institution-building, such as the strengthening of livestock auctions; encouraging a cost effective cooperative transport of livestock to markets, improving cattle marketing strategies, creation of associations and cooperatives, village banks, micro financing, revolving funds and de-stocking, saving and investment.

The PRA strategy and methodology is now a common tool in the design of all of Oxfam's new projects. It is used to select the beneficiaries (for instance, in Marsabit District) and to assist the designers in dealing with gender issues, especially on defining and sharing tasks between men and women. There are also ongoing attempts in Oxfam to strengthen the linkages and the responsibility sharing between the beneficiaries and Oxfam's project managers. For example, the community livestock workers and the women extension volunteers in the livestock loaning system in Samburu complement and supplement the project managers in extending technologies and interventions to the beneficiaries. Village implementation groups have been established in Oxfam projects in Samburu. Each village implementation group is composed of a village leader and a number of villagers responsible for accounting, women representation and technical matters such as livestock technicians and village vaccinators, or what are known popularly as pre-vets. These local cells play an important role in preparing the village development plans. The participatory approach in Oxfam projects also draws on input from local professionals and intelligentsia besides the regular beneficiaries, which gives it a wide range of ideas.

The inclusion of beneficiary representatives in project coordination committees by Oxfam is, in my opinion, one of the most useful innovations as this is a major vehicle for beneficiary participation in implementation. However, even this method of involving all levels of stakeholders in decision-making and project implementation has its shortcomings. For instance, elders have resisted some of the committees that marginalize them and where women and young men dominate. The model was also initially resisted in some parts of northern Kenya especially in predominantly Muslim societies such as Boran and Somali where women were not allowed to attend public development meetings. Only men turned up at consultation meetings in the 1980s before it occurred to NGO officials that it was a cultural obstacle that needed to be negotiated. On this, one NGO official said, "we used to invite specific women and instead of them showing up, it was their husbands who would show up. When we found out the reason, we laughed at our naïveté as development activists."[26] He adds, "among the Boran, you can invite a woman only through her husband or father. We tried this and it worked."[27] In other areas, Oxfam found an answer in creating single-gender groups in Isiolo, Wajir, and other dominantly Muslim areas. For the other areas, men started to realize that women were assets that they had not utilized in management of communal welfare. However, the PRA approach has some weaknesses. The lack of mechanisms to select the representatives and the small likelihood of the effective representation of tens of thousands of beneficiaries spread over a wide geographic area restrict the effectiveness of this approach. It is also predicated on the cooperation of the beneficiaries, and has to conform to their cultural and social dynamics.

Projects have a higher rate of achievement when designed with the full participation of the beneficiaries (both men and women) and national professionals and authorities, such as the Pastoralist Forum and local livestock associations. Interviews also revealed that many beneficiaries appreciated improved technologies and adopted them insofar as the technologies did not burden limited household labor resources. It was evident that success in implementing livestock projects depends on the availability of favorable policies (for instance, market pricing policies) and sustainable services to communities empowered through access to training, markets, and rural financing.

Furthermore, there is evidence that collaboration among donors and NGOs such as that between Action-Aid, Oxfam and World Vision in Isiolo and other pastoralist districts in supporting each other is essential to the success of development projects.

Oxfam has also lobbied the Kenya government on behalf of pastoralists in northern Kenya. It has called for cessation of importation of cheap meat and dairy products from abroad, for they mostly affect pastoralists. This has not been successful, as cheap South African livestock products have increasingly arrived in Kenya through common market agreements to which Kenya is a signatory. Oxfam has also initiated revenue-enhancing measures (for example, marketing, and the development of feeder roads) and drought contingency plans in many pastoralist districts.

Oxfam and other NGOs have also started some irrigation schemes along the Ewaso Nyiro and Turkwell Rivers in Kenya, schemes that initially allowed for the cultivation of many hectares of sorghum and millet by the Boran, Samburu and Turkana but which failed. The Perkerra Irrigation Scheme that was funded by Oxfam in the 1960s under Grant Number 4392 is one such failure.[28] The irrigation schemes have not been successful, as they are incompatible to pastoralist peoples' needs and lifestyles as Oxfam and other NGOs later realized. Many irrigation schemes have been abandoned, resulting in many problems as the de-stocked groups go back to pastoralism, often carrying out livestock theft through raiding. The pastoralists that continue farming have often been raided for food, making farming families vulnerable to attacks.[29]

Water is an important resource in northern Kenya and constitutes part of Oxfam's mission in the region. Oxfam has constructed boreholes and wells in the region and helped in ameliorating conflict over water in the region. However, some controversies and tensions still attend this sector. In an oral interview, an NGO beneficiary, Ewalam Lokolak, (Aged 83), complained about access to water particularly the arbitrary manner in which new boreholes are developed. Of course, Oxfam is at times in a dilemma since, when water is not available nearby, people are often forced to move to new areas where there is water.[30]

> When Oxfam officials came here, they asked if we needed water and where we wanted a borehole sank. They promised to sink a borehole for us here (Upper Ewaso Ng'iro River). But when they went to consult with *wakulima matajiri* (rich farmers) across the border in Nanyuki, they changed their mind and sank a borehole on the other side, near Kisima [National Sanctuary]. I think their intention was to make us move out of this [Ewaso Ng'iro] valley near this border area for we know these *wakulima matajiri* must have told them we are a source of

> trouble for them in the dry season They should realize that our animals also need pasture from this valley and water and not in Kisima where they want us to move.[31]

The response to this project's politics by Oxfam officials was that they operated under very fragile environments where there was a need to balance everything, from the government and from the people's view together with their own projected implications and use for projects.

> We have realized that boreholes constructed in border areas bring about conflict. We would like the Mgogodo Maasai and Kikuyu in Rumuruti and the Samburu to be as far away from each as possible because water sources exacerbate their conflicts. That is the policy of the [Kenya] government. Even though we consult with the people in planning and implementing projects, some of these projects have to fit in the government development plans, and have to be logical. They [Samburu pastoralists] wanted a borehole near the valley and we felt that it would not serve any useful purpose. Rich farmers did not influence us in the sinking of the boreholes at Kisima.[32]

Sometimes this can lead to serious congestions and conflict. Thus, it is when they participate in such conniving that one often wonders about Oxfam's (NGOs) self-proclaimed transparency, accountability and impartiality. There is no doubt that Oxfam has ameliorated the suffering of people in northern Kenya following failure by the state to provide essential services. Agnes Leshina, a beneficiary from Oxfam's benevolence felt that the government discriminated against pastoralists, especially women. Like many informants, she believed that the government was only interested in the collection of market fees and levying taxes on livestock products, but was not doing much to advance the course of pastoralists.[33] Of course the vast areas assigned to government administrators such as chiefs and their assistants in the semi-arid pastoralist areas do not make it possible for them to oversee everything because of a lack of resources.

Having enumerated what Oxfam has done in Northern Kenya over the years, I do not agree with writers like Dambisa Moyo who argue that aid alters incentives among technocrats and policy makers in African societies. I particularly object to the notion that aid makes African policy makers become reluctant and less innovative or creative. In fact, my experience has shown that the work of NGOs challenges government operatives to become more transparent and accountable, seeing that NGOs are able to achieve a lot with so little. My take is that writers who criticize aid per se fail to examine other factors that have undermined development efforts in Africa. For example, Dambisa Moyo's approach is one-dimensional for she wrongly believes that aid makes African governments less responsible to their citizens; and aid has led to underdevelopment and problems of instability such as civil wars, massive corruption and rot in African civil service that has led to the perpetuation of poverty. Of course none of these arguments are new, because scholars such as Walter Rodney in his *How Europe Underdeveloped Africa* have made these connections years ago, and I did the same more recently in *The NGO Factor in Africa*. Dambisa Moyo's ideas only seem to be new because of her heavy use of spin and PR.

Paradox of Development: Oxfam and Aid in Northern Kenya

Of course, there is a certain paradox in Oxfam's role in delivering development, with its work being praised by ordinary pastoralists in northern Kenya but vilified by the local intelligentsia and some government officials. Why is this happening? Elliot Fratkin has shown weaknesses and poor implementation of current development models in the region, and has suggested some alternatives focused on appropriate development that would not disrupt or end pastoral production in Africa's arid lands.[34] It seems that the development models that NGOs pursue are exclusively Northern in which local voices are excluded. This creates some tensions. How does one understand these tensions?

I utilize Mark Duffield's theory of "two-tier system of public welfare" in interrogating these tensions that attend Oxfam's development record in northern Kenya. Duffield has formulated a theory of the North's internationalization of public welfare through his study of the North's intervention in Africa and especially in the conflict prone areas, such as northern Kenya. In some studies, this approach is referred to as the "two-tier system of public welfare."[35] What makes Duffield's framework interesting and useful is that Oxfam is a British NGO that would be expected to carry certain trappings of "imperialism" and colonialism in a country like Kenya, a former colony of Britain. Duffield's major thesis and argument is that Northern NGOs play a major role in shaping policies and development processes of developing countries. He argues that the direct participation of NGOs in development processes of developing countries while at the same time keeping ties with the former colonial powers allows them to perpetuate certain aspects of "empire". Therefore, he argues, allowing NGOs to participate in this system has transformed these agencies from autonomous organizations striving to bring a "new vision" of development, into PSCs.

The twist here is the new role that NGOs acquire as PSCs. PSCs, he points out, are not people friendly nor are they Southern friendly because their new desire is just to fulfill contractual obligations, for example road building, construction of a bridge, or delivery of piped water. One cannot fail to see the profit motive that drives them in these contracting enterprises. This is because PSCs are market-driven, and profit-driven and mainly implement components of official aid programs, and to Duffield, this is where the problem starts.[36] When NGOs present themselves as PSCs, they cease to be philanthropic but instead act as business concerns. Throughout their operations in the South, it is often not easy to discern when NGOs are "contracting" or engaged in philanthropy. In 2000, the British DFID announced that it was releasing 200 million shillings to Kenya through Oxfam.[37] This was the largest amount ever to be dispensed through a single NGO in Kenya and this transformed the status of Oxfam in Kenya. It made Oxfam a PSC and at the same time made its linkage with British official aid explicit. Whatever pretenses it had at neutrality were now exposed.

There are numerous concerns that arise out of this public service contracting role, which many NGOs such as Oxfam are now performing in Kenya, clearly manifested in their official and unofficial roles. The official side targets areas that can reproduce results and which are economically viable whereas the other is interested in evening the social and economic fabric, and intervenes among the poorest of the poor without expecting much in return. Duffield traces the development of this two-tier type of welfare system that has now been globalized through NGOs, in the neo-liberal restructuring of the welfare state in the North. According to him, the system is composed of a dualistic pattern of provision of services, in which the economically active segment of the population must seek services in the market place directly, where market forces are fully unleashed. The remaining section of the population, often the so-called underclass or lower class, receive their due by way of a "safety net" put in place through contractual relations between local authorities and voluntary agencies, such as welfare or unemployment agencies.[38]

There are a number of concerns about this donor/NGO welfare system that is visible and strongly prevalent in Oxfam projects in Kenya over the years.[39] This is clearly so in northern Kenya where Oxfam has been involved in dispensing official British aid from the Department for International Development (DfID). In addition to increased official funding by Britain to Oxfam, the tendency to identify official aid with government foreign policy and economic interests cannot be waved away in Oxfam's mission in Kenya. Oxfam and the British Agency for International Corporation (DFID) has put in place collaborative mechanisms between itself and the British Government where Oxfam is more or less enhancing the UK's foreign and economic policy and official aid objectives in Kenya.

Even though Oxfam claims to represent an alternative radical approach to development that aims to empower the poor in northern Kenya, Westminster (London) cannot be completely overlooked in its operations. Officials interviewed insisted that Oxfam is autonomous and no one in the British government directs or interferes in its programs abroad. "We are autonomous in our operations and do not engage in politics."[40] Take for example that Oxfam receives part of its funds from the British government; the British government would obviously be interested and concerned with concrete programs that have identifiable socio-economic benefits. These projects/programs are, nonetheless, the type found within the conventional development model that Oxfam offers as an alternative. This tallies with what Charles Elliott notes about donor control: "The greater the dependence of Northern NGOs on government funding through co-financing, the greater institutional weight is likely to be given to modernization-type projects—and the more difficult the organization is likely to fund the rest of the spectrum."[41]

Autonomy of NGOs from donor-control is artificial. Duffield points out that the neo-liberal logic of the donor-led welfare system requires the provision of a minimalist welfare apparatus through careful targeting, by use of actors such as NGOs.[42] Therefore, whereas Oxfam projects are empowering in some respects, one cannot help to notice certain tendencies towards "welfarism." This targeting for minimum welfare provision, according to Duffield, serves no development purpose at all, particularly to the poor who are kept in a vicious cycle of poverty or condition of dependence. As Elliot Fratkin has argued, this is intentional:

> Following independence, Kenya was pulled directly into the global capitalist economy, with international development agencies such as the World Bank and United States Agency for International Development (USAID) encouraging continued production of export crops (coffee, tea, and cotton, aided by dams and irrigation schemes) as well as industrial development in manufacture and assembly of cars, fertilizers, and chemicals.[43]

Significantly, the role of Oxfam has increased from that of the 1960s, when it was regarded as a legacy of the declining colonial influence, to a more robust one. The legacy of the colonial state, it seems has been revived by NGOs. The growing tendency by Oxfam and other NGOs to recruit Kenyan civil servants, whom they pay, better, has raised eyebrows. Many see this as internal brain drain. Oxfam's operations and public contracting are controversial for two reasons. First, since one justification for Oxfam intervention in Kenya is the claim that there is lack of skilled personnel locally, its aggressive recruitment of the best and the very talented local personnel for their projects is paradoxical in some sense. This type of recruitment, which arises from public service contracting, defeats the very purpose for which NGOs are created especially with regard to capacity building and human resource development. One can argue that the assumption that the Kenyan government or public service is starved of skilled personnel is misplaced and should, therefore, not be used as justification for Oxfam intervention in Kenya. Further, the policy defeats the overriding aid objectives of institution building for sustainable development, which must include making the governmental bureaucracy work better and efficiently for the benefit of the people.

Second, the failure of government projects has been occasioned more by inadequate funds than inefficient project management, and yet Oxfam is now eating into the bilateral and multilateral donor component by competing with the government in public service contracting. Luckily, the NGOs' mandate and obligation goes beyond personnel or recruitment issues to include such critical matters as availability of funds, accountability and transparency. Similarly, even if bypassing the government somehow contradicts the very general policy of extending assistance to Kenya, it simply does not make sense when a government does not provide veterinary services, clean water, good roads, good medical facilities and other infrastructure to the taxpayers. Thus, anyone appearing to provide these services is justified in claiming legitimation as stakeholder to the local populations, occasioning admirations such as this: "If these people [Oxfam] did not come here, we would be dead by now ... our animals were gone, we had no water, and we were just waiting for time to die when God send them to us ... and gave us hope to live."[44]

Clearly, it would seem that Oxfam is creating parallel institutional structures in service delivery especially in the use of pre-vets in treating basic animal diseases in northern Kenya, a system that is more popular than the government-run ones. Some of the so-called development efforts are undoubtedly sub-standard such as the pre-vets who are unable to keep their artificial insemination (AI) kits safe just like government extension workers do when power suddenly goes off and they cannot maintain the required temperatures. In government run AI programs for instance, the farmer requires between 2 to 3 visits from the veterinarian for one conception for the family animal. Farmers also require between 2 to 3 visits for the Oxfam pre-vets, for one conception. It is obvious that the government of Kenya is viewed as lacking the required qualities, approach and skills by its own citizens, besides the reality that it lacks adequate resources in meeting the needs of its people. This obviously opens up questions of legitimacy by the pastoralists, and belief in their government. Pastoralists increasingly see NGOs as their "rescuers" and give more recognition to NGO program officials more than to government representatives. This is dangerous for Kenya's statehood and sovereignty.

However, it is Oxfam's success as PSC that has perhaps been its major undoing. Oxfam operates in Kenya with its own pre-determined objectives, work ethics, social demands, new models of development and certain values that have increasingly placed it at odds with Kenya's middle class and the government. The assumption of Oxfam project planners and managers is that disadvantaged rural communities have been progressively marginalized and are often ignored by policy-makers and decision-makers; that they have lost control over the use of natural resources, as well as their traditional coping strategies to mitigate the effect of uncertainties and disasters (for example, traditional restocking practices such as loaning and shareholding) and indigenous knowledge. Unfortunately, that is not entirely true. For example, the Turkana used to vaccinate their cattle against rinderpest and contagious bovine pleuro-pneumonia (CBPP) by injecting fluids from the lungs of infected animals into incisions in the snouts of healthy animals. Although those methods were not completely effective and have fallen into disrepute, they were free and easily accessible to everyone. This contrasts with modern methods that demand cost sharing by local farmers. Most poor herd owners cannot access veterinary services easily due to escalating costs of drugs by multinational drug companies. Thus, even though Oxfam has encouraged the use of modern medicine, most poor livestock-keeping communities such as Boran, Samburu, Turkana, Pokot and Rendille become economically, socially and politically disadvantaged as they lose the social and economic advantages that was previously the basis of their solidarity and traditional means of problem-solving, by being made to depend on drugs from abroad. Dambisa Moyo defines aid as the total concessional loans and grants but excludes emergency intervention e.g. famine, drought and floods for many African counties. There's no distinction within Dead Aid between grants, bursaries, budget support, infrastructure aid, person-to-person aid, heath related aid or concessional loans for discretionary spending. It is all discussed under one umbrella and handed the same fate, as bad. This is a remarkable assumption, especially given that the same book acknowledges the effectiveness of the Marshall Plan that largely focused on infrastructure spending. Surely the Marshall Plan demonstrates that a more nuanced assessment of aid has the potential to reach different conclusions.

For a scholar who argues that aid should be discontinued for African governments, the support for aid from China is rather odd. China is tying down many African governments into long term relations through program assistance direct aid and infrastructure development loans. In Kenya, China has embarked on aggressive prospecting for oil at the coast and in northern Kenya. China built Moi International Sports Center, Kasarani as well as Moi Teaching and referral Hospital in Eldoret, but the government of Kenya is still paying for the grants. China is involved in every new oil discovery on the continent such as in Sudan. It is now involved in almost all strategic mineral projects on the continent. That is not necessarily bad, but if the central worry is that dependency leads to ineffective governments with poor incentives we should be honest enough to consider the possibility that China's closeness may have the same effect to African governments (which are not all democratic) that Western aid has had on Africa. There are no structures and institutions in place that will make assistance from China not have similar negative impacts as aid from the West.

Dambisa Moyo's positions are not supported by proper evidence but some obscure statistical and anecdotal examples. NGOs became powerful in Africa largely as a result of neoliberal policies of the IMF and the World Bank, which Dambisa Moyo supports. Moyo argues that African governments could find money for development through financial markets, and through borrowing, both international and domestic. Moyo seems to suggest that if aid to African governments was cut, they would respond by turning to other sources of finance that would make them more accountable. This is so simplistic and exaggerates the opportunity for alternative finance and takes too lightly the difficulties African societies face. This is merely an academic rather than practical argument because of what we have seen of the impact of structural adjustment programs (SAPs) on Africa, with its market-oriented approach and for which mistakes the IMF and World Bank have apologized. The recent stimulus packages given out by the United States government to private firms are the clearest indication that market forces alone cannot bring about development. Even micro-finance projects such as the Grameen Bank in Bangladesh that Moyo sees as viable vehicles for development in Africa need starting capital. It is true that decades of direct foreign assistance to African governments have not delivered the required results. This is an argument I have made in my book *The NGO Factor in Africa*. Such aid, I have argued has often propped up inefficient, bloated and corrupt regimes, and shielded African leaders from the consequences of their own incompetence and delayed reforms necessary for proper development. NGOs that succeeded in assisting in development have worked through civil society instead of giving money directly to African governments.

Conclusion

From the foregoing, there is no doubt that Oxfam has done a good job in the development of livestock economy through the financing of massive restocking programs, the training of community pre-vets who assist in treatment of simple livestock diseases and the fight against ticks, etc since the 1950s. Oxfam has also trained pastoralists in livestock marketing skills. These skills help pastoralist livestock owners to sell or exchange their cattle for fair prices at markets particularly in fast growing urban areas. This helps them to continue their pastoralist traditions and avoid having to move to towns and becoming destitute, thereby adding to the urban poverty statistics.

In the general introduction to this volume, Emmanuel Mbah and Steven Salm posited that "Africa's experience at connecting with the rest of the world has been at worst pernicious, and at best contradictory and questionable." This is especially obvious in the role NGOs play in the continent, and particularly true with the case of Oxfam in Kenya. Throughout northern Kenya, interviews, conversations and observations revealed that Oxfam is indeed helpful. This is not however the position shared by the middle classes within these societies. There is certainly no choice for these rural poor but to support Oxfam. Some of them are dependent entirely on Oxfam's handouts. Oxfam has not included elders in its project decision-making and implementation phases at top level. This has moved it further and further away from finding local solutions to local problems. There is also the dependency element noticeable in CBOs such as women groups and livestock owners associations, to over-praise Oxfam since they are dependent on it for funding.

There are some shortcomings in Oxfam's performance of development in the region. Pastoralists in areas of northern Kenya where Oxfam works rarely have a voice in what they are given, be it veterinary services, water wells and boreholes, among others. In most cases, Oxfam identifies their needs for them. Whereas this could be acceptable to a people perceived not to " ... know what they want in a fast changing world" as one NGO executive told me, it is incorrect and undemocratic to impose decisions on a people the way NGOs do. Pastoralists are increasingly accepting everything that comes their way, becoming very dependent on aid in the process. This is dangerous as it is increasing the state of dependency of some welfare programs in Kenya. Besides, the selective and sometimes emergency makeshift structures that eventually become "permanent" are leading to some kind of "ghettoization" of development in Kenya. In northern Kenya such minimalist development programs are so prevalent.

In the past, Oxfam has been regarded as a small-scale operator, which has allowed it to be flexible, but not anymore, especially when it started becoming a PSC. The amount that Oxfam has been committing to projects has been increasing exponentially exceeding that of even some ministries' total annual budget. Besides being intimidating, it elevates the power and authority of Oxfam executives who have to be answerable to the various ministries' bureaucrats under which their projects fall. In addition, Oxfam is increasingly becoming bureaucratic in its own right. Increasingly, there are perhaps too many field officers and major decisions affecting the field are decided far away in Nairobi. Thus, Oxfam has been growing in size, due to handling of more funds and employing more people. Oxfam is becoming more bureaucratic in its structures across Kenya and getting complicated; an irony in that, NGOs once criticized governments of this same characteristic. In fact, as a result of public service contracting, the Oxfam budget in Kenya is larger than that held by some important government ministries, including water, health and public works put together. Incidentally Oxfam is a good example of effective aid that is unfortunately ignored by Dead Aid. Recent writings such as those of Dambisa Moyo do not have much traction because they lack practical facts from the ground. For example, Dambisa Moyo's proposed solutions do not offer much, if anything. Remittances or micro finance or international market finance will not be adequate, to turn off the global aid tap to Africa. Aid is still important and the challenge is how to make it work by making it reach the intended beneficiaries in rural areas.

Bibliography

Amin, Samir. *Accumulation on a World Scale.* New York: Monthly Review Press, 1974.

Amin, Samir. *Unequal Development: An Essay on the Social Formations of Peripheral Capitalism.* New York: Monthly Review Press, 1976.

Amutabi, Maurice N. *The NGO Factor in Africa: The Case of Arrested Development in Kenya.* New York: Routledge, 2006.

Bratton, Michael. "The Politics of Government: NGO Relations in Africa." in *World Development.* Vol. 17, No. 4, (1989), 569–587.

Bratton, Michael. "NGOs in Africa: Can They Influence Public Policy?" *Development and Change* 21, (1990).

Bratton, Michael. "The Politics of Government: NGO Relations in Africa", in *World Development.* Vol. 17, No. 4 (1989), 569–587.

Brodhead, Tim, Brent Herbert-Copley, and Anne-Marie Lambert. *Bridges of Hope? Canadian Voluntary Agencies and the Third World.* Ottawa: The North-South Institute, 1988.

Boyer, David. *The Role of Northern NGOs in the Promotion of Sustainable Development in Africa.* Edinburgh: Centre of African Studies, 1990.

Clark, John. *Democratizing Development: The Role of Voluntary Organizations.* London: Earthscan Publications, 1991.

Clark, John. *The State and the Voluntary Sector.* Human Resources and Operations Policy Working Paper No. 12. Washington DC: World Bank, October 1993.

Edwards, Michael and David Hulme, *Making a difference: NGOs and Development in a Changing World.* London: Earthscan, 1992.

Fowler, Alan. "NGOs as Agents of Democratization: An African Perspective." Mimeo (draft). University of Sussex, Institute of Development Studies, May, 1992.

Fowler, Alan. *Nongovernmental Organizations in Africa: Achieving Comparative Advantage in Relief and Microdevelopment.* IDS Discussion Paper No. 249. Brighton: Institute of Development Studies, 1988.

Fowler, Alan, P. Campbell, P. and B. Pratt. *Institutional Development and NGOs in Africa: Policy Perspectives for European Development Agencies.* Oxford: INTRAC, 1992.

Fowler, Alan. "NGOs as Agents of Democratization: An African Perspective." Mimeo (draft). University of Sussex, Institute of Development Studies, May 1992.

Frank, Andre Gunder. *Capitalism and Underdevelopment in Latin America: Historical Studies of Chile and Brazil*, rev. ed. New York: Monthly Review Press, 1969.

Frank, Andre Gunder. *Latin America: Underdevelopment or Revolution.* New York: Monthly Review Press, 1969.

Frank, Andre Gunder. "The Development of Underdevelopment." *Monthly Review*, 18 (September 1966): 17–31.

Hulme, David and Michael Edwards, (eds.), *Making a Difference? NGOs and Development in a Changing World.* London: Earthscan, 1992.

Irogbe, Kema. "Globalizatin and the Development of Underdevelopment of the Third World," *Journal of Third World Studies*, Vol. 22:1 (Spring 2005), 41–68.

Jackson, Robert H., and Carl G. Rosberg. "Why Africa's Weak States Persist: The Empirical and the Juridical in Statehood." *World Politics* 35 (1): 1–24 (1982).

Migdal, Joel. *Strong Societies and Weak States: State-Society Relations and State Capabilities in the Third World.* Princeton, NJ: Princeton University Press, 1988.

Moyo, Dambisa. *Dead Aid: Why Aid Is Not Working and How There Is a Better Way for Africa.* London: Allen Lane, 2009.

Tandon, Rajesh. *The Relationship between NGOs and Government.* Mimeo paper presented to the Conference on the Promotion of Autonomous Development. New Delhi: PRIA, 1987.

Tandon, Rajesh. *NGO Government Relations: A Source of Life or a Kiss of Death.* New Delhi, India: Society for Participatory Research in Asia, 1991.

Tandon, Rajesh. *NGOs and Civil Society*. Boston: Institute for Development Research, 1992.

Tandon, Yash. "Foreign NGOs, Uses an Abuses: An African Perspective", in *IFDA Dossier* 81, April/June 1991.

Tendler, Judith. *Turning Private Voluntary Organizations into Development Agencies: Questions for Evaluation,* AID Program Evaluation Discussion Paper No. 12. Washington: USAID, 1982.

Wallerstein, Immanuel. "Dependence in an Interdependent World." *African Studies Review* 17 (April 1974): 1–26.

Part B

Socio-Cultural and Intellectual Globalization

Chapter 6

Gender and Globalization in Africa

Bridget A. Teboh

Introduction

The history of gender and globalization is rife with competition and struggles between classes, genders and nations. How women and gendered practices interacted with the attitudes and structures of globalization is central to this discussion. Few studies of globalization address its impact on women, and gender and this has resulted in an incomplete understanding of the ways in which material life, cultural values, and political imperatives interact in a global context to affect the lives of women who make up 51 percent of the population of Africa.[1] In the few cases where women are mentioned, they are often depicted as victims of the hegemonic and exploitative forces of the world capitalist system and corrupt African governments.[2] The former Deputy-Mayor of Batibo town in Cameroon sums it up best for many African women: "Globalization is the extent to which improved technology can help humans connect with each other ... a situation in which African women can connect to the rest of the world, and have a say as equal partners, as human beings in matters that directly concern us or affect our daily lives."[3]

The main objective of this chapter is to explore the ways in which African women have protested their social, political and economic positions as they navigate multiple roads transiting to globalization in a process that links them to the rest of the world. I am, therefore, compelled to ask the following questions: How has Africa interacted with the outside world and what have been the gender implications of such interactions? What attempts at gender equality have been made within Africa since the 1970s? How have women responded to the increasing presence of global processes? As I sketch out available instruments in Africa to enable gender equality and equity, the underlying dynamic of attempts to liberate women, the constraints and biases towards men and also towards Western ideologies and culture become apparent. The power and dynamism of African women come to the fore as women respond to changes in an era of increasing global transformations and processes.

How then can we speak about globalization and gender relations in Africa without being trapped by generalizations? How can we highlight what is at stake for women while also being cognizant of the fact that every society is different and distinctive? Can we avoid the pitfalls of the homogenizing discourse of African women, and by extension, women of the developing world or global south and its simplifications, and yet recognize that African societies have been shaped by a common set of global processes, interactions and policies triggered by the west/global north?

Contextualizing Globalization in Africa: A Legacy of Exploitation

The chapter starts with this book's premise that as an economic, political and cultural phenomenon, globalization is not new, but it is a new name for a very old process, one that has always worked against the betterment of women and stripped them of power. Such a discussion can only be rendered fully comprehensible through the use of gender as an important category of analysis as well as a Gender Development Index (GDI) which makes it possible to measure comparatively the gender weighted impact of global processes on women in Africa. Gender is central to an understanding of power, and the historical processes linked to all phases of globalization that continue to transform African women's lives. Women's lives are not lived in a vacuum; their fate is tied to the fate of nation states and to the continent of Africa. As such, women have always been witnesses to the traumatic events in Africa and in most cases have picked up the pieces after such devastation.

Central to the dialectical relationship between Africa and globalization is the imbalance within the dogma of profit maximization, ethical values about human welfare and gender equality. Globalization demands that whatever the nature of their economies, level of development, and location in the global economy, all countries must pursue a common set of economic policies: the primacy of the free market and of private enterprise in all processes of human development. Some scholars argue that globalization offers opportunities for the poor to alleviate poverty while spreading democracy.[4] Others claim it has led to greater disparities within world regions and nation states while enabling greater accumulation of wealth for big corporations, wealthy nations and the privileged few.[5] Most fail to include gender and other issues not related to economic globalization.[6]

African countries did not recently enter into the global economy, their entry started a long time ago as disadvantaged partners or participants of European powers and western nations who controlled that economy and hampered Africa's growth and development.[7] One of the most damning critiques of colonization of Africa has been that colonial powers depleted African resources and left Africa with nothing but pain, artificial boundaries and bad debt—not even the requisite infrastructure or technology needed for development and modernization in a global age. Without appropriate technology Africans have been left out of the economic and technological innovations of the twentieth century. The link between technology and development in today's society has been underscored by many. According to Stross, the twentieth century was known variously in British and American history as "The Machine Age," or the "post-industrial Information Age," because such technological innovations were already available and in use in Britain and some European nations as well as in the United States, and therefore triggered development and industrialization in these places.[8] Real development did not come from European colonization of Africa. The new infrastructure introduced was to facilitate exploitation; and the new system of large-scale agriculture and extractive production were to benefit Europeans.[9]

In the Cameroons colonial economics, new industries, and the intervening hand of of British colonial administration intruded on once enterprising and self-sufficient communities, forcing new choices and redefining the roles of women.[10] Low grade technology requiring little capital intensive skill was introduced to the colonies—just enough to allow Europeans to fulfill their mission of exploitation through cash cropping and mining as well as taxation, wage and forced labor. These were all newly imposed policies to Africans and they transformed society profoundly.[11] After independence this pattern did not change until the 1990s, because colonies in Africa were set up to have a dependent economic relationship with former colonial powers and that undermined the economic, political, and social systems of independent African states. Traditional systems were undermined and new political entities created as different groups of people were thrown together or mothers and children separated by artificial boundaries.[12] It is within this particular context that we must examine African women's struggles for gender equality and the impact of globalization on women.

Contextualizing Women's Struggles, Development and Globalization

The impact of colonization on African women has often been studied through the lens of domesticity, a perspective that emphasizes the role that Christian missionaries and colonizers played in spreading Western education, culture and norms, and argues that such European influences narrowed women's sphere of activities and increasingly confined them to the domestic realm, the "housewifisation" of African women.[13] Such influences disseminated "an ideology of female domesticity that laid stress on women's reproductive and nurturing roles above their autonomy and productivity."[14] While some scholars have examined the diversity and roles of colonial European women in Africa, recent scholarship shows that some colonial European women's experiences of Victorians ideals and patriarchy in Europe made them to fight for African women's liberation through better education in the colonies.[15] As much as some colonial women wanted to improve these conditions, they could only attempt changes within the confines of colonial rule and colonial policies. Suffice it to say that recent, nuanced work on colonial encounters complicates relations between Europeans and Africans, demonstrating that "African women were frequently active agents, rejecting and transforming colonial ideologies" that did not meet their needs.[16] Such is the attitude that African women have adopted in this latest phase of globalization. Since the mid 1980s, they pick and choose what is right or good for their welfare and ignore the rest. It is no secret that in postcolonial Africa, poverty has been feminized. The colonial legacy and differential gendered impact of colonization and neocolonialism are to blame for this situation, and with obvious reasons: gender discrimination at all levels in the African economic and political spheres, and a disregard for basic human rights, especially those of women.

Feminist theorists and activists have been engaged with gender development theory, policies, and practices since the mid-1970s. The most salient development projects have often been state-led and the tendency among development practitioners has been to ignore the ways in which the processes of development impact women. In practice, development not only positions women very differently from men, but it is itself a profoundly gendered project. Since the 1990s, we have witnessed what many have called the "demise of the development project." Changes in the international political economy and within developing nations have transformed how development is now being constituted. The current ascendancy of the forces of globalization, with its concomitant regimes of neoliberal policies and structural adjustments, as well as a negative colonial legacy have threatened the ability of African nations to undertake meaningful development.[17] According to Osirim's feminist political economy perspective, "the global capitalist system then, in combination with domestic factors, reinforces inequality between the rich and poor as well as between women and men."[18]

Given these circumstances globalization is not a disembodied force. Globalization takes place through people, organizations and institutions, who together determine its direction. In the case of Africa globalization involves several key players: former colonial powers, western nations, IFIs like the Internal Monetary Fund (IMF), World Trade Organization (WTO), and World Bank (WB), the United Nations, TNCs/big corporations, African governments and Africans themselves, especially women. How various key players interact with Africans and how Africans have responded in an increasingly global context is important in the discussion that follows. Accounting for two percent of the world GDP, African countries have a limited voice in the financial institutions that govern flows of trade and capital, such as the World Trade Organizations (WTO), the World Bank and the IMF. Compared to other countries and areas of the world, African nations and their economies have benefited the least from such global economic linkages.

Economic SAPs developed at the behest of the IMF and WB, and represented one facet of globalization. This was characterized by the expansion of a world capitalist economy, economic restructuring, and the enactment of SAPs in Global South nations mandated or strongly recommended by the major International Financial Institutions, IFIs and the Global North as a solution to Global South problems. Equality and fundamental human rights became enshrined in the basic instruments of today's international community as cornerstones to the vision of any democratic society. But the carefully written words of these documents stand in sharp contrast to the daily reality of millions of women around the world especially in Africa. Of the 1.3 billion people living in poverty today, 70 percent are women, and most of them live in Africa. In terms of ownership, African women are constrained in their access to and control of resources, aggravated by entitlement systems that impose disparities in men's and women's access to common property resources, especially to productive assets. Women play important roles in agricultural countries where they grow, harvest and prepare almost all of the food consumed by their families but are rarely acknowledged as food producers. In sub-Saharan Africa women directly produce 80 percent of all food. According to Seager, "in official statistics women represent 40 percent of agricultural workers worldwide, but much of women's farm and food production work is unaccounted" or underestimated and overlooked by official agriculture aid agencies.[19] In the 1990s the proportion of agricultural tasks carried out by African women clearly told the unfair story: feeding the family—95 percent; fuel and water processing—90 percent; storing and transporting—80 percent; hoeing and weeding—70 percent; planting and domestic stock—50 percent; turning the soil—30 percent; hunting—10 percent and clearing fields—5 percent.

When women receive wages for their labor, they get the lowest pay. They are often employees not employers at the bottom of pay and power scales. This has led to the "feminization of poverty" as many women in Africa live in poverty in spite of long hours spent working. Labor is also increasingly feminized, in the absence of gender development or economic empowerment for women. The global exchange and interdependency of people, ideas, wealth, trade and capital flows, and technology which quickly intensified in the past two decades, poses a challenge for Africa because the continent is ill prepared to deal with these rapid changes. Technological innovation is not happening at the same pace as global exchanges. Although all the key components of the process of globalization have been implemented partly as structural adjustment programs, they have not only failed but have created more problems for African nations.

Section I: Globalization and the Push for Gender Equity/Equality

Here my focus is on the UN World Conferences on Women held between 1975 and 2000. These conferences and meetings created much needed buzz and awareness regarding gender and women's rights not only among women but also within African governments as they had to send delegates to meetings. Women in Africa, like women worldwide, live with de facto restrictions on their movement, public presence, dress, public and private behavior. In some countries they are faced with specific and legally encoded restrictions rooted in assumptions that men have the right to control women.[20] Particular restrictions are often symptomatic of broader human rights abuses and political repression. Global travel and gender segregation became an interesting part of the discussions as permits and visas were needed for travel to conferences. How African women navigated citizenship within a changing landscape of globalization to become world citizens, and the roads of transition to globalization are crucial to the following discussion.

The drive to promote women in decision-making positions worldwide gained momentum after the first UN International Conference on Women (Mexico, 1975) highlighted the devastating state of women around the world, and during the 1980s and early 1990s through a series of additional meetings.[21] For example, in Nairobi (1985), women from around the world gathered to mark the culmination of the UN decade for women. During the ten days of intense discussions, women brought diverse experiences, concerns, and visions as they focused on gender equality, development and peace, and ended with the Forward-Looking Strategies for the Advancement of Women. The diversity of voices was one of its strengths and challenges. For delegates, the Nairobi Conference was crucial as a marker, an assessment point and reality check. A key question that emerged was, "can we speak of feminism on a global scale?" If yes, what parameters are to be used to address the concerns of all delegates? UN Spokesperson, Margaret Papandreau, summed up the challenges and hopes for the future in the following words: "In the end we will find a way to be united, if even to be united in diversity and all of us will take home with us the richness of this experience, the awareness of the difficulties, and a renowned faith in the justice of our course."[22] Following Nairobi, women's efforts doubled as they came together and created independent movements to better push the women's rights agenda, serve women's needs and make demands on African governments.

Further impetus came a decade later at the Fourth World Conference on Women, held in Beijing, China, which called for at least 30 percent representation of women in national governments. UN World Conferences on Women thus served as catalysts for change and Beijing (1995) marked a watershed as governments went beyond national rhetoric with regards to initiatives regarding women. African nations sent delegates to these conferences and most of them were women. The Platform incorporated 'gender' and 'gender mainstreaming' that became popular in development cycles in the 1990s when the GAD framework for development was also adopted. These conferences were significant in terms of the buzz that they generated around women's issues and in terms of the increasing number of participants and countries that sent delegates. Figure 6.1 depicts the increasing interest over the years, and the participation of women and governments at the UN International Conferences on Women.

At the dawn of the new millennium, poverty and gender disparity had increased around the world, prompting more action. In September 2000 at the UN Millennium Summit in New York (also known as Beijing + 5 summit), world leaders pledged in a *UN Millennium Declaration* to "promote gender equality and the empowerment of women as effective ways to combat poverty, hunger and disease, and to stimulate development that is truly sustainable."[23] At that summit, world leaders also adopted the goal of gender equality and seven others, known collectively as *the Millennium Development Goals (MDG)*.

Figure 6.1 Conferences, Number of Women Delegates and Number of Countries Represented

1st Mexico, 1975	6,000 women	133 governments
2nd Copenhagen, 1980	8,000 women	145 governments
3rd Nairobi, 1985	15,000 women	157 governments
4th Beijing, 1995	30, 000 women	189 governments

Source: Joni Seager, *The Atlas*, p. 2

Since then, the number of women in leadership positions has been on the rise around the world.

UN Globalizing Mission and the Gender Implications for Africa

To promote women's rights, and enhance gender equality around the globe, the UN Assembly embarked upon a number of changes to help transform Africa. The "Decade for Women" (1975–1985), established at the first International Women's Conference in Mexico City, had the following goals:

- The eradication of underdevelopment.
- The quest for peace.
- The pursuit of equality for women in all spheres (political, economical, and social).

Delegates to the Mexico City conference laid out an ambitious "World Plan of Action" with a series of recommendations for Governments to follow during the next ten years. A parallel NGO forum also took place in which women activists raised and discussed issues similar to those on the UN agenda. *The Convention on the Elimination of All Forms of Discrimination Against Women* (CEDAW) was adopted in 1979 by the UN Assembly and is often described as the International Bill of Rights for women; it stands as one of the available basic legal and political instruments for the promotion of women's rights. It was the result of years of organizing within the UN and in many countries around the world. The final impetus for drafting the treaty was the first UN Women's Conference in Mexico in 1975. CEDAW established a set of standards and principles that are intended to serve as a template for shaping national policies towards the long-term goal of eliminating gender discrimination in every country. The preamble to the 30 articles defines discrimination and sets up an agenda for national action to end discrimination. Simply put, discrimination means,

> Any distinction, exclusion or restriction made on the basis of sex which has the effect or purpose of impairing or nullifying the recognition, enjoyment or exercise by women irrespective of their marital status, on basis of equality of women and men, of Human Rights and fundamental freedoms in political, economic, social, cultural, civil or any other field.[24]

Countries that have signed and ratified CEDAW are not only held to the set standards and are obliged to pursue policies that eliminate discrimination, but they must also report their progress or lack thereof once every four years to a CEDAW committee.[25] It is certainly true that many countries that have ratified CEDAW have nothing much to show for it in terms of evidence of genuine efforts towards compliance with the terms of the treaty. Like many international agreements, the practical effectiveness and implementation leaves much to be desired. However, "it sets a platform of 'minimum expectations,' and it stands as an important document to which women's pressure groups can hold governments responsible."[26] Most of the world's governments and most African governments have signed and ratified the CEDAW. Oddly enough due to internal politics the USA has not yet ratified the CEDAW because it would require a substantial overhaul of the legal structure of the country. Yet in the eyes of Africans and the rest of the world, the USA is generally considered to have progressive policies on gender.

The Beijing Declarations and Platform for Action

Women's struggles worldwide coalesced around the 1995 UN conference and the adoption of the Platform for Action (PFA), a document that brought together most of the previous commitments that women had secured at different world conferences. According to its mission statement:

> The Platform for Action is an agenda for women's empowerment. It aims at accelerating the implementation of the Nairobi Forward-looking Strategies for the Advancement of Women and at removing all the obstacles to women's active participation in all spheres of public and private life through a full and equal share in economic, social, cultural and political decision-making. This means that the principle of

> shared power and responsibility should be established between women and men at home, in the workplace and in the wider national and international communities. Equality between women and men is a matter of human rights and a condition for social justice and is also a necessary and fundamental requisite for equality, development and peace.... A transformed partnership based on equality between women and men is a condition for people-centered sustainable development.... A sustained and long-term commitment is essential, so that women and men can work together for themselves, for their children and for society to meet the challenges of the twenty-first century.[27]

The Platform had two-pronged aims: first, accelerating the implementation of the 1985 Nairobi forward-looking strategies for the Advancement of Women and, second, removing all obstacles to women's active participation in all spheres of public life. It reaffirmed the fundamental principles set forth in the Vienna Declaration and the Program of Action that the human rights of women and the girl child are inalienable, integral, indivisible parts of human rights. The Platform identified twelve "Critical Areas of Concern" that were seen as the main obstacles to the advancement of women the world over: poverty, education, health, violence, armed conflict, economic structures, power sharing, institutional mechanisms, human rights, media, environment, and the girl-child. The Platform offered corresponding strategic objectives and actions to be taken by national and local governments, the international community, NGOs, and the private sector over a 5-year period in an attempt to remove existing obstacles to women's advancements.

The summary in Figure 6.2 of the 11 October 2004 Cameroon presidential results includes names of political parties and party leaders, and is evidence of underrepresentation of women in politics.

As the case of Cameroon shows, there is a big difference between identifying and 'domesticating' these priorities. Despite all these measures, studies show women's rights and women's status as low when compared to that of men. In 1975 Cameroon heeded the UN push, and created a national machinery by forming a women's unit within the Ministry of Social and Women's Affairs. In 1994 Cameroon ratified the CEDAW and in December, 1997, created the Ministry of Women's Affairs.[28] Since 2004 its current designation is Ministry of Women's Empowerment and the Family. Such name changes and designations are disruptive because they entail new structures, new bosses and personnel. However its mission has remained the same, the advancement of women and the reduction of the gender gap in Cameroon by:

- Ensuring that women's rights are protected and respected;

Figure 6.2 Presidential Elections in Cameroon: Party Leaders and Candidates, 11 October, 2004

Candidates and Parties	Votes	%
Paul Biya—Cameroon People's Democratic Movement (Rassemblement démocratique du Peuple Camerounais)	2,665,359	70.92
Ni John Fru Ndi—Social Democratic Front (Front Social-Démocratique)	654,066	17.40
Adamou Ndam Njoya—National Union for Democracy and Progress (Union Nationale pour la Démocratie et le Progrès)	168,318	4.48
Garga Haman Adji—Alliance for Democracy and Development (Alliance pour la Démocratie et le Développement)	140,372	3.74
12 Others	130,106	3.46
Total (turnout 82.2%)	3,758,221	100.00

Source: Cameroon Supreme Court

- Advocating the eradication of all forms of discrimination against women;
- Contributing to political, economic and socio-cultural advancement of women;
- Working for the autonomy of women;
- Participation in drawing up policies and programs that consider gender approach (Mainstreaming);
- Training and supervising different trades for young girls and women in empowerment centers; and
- Providing support to small scale businesses through financing of income generating activities.

Despite the rhetoric, the budget of this ministry has always been insufficient to carry out the stated goals.[29] In 1997 for instance, its budget was 40 percent of the already meager Ministry of Youth and Sports' budget.[30] The creation and budget of the Ministry of Women's Affairs showed little more than a token creation to please women and international/external donors and observers. Despite the best efforts in Cameroon with respect to women's rights and gender issues, the results have been unimpressive and minimal to say the least. After Beijing 1995, Cameroon made two reforms regarding pregnant girls and women workers. Girls who left school due to pregnancy could be re-admitted and female workers could claim housing benefits on equal terms with men. Women were still poorly represented in the legislature and within government in Cameroon.

Gender Problematic and the Plight of Women in a Globalizing Era

UN Secretary-General Kofi Annan notes that "there is no effective development strategy in which women do not play a central role." When women are fully involved, he continues, the benefits are immediate—families are healthier and better fed and their income, savings and investments go up: "And what is true of families is also true of communities and, in the long run, of whole countries."[31]

It is not easy to measure the plight and status of women in Africa or worldwide. Nonetheless, there are approximations. The UNDP has created a gender sensitive development index (GDI), informed by feminist critiques of the many cross-national measures in standard of living. The GDI is not a status of women index, but is rather "an index, in which countries are ranked according to a set of basic 'quality of life/development' measures, including life expectancy, educational attainment and income." These are then adjusted according to the degree of gender disparity in each measure. Thus, the result is a "gender weighted index of country by country standards of development."[32] Gender equality does not depend on income level of a society but rather on state policies. Since the 1970s thanks to the UN conferences and women's organizing, GDI values for all countries have improved, but the pace of progress has been uneven. For Africa it has been very slow and in some instances it stopped completely. Unemployment and poverty among women has increased, and violence against women has also increased while government support for health care, child care, and food subsidies have been eliminated often as part of economic policies imposed by SAPs.[33]

Wage gaps persist between men and women. In fact, women have seen their wages decline and their workload double through trade liberalization. This is evidence that women are still perceived as secondary wage earners whose income should supplement a household rather than support it. The deciding factor in women's labor woes and economic challenges today is the difference between paid and unpaid labor.[34] Unequal power relations therefore remain entrenched at the household and community level—a problem which underlies other forms of inequality. African women have a lot of responsibilities, yet in most countries women do not have the rights that will allow them to handle these responsibilities. As a result, women continue to struggle in contestations over power or scarce resources.[35] Economic freedom for women is therefore a better starting point to addressing some of these issues.

Section 2: Women and the Global Economy

Since the 1980s African nations have been battling a political and an economic crisis. The reasons for the crisis are many and multi-faceted, triggered by internal and external factors—ranging from bad governance and corrupt African governments, gender segregation and bias, neo-liberal economic policies and structural adjustments, to neo-colonialism, globalization and attendant unfair terms of trade. We cannot emphasize enough the devastating impacts of all these on African women and on gender relations in Africa. An upsurge in new women's organizations and NGO activities in the 1990s helped a little but was not enough to change the direction of the feminization of poverty in Africa. With increasing trends of globalization, the gendered nature of migration has been accentuated. Current world systemic political and economic dislocations generate large population movements, most of these punctuated by gender differences. African women have become part of an increasing pool of women from all over the world, (mainly from Asia, Eastern Europe, the Caribbean, and Latin America) who migrate internationally in search of better jobs in wealthier countries of the west.

This is not surprising given that globally since the 1960s the rich have become richer and the poor have become poorer, thus increasing the gap between the two. Income levels of the poorest 20 percent of the world's population declined from 2.3 to 1.4 percent while the income of the richest 20 percent rose from 70 to 85 percent. Overall poverty increased in Africa between 1981 and 2005, whereas poverty decreased from 40 to 28 percent worldwide. Some 50 percent of sub-Saharan Africans lived below the poverty level in 2005, most of them women who constitute the poorest of the poor.[36] They do not have the same access to credit as men and in many countries women are still minors in financial matters and are not allowed to make financial decisions.[37] While the debates regarding the pros and cons of globalization rage on, and African governments take their time deciding whether or not to domesticate and implement UN instruments and ratify bills (national and international) that protect women's rights and guarantee gender equality, African women have continued to do what they do best—take care of financial and other problems, while managing poverty.

Njanggi Credit System in a Global Context

In this part of the chapter I focus on *njanggis,* savings clubs and their usefulness for Cameroonians abroad, to demonstrate the extent to which the *njanggis* have become part of global processes and the ever-expanding transna-

Figure 6.3 Entry of Africans into the United States (2000)

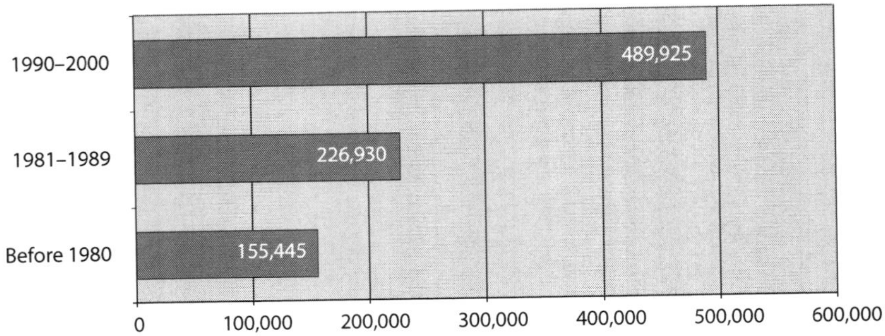

Source: United States Census 2000, table FBP-1.
* Bridget Teboh, "Reproducing African Communities in the US: Settlement Patterns, Reproduction and Social Organizations," in Emmanuel Yewah and Dimeji Togunde (eds.) *Across the Atlantic: African Immigrants in the United States Diaspora* (Champaign, IL: University of Illinois Press, November 2010), 79.

tional pursuits and remittances by African women.[38] Many Africans travel to and live in far-away places. African women therefore had to find alternative methods to take care of themselves and their families as well as to meet other obligations expected of them. Elsewhere I argue that women living abroad still depend on *njanggis* and other forms of African cultural know-how to create a home away from home—Africa.[39] Women increasingly find themselves heading households in these places, working day and night to make it possible for the family to be reunited. Others try to make a living and build a new home. In both cases, they still have to help people back in Africa, and that is where the *njanggis* play an important economic role, one that highlights women's active participation and struggles to resist poverty and produce change in their circumstances. Figure 6.3 shows the dynamics of African immigration in the United States in the post-1965 Immigration Act.

Women have been a part of travelling or migratory Africans since the era of the Trans-Saharan trade. In recent times, the movement of Africans to the USA increased after the 1965 Hart-Cellar Immigration Act,[40] which eliminated national-origin quotas, and opened up migration from developing and African nations.[41] This bill is important because after 1965 Africans came to the US as skilled workers and professionals attracted by the possibility of higher earnings. Leaving their countries in frustration, by 1995 an average of 40,000 Africans, mostly skilled workers and professionals arrived annually to the US. The reasons for leaving are many. Some are internal such as, the decline in real income; increasing high prices for consumer/basic needs; lack of merit based promotion practices; political interference; inadequate higher education facilities and opportunities; political upheavals and general instability. Others are external and multifaceted. The articulation of African economies with the wider economic global system has never been based on equality. The economic pressures of the 1970s including "structural adjustments" imposed on many African economies by the International Monetary Fund (IMF) triggered hardship and fueled migration from the continent. These "adjustments," which theoretically were designed to realign the African economies with the so-called "developed" world, further opened the African market to deregulation and liberalization favoring the final penetration of capitalist relations into the remotest hamlet. These strategies failed to bring the necessary readjustments, and, while unable to rearticulate the African economy, left the majority of the population especially women, in abject poverty. Unable to manage their affairs, most African nations were heavily indebted by the 1980s. This cycle saw the state decline and the neoliberal hegemony of international organizations such as the IMF and World Bank increase as these banks rushed in to 'rescue' African nations and their economies.

IMF and World Bank loans came at a very high cost, with conditionality clauses and Structural Adjustment Programs that required African governments to diminish state subsidies and social spending, and to increase economic growth through privatization and international trade. According to Seager, adjustments in the economic and social domains affected particularly "those most vulnerable to cuts in social services and government support: the poor, single-earner households, and those on the economic margins."[42] It is therefore no surprise that women are among the hardest hit by SAPs. When compared to 1983 standards, IMF and World Bank SAPs led to a general decline in the standards of living in almost all of West Africa in 1993.[43]

Given these circumstances women have continued to rely upon traditional African self-help groups and associations such as the *njanggis* in Africa and outside Africa. In the face of failed capitalist economies these groups are indispensable for women's survival.[44] They are popular in Cameroon because of their unique rotating feature and scheduled monthly meetings.[45] Other places in Africa have different names for them.[46] There is a growing literature on *njanggis* and some scholars now distinguish between the rotating clubs—ROSCAs and the non rotating clubs—ASCRAs (Accumulating Savings and Credit Associations). Ardener in her pioneer work on ROSCAs in Africa defines them as follows: "ROSCAs are associations in which members regularly contribute to a fund that is given in whole or in part to each contributor in turn."[47] When compared to ROSCAs, ASCRAs are microcredit clubs which do not rotate. They tend to be more businesslike and do not immediately help participating members. ASCRAs are often too involved with banks and NGOs.[48] The simple premise—and in particular its rotating feature—has made it an incredibly resilient and flexible tool of empowerment for people across all classes and genders in Africa. Several hundreds of thousands of African immigrant women have benefitted from *njanggis* which are life-savers for most. As Beatrice G. aptly explains,

> My njanggi picks are the reason I can afford a car to go to work and school. I depend on my njanggi groups for continuous support and networking. When I first arrived from Cameroon to Boston, I knew few people and they could not help me financially. The njanggi group members became close friends. The money from the two njanggis is the main source of funding for my college training.[49]

What are *njanggi* picks? How important are they for African immigrant women? Why are they so popular? Many of the African adults that I interviewed in the US belonged to one or more *njanggis* and 60 percent of them were women.[50] Picks rotate among members in turn. First, the members (say twelve in all) form a group and elect officials. Then, they choose an amount of the monthly dues—say $20, and select numbers to determine the order of their pick. Each month for twelve months, these twelve people meet and contribute a total of $240 that is given to the first person and later to each in turn every month. Members feel a sense of belonging with the community or group. They eat, work and play together. The larger group of Cameroonian friends forms an important social network for them, and really are their "social capital." This is even more significant in a foreign land as many Cameroonians and Africans now reside outside the continent. As foreigners and immigrants, they do not quickly benefit from bank loans or social welfare services.

Njanggis therefore provide money to their members for all kinds of necessities: medical bills, start-up funds for small income-generating projects, school fees, books, construction of homes and purchase of building materials, etc. Today, *njanggis* are very important in the context of immigration and globalization as they constitute local forms of self-help and credit which have been transported abroad by immigrants.[51] An asylum seeker recounts how she came to Boston in winter and was rescued by the *njanggi* group:

> I left Oshie in the Northwest Province of Cameroon in December 2006. It was my first time to venture out of the country. In Cameroon we have the rainy season and dry season. I was told it was winter in Boston.You think I had an idea what that meant?! When the plane finally landed after what seems to be an endless flight on December 12,

> I was confronted by harsh reality. There I was at Logan International Airport, waiting for my aunt's husband to pick me up in the snow, without a winter coat! I had on a beautiful wrapper skirt suit, specially sewn for the occasion. It felt like I had no clothes on, nothing compared to the biting cold outside. I felt my teeth chattering. He finally arrived with an extra jacket for me ... not a winter jacket though. I was glad we were on our way 'home'—a tiny two-bedroom apartment in Dorchester. The next day, we went to our monthly meeting where I was introduced to everyone. I got help and advice from members. I felt at home. I joined the group and later took money from the *njanggi* to buy a winter coat.[52]

On arrival therefore in the USA or any foreign country, the first thing immigrant women do is to seek and join existing national or ethnic social groups and *njanggi* groups in their city, or create one with other Africans. These groups are important loan providers for such necessary material things as winter jackets and boots purchase, car purchase, rental deposit, and education fees. Group members also help by explaining cultural differences and proper behavior to new-comers fondly known as JJCs or Johnny-just-come. *Njanggis* challenge traditional notions of femininity as most women have been able to raise enough money through these *njanggis* to not only supplement low incomes but also to accomplish 'masculine' duties back in Cameroon, such as land purchase, house construction, sponsoring students and other children through college/university, and starting businesses and commercial trips to Dubai and Europe.[53] Female political candidates have increasingly benefitted from *Njanggis* during campaigns. In the USA, even with the collapse of the real estate market in 2007, more African women have bought their own homes. *Njanggis* constitute a significant portion of remittances to Cameroon from abroad. *Njanggis* thus enable the socio cultural value of remittances to be captured. Remittances are "that quantity of currency that migrants earn abroad and then send home to their families and communities."[54] A World Bank Report of 2009 provides figures on remittances to Africa from Africans as follows: Nigeria $10 billion to Nigeria, the highest in sub-Saharan Africa, and "the 6th highest from citizens of developing nations in the Diaspora." In 2008, according to a 2008 World Bank Report, Sudan received remittances of $1.2 billion, Senegal and Uganda $0.9 billion, and South Africa $0.7 billion.[55]

Section 3: Women and Political Activism: Breaking New Ground

An examination of the intersection of constitutionalism and global political ideas of Democracy is required at this time in order to demonstrate how women went from victims and the marginalized to political champions in places like Rwanda, Uganda, South Africa and Liberia. It portrays what women are doing as active agents of resistance and change and explores women's political participation and activism since the 1990s leading to the explosion of women on the political scene in Africa. It captures female agency in Africa—exploring both action and representation, and calls for the investigation of both the strategies used (such as quotas, etc.) and the subject position of African women as agents in Africa. African women presently are moving away from and protesting those barriers that have rendered them subordinate to men politically and legally (traditional, religious, cultural barriers) by using a gendered perspective aimed at transforming existing gender inequalities, building coalitions and networks among themselves and other national and international organizations. Positive changes occurred in the 1990s due to women's activism and the push from UN international conferences and UN development agenda for women. The focus became not to organize for improvement in the status of women, but to organize and demand total transformation of existing unequal gender relations.

By Nairobi 1985, it was obvious that poverty and gender inequality were on the rise instead of decreasing. Many development projects had failed, leaving people to question the existing conceptual framework for development that was state-led, and wanting a new framework to solve the problem. This is when the GAD (Gender and Development) framework was adopted. Together with the drafting of the CEDAW, and the publication and dissemination of the Nairobi 1985 Forward-Looking Strategies for the Advancement of Women, these were powerful tools in favor of gender equality. From Nairobi things changed quickly as women mobilized around specific issues and organized as groups and forged partnerships with other women worldwide who had the same goals. Women started challenging the status quo, focusing on issues relevant to their lives and on agendas discussed at the UN Conferences. Women's struggles worldwide culminated in the 1995 conference and the adoption of the Platform for Action (PFA), a document that brought together most of the previous commitments that women had secured at different world conferences.

African women benefitted somewhat from these globalizing conferences and processes and have been empowered by global ideas of democracy. In African nations, even those that consider themselves democracies, policy and gender have a contested relationship. Therefore any help that could push forward gender awareness and political representation was welcomed. While it can be argued that international conferences helped African women to refocus on women's issues, a wide range of policies play a significant role in entrenching women's subordination. The policy process involves well-considered legislative and legal responses to social problems and social needs. In this understanding, rational and detached policy-makers should make well-intentioned attempts to improve the lives of all citizens. A close analysis of policies in Africa suggests gender bias in favor of male citizens. The paradoxes of African women's status, struggles and gender inequality within all spheres of life in spite of their hard work, mirror Africa's plight and status as the poorest continent when compared to her relative wealth and natural resources.

Globalization and Women's Political Struggles and Agency

The UN International Conferences on Women and other conferences have helped to push forward the agenda of equality between women and men, and women's rights by creating and fostering gender awareness and the implementation of gender sensitive policies at local, national, international and organizational levels. In spite of such attempts and laudable efforts, gender inequity and inequality still prevail. Despite the few successes, women's political participation in modern African politics remains limited due to lack of resources and economic power, government crackdown, lack of confidence, and mistrust. As a result several strategies have been used to encourage women to participate in politics. One such strategy is the use of gender quotas.

The UN 1995 Conference in Beijing adopted a Platform for Action (PFA) to ensure women's equal participation in all forms of "power structures and decision-making."[56] This conference helped to foster positive changes and, between 1995 and 2005, 23 of 48 sub-Saharan African countries adopted quotas. Worldwide, about 30 countries apply some form of female quotas in politics. Why are gender quota's only taking off now in Africa? How important are they to bridging the political gap between women and men? Looking at recent success stories in Africa the possibilities are endless.

Quotas were initially introduced to create a critical mass of 30 to 35 percent in political representation, enough to bring about needed momentum for campaigns and advocacy for gender parity. The tension between democratic and repressive tendencies all over Africa has raised the stakes of political contest. This in turn has rendered the gender issues that have been a part of this contest all the more fascinating and challenging. The use of gender quotas has increased in the last two decades. Many reasons have been given for this trend, all of them different, all of them yielding positive results. In Africa, a continent known for its many patriarchal societies and constraints on women's lives and their participation in public affairs, women are still struggling politically. Gender quotas have been very useful in bridging and reducing the political gap between women and men.

In Africa, there are four main quota systems all of which are promoted by women's movements to promote issues of justice, development, equity, and democratization. These include: 1) *constitutional quotas:* Some countries, including Burkina Faso, Burundi, Rwanda, Tanzania, and Uganda, have constitutional provisions reserving seats in national parliament for women; 2) *reserved seats*: From the outset the number of seats to be won by women is pre-determined; 3) *election law quotas:* Provisions are written into national legislation, as in Sudan, Eritrea, and Mauritania; and 4) *political party quotas* (compulsory and voluntary): Parties adopt compulsory internal rules to include a certain percentage of women as candidates for office, through measures determined by national legislation or constitutional mandates. Parties may also adopt voluntary quotas to influence the number of female candidates. Some examples include the governing parties in fourteen African countries including South Africa, Mozambique, and Cameroon.

Politically, women have done much better in certain contexts and countries in Africa. In countries where they played historically important roles during protest movements, women's status was enhanced and their political participation saw a similar rise. For instance, women played important roles in anti-colonial campaigns in Nso (the ANLU of Cameroon, 1958) and Igboland (The Aba Women's War of Nigeria, 1929), in Kenya (the Mau-Mau Uprising, 1952–56) and in Uganda (the National Resistance Army, 1980s–90s), and in South Africa's anti-apartheid struggles. In other instances gender quotas were deemed necessary to correct gender gaps and include women in politics and development agendas of various African nations.

Uganda's quota for example, grew out of the NRA's war in the 1980s. During that struggle, women fought alongside men to achieve victory, and it was expected that they would be recognized and compensated for their efforts. In recognition of their role during the guerrilla war, Rebel Councils set up in the liberated zones included a Secretary for Women's Affairs. After the NRA victory, which led to NRA gaining power in 1986, Yoweri Museveni, the new President, applied "the bush measure" to national politics. This strategy worked to the advantage of women, as it enabled them to participate fully in the newly formed government. Museveni summed up his decision and reasons as follows: "There was always a distortion. Women were left out, yet they're the producers of wealth in the countryside. So it was a must that we empower 51 percent of our people."[57] In Uganda, quotas initiated the process of improving women's participation in national politics. According to Beatrice Kiraso, elected to parliament in 1996, a cycle began in which "women gained confidence in women, opening up even more avenues."[58] By 1994, the government of President Yoweri Museveni appointed Dr. Wandira Kazibwe as Vice President, making her one of the highest-ranking women in politics on the continent at that time. The timing of the implementation of quotas is linked to the 1995 UN conference in Beijing as well as the end of war or conflict.

In South Africa, both Houses of Parliament are one-third female. The reason behind the high numbers is probably not obvious to most people, but women played a key role in the national liberation struggle and today are benefiting from a quota system adopted by the ruling party, the African National Congress (ANC). Women in South Africa were prominent in the fight against Apartheid, and therefore became part of the new government once apartheid collapsed. The new constitution of South Africa made provisions for women and for gender equity. In many ways it is the best in the world in terms of individual freedoms. Case in point, the Speaker of the House (for Parliament) is a woman. Additionally, the new constitution bars discrimination on the basis of gender, marital status, sexual orientation, or pregnancy. South Africa has the eighth highest percentage of female Members of Parliament, while the United States of America for instance is tied with Jamaica and St. Kitts in 42nd place. One of the key strategies of female activists in Africa was therefore advocating for the adoption of gender quotas and other instruments to advance female representatives. Quotas account for most of the increases in female representation in African legislatures. As per Tripp et al., "In sub-Saharan Africa, countries with quotas have an average of 19 percent female-held seats compared to 11 percent female-held seats in countries without quotas."[59] Approximately 28 countries now have some form of quotas.

As the world marched into the twenty-first century African women experienced hope for the future because of the recent turn of events on the continent and around the globe. In January 2006, Ellen Johnson-Sirleaf of Liberia became Africa's first elected woman head of state, having beaten a Liberian football star in the 2005 election with 59 percent of the vote. She came into office articulating a peace agenda for her war-scarred country. While she has a reputation for strength, she also asserts the necessity of inclusion, political diversity and tolerance.[60] In a country whose confidence in its political leaders has been shattered repeatedly, Sirleaf faced a long and challenging process to build public trust and create constructive roles for Liberia's many combatants. Challenging as the prospects were, her election and subsequent reelection in 2011 are a testament to hopes that women can forge change in African nations.

In 2004 women in Rwanda topped the world rankings of women in national parliaments, with 49 percent representation compared to a world average of 15.1 percent. This success mirrored the trend of a small, but growing number of countries in sub-Saharan Africa, where women made history by breaking into politics.[61] The case of Rwanda is not only special but interesting as it sheds light on women's involvement in politics in Africa. Following the genocide of 1994, when Rwandan women suffered death, humiliation, persecution and sexual abuse during a 100-day massacre that left more than 800,000 people dead, the country entered a period of reconstruction. During that period women took an active role and participated in all spheres of life. They headed about one-third of all households, took up many jobs that were formerly the preserve of men, such as in construction and mechanics. Thanks to a new constitution, 24 out of 80 seats in the lower house of parliament are reserved for women. During the country's September 2003 general election, the first after the genocide, an additional 15 women were voted into non-reserved seats, bringing the total to 39 into the lower house. In the upper house, 6 out of 20 seats are reserved for women. The entry of so many women in the national assembly was a positive sign for politics in Rwanda and women's agency and participation. According to Inter-Parliamentary Union President Anders Johnsson, Rwanda managed to beat the long-time leader, Sweden, where women constitute 45 percent of parliamentarians.[62] For that to happen, Rwandan women lobbied tirelessly, helped to draft the new constitution, and developed voting guidelines that guaranteed seats for women candidates. They also pushed for the creation of a government ministry of women's affairs to promote policies in favor of women's interests. This worked for Rwanda and other nations that saw an end to a long conflict. According to Noeleen Heyzer, "in post-conflict situations, where new constitutions and legislative structures are being created, it is critical that women are present at the peace table and in post-war policy-making."[63] UNIFEM participated in post-genocide reconstruction in Rwanda, by helping women to prepare for political office.

Women's representation in national parliaments across sub-Saharan Africa equals the world average of about 17 percent but it has risen steadily since 1960. The percentage went from 0.6 in 1960, to 1.6 in 1970, 5 in 1980, 6 in 1990, 10 in 2000 and 17.8 in 2007; the level of women's representation in parliament is now higher than in many wealthier countries today.[64] According to Tripp et al., these changes are linked to the influences of domestic and international women's movements which themselves are related to three key factors: "the introduction of electoral quotas for women; opportunities emerging in the process of ending major armed conflicts after 1986 in some countries; and pressures from regional bodies" such as SADC or pan-African organizations.[65] Women's movements in Uganda, Kenya, and South Africa are becoming more assertive and they now demand 50 percent representation in government today.[66] Since the goal of these groups is to have equal representation at every level of decision making, they have to prepare and train women for political office. In Sierra Leone women's groups have recruited, trained and taught women how to raise funds to reach their goal.[67]

Institutional and legal measures are now being taken by African nations to support gender equity and women's rights. The attempts of the past four decades have failed to push most African nations to action. The goals of the UN Conferences on Women, CEDAW, Beijing platform for Action, the UN Millennium Declaration in New York, and the Millennium Development Goals, remain largely underachieved. In addition to domesticating and adhering to the terms of these plans, African nations must find a way to deal with globalization. To this end, African nations have done four important things:

1) Changed from the Organization of African Unity (OAU) to the African Union (AU) (2002);
2) Adopted the Protocol to the African Charter on Human and People's Rights on the Rights of Women in Africa (2003);
3) Made the Solemn Declaration on Gender Equality in Africa (SDGEA) (2004);
4) Declared 2010–2020 as the "African Women's Decade." (2009)

Taken as a whole these are significant decisions and shifts that are capable of engendering positive changes within the continent when and if properly implemented and supported by various governments. This could be a second chance for African nations to implement existing commitments on gender equality and women's rights, and engage sustainable development.

The change from the Organization of African Unity (OAU) to the African Union (AU) in 2002 marked a major shift at the continental level in addressing women's human rights. For example, AU's commitment to gender parity was backed by the election of five female Commissioners to the AU Commission. Also within one year of its existence, the AU adopted the Protocol to the African Charter on Human and People's Rights on the Rights of Women in Africa in (known as the Protocol). Member states at the 2004 AU Summit in Ethiopia adopted the *Solemn Declaration on Gender Equality in Africa* (SDGEA) with the commitment to hold each other accountable on progress made in terms of gender mainstreaming. The Summit in Ethiopia also agreed to:

> Sign and ratify the Protocol to the African Charter on Human and People's Rights on the Rights of Women in Africa by 2004 and to support the launching of public campaigns aimed at ensuring its entry

> into force by 2005 and usher in an era of domesticating and implementing the Protocol as well as other national, regional and international instruments on gender equality by all States Parties.[68]

The Protocol's entry into force was achieved on November 25, 2005, not because member-states actively pushed such an agenda as part of states' campaigns, but mainly because of the advocacy of women's organizations under the Solidarity for African Women's Rights Coalition (SOAWR).[69] The date coincided with the International Day for the Elimination of Violence against Women that marks the beginning of the annual 16 days of activism on violence against women, observed in many countries around the world. According to a SOAWR Policy Briefing, "the era to ensure its [the Protocol's] domestication and implementation is yet to be set, to date only 27 countries have ratified it."[70] Additionally, governments have not made deliberate attempts to domesticate and implement the Protocol or to protect women's rights. Even with such positive signs, gender equality is still an elusive goal.

The declaration of the African Women's Decade is a huge step forward as it implies that African governments do finally realize there is a gender problem, and that women's rights are human rights and this problem must be resolved for the greater good of the continent. The AU summit called on all interested parties (Member States, AU Organs, and RECs-Regional Economic Communities) to support the implementation of Decade activities.[71] Like the UN Declaration of 1975–1985 as Decade for Women, in 1975 in Mexico, this AU declaration is particularly meaningful and insightful. It builds on past attempts and allows us to see the progress made and to compare how far women have come since 1975.

SOAWR's policy briefing suggests that the implementation of the Beijing Declaration and Platform for Action in Africa, the AU Women's Protocol and the Solemn Declaration on Gender Equality in Africa should be the focus of the African Women's Decade. For this to happen, it is crucial for African governments to implement thirteen measures between 2010 and 2020.[72] I draw attention here to the first six recommendations which are short-term and are instrumental to achieving gender equality and women's rights in Africa in the long run:

1) With a sense of urgency, sign and ratify the Protocol and other international instruments that protect the rights of women;
2) Build capacity of Gender Machineries/Ministries/Focal points in the use of a multi-sectoral approach in implementing women's rights commitments in order to coordinate implementation and monitoring by all sectors in government;
3) Put in place effective monitoring mechanisms to measure the implementation of the Protocol and SDGEA including adopting best prac-

tices on implementing women's rights such as establishing performance contracts for all stakeholders in the multi-sectoral approach;

4) Strengthen capacity to coordinate integration, analysis and periodic reporting on the Protocol and SDGEA;
5) Develop and include gender-sensitive indicators and sex-disaggregated data on women's rights into national statistics, national development plans and national budgets; and
6) Build the capacity of Ministries of Finance in gender budgeting to ensure that women's rights priorities as set out in the Protocol and the SDGEA are fully financed.

These multi-level and multi-sectoral measures when implemented properly can make the African Women's Decade truly meaningful. However, one can be fooled into thinking this seems easy to do. History has taught us that since independence in the 1960s, numerous issues have supplanted gender issues in importance. In any case, these are different historical times. Since the 1990s, women have burst onto the political scene. In November 2009 in the Gambia, African Ministers in charge of Gender and Women's Affairs met to discuss women's issues at the 8th African Regional Conference on Women. This means that more serious thought is being given to these issues with African governments doing their best to find solutions. This also means that the continent has more ministries dedicated to women's issues—enough to warrant regular meetings of Ministers in charge of Gender and Women's Affairs. That is good for gender mainstreaming, with broader implications for women's rights and well being.

The African Women's Decade marks a new opportunity for African nations to make a difference in the lives of women. As in the past, such laudable declarations do not mean much if there is no clear-cut budget and written agenda to support activities. In fact, there is no shortage of good, well-intentioned and written documents to support the idea of gender equality among other pressing needs on the continent. The aforementioned documents, bills and declarations are proof of that. The problem in Africa however is and has always been making the transition from theory to practice. In other words, how can African nations and AU member-states go beyond the written document and actually implement the actions? The answer requires stronger institutional and governmental will. The AU has set a positive example during its first few years of existence and African governments should emulate that.

Conclusion

Although some aspects of globalization may offer positive benefits, these benefits have not been equitably distributed between genders and between nations of the world. Women have benefitted the least from globalization and remain disadvantaged in many areas of life, including politics, economics, education, employment, health, and basic human rights. Each new opportunity for development—such as communications technology, greater ease and speed of transportation, diminishing cultural barriers, and the spread of democratic ideals—seems to produce more negative outcomes for women. Particular insights into Africa's history since 1970 have enabled us to focus on Africa's place within the processes of globalization in order to look forward to a better future. Important features of globalization such as capital flows, trade liberalization, and increased trade must therefore be managed in a gender-sensitive way that involves and acknowledges gender and women's rights. Globalization must take into account cultural integration, changing consumption patterns, and increased flows of labor, and enable proper use of information and new technology. As long as trade and other negotiations continue to treat all world countries as equals (when it suits them), and ignore African countries and women when it comes to important decision making processes (thus rendering them voiceless), globalization will remain a vehicle of inequality between nations and between genders.

For this reason, economic, political, and socio-cultural globalization bear striking similarities to the era of colonialism in Africa with all the processes of domination, exploitation and gender discrimination firmly put in place and unchanging. Scholars and policy-makers must reflect on the increasingly diverse perspectives of globalization as a multifarious force affecting African societies and especially women at all levels. Strategies to confront such a force should also be multifarious in nature. African nations must identify and elaborate on the strategic place of Africa and African women in a global world, and in the constantly shifting perspectives prompted by globalization. President Obama shed some light on his and US expectations of African governments on the eve of a visit to Ghana, his first visit to Africa as a US President: "I think that the new president, President Mills, has shown himself committed to the rule of law, to the kinds of democratic commitments that ensure stability in a country. And I think that there is a direct correlation between governance and prosperity."[73] African nations and governments MUST create governments with more diversity, more women and sensitivity to the needs of poor. They MUST recognize the need for social justice as well as economic growth, addressing gender issues to do with both practice and representation, with the example set by the African Union to advance the African women's decade.

In this chapter I have explored the ways in which African women have protested their socio-economic and political positions, and how they have and continue to navigate multiple roads of transition to globalization, a process that links them to the West and the rest of the world. I have argued that the UN conferences on women globalized the push for gender equality, driving the message home in Africa through bills, declarations and treaties. I have also argued that in a globalizing economy African women used traditional survival strategies such as *njanggis*, as transnational pursuits. Finally, I discussed women's political participation and activism and how global political ideas of democracy became concretized in Liberia, Rwanda, South Africa and Uganda. In the end I demonstrated that African women and women's groups are a force to reckon with, playing important roles as actors within globalization, adapting to, and reshaping global policies to their advantage. This chapter serves as a review of the struggle for gender equity and the advancement of women in Africa and a reminder of the work that lies ahead. In doing so, this chapter has opened up new avenues of inquiry that can help to pave the way for a gender-friendly and politically stable Africa capable of participating fully in a rapidly changing global setting.

Bibliography

A. Mama. "Women's Studies and the Studies of Women in Africa during the 1990s," Working Paper Series 5/96, Dakar, Senegal: CODESRIA, 1996.

Adams, M. "Colonial Policies and Women's Participation in Public Life: The Case of British Southern Cameroons." *African Studies Quarterly*, 8, no.3 (2006) http://web.africa.ufl.edu/asq/v8/v8i3a1.htm.

Adams, Melinda. "Appropriating Global Discourses for Domestic Aims: National Machinery for the Advancement of Women." In *Annual Meeting of the American Political Science Association*. 2004a. 12.

African Union. Decision on the African Women's Decade, Assembly/AU/Dec. 229 (XII).

African Union. *Solemn Declaration on Gender Equality in Africa*. 2004.

afro1 News/Africa Recovery, 10 May.

Ardener, Shirley and Burman, Sandra, eds. *Money-Go-Rounds: The Importance of ROSCAs for Women*. Berg: Oxford/Washington, DC. 1995.

Bhagwati, Jagdish. *In Defense of Globalization*. Oxford/New York: Oxford University Press, 2007.

Beatrice G., student and single mother, interview by author, July 08, 2008, Boston, USA.

Boyd, N. *Emissaries The Overseas Work of the American YWCA 1895–1970.* New York: The Women's Press, 1986.

Callaway, H. *Gender, Culture, and Empire: European Women in Colonial Nigeria.* Urbana and Chicago: University of Illinois Press, 1987.

Chase-Dunn, Christopher. *Global Formation: Structures of the World Economy.* Lanham, MD: Rowman and Littlefield, 1998.

Chaudhuri, N. and Strobel, M. (eds.), *Western Women and Imperialism: Complexity and Resistance.* Bloomington: Indiana University Press, 1992.

Chen, Shaohua and Ravallion, Martin. "The Developing World Is Poorer Than We Thought, But No Less Successful in the Fight against Poverty." *Policy Research Working Paper* 4703, August 2008.

Communique of the *"Stakeholders Meeting on Domestication and Implementation of the Protocol to the African Charter on Human and Peoples' Rights on the Rights of Women in Africa,"* 16–18 July 2009, Kigali, Rwanda.

Communiqué of the SOAWR Annual Review and Agenda-Setting Workshop, Theme: *"Spreading Our Wings: A Multi-Sectoral Approach to Women's Rights"* 5–7 October 2009, Panafric Hotel, Nairobi, Kenya.

Cooper, Frederick. "What is the Concept of Globalization Good For?" *African Affairs* 100, 39 (2001), 189–213.

Cooper, Frederick. *Africa Since 1940: the Past of the Present.* Cambridge: Cambridge University Press, 2002.

Coquery-Vidrovitch, Catherine. *African Women: A Modern History.* Boulder, Colorado: Westview Press, 1997.

Dasgupta, Samir. *The Changing Face of Globalization.* SAGE, 2004.

Decree N°97/205 of 07 December 1997. Presidency of the Republic of Cameroon.

Duignan, Peter and Gann, Lewis. *The United States and Africa: A History.* New York: Cambridge University Press, 1984.

Eliza, Paul. *Rethinking Africa's Globalization.* Trenton, NJ: Africa World Press, 2003.

Falola, Toyin. *Britain and Nigeria: Exploitation or Development?* London: Zed Press, 1987.

Falola, Toyin ed. *Africa, Volume 4, The End of Colonial Rule: Nationalism and Decolonization.* Durham, NC: Carolina Academic Press, 2002.

Falola, Toyin ed. *Africa, Vol. 5.* Durham, NC: Carolina Academic Press, 2003.

Falola, Toyin and Salm, Steven J. eds. African Urban Spaces In historical Perspective. New York: University of Rochester Press, 2005.

Graham Jr., Otis L. "Tracing Liberal Woes to '65 Immigration Act." In *Christian Science Monitor,* v 88, n 23, (1995), 19–23.

Held, David, Anthony McGrew, David Goldblatt and Jonathan Perraton. *Global Transformations: Politics, Economics and Culture.* Stanford: Stanford University Press, 1999.

International Monetary Fund, "World Economic and Financial Surveys: Regional Economic Outlook: Sub-Saharan Africa Back to High Growth?" (April 2010), http://www.imf.org.

Inter-Parliamentary Union (IPU). *Women in Parliament. 1945–1995.*

Jayawardena, K. *The White Woman's 'Other' Burden: Western Women* in *South Asia during British Rule.* New York: Routledge, 1995.

Kenneth Ruffing, "Africa in 2008: Breaking Down the Growth," *OECD Policy Insights,* No. 64 (April 2008), http://www.oecd.org/dataoecd/55/15/40583776.pdf.

Khapoya, B. Vincent. *The African Experience: An Introduction.* 2nd Edition. Upper Saddle River, NJ: Prentice Hall, 1998.

Kieh Jr., George (ed.) *Africa and the New Globalization.* New York: Ashgate Publishing, 2008.

Krome, Margaret. Madison semimonthly column for *The Capital Times.* E-mail: mkrome@inxpress.net Published: January 18, 2006.

Madam Esther Teboh, Deputy-Mayor, 2002–2008, Interview by author, December 29, 2010, Batibo, NWP, Cameroon.

Martin, Meredith. *The Fate of Africa: A History of Fifty Years of Independence.* Cambridge, MA: Public Affairs, 2006.

Mbaku, J. Mukum and Saxena, S. Chandra. *Africa at the Crossroads: Between Regionalism and Globalization.* New York: Praeger, 2004.

Moghadam, Valentine. "Gender and Globalization: Female labor and Women's Mobilizations." *Journal of World Systems Research* 5, no. 2 (1999), 367–88.

Moghadam, Valentine. *Gender and Globalization: Female labor and Women's mobilization.* Occasional Paper 11. Normal: Women's Studies Program, Illinois State University, 2000.

Moghadam, Valentine. *Globalizing Women: Transnational Feminist Networks.* Baltimore: Johns Hopkins University Press, 2005.

Nathan Nunn, "The Historical Origins of Africa's Underdevelopment," Nov 8, 2007, http://www.voxeu.org/index.php?q=node/779.

Ngwa, Bernadetta. Retired teacher, interview by author, July 10, 2008, Boston, MA, USA.

Nugent, Paul. *Africa Since Independence: A Comparative History.* Basingstoke: Palgrave, 2004.

Obama, Barack, Interview with AllAfrica's Charles Cobb, Jr., Reed Kramer and Tami Hultman, Blue Room, the White House, 2008.

Osirim, Mary Johnson. *Enterprising Women in Urban Zimbabwe: Gender, Microbusiness, and Globalization*. Bloomington and Indianapolis: Indiana University Press, 2009.

Pádraig Carmody, *Globalization in Africa: Recolonization or Renaissance*? Boulder, CO: Lynne Rienner, July 2010.

Sinn, B. Maxine, Hondagneu-Sotelo, Pierrette and Messner, A. Micheal, eds. *Gender through the Prism of Difference*. Oxford and New York: Oxford University Press, 2005.

SOAWR, Policy Briefing, 3. SOAWR, Solidarity for African Women's Rights Coalition, www.soawr.org.

Special Issue on "Gendered Colonialism and African History," *Gender and History*, 8, no. 3 (1996).

Special Issue on "Indigenous Women and Colonial Cultures," *Journal of Colonialism and Colonial History*, 6, no. 3 (2005).

Special Issue on "Revising the Experiences of Colonized Women: Beyond Binaries," *Journal of Women's History*, 14, no. 4 (2003).

Steady. *Women and Collective Action in Africa*, 56.

Steger, B. Manfred. *Globalization: A Very Short Introduction*. Oxford: Oxford University Press, 2009.

Strobel, M. *European Women and the Second British Empire*. Bloomington Indiana University Press, 1991.

Stross, E. Randall. *Technology and Society in Twentieth Century America: An Anthology*. Richard D. Irwin, Inc., 1989.

Teboh, Bridget "Reproducing African Communities in the US: Settlement Patterns, Reproduction and Social Organizations." In Emmanuel Yewah and Dimeji Togunde (eds.). *Across the Atlantic: African Immigrants in the United States Diaspora*. Champaign, IL: University of Illinois Press, Nov. 2010.

Teboh, Bridget, "Science, Technology and the African Woman during (British) Colonization: 1916–1960: the Case of Bamenda Province." In Toyin Falola and Emily Brownell (eds.) *Landscape and Environment in Colonial and Post Colonial in Africa*. London and New York: Routledge, August 2011.

Teboh, Bridget. "African Women's Survival 101: Tontines, *Njanggis*, Money-Go-Rounds as Alternatives to Failed 'Capitalist' Economies," at the SASE Conference on *Capitalism in Crisis: What Next? Economic Regulation and Social Solidarity after the Fall of Finance Capitalism*, Paris, France, July 16–18, 2009.

Teboh, Bridget. "Historicizing 'The Moghamo-Bali *ibit* /Conflict: German Encounters with 'Rebellious Vassals.'" In Toyin Falola and Raphael Chijioke Njoku, (eds.). *Wars and Peace in Africa: History, Nationalism and the State*. Durham, NC: Carolina Academic Press, Jan. 2010.

Teboh, Bridget. "*Money-Go-Rounds*: Navigating a Hostile Gendered Economic Environment in the Grassfields [Cameroon]. "Gendering African History: In Honor of E.A. Alpers and Christopher Ehret" paper presented at African Studies Association (ASA)'s 50th Annual Meeting, on *21st Century Africa: Evolving Conceptions of Human Rights* at The Sheraton Hotel and Towers, New York, NY, October 18–21, 2007.

Teboh, Bridget. "Reproducing African Communities in the US: Settlement Patterns and Social Organizations." In Emmanuel Yewah and Dimeji Togunde, (eds.). *Across the Atlantic: African Immigrants in the United States Diaspora*. Champaign, Illinois: The University Press/Common Ground, 2010.

Teboh, Bridget. "Science, Technology and the African Woman during (British) Colonization: 1916–1960: the Case of Bamenda Province." In Falola, Toyin and Brownell, Emily, (eds.). *Landscape and Environment in Colonial and Post Colonial in Africa*. London and New York: Routledge, August 2011.

Teboh, Bridget. "Women and the *Njanggi* Phenomenon in Cameroon," Unpublished Paper.

Teboh, Bridget. "Women and the *Njangg*i Phenomenon in Cameroon." Paper presented at the (AAA), African Activist Association, 3rd Annual Young Scholars Conference at UCLA, April 7–8, 1995.

Tripp, A. "A New Look at Colonial Women British Teachers and Activists in Uganda, 1898–1962." *Canadian Journal of African Studies* 38, no. 1, (2004).

Tripp, M. Aili and Kang, Alice. "The Global impact of Quotas: On the Fast Track to Increased Female Legislative Representation." *Comparative Political Studies* 41, 3 (2008), 338–61.

Tripp, M. Aili; Casimiro, Isabel; Kwesiga, Joy; and Mungwa, Alice. *African Women's Movements: Changing Political Landscapes*. Cambridge and New York: Cambridge University Press, 2009.

UN Millennium Declaration and Millennium Development Goals (MDGs), New York, 2000.

UNDP, *Human Development Report, 1995, 1996*, NY: OUP, 1995, 1996.

UNICEF, *The progress of Nations 1996*, NU: UNICEF, 1996.

UNIFEM, Progress of the World's Women 2002 Report.

United Nations, UN Treaties Office, December 1996.

United Nations. *The Beijing Declaration and the Platform for Action*. New York: UN Department of Public Information. 1996.

United Nations. The UN and the Advancement of Women, 1945–1995, NY: UN, 1995.

Walker, *Women and Gender*, 1990.

Yewah, E. And Togunde, D. "Towards a Fresh Perspective in Understanding African Migration to the United States Diaspora." In Yewah, Emmanuel and Togunde, Dimeji (eds.) *Across the Atlantic: African Immigrants in the United States Diaspora.* Champaign, Illinois: The University Press/Common Ground, 2010.

Young, Crawford. *The African Colonial State in Comparative Perspective.* New Haven: Yale University Press, 1994.

Chapter 7

Impacts of Globalization on Health, Food Security, and Biomedicine in Africa

Karen Flint & Bridget A. Teboh

Introduction

Globalization, a process usually associated with the movement of peoples, goods, and ideas, also contributed to the spread of pests, microbes, and disease. While trade was the main engine of communicable disease, globalization also created long term changes in local disease environments which allowed parasites and bacteria to thrive on new hosts and in different lands. As global trade intensified, particularly during the age of capitalism, and in the post-colonial period, so too did its impact on African health. Thus early global trade routes exposed Africans to Afro-Eurasian diseases, while the Columbian Exchange and colonialism spread new diseases and epizootics throughout the continent and intensified the impact of older ones. Likewise, human manipulation of the environment through settlement, colonialism, and post-colonial development projects such as the building of dams, or irrigation projects created conditions for certain pests or diseases to thrive where they had previously been limited or non-existent.[1] More recent migration patterns in and out of Africa, but particularly those involving migrant labor have assisted with the spread of the AIDS pandemic.

Globalization not only led to the spread of infectious diseases and changes in the disease environment, it also greatly increased disparities of wealth and health around the world and within national borders. National wealth, as can be seen in the petrol rich nations of Angola, Chad, Cameroon, or Nigeria, or in a country like South Africa, does not necessarily translate into national health or prosperity. Poverty, however, is often an indicator of health; and Africans have on average gotten poorer. As recently as 2007, over 40 percent of sub-Saharan Africans survived on less than $1 a day and could not meet minimal daily food requirements.[2] Poverty and the failure to distribute resources globally and locally have meant that many Africans do not have access to reliable medical personnel, vaccines, or medicines. Furthermore the lack of public health measures to ensure safe food and drinking water, and prevention of epidemics, has meant higher mortality rates on the continent. Individual poverty often means living in crowded conditions which leads to a greater susceptibility to diseases like tuberculosis (TB), an inability to afford medicines even when they are available, and a focus on short term gains such as access to food or money at the expense of long term health. Finally, endemic hunger is a major contributing factor to disease as malnutrition weakens the body's immune system, making it more difficult to fight off parasites, microbes, and viruses. Indeed as many African countries have become increasingly dependent upon imported food stocks, their populations have become more vulnerable to local ecological disasters and fluctuations in global food prices resulting in food shortages and the diseases that accompany malnutrition. According to Kofi Annan,

> AFRICA is the only continent unable to feed itself. Agricultural productivity has failed to keep pace with a growing population. Hunger has never been worse. Around 300 million people will not have enough to eat today. Despite millions of hectares of unused cultivated land, Africa spends $20bn each year buying food. This is simply not sustainable, economically nor politically. It is the cause of terrible human suffering and is a catastrophic brake on Africa's development.[3]

Theoretically global transportation networks and flows of money should allow for the quick movement of medicines and food stores from one region to another, and in times of well publicized crises this does happen. But such help, often too little too late, does not address the historical causes that enable these crises and pandemics to occur and reoccur, or the issue of hunger found throughout much of the continent. This chapter argues that the political and economic repercussions of globalization have had important and long-lasting implications on the health and well being of Africans. This chapter seeks to understand how and why Africa has borne the brunt of such global disparities in health and how Africans have responded to these health crises. We argue that many of Africa's contemporary health dilemmas can be traced to a combination of local and global factors, including: 1) Africa's participation in global trading patterns; 2) colonial measures and an infrastructure that focused on maximum short-term production of raw materials for export; 3) the intervention of international financial institutions like the International Monetary Fund, Word Bank, or World Trade Organization that often restructured African economies, food production, and restricted governments' prioritizing and spending on healthcare; 4) the ineptitude or corruption of various postcolonial African governments who either ignored public health needs or used food or health resources as a form of political punishment or patronage; and 5) Africans' skepticism and in some cases resistance or non-compliance with biomedical interventions. While these factors are complex and vary from nation state to nation state, there are similarities in the ways in which global forces have impacted African health and likewise, how Africans have responded to certain health crises.

This chapter begins by examining the ways in which globalization, from the pre-colonial through the postcolonial period, impacted African health and the spread of communicable diseases. We then turn our attention to the issue of food insecurity and seek to understand why Africa can no longer feed itself. We ask whether foreign food aid and current discussions of a Green Revolution for Africa has, or can help Africa to obtain food security as it did in Cameroon in the 1970s and early 1980s. We conclude by examining the HIV/AIDS pandemic as a current disease of globalization. While the global reach of biomedicine has provided lifesaving medicines, African responses to this pandemic also show a public alienated by biomedical explanations and curatives.

Health and the Spread of Tropical and Communicable Diseases

Africa's participation in early global trade routes is perhaps most important for its role in effectively exposing Africans to communicable diseases found in Europe, the Middle East and India. This exposure helped confer future generations with a degree of biological immunity against potential epidemics, thus enabling Africa to largely avoid the virgin soil epidemics that so devastated peoples in the Americas and Oceania. Given that "globalization" in the early period was largely restricted to regional trade and to times dictated by yearly weather patterns; the spread of infectious diseases and changes in the disease environment happened relatively slowly. Consequently, disease organisms that killed their hosts too quickly were unlikely to survive the long voyages across the Sahara Desert or Indian Ocean. Thus while much of sub-Saharan and East Africa escaped bubonic plague, the first global epidemic in the 1300s, smallpox whose incubation and contagion period lasted much longer occurred throughout much of the continent.[4] While the African environment has hosted and spawned new and dangerous microorganisms, many of which led early European explorers and traders to dub West Africa "the white man's grave," it also exhibits great ecological diversity and various disease environments. Consequently, Africans learned to control or at least limit certain environmental hazards through settlement patterns, management of domestic animals, and ecological interventions. While these measures developed locally over time through careful observation, others such as variolation, a medical technique used to inoculate individuals against smallpox, emerged as a result of Africa's participation in trade routes across the Sahara Desert and Indian Ocean.[5]

Direct European contact with sub-Saharan Africa, first through the trans-Atlantic slave trade and later the imposition of European colonialism, greatly intensified the degree of interaction between the continents. Similar climatic environments in parts of Asia, Africa, and the Americas as well as new movements of peoples and goods enabled the spread and proliferation of microbes, parasites, and pests. Europeans introduced contagious diseases such as measles, whooping cough, and small pox from Europe; jigger fleas and syphilis from the Americans; and cholera, leprosy, and hookworm from the Indian subcontinent.[6] The Trans-Atlantic slave trade itself greatly deteriorated the health and wellbeing of Africans who lived and traveled along its slave trading routes. Not only were some of Africa's healthiest men and women of childbearing age taken from the continent, but demands for slaves increased warfare, famine, and disrupted social and economic security. As a result, historian Patrick Manning estimates that Africa's population declined from 30 percent to 10 percent of the total world population between the years 1600 to 1900.[7]

As destructive as the slave trade had been on Africa, historians Hartwig and Patterson argue that the greatest impact and deterioration of African health occurred with the imposition of colonialism between 1880 and 1920.[8] Pressure for windfall profits led colonists to place great demand on the land and peoples of Africa. Consequently, Europeans not only introduced new epidemics and epizootics, they helped spread new and old diseases, and create the conditions for malnutrition and disease. As Europeans destroyed pre-colonial states; cleared forestland and villages for plantations; built roads and railway tracks; imposed cash crops, forced labor, migration, taxation, colonial legislation, and urban planning; they destroyed local forms of public health and ecological controls.[9] The Gaza of Mozambique, for instance, had used ecological controls to minimize the threat of the tsetse fly that caused sleeping sickness by creating buffer zones between residential and farming areas and uncultivated areas that contained game. When the Portuguese destroyed these controls with the forced evacuation of Gazaland in 1889, sleeping sickness broke out in epic proportions.[10] Nor is it not coincidental that the use of 50,000 "volunteers" which provided 236,388 days of work along the route du Tchad in 1912 coincided with frequent famines in the area that could be directly correlated to the local population's inability to mobilize labor for their own food production.[11] Likewise, the mixing of people on plantations, mines, factories, and in the urban areas not only increased Africans' exposure to new diseases and the likelihood of epidemics in population dense areas; it affected the health of communities away from these centers. As migrant workers returned to their homes at the end of employment contracts or when employers sent ill workers home, they often spread contagious diseases like hookworm, tuberculosis, sexually transmitted diseases, or pneumonia to rural areas unable to cope with such outbreaks.[12]

Colonialism also contributed to declining rates of nutrition as Africans lost control and access to their own land and labor. Cash crops, like cotton or sisal, replaced fields of edible crops and Africans made to grow these crops or work on plantations derived little income from their labor, as money disappeared to pay for taxes or the inflated price of goods and food.[13] Decreases in land and labor led to changes in agricultural practices as many Africans moved away from labor intensive but nutritious millet and sorghum, towards labor saving but less nutritious corn and cassava.[14] Farmers seeking to maximize cash-crop production abandoned farming practices that had maintained soil fertility, depleting the land and decreasing agricultural output.[15] Furthermore, game, which had been depended upon for protein and particularly during times of famine, rapidly diminished during the early years of colonialism, a result of overhunting for sport and trade. Likewise as Africans moved to urban areas in the twentieth century, nutritional levels fell even more as many people removed from subsistence agriculture added refined white bread and soda to their diets. This nutrition deficit like hunger greatly increased African vulnerability to both communicable disease and the impact of parasites.

In the post-colonial period, new independent African states faced a variety of challenges that directly impacted African health and food security. While a virulent disease environment and ecological events such as drought or locust invasions were beyond human control, the ability to meet many of these challenges can be directly tied to Africa's colonial legacy while others are related to decisions made by African governments. Africa had inherited colonial economies that were short term and externally focused, lacked adequate healthcare infrastructure, were dependent upon infertile land, and faced growing populations who needed and expected access to education and healthcare.[16] While colonial powers had diversified economies of scale, many post-colonial African states were based on single-export economies that made them particularly vulnerable to the whims of the global economy. Furthermore, colonialism had not only disrupted regional trade networks and consumption patterns, but introduced new and alluring commodities from abroad. All of these factors contributed to Africa's economic decline, making African governments particularly susceptible to outside intervention from international financial institutions (IFIs) such as the IMF and World Bank—the purveyors of economic globalization.

Guided by neoliberal policies, IFIs of the 1970s and 1980s insisted that indebted African governments radically alter their economies through Structural Adjustment Programs (SAPS) in exchange for further loans.[17] While the economic and political impact of these programs has already been described in detail in other chapters in this volume, these changes also had profound impacts on African health. Working from the premise that ill health was a consequence of poverty, IFIs ignored the ways in which improvements to sanitation and health programs can also generate national wealth. For instance, access to safe/clean water and control over debilitating diseases like malaria can greatly increase national productivity, and also attract foreign investment and tourists.[18] Instead, SAPs sought to restructure African economies with little regard to safeguarding food supplies, or protecting public health or the public's access to medicines or medical practitioners. The results were disastrous on a variety of different levels, leading institutions like UNICEF to declare in 1990 that SAPS could be linked to rising infant mortality rates. Even in countries like Ghana which showed improvements in mortality and immunization compliance rates, such changes were limited and uneven, largely benefitting urban residents at the expense of rural ones.[19]

To the detriment of African health, SAPs forced countries to reprioritize their spending, and privatize various aspects of their economies. This included healthcare and even water. Thus Mozambique, which ranked fourth in the world for the highest infant mortality rate in 2001, was forced to increase user fees five-fold as a condition for partial debt forgiveness as determined under HIPC.[20] Reduced government spending on healthcare has meant fewer doctors and nurses, less essential medicines and vaccines, and a healthcare system that cannot adequately meet the populations' needs. One consequence is that African women have some of the highest death rates in pregnancy and childbirth. In Tanzania, pregnant women are expected to bring their own "delivery kit" to the clinic, and the shortage of personnel and drugs means that caesarean sections are performed with ether and by assistant medical officers rather than surgeons.[21] Such working conditions lead qualified doctors and nurses, many of whom are educated in Africa, to leave for Europe or the United States where they earn higher wages within a better work environment. The result is an appalling doctor-patient ratio with places like Malawi and Mozambique maintaining only three physicians per 100,000 people.[22] Perhaps more alarming is the privatization of water which unsurprisingly has resulted in higher water prices. In 2000, IMF loan stipulations forced eight African countries to either privatize water or impose full cost recovery. Given that so few Africans can afford to pay the full costs of water, privatization in effect has made safe water less accessible; forcing those who cannot afford privatized water to secure water from even less safe sources. This is particularly concerning given that water contamination is one of the leading causes of disease in sub-Saharan Africa, often carrying threats of typhoid, cholera, dysentery, gastro-enteritis, polio, hepatitis, and various parasitic pests.[23]

Food (In)Security in the Post-Colonial Period

One irony of modern globalization is that it is cheaper to import a ton of grain from Chicago, Illinois to Mombasa, Kenya than from Kampala the capital city of Uganda, Kenya's adjacent neighbor.[24] The same can be said for importing grain from Houston, Texas to Bamenda, Cameroon, than from its neighbor to the west, Nigeria. This is due in part to a transportation infrastructure built during the colonial period that privileged and continues to privilege exports out of Africa rather than internal or regional trade. The colonial period radically disrupted African forms of farming as demands for cash crops meant that land used for food production was turned over for "commercial" purposes. In many African countries this resulted in small peasant farmers, who abandoned traditional farming methods and crops for intensive farming of a few commercial crops and an increased reliance on external inputs such as pesticides and fertilizers. Within the former settler states, Africans found themselves dispossessed of the most productive land by white farmers who implemented large-scale farming. Yet, to understand the way in which globalization has contributed, exacerbated, and remedied African food shortages, as well as some of the solutions being put forward, we will examine challenges in the post-colonial period. This includes the exploitation of African farmers by domestic market boards, competition from imports, and the imposition of economic liberalization that thrust African farmers into a "free" and largely unfriendly global market place.

In the postcolonial period, new supports were put into place to help African farmers. African governments and Western donor agencies sought to support and "modernize" rural producers, in part because rural agricultural producers had played important roles in national independence movements and to prevent future famines as had been experienced seasonally and dramatically in the colonial and early postcolonial period. Furthermore, African governments often depended upon agricultural export production as a basis for their national economies. Government subsidies on fertilizer and seeds, combined with staple food improvement packages and guaranteed fixed prices by government marketing boards, encouraged African farming.[25] Marketing boards guaranteed quality control of African products and mediated the impact of the global market, not only guaranteeing crop prices but also building up food reserves for emergencies. Countries such as Sudan sought food and economic security by moving away from the production of cotton—a colonial cash crop. Instead they diversified their crops to include sorghum and wheat, supplying internal and regional markets rather than just increasing export production.[26] In Cameroon, as will be discussed shortly, food self-sufficiency evolved within a development-oriented framework of what former President Ahmadou Ahidjo officially labeled "Sahel Vert" and the "Revolution Verte."[27] Despite numerous challenges, African economies initially did well and agricultural yields increased. By the mid-1970s and 1980s, however, Africa's ability to feed itself was compromised as export earnings fell dramatically and Africans became gradually more dependent upon imported foods. Likewise, African countries particularly along the Sahel suffered massive food shortages as a result of drought and conflicts. By 1984 some 140 million Africans out of 531 million were living off of imported grain.[28] The issue of endemic hunger, however, only increased as Africans fell further into poverty—making it increasingly difficult to afford basic dietary staples.[29] Between 1990 and 2006, the numbers of people going hungry increased from 169 million to 206 million.[30]

The oil crises of the 1970s brought new challenges as commercial rural agricultural production deteriorated and Africans increasingly moved to the cities. While African farmers had considerably cheaper inputs in terms of labor and government subsidized seed and fertilizer, poor internal transportation networks and the long distances needed to move produce to both international and domestic markets disadvantaged them. Increased oil prices meant African exports became less competitive on the global market, and African countries found it cheaper to import international grain to its urban centers.[31] Declining export revenue coupled with increases in import expenditures, led many African states to fall further into debt. To make up for lost revenues market boards squeezed African farmers even more. In The Gambia, whose main export was peanuts, market boards set the price of this crop below what the government received for them on the global market. In 1967, a bumper crop year, farmers got 46 percent of the market price. For the next 15 years the government, who needed monies for food subsidies and amenities that favored city dwellers, consistently reduced the percentage that farmers received. This had the impact of increasing the amount of rice that was imported each year, and discouraging peanut farmers who left agriculture for more lucrative and non-agricultural fields.[32] As in many other areas of Africa, Gambians moved to the cities, where they too came to depend upon imported food. African farmers, however, stopped growing food for a number of reasons; some of them were internally generated such as we see with the market boards, while others can be tied more directly to the power and influence of global institutions.

African debt gave tremendous leverage to IFI's who used it to remake African agricultural markets that generally favored northern farmers and industries while increasing food insecurity on the continent. Loans were predicated on the principle of "comparative advantage," thus encouraging a return to colonial cash crop production rather than self-sufficiency in food. When Sudan, which suffered political instability, civil war, and declining export earnings, turned to the World Bank they were advised likewise.[33] The 1978 World Bank "stabilization plan" for Sudan included devaluations, removing government subsidies on food, a moratorium on new development projects, and a return to exporting cotton.[34]

Sudan was thus encouraged to move away from food self-sufficiency even though they had already experienced the volatility of the cotton market shortly after independence. In fact they were one of the few Sahelian countries that had escaped major famine during the droughts of the 1960s and 70s, because of their focus on food production.[35] Generally export-led growth strategies favored by IFIs did not have favorable results but instead led African producers to flood markets with their goods. African exports proved twice as volatile as East Asian commodities and four-times that of rich industrial countries.[36] In the case of Sudan, however, it led the country to become vulnerable to the drought-induced-famine of the 1980s.[37] Despite decades of failure, IFIs continued to promote neoliberal remedies for ailing and indebted African economies. Governments reduced or eliminated subsidies for fertilizers and seeds, dismantled market boards, and were discouraged from keeping food reserves. The IFIs required the same remedy for Malawi, and insisted in 2001 that they sell their reserve grain stocks to pay their foreign debt. A year later, Malawi suffered drought and flooding and a devastating famine, leading them to import grain from South Africa.[38]

This dismantling of agricultural supports was coupled with demands for African countries to open their markets to international and regional trade. Domestic as well as international agricultural aid decreased, as can be seen by the 98% drop in U.S. agricultural aid between 1980 and 2003.[39] While IFIs insisted that Africa liberalize its markets, American and Europe countries could afford to ignore their advice. Consequently, the North continued to subsidize its own farmers and erected protective tariffs and non-tariff barriers that restricted African agricultural exports. Despite the formation of the World Trade Organization, and a steady rhetoric of free market ideology, the developed world continued to spend $350 billion a year on agricultural trade subsidies in the early 2000s.[40] As of 2006, the US government was spending $17 billion a year on commodity subsidies.[41] This included subsides for peanuts and tariffs that prevented the selling of Gambian peanuts in the U.S. the largest peanut consuming market. In effect this deflated the price of Gambian peanuts on the world market; consequently they were crushed for oil and sold in Europe where they competed with locally produced, protected, and subsidized olive oil.[42] While northern producers flooded world markets with subsidized and protected industrial agricultural goods—corn, wheat, or cotton—African farmers found themselves paying full market price for seeds and agricultural inputs.

The Case of Cameroon: From Green Revolution to Food Crisis

Launched in the mid-1970s, by former President Ahmadou Ahidjo, the Sahel Vert project aimed at fighting gradual desertification in northern Cameroon by planting trees. Since its inception at the Buea agro-pastoral show of March 1973, the Green Revolution aimed at the mass production of high consumption commodities such as rice, wheat, bananas, tomatoes, vegetables, and corn. Even though rice production was dismal prior to 1971, the state had identified various sites for extensive cultivation and major corporations became involved.[43] Their primary goals were to increase the market share of Cameroonian rice, enhance agricultural revenues in the isolated regions, provide jobs, supply the local consumption market with adequate food, and bring large scale imports under control.[44] Blessed with natural resources, especially oil, Cameroon could afford to indigenize its agricultural technology sector as well as embark on a socio-economic development plan. From a historical perspective Cameroon provides an interesting case study that is typical of other African countries' agricultural successes and failures, as well as current rethinking and renegotiation of issues around food security.

Ahidjo's socio-economic development was based on two primary ideologies: planned liberalism and self-reliant development. Under the former, the state regulated and managed natural resources and oriented foreign investment to-

wards the common interest. The state also partnered with foreign entities setting up various parastatals to provide jobs. Planned liberalism encouraged private enterprise and investment and the rational exploitation of production factors and market forces.[45] *Food self-sufficiency, reached by Cameroon in the 1970s, rested on the country's ability to grow adequate food for the consumers or to have stabilized its trade balance. A long–awaited dream for many developing countries, easy access to food became a reality in the daily life of the population. Self Reliant Development launched in 1975 as "an integrated national development through effective control of the main factors of production by the government and the people."*[46] *Interestingly, self-reliant development subordinated "Cameroon's international economic relations to the objectives of domestic development, depending principally on local efforts and labor."*[47] *Self-reliance favored a production policy more sensitive to local consumption, a greater mobilization of financial and monetary policy toward savings and investment, and an enhanced labor and income policy in the labor market.*

Required and necessary training of rural consultants, agricultural technicians and engineers was carried out through various academic and professional institutions that emerged nationwide under state support.[48] *C. Dongmo has argued that another important aspect of the Green Revolution was the institutionalization of agro-pastoral shows in the country's socio-economic and political agenda. Jointly organized by the Ministries of agriculture and livestock, fisheries and animal industries, Buea hosted the inaugural agro-pastoral show on March 1973.*[49] *Subsequent shows took place at Ngaoundéré (1976), Bafoussam (1977), Bertoua (5-8 February 1981), Bamenda (1984), Maroua (1987), and Ebolowa (2010).*

Using the traditional Five-Year Development Plan, self-reliant development and planned liberalism were successfully implemented and enforced by various state organs. The Green Revolution reflected in part the deep concern that Cameroon's decision makers wanted to accommodate the demands of large, medium and small size farmers in search for self-determination and the right to sustainable development. Thus, the Green Revolution led to the establishment of many agricultural parastatal institutions.[50]

Cameroon's apparent sudden rise to agricultural prominence was primarily the result of the activities of the National Produce Marketing Board (NPMB). Created on September 9, 1972, it was not until 1978 that this agency was formally organized through a presidential decree. The NPMB collaborated with various agricultural cooperatives and large plantations nationwide as the principal buyer and exporter of consumption and non-consumption commodities: coffee, cocoa, cotton, palm oil, sugar, banana, maize, sugar, rubber, and peanuts among others. The sale of highly demanded crops brought in substantial returns to the national economy. This air of success is clearly captured in the words of DeLancey who stated that there is no doubt that by 1984 the NPMB "enjoyed economic prosperity and maximized benefits under its ostentatious price policy that substantially raised the income of the local consumers in net value."[51] *Consequently, this allowed farmers to "enjoy the fruits of their labor, send their children and relatives to schools of their choice, develop both a horizontal and vertical support base within the family, take care of siblings, invest in small and medium size enterprises, acquire more lands, build homes, and most importantly, live an honest and prosperous life."*[52]

During Cameroon's Green Revolution, claims pertaining to Food Self Sufficiency became a leitmotiv of Ahmadou Ahidjo's political discourses.[53] *Being already able to feed its own population without any external conditionalities and fear, Cameroon evolved as the main food provider of Central Africa by exporting commodities to neighboring countries: Gabon, Equatorial Guinea, Congo, Nigeria, Chad and the Central African Republic. In Santa and Kongmbuh (Bamenda grassfields region), market women recounted how many trucks came from neighboring countries to the markets and farms to purchase cabbage, vegetables, tomatoes, and plantains. Those were indeed happy times!*

When the Cameroon Green Revolution was launched in 1972, the government encouraged mono-cropping and the use of chemical inputs, subsidizing up to 65 percent and 100 percent of the cost of fertilizer and pesticides, respectively. With government subsidies and credit, many farmers shifted toward producing export crops and became heavily dependent on external inputs. By the late 1980s, many African nations began to experience falling prices for their export crops and other commodities and economic and political crises emerged. In 1986, a serious economic crisis struck Cameroon as a result of changes in the world commodity market and the oil crises. The value of export products such as oil, cacao and coffee fell drastically and remained low. The consequences were felt throughout the countryside. Subsidies were completely removed and most agricultural development projects collapsed. Poverty increased in the rural areas and thousands of people had to receive food aid. The foreign food aid programs damaged local food production. Foreign rice, for example, was sold at a cost lower than the cost of producing it in Cameroon, forcing some farmers to abandon farming and making communities increasingly dependent on imported food. With the termination of subsidies and the subsequent devaluation of the Franc CFA, peasant farmers could no longer afford the agricultural inputs upon which they had based their agriculture. In many areas where heavy use of external inputs was common, soils were los-

ing their fertility and yields decreased. As such Cameroon went from great success in the 1970s to a failure triggered by broken promises in the late 1980s.[54]

Initially in the case of Cameroon, government was confident in the wake of the oil crises of the mid 1980s, and promised to fight global recession by all means. President Paul Biya every now and then borrowed from the traditional reference to "auto-suffisance alimentaire" or food self-sufficiency in his initial speeches. However, he soon resorted to blanket statements with global impact such as, "Le Cameroun se porte bien/Cameroon is doing well" and "Le Cameroun n'ira pas au Fonds Monétaire International/Cameroon will not go to IMF (for financial aid)." Such rhetoric was easily accepted by political accomplices of the ruling party, CPDM, who were quick to applaud. However, the applause was short-lived as things went rapidly from bad to worse leaving a lot of hungry and angry people in the country asking: "what happened to all our oil money?" A series of interlocking and unfavorable market hazards finally forced Paul Biya to implement the policy of "budget constraints" from the top down. In 1987, however, he openly declared that the economy was in dire economic crisis and instructed a series of IMF/WB measures aimed at reducing state spending: repossession and sale of administrative cars, curtailment of employment benefits, and the rationing of administrative consumption on energy, telephones, and office supplies.

Like most state-run corporations, the global economic recession of the late 1980s hit agricultural and rural development agencies hard. One parastatal, FONADER, was reorganized in 1987 under the Credit Foncier du Cameroun, geared particularly towards the financing and acquisition of land, community, and private housing. In 1990, the Cameroon Agricultural Bank opened and took over most of FONADER's listed missions.[55] *Being unable to stabilize prices and subsidies provided by international donors and meet its running budget, the NPMB closed down in 1991. Bankruptcy also hit the financial sector.*[56] *Besides the disastrous global economic factors, and the 50-percent devaluation of the CFA currency in early 1994 by the French Central Bank, state-run corporations and other agricultural projects suffered from mismanagement, diversion of public funds, and state-sponsored corruption, including nonguaranteed excessive borrowing. The government established Cameroon's Debt Collection Agency on August 19, 1989 and extended its mandate with another Decree on January 23, 1991 in an attempt to recover the huge amount of money lost to mismanagement.*[57]

The prevailing land tenure system is another factor which, coupled with an increase in population, was a constraint to food production because it placed women and poor farmers at a disadvantage. Women were the main producers of food crops but according to traditional custom, they could not own land.

Moreover, the average farm size was less than one hectare for many families. The small size of these landholdings made it difficult to feed the family throughout the year. With decreasing land availability, in areas where traditional shifting agriculture was still practiced, fallow periods were reduced or were non-existent. Thus, soil fertility in the cleared land could not recover to optimal levels and slash-and-burn farming systems were becoming unsustainable. In some areas of Cameroon, this process contributed to deforestation.

Thus faced with a food security crisis, the government started in 1990 to encourage research and extension on food crops such as maize, beans, potatoes, soybean, and tubers. It also emphasized increasing livestock production and the consumption of animal protein while encouraging the production of non-traditional agricultural exports such as green beans, flowers, tropical fruit, banana, and cassava chips to neighboring African countries as well as to European nations. To increase the adoption of innovations, a new extension system was set up to bring extension workers in closer contact with farmers. Some farmers have benefited from this new approach but the great majority have remained untouched. A lack of funds has also limited the effectiveness of the new extension system. Today in Cameroon there are about 73 NGOs distributed throughout the 10 provinces of Cameroon. Most of them are less than 10 years old and local, while a few cover the whole country. Twenty of these NGOs focus their efforts on sustainable agriculture.

While the forces of colonialism, post-colonial domestic priorities, and neoliberal policies of global financial institutions shaped Africa's agriculture, food security depends less on where food is produced than access to that food. In effect, markets respond to demand not needs. Those wishing to sell do so to those who can afford to buy. Why would Africans sell green beans domestically when they could get a higher price from French brokers? This has resulted in the perverse irony that food crises do not always mean that food is not produced locally, just that most people can't afford it. During the Ethiopian famine of the 1980s, Ethiopia continued to export green beans to Europe. This is the result of a free market that seeks to maximize profits, and poor indebted African farmers who bare that burden. Such farmers pay higher market prices for seed and food during periods of scarcity while selling their crops shortly after harvest in order to repay debts, pay taxes, or pay for other necessities such as health or education. No longer protected by subsidies or market boards, farmers are forced to buy high and sell low thereby increasing their debt burden. Wholesale buyers, however, buy low and wait for commodity prices to increase before releasing their produce to market. Consequently the price of cereals in places like Niger, which suffered an epidemic of starvation in 2005, were 90 to 130 percent higher between 2000 and 2004 than a decade earlier.[58] In the 2005

Malian food crisis, Pablo Recaulde, head of the UN World Food Program in Mali, commented that the crisis stemmed not only from drought and locusts: "I could buy food in-country and distribute it immediately but I need the resources to do that."[59] Until 2007, U.S. law mandated that emergency food aid be produced and transported by US companies. This meant longer wait times for those in need, and that aid dollars went for the costs of transportation rather than food. Against strong agricultural and transportation lobbying interests, the US Congress adopted a five year trial to allow 25 percent of emergency aid to be purchased from local producers.[60] While this helps mitigate acute crises, the underlying causes of endemic hunger and famine remain.

The political implications of food insecurity became apparent when a spike in world oil prices and rice shortages in 2008 not only increased food prices but also led to food riots around the world including some West African cities. Africa's declining food security is of great concern not only to African governments, but also to economically powerful nations who recognize that food insecurity can have grave implications for world stability. Unfortunately, there are those who recognize market opportunities in a crisis. In the name of food security, the Rockefeller and Gates foundations have partnered with multinationals Monsantos and Cynergy to propose a "Green Revolution" for Africa that promotes selling genetically modified seeds and products to African farmers. Such seeds cannot be replanted due to a "terminator gene," and others would depend on commercial inputs to allow the plants to fully germinate.[61] Likewise recent African "land grabs," where African countries provide long-term leases of valuable agricultural land, have been loosely glossed in the name of development. In such cases, cash strapped African nations sell land to wealthy individuals or nations with the aim of moving away from small scale peasant production towards large scale industrial agriculture. One wonders what ecological or human impact such market solutions would bring, particularly if Africans cannot afford to purchase what is produced. Given the volatility in the grain markets, and increased world population, it is more likely that Africans are not the intended recipients of such food, but their land will be used to provide food security for other nations.

After years on the losing end of globalization, many African countries and communities have sought to reassess how they could produce local food for local markets. In Malawi, a new president decided that rather than following what the West preached—free markets—he would follow western practices and subsidize his farmers. Assistance was given in the form of subsidized fertilizer and seed. Combined with a good rainy season, Malawi enjoyed a bumper corn harvest in 2006-2007, which decreased local food prices and enabled them to export maize to their neighbors.[62] This practice has continued with mixed reviews, unfortunately rising oil costs in 2008, led to higher fertilizer prices, making Malawi more vulnerable to pressures of land grabs. Local African communities as well as The International Assessment of Agricultural Knowledge, Science, and Technology for Development (IAASTD), an organization of 900 scientists funded by the World Bank and United Nations, have advocated "agroecology" to tackle issues of food security. Such farming techniques are organic and rely on and resurrect the use of traditional seeds and local farming methods that have been adapted over thousands of years. Consequently, indigenous crops tend to be more drought and pest resistant. By using intercropping techniques that complement each plant, and using food crops as mulch, farmers are able to grow more robust harvests with greater yields. The upside of such farming techniques is that it is free, less labor intensive, better for producer and consumer health, and it provides long term sustainability. The downside for African nations, however, is that current initiatives are aimed at small producers and for local consumption. Thus while it may help African farmers to lessen their debt and provide more food security, it is unlikely to contribute to GDP in the same way that commercial industrialized agriculture could.[63] Fortunately globalization has empowered local communities by creating networks of knowledge and activists to pursue what the international grass roots organization Via Campesina calls *food sovereignty*. This includes the notion that local producers have the right not only to food security, but to determine their own food systems rather than being subject to the market.

African Perspectives of Globalization through the HIV/AIDS Pandemic

Many people have compared the impact of HIV/AIDS in South Africa to Black Death, an earlier disease also facilitated by the process of globalization. The death rate has been incredibly high, and it has impacted all segments of society from the most impoverished to white collar workers. Its spread, however, has been slower and more insidious. One cannot tell by looking at someone whether they carry the virus. Furthermore HIV/AIDS is a biologically complex disease that mutates making it nearly impossible to develop a vaccine, and the strain prevalent in sub-Saharan Africa is more virulent and deadly than others. While treatment costs have recently come down, treatment is still expensive and requires a daily regimen often accompanied by unpleasant side effects, as well as the need to change medicines as old ones become ineffective. The fear and frustration engendered by this disease recently led a Swazi parliamentarian to suggest branding the buttocks of HIV/AIDS carriers as a means of thwarting the disease. A suggestion he quickly rescinded.[64]

As a disease of globalization, HIV/AIDS has often followed the tracks of long distance truckers throughout parts of Africa and evaded communities too poor to be visited or too impoverished to travel. Clearly, unprotected heterosexual sex mixed with the movement of people has been a major contributor to the spread of disease in Africa. Perhaps it is not surprising that given South Africa's history and its role as an economic powerhouse in the region, that Southern Africa would claim some of the world's highest HIV/AIDS rates.

Globalization has also impacted the ways in which Africans have responded to the disease. Shortly after winning the 2004 Noble Peace Prize, Wangari Maathai, the Kenyan environmentalist, shocked much of the Western world by suggesting that the West had crafted HIV as a biological weapon to be released on Africa. Such beliefs, however, are largely accepted in many parts of Africa where the acronym AIDS has been dubbed the "American Invention to Discourage Sex" and the French acronym SIDA is translated equally cynically as the "Imaginary Syndrome for Discouraging Lovers." In Cameroon for instance, on the radio and on TV one heard daily as late as the 1990s the following statement, "Le SIDA est un Syndrome Inventé pour Decourager les Amoureux." Many African countries initially denied HIV/AIDS rates for fear of its impact on tourism and foreign investment yet popular memories of moralizing missionaries and colonists, who not only introduced the "missionary position," but also condemned polygamy, premarital sex-play, and education led Africans to a skeptical. Furthermore much western scientific and non-scientific discourse surrounding AIDS has blamed Africans for the epidemic—both in terms of their behavior and as the origin of the virus. Only in late 2006 did the medical journal *Lancet* publish a study proving that Africans were no more sexually promiscuous than other population groups—a long pondered question by researchers who sought to explain why Africans had higher rates of the disease than other population groups.[65]

Within South Africa skepticism also can be seen in the limited numbers of people who initially took advantage of free anti-retrovirals. During the first two years (2002–2004) that Anglo-America, a South African mining company, offered free anti-retrovirals to all employees, there were few takers. Of 140,000 employees, of which 34,000 employees were infected with HIV, and 8,500 had reached the stage of the disease where they should be taking the drugs, only 2,050 received them, which means that 75 percent of those in need were refusing the drugs. Likewise a doctor at Johannesburg General Hospital in that same year estimated that one out of three patients who were offered the free anti-retrovirals refused them. While use of anti-retrovirals has gone up, doctors speculated that those rejecting biomedical treatments do so out of fear of the stigma still attached to AIDS, for fear of side effects, and skepticism regarding its efficacy. Much of Black South Africa's initial cynicism towards biomedicine and messages on HIV/AIDS and how to practice safe sex were in response to apartheid's coercive and racist Population Control Program.[66] In the 1960s, the government encouraged white women to reproduce while forcefully removing black women and children to the rural areas. This Population Control Program was intensified in the 1970s through state sponsored contraception that aimed to regulate 50 percent of black women's fertility by 1980. Concern over reducing the black population led the apartheid government to make fertility clinics widely available and to offer free sterilizations. Thus in a country where medical care remained underfunded and largely inaccessible to South Africa's communities of color and did not include access to regular gynecological care, the offer of these services in both urban and rural areas stood out as an obvious attempt to reduce the black population. Furthermore, doctors and family planning centers that prioritized a low birth rate, as opposed to women's health or the prioritizing of her individual body needs or lifestyle, chose birth control methods based on the provider's preference and assumptions about women of color. In the 1970s, one doctor fitted 25,000 African women with the Lippes loop and the Dalkon shield because he said they required "less patient responsibility."[67] While compulsory sterilization never became government policy, many white doctors acted on their own accord inserting IUDs and performing tubal ligations without patient consent, and the private sector sometimes used coercive measures to ensure that black women remained infertile.[68] Given that biomedical practitioners were very much on the frontlines of this population control movement, despite that many of them have done much since then to counter the negative history of this era, many South Africans of color remain skeptical of anything that can be interpreted as "Fertility Control" and weary of biomedicine in a post-apartheid era.

Mbeki's popular disgust for anti-retrovirals made sense to many South Africans who saw pharmaceutical companies as greedy. Certainly, the decision of multinational pharmaceutical firms to sue South Africa in the late 1990s to prevent it from purchasing more affordable generic HIV/AIDS drugs added to these ideas. Even though this pharmaceutical suit was eventually withdrawn, these last actions, coupled with biomedicine's focus on sexual control while ignoring issues of fertility, exacerbated public skepticism.[69] While African governments welcomed global assistance, some aid came with restrictions. The US PEPFAR program had an anti-prostitution pledge, no funding for needle programs, and mandated one third of prevention spending go towards abstinence only messages. Only in recent years with changes in government policies, the destigmatizing of HIV/AIDS, and declining pharmaceutical prices has public opinion begun to change.

Conclusions

In a global capitalist system, market *demand*, not *need* determines how medicines and food are produced and distributed. It is more profitable to produce something taken everyday than antibiotics that only need to be taken when one falls sick. Drug discovery and regulation are a long process, and pharmaceutical companies seek a good return on their investment. Curatives for diseases and parasites that afflict the world's poor and dispossessed thus have a low priority. Of 1,233 new medicines patented between 1975-1997, only 13 or 1% were for tropical diseases.[70] Despite the World Health Organization's support for incorporating traditional medicines into national healthcare systems, health research continues to be largely market and biomedically oriented. Consequently we see continued testing for anti-retrovirals rather than indigenous herbal remedies, even though neither can cure HIV/AIDS and both can effectively treat its symptoms. This is important given that many African HIV/AIDS sufferers use traditional medicines to treat their symptoms, and often times in conjunction with anti-retrovirals. Likewise, the global food system will continue to offer food solutions that privilege multinational grain traders, industrial agriculture, and producers of genetically modified seeds at the expense of small-scale African farmers. And despite the best of intentions, that same system will force African governments to pursue market-based "solutions" to Africa's issues of food (in)security, rather than supporting small scale agro-ecology.

While globalization has increased global disparities in health and food security, it has also created the vehicle for change. HIV/AIDS activists around the world fought for accessible treatment of all HIV/AIDS sufferers regardless of race or national origin. Their work helped to spur bi-lateral aid programs like PEPFAR, while also embarrassing and convincing pharmaceutical companies to decrease their prices for anti-retrovirals and drugs used to treat common secondary infections. In South Africa, HIV/AIDS activists and traditional healers, combined with global support, convinced the state to fund and test indigenous remedies for HIV/AIDS. Global activists have also been at the forefront of publicizing the inequities of the global food system, and mounting international campaigns against genetically modified foods and seeds in Africa. This activism has created greater support for "fair trade" companies in the North who collaborate with small scale producers in the South to encourage organic farming and sustainability while guaranteeing a living wage. And African farmers, buoyed by global food activists like Vandana Shiva and organizations like Via Campesina, have begun their own food sovereignty movements. Farmers are thus rediscovering indigenous crops, while borrowing techniques for intercropping, organic fertilizers, and activism from other farmers across the world.

Bibliography

Abu-Lughod, J. *Before European Hegemony: The World System AD1250–1350.* Oxford: Oxford University Press, 1991.

Ahidjo, A. *Anthologies des Discours, 1957–1979.* 4 Volumes. Dakar: NEA, 1980.

Andrae, G. and Beckman, B. *The Wheat Trap: Bread and underdevelopment in Nigeria.* London: Zed Books, 2008.

Annan, Koffi. Speech "The Green Revolution—Africa to Feed Itself." May 05, 2010.

Ashton,G. "Bill Gates' support of GM crops is wrong approach for Africa." *The Seattle Times.* Feb 27, 2012.

"A Perfect Famine—Malawi," 2003 Journeyman pictures.

Bell, Jacques Doo. "Impunité: Voici les Barons qui ont Pillé nos Banques." *Le Messager*, July 27, 2006.

Bond, P. and Dor, G. "Uneven Health Outcomes and Political Resistance Under Residual Neoliberalism in Africa." In Navarro, Vicente ed. *Neoliberalism, Globalization and Inequalities.* Amityville, NY: Baywood Publishing, 2007.

Bradford, H. "'Her Body, Her Life': 150 Years of Abortion in South Africa." In Meade, T. and Walker, M. eds. *Science, Medicine, and Cultural Imperialism.* New York: Palgrave MacMillan, 1991.

Bryceson, B. Food Insecurity and the Social division of Labor in Tanzania, 1919-1988. London: MacMillan, 1990.

Burke. T. *Lifebuoy Men, Lux Women: Commodification, Consumption, and Cleanliness in Modern Zimbabwe (Body, Commodity, Text).* Durham: Duke University Press, 1996.

Davis, M. *Late Victorian Holocausts: El Niño Famines and the Making of the Third World.* London, New York: Verso, 2002.

DeLancey, M. *Cameroon: Dependence and Independence.* Boulder: Westview Press, 1989.

DeLancey, M. *Historical Dictionary of the Republic of Cameroon.* Lanham, MD: The Scarecrow Press, 2000.

Dembele, D. M. "The International Monetary Fund and World Bank in Africa: A "Disastrous" Record." In Navarro, Vincente ed. *Neoliberalism, Globalization and Inequalities.* Amityville, NY: Baywood Publishing, 2007.

Dongmo, C. "Green Revolution and Food Self-Sufficiency: Cameroon's Land Theory of Economic Development." CL-Experts: 24.06.2008. http://www.CamerounLink-Experts.com/docs01/.htm.

Doo Bell, Jacques. "Impunité: Voici les Barons qui ont Pillé nos Banques," *Le Messager*, July 27, 2006.

Dugger, C. "Ending Famine, Simply by Ignoring the Experts." New York Times, 12/2/07.

Feierman, S. and Janzen, J. (eds.). *Social Basis of Health and Healing*. Berkeley: University of California Press, 1992.

Flint, K. *Healing Traditions: African Medicine, Cultural Exchange, and Competition in South Africa, 1820–1948*. Athens: Ohio University Press, 2008.

"Food Security in Africa: the impact of Agricultural Development: A hearing before the subcommittee on Africa and Global Health of the Committee on Foreign Affairs House of Representatives." July 18, 2007.

Fourshey, C. " 'The Remedy for Hunger is Bending the Back:' Maize and British Agricultural Policy in Southwestern Tanzania, 1920–1960." *International Journal of African Historical Studies*, Vol. 41 No. 2, 2008.

Franke, R. and Chasin, B. *Seeds of Famine: Ecological Destruction and the Development Dilemma in the West African Sahel*. Montclair, NJ: LandMark Studies, 1981.

Grady, D. "Where Life's Start is a Deadly Risk." New York Times, 5/23/09.

Hartwig, G. and Patterson, D. *Disease in African History*. Durham, NC: Duke University Press, 1978.

Hennig, R.C. "IMF forces African countries to privatize water." http://www.africaaction.org/docs01/wat0103.htm [last accessed July 15, 2009].

Herbert, E. "Smallpox inoculation in Africa." *Journal of African History*, vol. 16, 4 1975.

Kipple, K. *The Cambridge World History of Human Disease*. Cambridge: Cambridge University Press, 1993.

Klugman, B. "The Politics of contraception in South Africa," *Women's Studies International Forum*, Vol. 13 No. 3, 1990.

Lindsay, L. *Captives as Commodities*. Upper Saddle River, NJ: Pearson, 2008.

"Mali: No famine, but a perennial problem of poverty" from IRIN, humanitarian news and analysis, a project of the UN Office for the Coordination of Humanitarian Affairs http://www.irinnews.org/report.aspx?ReportId =55852.

Mousseau, F. and Mittal, A. "Sahel: A Prisoner of Starvation." 2006. http://www.oaklandinstitute.org/pdfs/sahel.pdf.

Nugent. P. *Africa Since Independence*. New York: Palgrave, 2004.

O'Brien, J. "Sowing the Seeds of Famine: the political economy of food deficits in Sudan." In Lawrence, Peter ed. *World Recession and the Food Crisis in Africa*. London and Boulder: Review of Africa Political Economy and Westview Press, 1986.

O'Brien, J. and Gruenbaum, E. "A Social History of Food, Famine, and Gender in Twentieth Century Sudan." In Downs, R. E.; Kerner, D.; and Reyna,

S. eds. *The Political Economy of African Famine*. Amsterdam: Gordon and Breach Science Publishers, 1991.

Packard, R. *White Plague, Black Labor: The Political Economy of Health and Diseases in South Africa*. Berkeley: University of California Press, 1989.

Patel, Raj. *Stuffed and Starved: The Hidden Battle for the World Food System*. Brooklyn: Melville House, 2007.

Phillips, H. & Killingray, D. *The Spanish Influenza Pandemic of 1918–19: New Perspectives*. London and New York: Routledge, 2003.

Prins, G. "But What Was the Disease? The Present State of Health and Healing in African Studies." *Past and Present*, No. 124, August 1989.

Rees, H. "The Abortion Debate in South Africa." *Critical Health*, 34, June 1991.

Rivoli, P. *The Travels of the T-shirt in the Global Economy*. Wiley Press, 2009.

Robbins, R. *Global Problems and the Culture of Capitalism*. Boston: Allyn and Bacon, 2002.

Rodney, W. *How Europe Underdeveloped Africa*. London: Bogle-L'ouverture, 1972.

SODERIM Report, May 1997.

Teboh, B. "Reproducing African Communities in the US: Settlement Patterns and Social Organizations." In Yewah, Emmanuel and Togunde, Dimeji eds. *Across the Atlantic: African Immigrants in the United States Diaspora*. Champaign, Illinois: The University Press/Common Ground, 2010.

"The Politics of Food." Yorkshire Television, 1988.

The Trade Trap, Bullfrog Films, 2003.

Timberlake, L. *Africa in Crisis*. Philadelphia: Earthscan, 1986.

"USDA News Release: International Assistance Announcement for 2007 and 2009."

Wellings et al. "Sexual Behaviour in Context: a global perspective." *The Lancet*, 11 November 2006, 368, 9548.

World Bank and World Health Organization in Dying for Change? Poor People's experience of Health and Poor Health. Washington, DC, 2002.

Wright, D. *The World and a Very Small Place in Africa: The History of Globalization in Niumi, the Gambia*. New York: ME Sharpe, 2004.

Chapter 8

African Cultures, Modernization and Development: Reexamining the Effects of Globalization

Seth N. Asumah

Introduction

> Globalization is a phenomenon and a revolution. It is sweeping the world with increasing speed and changing the global landscape into something new and different. Yet, like all such trends, its meaning, development, and impact puzzle many ... Local cultures who believe that Wal-Mart and McDonald's bring cultural change and harm rather than inexpensive products and conveniences criticize the process. In this way, globalization, like all revolutionary forces, polarizes people, alters the fabric of our lives, and creates rifts within and between people.[1]

> The West thinks it does the world a favor by exporting its culture along with the technologies that the non-Western world wants and needs. This is not a recent idea ... Political imperialism died in the wake of World War II, but cultural imperialism is still alive and well.[2]

Cultural values, norms, and practices characterize African peoples and societies. Culturally, there are similarities and difference among African people, so it is important to make reference to African histories and cultures, since one cannot find a monolithic culture and history in Africa. The process of settling in different economic zones and indigenous entities was concomitant with different socio-historical, cultural developments and lifestyles. These cultural developments, histories and lifestyles shaped kinship relationships, forms of marriage, family life, socialization, religious beliefs, economic activity, political culture and the modus operandi of the people. Yet a critical evaluation of cultures in Africa would lead some observers to question the relevancy of many practices in the decolonization and postcolonial era that tend to stifle the process of modernization and development. In this connection, the plethora of problems confronting Africans in times of development and in the era of globalization may be associated with traditional, historical, and cultural practices within Africa. Nevertheless, the forces of colonial legacy, modernization, and globalization have adverse multiplier effects on African cultures and traditions.

In the balance of this chapter, I will argue that even though African cultures and histories could interfere with the processes of development, the forces of modernization and globalization are contributing to the bastardization and gradual extinction of African cultures, and unless Africans are able to navigate the dynamics of cultural imperialism from the United States, Europe and China to become true development partners of the West and China and not just exotic "cultural objects" for the global village, African histories and cultures will reach a stage of extinction and African development problems will continue to be irrepressible, absent historical and cultural contexts for solving such problems. A deliberate agenda to reconcile the forces of African cultures and developmental goals is needed urgently to maintain a balance between African histories and cultures on one hand and the process of modernization and development on the other. One may characterize the theme of this chapter and the apparent rift between African cultures and the process of Anglo-American/Chinese development and modernization as another form of the "culture wars" waged around the world between different civilizations. In this case, it is African traditional and contemporary cultures vis-à-vis Anglo-American/Chinese processes of modernization and development that are at "war". "Culture wars" as a phrase is a neologism with roots from the German transliteration-*Kulturkampf*, which translates into a "struggle for the control of the culture." A reference to German Chancellor Otto von Bismark in 1871 is appropriate in this perspective, in that he waged a *Kulturkampf* against the Catholic Church's imposition of Roman-style education and politics on Germany. Nonetheless, Bismarck's culture wars were discarded in 1878 because the general populace stood against it.[3] The recent culture wars between African cultures on one side and Western/Chinese modernization, development and globalization processes on the other are subterranean and yet more lethal to the African human condition and sustainable development because they evade the discourse over both discursive consciousness and practical consciousness.

With reference to the disregard for discursive consciousness, most Africans are not taking the discussion of Western/Chinese cultural imperialism seriously now and many have already succumbed to verbalizations from the Anglo-American and sometimes Chinese cultures that are more palatable to their worldviews. Neglect for practical consciousness ensues because there are no structured institutional arrangements to reconcile the forces of African historical, traditional and contemporary cultures and the effects of modernization, development and globalization on Africa. There are no known historical arrangements or policies established by African nation states to mitigate the adverse effects of globalization and development on African cultures. Perhaps, because culture is about everything we do, say, use, and acquire individually and institutionally and it evolves slowly, it is so elusive to realize when it is affected by outside agents and processes, especially in a time when global cultures are establishing hegemonic relations with indigenous African cultures. Social and cultural capitals are important for the sustainability of any civilization in the era of globalization; nonetheless, the process of acquiring cultural capital has been distressing to many Africans because of global forces and the ease by which subordinate cultures often dislocate the meaning of their existence in order to participate in global enterprises.

Moreover, when global culture becomes synonymous with Westernization and/or Americanization and more recently, Chinanization, and the West and China have presumably convinced themselves that their cultures are superior and would therefore benefit Africans, then one has to revisit the old attitudes that were historically manifested in the actions of Western slave traders and colonialists in Africa in order to adequately understand the contemporary effects of globalization on African cultures. Anglo-American cultural imperialism and attitudes of the late nineteenth century "manifest destiny" and social Darwinism promoted expansionism and jingoist views of "survival of the fittest" cultures. This Anglo-American arrogance has not diminished in many economic, political and cultural interactions in the global village today. Anglo-American cultural imperialism in Africa is one thing, but another thing that Africans must not neglect is China's benevolent neo-imperialism on the continent.

Ironically, where Anglo-American cultural imperialism in Africa may have failed, Chinese benevolent neo-imperialism is succeeding. As Michael Elliot reports in *Time* magazine, January 11, 2007, a senior member of the United States National Security Council under President Bill Clinton, Kenneth Lieberthal notes, "The Chinese wouldn't put it this way themselves. But in their hearts I think they believe that the 21st Century is China's century."[4] Even though China's benevolent neo-cultural imperialism is unlike Anglo-American pomposity in cross-cultural interactions, Chinese traditional cultures and the history of the "Middle Kingdom" (in the middle of the heavens), guided parts of the Chinese people's perception of themselves as a great civilization. However within China, ethnic differences among Cantonese, Shanghainese, and Hunanese, for instance, could count for internal cultural and historical intolerance. Consequently, these internalized attitudes are easily transformed into benevolent neo-cultural imperialism when Chinese of all ethnicities, regardless of "all their differences and mutual snobberies ... think of themselves first and foremost as Chinese—as *Zhongguo ren*, literally, 'people of the Middle Kingdom'" when the Dragon enters the "Dark Continent"—Africa.[5] Lucian Pye asserts that, "China is not just another nation state in the family of nations," rather, China is "a civilization pretending to be a state."[6] A civilization of that unique Chinese persona maintains a culture that sometimes interrogates African cultures in the global village.

Culture Revisited

What then is culture? How can a group determine when it is losing its culture? Put simply, Gary Wederspahn defines culture as the "shared set of assumptions, values, and beliefs of a group of people by which they organize their common life."[7] Robert Kohls describes culture as "... an integrated system of learned behavior patterns that are characteristic of the members of any given society. Culture refers to the total way of life of particular group of people."[8] Historical archaeology characterized societies historically by stratifying them into distinctive ethnic and cultural groups based on the material possession of a particular culture. Yet its position in studying cultures by linking them to racial categories was challenged by archaeologists in the early twentieth century and its conceptual framework fell into disuse in the mid-twentieth century.[9] Nevertheless, culture is central to understanding human life in the global village. This is the reason why it is pertinent to define culture, a term that could mean different things to different people and different disciplines. Anthropologists, traditionally, make reference to Edward Tylor who defines culture as, "that complex whole which includes knowledge, belief, art, morals, law, custom, and any other capabilities and habits acquired by man as a member of society."[10] Culture is then both a process and an institution. Culture is as much a structure as the institutional arrangements of the economic system or political institutions of any given society. Its roots lie within families, learning institutions, music, art, and sociopolitical institutions of the society. Culture is therefore important to social domination or the emancipation of a group within the global village. The complex question here is what kind of culture—global or indigenous or perhaps a combination of the two could enhance the people's ability to deal with both domestic and global issues in the era of globalization?

Iris Marion Young cautions us that culture is such a broad category that it is difficult to give a precise definition of it. She nonetheless refers to culture as "all aspects of social life from the point of view of their linguistic, symbolic, affective, and embodied norms and practices. Culture includes the background and medium of action, the unconscious habits, desires, meanings, gestures, and so on that people grow into and bring to their interaction."[11] In their work on multiculturalism and diversity, Asumah and Johnston Anumonwo make reference to Thomas Sowell's (1994) characterization of culture by defining it as an accumulation of observances and institutions "concerned with socio-economic and political construction, moral arrangements, precepts, norms, practices, and shared ideas of a particular group of people."[12] And Richard Fredland is certain that culture is the "cumulative practices and beliefs of a fairly homogeneous group."[13]

What is common among these definitions is the evolution of practices and institutions that give meaning to people's existence and how they adapt to their environment. Nevertheless, this evolution can easily be affected by other outside agents and forces such as development and globalization. African cultures have historically been more vulnerable in the process of development and globalization in that the subversive global forces have little consideration for the interpretation of a particular people's culture because most cultural outsiders primarily see and deal with "surface culture" and not "deep culture". Surface culture and deep culture are derived from analyzing culture from a structural perspective and a conceptual framework of culture as a metaphoric iceberg.

The iceberg concept of culture (see figure 8.1) provides an in-depth analysis of how cultures evolve and operate in most parts of the world. Like an iceberg, the greater proportions of most cultures are hidden below the surface of the water. Furthermore, culture could be structured by both individual and institutional patterns of interaction. On surface culture, individual levels of interaction, a particular group's language, accent, behavior, food, dance, visual arts, performing arts and physical appearances are very visible. Surface culture for the institutional portion of the iceberg includes those rules and regulations, policies, mission, and key institutions that are visible. Under deep culture, the individual and institutional portions of culture that are hidden beneath the water are difficult to see and comprehend by cultural outsiders and these tend to create the greatest misunderstanding and disrespect for other peoples' cultures. The individual side of deep culture may include value systems, beliefs, perceptions, emotions, and assumptions. On the institutional side of deep culture, hiring practices through lineage systems, benefit systems to particular sectors of the population, attitudes toward elders, class distinctions and the concept of societal relationships and organizational norms are difficult to assimilate. Again, cultural outsiders could be at a loss for not understanding the dynamics of how institutional deep cultures work.

Since culture defines a particular group of people who have different precepts, norms, behaviors and institutions, both conflicts and harmony are embedded in cross-cultural interactions. Western cultures have many differences from African ones. As Fredland correctly notes,

> European.... culture evolved in a temperate climate, over a long period of conflict and contact, and it developed to maximize certain values which are traceable to Greece, Rome and early Israel.... African cultures (and they are perhaps a thousand) evolved in greater isolation from one another as well as from outsiders and on generally smaller scales.... Depending on how we measure contact, we could say that these cultural traditions—European and African—have interacted for a hundred to five hundred years. However, whenever they have met, the Europeans have clearly triumphed—at least in terms of European values. The Europeans control the land; they have subjugated the African economically, socially, and militarily virtually whenever they have confronted one another.[14]

Fredland's assertion is troubling in this era of globalization, Sino-Africanization and development. It is indicative that Africans will continue to be at the losing end of the culture wars if the forces of globalization and development are mostly directed from Anglo-American and Chinese spheres. Yet it is not only systemic variables, the forces of the global system that affect African cultures negatively; it is also how Africans themselves have perpetuated the dysfunctional capacities and bastardization of African cultures in the global village. Whether it is language, behavior, style, governmental institutions, education, music, aesthetics, or architecture, there is apparently a strong movement by most Africans to submit to Western cultural preference, and more recently the Chinese ways of doing things, at the expense of African ones.

Historically, during the Neolithic times more than 10,000 years ago, African families developed settlements around different ecological zones on the continent. These settlements were concomitant with the diversity of cultures, precepts and histories that permeated the ancient empires and kingdoms of Egypt, Ethiopia, Mali, Ghana and Songhai until the European Scramble for Africa (1880–1900) drastically interrupted the socio-cultural development of African peoples. If the first half of the nineteenth-century history of Africa was submerged in international interaction adorned by slavery and European demands for African goods, then the earlier form of globalization started during the

Figure 8.1 Culture as an Iceberg

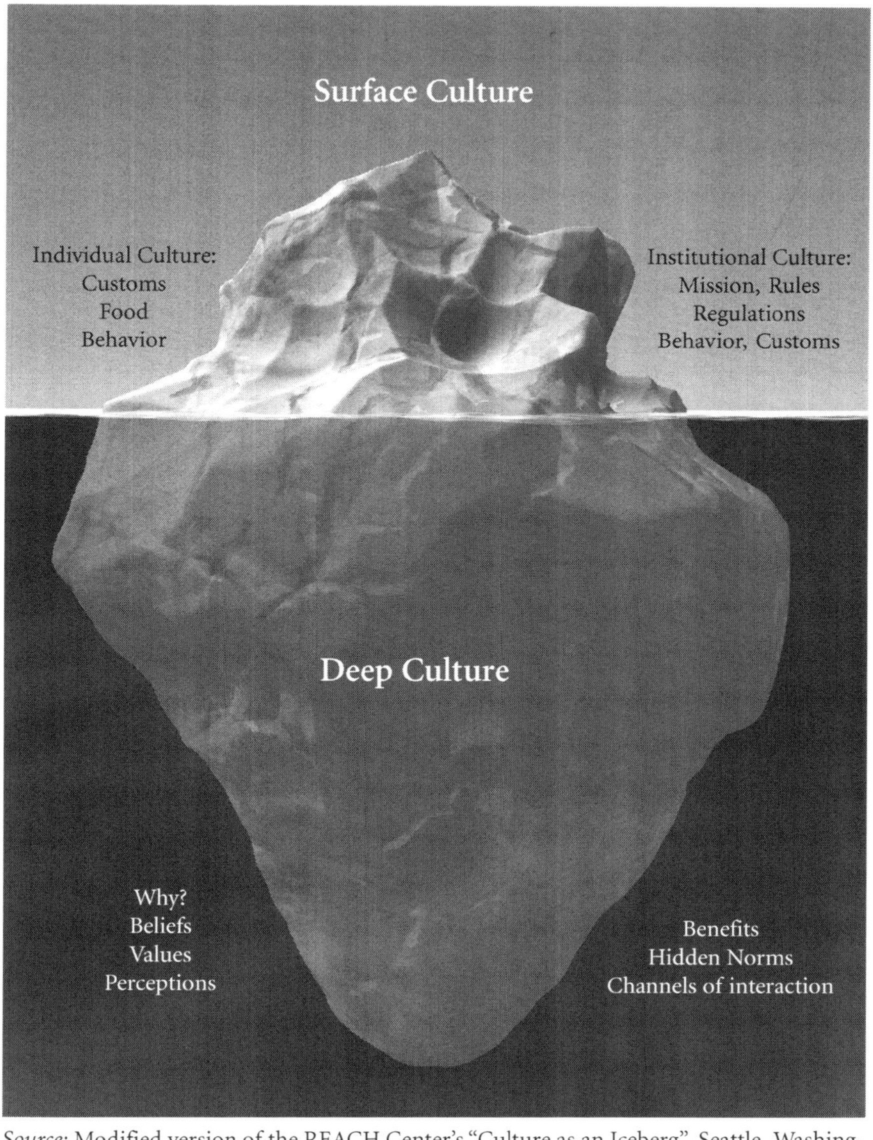

Source: Modified version of the REACH Center's "Culture as an Iceberg", Seattle, Washington, 2002. Iceberg image ©Sebastian Kaulitzki/Fotolia.

above-mentioned time period. I will return to the periods of globalization later on in this chapter. In the decolonization discourse, the search for African identity, history and culture continue to evade scholars because of the punctuation of the African human condition by the European presence on the continent. In examining postcolonial African perspectives on traditional cultures vis-à-vis Western political philosophy, for instance, Kwame Gyekye carefully notes that African people continue to struggle with reconciling the difference between their behaviors and actions and those of globalized cultures from the West. Gyekye, *inter alia*, identifies the following philosophical problems in African cultures that have to receive urgent attention in order for Africans to be accepted as partners in the global village:

- Correctly assessing inherited cultural practices and traditions in order to come to terms with modern societal realities and judiciously using traditional cultural practices to create visions for the future;
- Inability to utilize traditional forms of arrangement and institutions, tribal and ethnic groups, and adoption of cross-cultural approaches for nation-building processes;
- Creating ideologies from African traditions and worldview that would serve as building blocks for philosophical positions for mission and visions for contemporary Africa;
- Inability in adopting cultural categories that could enable Africans to strengthen their moral compasses and behavior in order to eradicate corruption; and
- Lack of concerted efforts and structures that would deal with African traditional and contemporary cultures in the era of globalization and rapid socio-political change.[15]

Culture wars between the African continent and the West in the process of modernization and development tend to create an unfortunate reservoir of psychic disequilibrium for Africans as they struggle to reconcile the effects of global cultures on traditional and contemporary African cultures. The structural variable within Africa and systemic dynamics in the international arena tend to compound this problem. Gyekye, again, notes that the "resiliency of these and other problems in postcolonial Africa has brought confusion on African life and left many to wonder why."[16] As African nation states are almost forced to keep up with the West in the process of modernization and development, they are left with limited options in balancing the dynamics of globalization with maintaining their indigenous cultures partly because the successes of development and advancement have been historically characterized in Western terms. Consequently, most of the theories of development and modernization have been culturally biased, giving preference to Western value systems and currencies.

The development of underdevelopment of Africa and the gradual dissolution of African indigenous cultures, some may argue, are attributable to traditional cultural values that tend to impede the process of modernization and development. Eminent Western scholars such as Talcott Parsons, Max Weber, Samuel Huntington, David Apter and Lucian Pye have suggested that the transformation of traditional African cultures is "the most crucial step in the modernization process."[17] These scholars argue that traditional African cultural values are somewhat irrational and unscientific to facilitate the process of modernization and development. Indubitably, the positions of the scholars above are at worst ethnocentric and at best Eurocentric—affirming Anglo-American cultural superiority while debunking African cultures. Whatever happened to cultural relativism?

The German American, Franz Boas' characterization of cultural relativism is that each particular group's behavior, values, and activities should be analyzed in terms of its own cultural standpoint and worldview. Boas' initial conceptualization of the idea in 1887 included the position that "civilization is not something absolute, but ... is relative, and ... our ideas and conceptions are true only so far as our civilization goes."[18] Yet it is argued that Boas did not actually coin the term "cultural relativism." The term gained coinage among anthropologists after Boas' death in 1942, to galvanize the corpus of ideas that Boas had developed and the first usage of "cultural relativism" appeared in the professional journal of American anthropologists in 1948.[19] Yet, if cultural relativism is a philosophical position contending that there is some logic to the notion that all cultures should be viewed equally, that same logic could be defeated if one views the assertion that all cultures can also not be viewed equally, especially in the global village where hegemonic cultures prevail. If cultural relativism is true and all cultural values are meaningful, then the assertion that cultural relativism could be false is also true because relativists believe that all truth is relative and that it is therefore impossible to establish absolute truths. Nonetheless, one can establish a statement that contains absolutism, which could also be true because one can argue about an absolute truth. *Ceteris paribus*, a logical conclusion could be reached that if there is an absolute truth, then that statement could also be false. All in all, the forces of globalization and development stand the reality of cultural relativism on its head.

The challenges for development and modernization for African nation states in the era of globalization invite several questions about the state of African cultures in these complex processes. Questions about Africa's warped economies that are associated with the learned behaviors of the people who depend too much on governments as providers of welfare are rampant. In that perception, African governments become anthropomorphic, in that they act as father figures and providers for the needs of the extended family. Other questions about political instability are mostly linked to cultural and behavioral values of African leaders and their relations with the general populace. An important question in this perspective is: how can African cultures modernize their values without sacrificing their own cultural traditions? In attempting to respond to these questions, development and modernization theorists have given us a sufficient premonition that the forces of "cultural sameness" are inevitable. Marion Levy, for instance, makes a projection that at the highest point of modernization, development and globalization, African countries and nation states in the developing world will resemble the West even more. He claims that, "they and we will increasingly resemble one another. [The] more highly modernized societies become, the more they resemble one another."[20]

Even though social scientists today do not totally subscribe to the convergence theory as they did in the 1950s and 1960s, the new forces of globalization have reignited the debate that as societies modernize and industrialize; they will become more alike culturally; they will converge. Hitherto, in recent times we have witnessed the aspects of the convergence theory working in many African countries. Today Anglo-American and Chinese values have indeed swept Africa. Most cities and villages in Africa are submerged in this neo-convergence era, adorned by *McCulturization*, *Coca-colization*, *Americanization*, *Chinanization*, computer technology, Internet cafés, hip-hop music, rock music, Hollywood films, Eurostar, MTV, soap-operas, blue jeans, and the values of democratic capitalism. As Handelman puts it, the "prophesy [of the convergence theory] may seem accurate."[21]

So, from Algeria to Angola, and from Zambia to Zimbabwe, people of the African world are adopting similar tastes in food, dress, art, popular music, and entertainment. These tastes are specifically Western ones. Paradoxically, there seems to be a trend toward "cultural sameness" in our multicultural world. The African world is experiencing a cultural disintegration in order to adopt Western forms of life-style and protocol, and most African nation states are losing their raison d'être as sovereign states. African nation states' susceptibility to global forces has facilitated the Anglo-Americanization, dollarization, *Coca-colization*, *McCulturalization* and *Chinanization* of the African world—making them even more vulnerable to the processes of globalization. African countries are converging at a very fast rate with the West and China, but they, nevertheless, remain underdeveloped according to the measures of development. What therefore is development? Development is a process of reaching self-sufficiency, self-reliance, and advancement. Development may include growth, but growth itself is not a necessary condition for development. Growth is an increase in productivity measured in gross national product (GNP), gross domestic product (GDP) or physical quality of life index (PQLI).

Impacts of Development and Modernization on African Cultures in the Era of Globalization

The 2001 protests in Genoa, Italy against the uneven effects of development and globalization on developing nation states, where the G8 nation states were meeting to shape the political economy of the world, were not epiphenomenal, nor were they an aberration. While the G8 nation states of the United Kingdom, the United States of America, Germany, Italy, France, Canada, Japan, Russia and their cohorts, transnational corporations, are celebrating the apparent benefits of globalization, most African nation states are experiencing a new form of colonialism, exploitation and cultural imperialism by the core nation states against the periphery—Africa and the Third World. In this section of the chapter, with reference to globalization, I argue that the global village presents a meretricious burlesque of so called "prosperity" for African nation states and cultures, while the world's hegemonic countries are hiding behind the façade of equal benefits of globalization to further their exploitation and marginalization of the more vulnerable African nation states. The world's hegemonic nations' actions in globalization are tantamount to quasi colonialism and cultural imperialism. Furthermore, African nation states are relinquishing their sovereign authority and cultural values to transnational corporations, the West and China in order to be accepted within the global village.

Similarly, the trends in today's political economy, coupled with the economic integration of the world, and trade policy liberalization have all combined to produce an unstoppable movement toward globalization. Globalization has become a buzzword for academicians, consultants, journalists and policy analysts. Globalization has gained currency with statesmen and stateswomen. The term globalization, which could not be found in a respectable English dictionary a few years ago, now has acquired both legitimacy and an added aura of sacred, enigmatic desirability, concomitant with Western media propaganda. Is globalization beneficial to the African economy? Is the process of globalization so inevitable and irreversible that African nation states have declared it a *fait accompli*? Has globalization increased the gap between poor African nation states and the rest of the world? In the balance of this article, the questions above will be tackled in addition to examining the different phases of Western intrusion into the African world and the emergence of global apartheid.

Rethinking Globalization

Globalization is the international reordering of priorities, values, cultures, technology, trade, communication, and the interdependent nature of international interaction. Friedman's characterization of globalization as "a dynamic ongoing process [which] involves the inexorable integration of markets, nation states and technologies to a degree never witnessed before, ... and in a way that is also producing a powerful backlash from those brutalized or left behind by this new system"[22] is meaningful to the theme of this chapter. The nation states and cultures that are brutalized and marginalized in the process of globalization are, without question, those on the continent of Africa. Because of the complex interdependence of hegemonic and peripheral nation states, global forces affect subordinate cultures and nation states in unprecedented proportions owing to the weaker positions of the marginalized entities in the global bargaining process.

Held, McGrew, Goldblatt, and Parraton correctly note that globalization is not a single process, but it involves four different types of change:

1) It stretches social, political and economic activities across political frontiers, regions, and continents;
2) It intensifies our dependence on each other, as flows of trade, investment, finance, migration, and culture increase;
3) It speeds up the world to a point where new systems of transport and communication provide the means for ideas, goods, information, capital, and people to move more quickly; and
4) It means that distant events have a deeper impact on our lives. Even the most local developments may come to have enormous global consequences. The boundaries between domestic matters and global affairs become increasingly blurred.[23]

Globalization, therefore, places emphasis on the universal application of national policy for a proper sphere of political influence. With the universalization of domestic policy, a more comprehensive view of globalization steers the world toward a global village. The world is expanding, but the expansion is geared toward a village community of inequality. The expansion of the world is concomitant with a convergence of the political economies of different nation states within a global village community. Producers and consumers, cultural imperialists and imitators, pauper nations and rich nations all come face to face in a supposedly free but unequal market. Ali Mazrui asserts, "Globalization is thus the villagization of the world.... What has been happening in the twentieth century is a more extensive globalization of Global Africa, making the African factor on earth more truly omnipresent and omni-directional."[24] Although global Africa has become a reluctant participant in the global village, there are a few African predatory regimes that benefit from their association with other global actors. Predatory regimes are African governments that have facilitated the marginalization of the African people by colluding with external agencies in the process of exploitation. Yet, Africans have provided moral leadership in the global village, from the United Nations to the World Court, and over the world, Black *faces* are becoming more common. Nonetheless, the aggregate effect of global Africa on the global village is negligible.

However, the African concept of the village is not the same as what is envisioned in the global village. The African village is more sociocentric and less exploitative. The global village, on the other hand, is just the most recent development of global political economy designed by Western imperialism and mercantilism over the past five hundred years.[25] Furthermore, Immanuel Kant over two hundred years ago, in his *Essay on Perpetual Peace*, projected socioeconomic development, interdependence, and the evolution of international law and organization into a system that binds all sovereign states.[26] Although Kant's vision about globalization is fast becoming a reality, given his Eurocentric and racist ideas, he could not have imagined African nation states as coequals in the global village. Furthermore, these African nation states have lost their raison d'être as sovereign states in the present global village because of systemic dynamics beyond their control.

In order to comprehend the impact of globalization on the nation states of Africa and their cultures, one has to analyze the historical context of global interaction during the past five hundred years. The present global village, as William Nester notes, is a continuation of a process that started five centuries ago.[27] Today's globalization is actually part of the fourth phase of Western imperialism and penetration into Africa by superordinate forces that used Africa as a platform for exploitation. The first phase of globalization's effect on Africa was during the period of slavery, when Africa's human and material resources were taken by global traders and slavers, whose work only benefited Arabs, Europeans, and North Americans.[28] The second phase of globalization was the period of colonialism, when Europeans divided and conquered the African continent for their self-interests beginning with the Berlin Conference in 1884–85. Just as the present form of globalization indicates, the benefits for the West always outweighed what the African people acquired through the other processes. The third phase of globalization was the period of neocolonialism, the post independent era, where Africa's fate was still controlled by alien transnational companies and foreign nation states. Trade patterns, debt arrangements, investment policies, and the general political economies of African nation states were primarily controlled by former colonial powers in the neocolonial era. The fourth, the present phase of globalization, is a global village where interdependence has made Africa even more dependent on foreign powers and resources than the period of colonialism. Financial flows, technology, information highways, byways, and thoroughfares, movement of people, and cultures have direct benefit to the Western countries and corporations that have very little in mind about Africa. Moreover, the global village would be dysfunctional if the dominant actors failed to carefully implement the tenets of the catalystic agent of globalization—liberalization.

The global village is considered a gigantic market place where profit maximization of private corporations and nation states advocate laissez faire principles through liberalization. This "free" market has no deference for the nature and function of non-Western nation states and cultures. The global village has all the qualities of global apartheid in the sense that its sustainability is predicated on race, geography, as well as markets.[29] In a neo-liberal marketplace affirmed by the norms, ideas and precepts of Anglo-American and Chinese cultures, African vision for prosperity is infinitesimally dilute. Liberalization, therefore, drives the free market of the global village to the desired destination of hegemonic, Euro-American, democratic, capitalist nation states.

What Then Is Liberalization?

Liberalization is a paradigmatic shift by government in social and economic policies to a noninterventionist stance. Frances Stewart writes that:

> "Liberalization" encompasses all these moves toward reduced state intervention. It has both a domestic and international component. The international component comprises reduced restrictions on trade, capital flows, and technology movements (but, significantly, not labor). These changes, along with new communications technologies and reduced transport costs, are responsible for the "globalization" phenomenon.[30]

Although Stewart does not clearly outline the domestic component of liberalization in the quotation above, paradoxically, the African nation states have become victims of the forces of liberalization in the domestic arena equally as well as in the international sphere. In the process of liberalization, African nation states that are producers of raw materials with relatively low value and sources of cheap labor set themselves up for exploitation with little state intervention.

The policy changes of liberalization, to facilitate globalization in Africa, have pervasive effects on the general political economy and social capital of these nation states. Despite liberalization, the markets for African products have not increased significantly as those nation states with well developed manufacturing sectors and a strong technological base. The developed nation states always have the comparative advantage precisely because they obscure and fiercely defend protectionism. Liberalization has a strong effect on growth without much development in Africa. It has a direct impact on poverty and income distribution within African nation states.[31] Growth without development, poverty and an uneven distribution all contribute to sociopolitical instability in Africa.

Liberalization's impact on income distribution is one of the most important effects globalization has on Africa, since changes in poverty levels are concomitant with changes in income distribution and economic growth. While Western nation states have increases in goods and services during the process of liberalization, because they could easily penetrate the poorer countries of Africa, the nation states of Africa only have to succumb to the dynamics of interaction dictated through Western liberalization policies. Recent evidence in developed nation states indicates that more equal income distribution tends to be associated with higher growth rates. Meanwhile, in African nation states, it could be argued that the effects of poverty have a more lasting impact on the society than that of income distribution.[32] Nonetheless, the changes in poverty levels during the process of liberalization are the combined outcomes of changes in economic growth and income distribution. Yet, for the poor countries in Africa, changes in income levels provide less in terms of meeting basic needs because of the differences in needs of richer nation states in the same global entity.

In general, African nation states that are primary-goods export producers (PEP) suffer the effects of liberalization more than Western nation states that are manufacturing-goods export producers (MEP), because MEP nation states have the ability to penetrate the global market without much trouble. In fact, MEP nation states control the global market. During liberalization, African countries, such as Ghana and Uganda that are primary-goods export producers (PEP) may experience a slight improvement in income distribution in the short run because the incomes of small peasant primary goods exporters may increase. However, in the long run, income distribution among these peasants may worsen with liberalization in that transnational companies enter the market, displacing the small peasants. Since trade liberalization favors Western developed countries more than African countries because of comparative advantage, the nation states of Africa would generally suffer the effects of liberalization and globalization. N. Birdsal notes:

> In short, the effect of trade liberalization on inequality depends on the extent to which a country's comparative advantage lies in labor-intensive agriculture or manufactured exports; on the extent to which education has been increasing and is already shared; and, ... on the extent to which the opening of markets is part of a much larger economic adjustment, implying widening income differences between those able to adapt and [those] less able.[33]

With reference to Birdsal's statement above, one can only inquire about how African nation states and cultures could muster courage in the socio-political game of comparative advantage if they are already disadvantaged in the global village. In preparing themselves to deal with the exigencies of the global village, African nation states and cultures must deal with the forces of the global village in order to maintain their raison d'être. These following questions are inevitable:

1) How does the nation state maintain its raison d'être in the global village?
2) How are the nation states' authoritative actions and inactions understood in reference to internal and external constraints during the process of globalization?
3) To what extent do African nation states still maintain their sovereignty in dealing with socioeconomic and political forces in the global village?

I will attempt to answer these questions in the balance of this chapter.

The Fate of African Nation States and Cultures in the Era of Globalization

Earlier in the twentieth Century, both Vladimir Lenin and many internationalists projected the gradual demise of the nation state and national cultures. In the 1990s, observers started revisiting Lenin's position and management consultants, such as J. Naisbits have suggested that the contemporary advancement of globalization and the activities of transnational corporations are creating a world beyond nation state, cultures, and nationalities.[34] The present effects of globalization on the African nation state only beg for revisiting the Weberian conceptualization of the state in order to determine the fate of the nation state within the global village. Max Weber's defining properties of the nation state include:

1) Defined boundaries under the state's control and an unchallenged territorial area. This property has been almost meaningless in the process of globalization in Africa since globalization supports economic, social, and political activities across frontiers, regions and continents.

2) The nation state's monopoly of legitimate use of force to control its borders and general populace within its territory. Here, African nation states, because of the forces of interdependence, have little monopoly of legitimate use of force and influence even within their own borders. Great powers and transnational corporations' irrepressible activities in Africa have diluted the nation state's authority and the use of legitimate force in conducting its affairs.
3) The reliance upon rules and regulations in the governance of its citizens and nationals. Here again, in the global village, the rules and regulations propounded by transnational corporations and Western nation states prevail in the global village. The boundaries between domestic matters and global affairs have become increasingly blurred to an extent that the movers and shakers of the global village carry the day.

In reviewing the Weberian properties of the nation state and how globalization has made the function and authority of the African nation state questionable, one cannot confide in the sustainability of these nation states. However, it would be erroneous to perform a premature autopsy on the African nation state, even though there is sufficient evidence that globalization has intensified the crippling effect and paralysis of states and cultures in Africa. In general, globalization has uneven effects on African nation states vis-à-vis the Western industrial ones that are clearly the winners in the global village. This means that African ways of life are under lethal attack from the forces of globalization. There is an internecine cultural warfare in the global village and most of the casualties are African cultures. The chart below demonstrates the reason why African nation states and cultures are ultimate losers in the globalization movement.

Mutatis mutandis, African nation states and cultures will continue to be victims in the globalization revolution. Africa's primary drawing card in the global market is as a source of cheap labor and producer of raw materials, which are relatively low in value vis-à-vis finished goods from the West. Despite the liberalization effort in the past ten to fifteen years, the markets for African products have not increased significantly compared to those countries with a well developed manufacturing sector and technological base coupled with comparative advantage.[35] Even though fiscal trade liberalization has increased financial mobility in recent years, African markets are vulnerable to external changes, dollarization, and external shocks. The facts below will not dissipate; they are the realities of globalization that African nation states have to come to terms with before blindly embracing the global village:

> According to the 1999 Human Development Report of the United Nations, one-fifth of the global village inhabitants live in the world's rich-

Figure 8.2 Uneven Effects of Globalization on Africa and the West

African Nation States: Non-Beneficiaries	Western Nation States: Beneficiaries	Reasons Why
1. Primary-goods Export Producers (PEP)	Manufacturing-goods Export Producers (MEP)	MEP nation states control prices and access in the global village.
2. Consumer culture	Productive Output	Nation states with productive output make profit, while those with consumer culture lack savings and investment.
3. Unskilled workers	Skill workers	Nation states with skilled workers capitalize on information technology and technocratic establishment that make gains faster than nation states with unskilled workers.
4. Debtors	Creditors	Most African nation states are characterized as heavily indebted poor countries (HIPCs) that are at the mercy of the IMF, World Bank and creditor nations of the West.
5. Small companies	Large companies	The economies of scale favor large companies in the global market.
6. Local Markets	Global Markets	Western nation states and transnational corporations have the ability to penetrate the global market.
7. Women and Children	Men	Men have more influential positions, assets, and power than women and children in the global village.
8. Indigenous culture	Global culture	Cultural imperialism prevails in the global village, where the dominant nation states' cultures are synonymous with Western culture and remain as the norm.

est nation states. This fifth controls 82 percent of the world's export market, 68 percent of international direct investment and 75 percent of all the telephone lines. The bottom fifth in the global village are mostly African nation states with the lowest human development indices and have less than 1.5 percent shares in the three categories mentioned above.[36]

The evidence above indicates that the global village is not what some observers paint it to be. Africans are receiving a raw deal; a deal that may be worse than all the deals in the three previous phases of Western interaction with Africa combined. How does the global village affect subordinate cultures? How does cultural imperialism affect the psyche of the African people in the global village? The next section of this chapter will briefly examine the effects of global culture on Africans in the global village.

Global Culture, African Cultures and the Global Village

The euphoric prognoses by statesmen, stateswomen and political economists about the benefits of globalization to all the members of the global village are beginning to subside because many developing nation states and African nation states in particular have realized the extent of exploitation, marginalization, and cultural imperialism associated with globalization.

Transnational and multinational corporations move from one place to another. When these movements occur, those engaged in them take their precepts, norms, and cultures with them. Globalization of cultures, therefore, has a long history. At the advent of the nation state in the eighteenth century, few distinctions stood between ethnic groups and stateless entities in Africa. Now many people may identify with the nation state. The emergence of the nation state and nationalism facilitated the process of cultural globalization. Nation states in Africa have attempted to control language, forms of communication and education. Colonialism has complicated the process because all African nation states had to deal with alien institutions and cultures. V. Sundaram asserts that "British Imperialism or Western Colonialism did not die after the end of World War II when the West gave up its colonies in Africa ... Gradually it changed itself into a more subtle form which is proving to be more harmful to all non-Western cultures."[37]

Many Africans continue to suffer what W. E. B. Du Bois called "double consciousness"—the struggle with the African self and the European other. European cultural globalization rose with technological advancement in transportation and communication systems, which helped the West expand into Africa and other areas with new ideas of liberalism, capitalism, socialism, and science. Now the Internet, satellite and digital technology have enhanced the process of global culture. Through radio, television, movies, and the Internet, exposure to different cultures and values has been more rapid than ever. In a similar vein, globalization has contributed to the dissipation of indigenous languages and cultures of Africa. *McCulturalization*, *dollarization*, *Coca-colization* and *Chinanization* all pose a threat to indigenous African cultures. We should not forget that fast food in McDonald's is not only about hamburgers or French fries—the food—it is more about "fast." Yet this "fast" that is designed for busy Western industrialized life-styles is now distorting the African cultural life of celebrating food culture and good communal eating.

The recent globalization of culture is spearheaded by transnational corporations, Western nation states and China. Cultural imperialism has been more rampant than ever, where the dominant corporations and superordinate cultures' practices, institutions and processes have become the norm for the rest of the global village. What does this mean to personal and national identities in the global village? Perhaps the recent rise of multiculturalism and the assertion of affinity politics (race, ethnicity, and gender) are challenges to the cultural imperialism of the West in the global village. T. Cowen suggests that global markets support multiculturalism and diversity in that they permit participants freedom of choices in the global village. He claims that "When two cultures trade with each other they tend to expand the opportunities available to individual artists."[38] Yet, the meetings of African cultures and Western ones have never been on equal footing. Most of the time the West, armed with both soft and hard power and leading by a vanguard of economic and military hegemonic powers, can easily manipulate African nation states with little to offer in such an encounter, discouraging true cultural partnership in the global village.

Conclusion

The process of globalization is unstoppable and inevitable. Globalization is transforming the world but the transformation is concomitant with prosperity and gains for a few Western nation states and China while most African nation states are entrapped in a pool of destitution and instability. Globalization has increased the gap between the wealthy nation states and the poorest ones, who are predominantly African. As Held et. al. correctly note, "globalization has disrupted the neat correspondence between national territory, sovereignty, political space, and the democratic political community."[39]

Today it is fashionable to speak of the global village—yet African nation states and cultures are not *bona fide* members of the village because, as the United Nations Human Development Program indicates, out of the 182 nation states ranked on its human development index, the twenty-two lowest nation states are African. The 2009 United Nations Least Developed Countries Report also notes that 33 of the 48 least developed countries (LDCs) are in Africa.[40] Henriot sums up this bleak picture for Africa in the era of globalization as:

> "economic fundamentalism" that puts an absolute value on the operation of the market and subordinate people's lives, the function of society, the policies of government, and the role of the state to this unrestricted free market. Throughout Africa, this ideology governs not only economic structures but also political arrangements. It assumes almost a religious character, as greed becomes a virtue, competition a commandment, and profit a sign of salvation. Dissenters are dismissed as non-believers at best and heretics at worst.[41]

Also, when global culture becomes synonymous with Western culture, there is a need for subordinate cultures to go back to their source of the essence of being *(Sankofa)* to search for productive elements that will bring new meanings to their lives. Indubitably, this is not the time for pessimism. Nevertheless, the nostalgia and trauma of slavery, colonialism, neo-colonialism, cultural imperialism and now globalization should always remind Africans that they have to take proactive policies to reconcile those differences between structural variables in their countries and systemic dynamics in the international arenas. In a similar vein, Booker and Minter document the inequalities in today's global village as part and parcel of the "foundation of the old inequalities of slavery and colonialism.... Like apartheid in South Africa, global apartheid entrenches great disparities in wealth, living conditions, life expectancy and access to government institutions with effective power"[42] Globalization is not a panacea to most of Africa's problems, as the winners of the global movement would like to make the world believe. Africans should be careful in participating in a movement that champions the style of globalization that is blind to the needs of the majority of the members of the global village. If this present process of globalization continues into the next twenty-five years, African nation states are likely to be permanently reinscribed in a position of subjugation, exploitation, marginalization and life-threatening status that is mystified by Western rationalization of a free market and equal benefits for all members of the global village.

In this perspective, number eight of the Millennium Development Goal to develop partnership for development should be seriously revisited. The G20 nation states that control most of the global village must be held accountable for the promises they made at the London, England summit in April 2009 to refrain from exploitative measures and to allow African countries to be true partners of the global village. African countries must be true partners in setting development goals that will take their cultures into consideration. African cultures must be realistically integrated into the Millennium Development Goals and the process of globalization through renewed emphasis on African development and the promotion of arts, indigenous dressing, and cultural festival.

Nevertheless, Africans must also take into the account deep cultural forces, how those forces affect the process of modernization, and how the processes of development is stifled because of certain cultural settings that are not conducive to the process of modernization and development. There is a plethora of evidence that African nation states are vehemently endeavoring to develop and become modern. Yet the issues and problems of the cultural divide between Africans and the West are being neglected because of global hegemonic cultures and the complacency of African nation states to start a new conversation over cultural imperialism. To be true partners in the global village, a new conversation about cultural partnerships and development must begin now.

To enable the impact of globalization to be meaningful to Africans in the global village, local cultures should be juxtaposed with global cultures through deliberate discourses and policy goals. Furthermore the values of Western cultures on African ones should be studied and analyzed constantly through institutional frameworks to determine the lethal impact of globalization on African cultures so that prudent decisions could be made about mitigating the differences. Lastly, African nation states must utilize the African Union in cooperation with the private sectors, China and governments from the West to create their own strategic plans that address their special needs and cultural preservations in order to remain as authentic players in the global village. Africans must continue to reexamine the global forces today in addition to returning to the African essence of community sustenance, reliability, and African worldview.

Bibliography

Asumah, S. N. and Johnston-Anumonwo, *Issues in Africa and the African Diaspora in the 21st Century.* Binghamton, NY: Global Publications Inc, 2001.

Birdsal, N., "Managing Inequality in the Developing World," in Griffiths, R. ed. *Annual Editions: Developing World. 01, 02.* Guilford, CT: McGraw Hill/Dushkin, 2001, 42–46.

Boas, Franz, "Museums of Ethnology and their Classification," *Science* 9 (1887): 589–592.

Chua, A. *Day of Empire: How Hyperpowers Rise to Global Dominance and Why They Fall.* New York, NY: Doubleday, 2007.

Cowen, T. "Globalization and Culture," in *Policy Forum: Cato Policy Report,* July 200, 8–16.

Booker, S. & Minter W. "Global Apartheid," in *The Nation,* July 9, 2001, 11–17.

Elliot, M. "The China Century" *Time* January 11, 2007, 1–9.

Fredland, R. *Understanding Africa: A Political Economy Perspective,* Chicago, Il: Burnham Press, 2001.

Friedman, T. "The World is Ten Years Old: The New Era of Globalization." In Kegley, C. and Wittkoft, E. *The Global Agenda: Issues and Perspectives.* New York: McGraw Hill, 2001, 297–306.

Gyekye, K. *Tradition and Modernity: Philosophical Reflections on the African Experience.* New York, NY: Oxford University Press, 1997.

Harf, J. E and Lombardi, M. O. *Taking Sides: Clashing Views on Global Issues.* New York, NY: McGraw-Hill, 2009.

Handelman, H. *The Challenges of Third World Development. Fifth Edition.* Upper Saddle River, NJ: Prentice Hall, 2009.

Held, D., McGrew, A., Goldblatt, D. and Parraton, J. in"Managing the Challenge of Globalization and Institutionalizing Cooperation Through Global Governance". In Kegley, C. and Wittkopf, E., eds. *The Global Agenda: Issues and Perspectives.* New York, NY: McGraw Hill, 2001, 134–146.

Henriot, P. Globalization: Implications for Africa, 2001. http://www.sedos.org/english/global.html.

Hyden, G. & Bratton, M. eds. *Governance and Politics in Africa.* Boulder, CO: Lynne Rienner Publishers, 1992.

Kant, I. Essay on Perpetual Peace. 1795, in Gay, P. ed. *The Enlightenment.* New York: Simon and Schuster, 1974.

Kohls, Robert, *Survival Kit for Overseas Living: For Americans Planning to Live and Work Abroad, Fourth Edition,* Yarmouth, Maine: Intercultural Press, Inc., 2001.

Levy, M. Social Patterns (Structures) and Problems of Modernization, in *Readings on Social Change.* Wilbert Moore and Robert Cooke, eds. Upper Saddle River, NJ: Prentice Hall, 1967, 180–195.

Marglin, S. A. Development as Poison: Rethinking the Western Model of Modernity, in Griffiths, R. J. Annual Edition: Developing World, New York, NY: McGraw Hill, 2010, 25–29.

Mazrui, A. "Africans and African Americans in the Changing World Trends: Globalizing the Black Experience," in Asumah, S. and Johnston-Anumonwo, I. *Issues in Africa and the African Diaspora in the 21st Century.* New York: Global Publications, Inc. 2001, 3–20.

Mwangi, W. "Who Gains and Who Loses from Globalization and Liberalization" in *EcoNews Africa,* 5. January (1996), 1–3.

Naisbits, J. *Global Paradox: The Bigger the World Economy, the More Powerful its Smallest Players.* London: Brealey. 1994.

Nester, W. *International Relations: Politics and Economics in the 21st Century.* Belmont, CA: Wordsworth, 2001.

Nordlinger, E. "Taking the state seriously," in Weiner, C. & Huntington, P. eds. *Understanding Political Development.* Boston, MA: Little Brown & Company, 1987, 353–398.

Outlaw, L. "Philosophy, Ethnicity, and Race," in Fred Lee Hord and Jonathan Scott Lee, eds. *I Am Because We Are: Readings in Black Philosophy.* Amherst, MA: University of Massachusetts Press, 1995, 304–328.

Pye, L. "Erratic State, Frustrated Society" *Foreign Affairs,* Vol. 69, No4, Fall 1990, 56–74.

Sowell, T. *Race and Culture: A Worldview.* New York: Basic Books, 1994.

Spiro, M. "Cultural Relativism and the Future of Anthropology, "in *Cultural Anthropology,* Vol. 1, No. 3. Blackwell Publishing, American Anthropological Association, Aug., 1986, 259–286.

Stewart, F. Globalization, Liberalization, and Inequality: Real Causes, Expectations, and Experience. (January 2000), http://www.findarticles.com/cf_0/m1093/1_43/59480145/print.jhtml.

Sundarum, V. "Impact of Globalization on Indian Culture." *Perspective* (2006). www.boloji.com/perspective/233.htm.

Tylor, E. *Primitive Cultures.* London: John Murray, 1871.

Trigger, Bruce. *A History of Archaeological Thought, Second Edition.* New York, NY: Cambridge University Press, 2007.

United Nations Development Program, *Human Development Report Index,* 1999.

United Nations, *United Nations Least Developed Countries Report,* 1997.

Von Glahn, G. *Law Among Nations.* New York: MacMillan Publishers, 1981.

Wederspahn, G. *Intercultural Services: A Worldwide Buyer's Guide and Sourcebook.* Houston, Texas: Gulf Publishing Company, 2000.

Williams, M. *Culture Wars: Opposing Viewpoints.* Farmington Hill, MI: Greenhaven Press, 2003.

World Bank. *World Development Report.* Washington, D.C., 1999.

World Bank. *Monitoring report 2009 factsheet,* Washington, D.C., 2009.

Young, I.M. *Justice and the politics of difference.* Princeton, New Jersey: Princeton University Press, 1990.

Chapter 9

Africanizing the West: Changing Expressions of Popular Culture among Urban Youth

Steven J. Salm

Introduction

This chapter reinforces the point that globalization is not a new phenomenon and that the spread of global cultures, even those emanating from dominant countries, must not simply be viewed as cultural imperialism. Sounds and images from around the world have had a profound influence on the development of popular culture forms throughout Africa since at least the late nineteenth century when the American Virginia Jubilee Singers and the Vaudeville team of Glass and Grant toured South Africa and Ghana respectively. Global cultural interactions accelerated after the Second World War and spurred increased exchanges of media, people, and ideas. Observers often bemoan these exchanges between the forces of globalization and the agents of popular culture—both the producers and the consumers—as hegemonic cultural imperialism of the Western world that, consciously or unconsciously, will result in the destruction of indigenous cultures. On the contrary, I argue, Africans, and especially African youth, act as cultural brokers in deciding what to accept and reject from outside cultures; deciding what can be *retained* from the past and present and what can be *obtained* for the future. In doing so, they create new cultural products by invoking processes of adoption and adaptation, selecting from the Western world that which they can utilize and discarding that which they cannot.

This chapter addresses the way in which youth in Accra, Ghana have increasingly turned away from the culture of the colonizers and toward that of the United States since the Second World War. As American films became more available, unique youth cultural expressions like *kpanlogo* began to appear in the 1950s. The first half of that decade represented a transition period when youth were forming their ideas and trying on new representational clothes such as zoot suits. The overall vibrancy of Accra nightlife varied throughout the 1950s, but by the middle of the decade, there was little to attract youth interest and they sought out new forms of cultural expression that could better meet their needs for a new and modern identity. Cinemas provided a window into American culture and youth began to model expressive styles in popular films. Although older generations and government officials often saw the increased flow of American cultural products as the cause of a general decline in youth morality and an increase in delinquency, youth viewed them as a means to express their changing worldviews within the urban milieu and as a way to distinguish themselves from the rest of the urban population.

By the early 1960s, *kpanlogo*, a unique form of music and dance, had become part of popular culture throughout Accra. Today, many see it as a traditional form of drumming and dancing that has been in existence for centuries. This, however, is far from the truth. It was created by underclass youth from the Bukom Square area of Old Accra, the central and oldest part of the city, in the late 1950s, when urban underclass youth merged aspects of American, diaspora, and African influences into a distinct popular culture genre. I have shown previously that rock 'n' roll and *kpanlogo* groups played a significant and positive role in the identity formation of Bukom youth and that this identity, very much rooted in the growing American influence of that era, also found strong foundations in more traditional forms.[1] This chapter establishes the larger turn toward American cultural forms in the early 1950s and emphasizes the creation and growth of a new class of urban youth with a very different worldview.

Colonial officials and African elites first began to acknowledge the existence of a youth class early in the post-war era. They viewed the growing youth culture (as opposed to "youth cultures") with alarm and homogenized all youth into a single class in the media and in government records.[2] They relegated urban youth to the margins, seeing them as delinquents and "hooligans" who symbolized the decay of modern life and made no positive contributions to society.[3] In general, it was less threatening for authorities and older generations to view changes in youth behavior as simply part of being young or as part of a trend of juvenile delinquency than to admit that youth had begun to assert themselves as agents in the construction of urban culture.

Youth and popular culture grew in contrast to that of the elite and older generations. The Western influences of previous generations came mainly from the colonial metropole. For many Accra residents, British culture still defined superior and sophisticated attitudes toward film, dress, music, and dance. British informed culture was set up in opposition to African culture in a modern-traditional binary. The Second World War brought new American influences to Ghanaian highlife. For some, it became the ultimate expression of Ghanaian modernity, combining aspects of local and global cultures to produce a music and dance form that fit well with the changing political environment. For others, highlife was still just that: music and dance for high classes. Some youth began to see it as too "colo", associating it with colonial culture and the new African elites. By the early 1950s, they began embracing a new set of cultural resources previously unavailable to them and attempted to create leisure space free of outside influences—free from elite and colonial control and free from older generations. Encouraged by a growing variety of cultural resources and increasing class and generational divides, the 1950s saw the immersion of youth into cliques that revolved around new styles of dress and sparked new tastes in the consumption of popular culture.

The 1950s-era youth grew up with the increasing presence of Hollywood movies and American music. The decade marked a rise in Ghanaian's acceptance of American culture and showed a sharp decline among the youth in their attitudes toward the British. The American author, Richard Wright, related his version of a 1953 conversation with a young man in Accra: "We don't like the British. I met American soldiers during the war and they were nice, sar." The young man told Wright that he wanted to become a detective by taking a correspondence course from America, a concept that he had read about in an American magazine. Wright inquired further as to why he wanted to study this profession and the young man responded: "To catch criminals, sar.... The English sar! ... It's the English who came here and fought us, took our land, our gold, and our diamonds, sar. If I could be a good detective, sar, I'd find out how they did it. I'd put them in jail, sar."[4] After his discussion with the young man, Wright stood perplexed:

> Where could I start with the boy? His view of reality was warped; it was composed of fragments of Hollywood movies and American pulp magazines and he had lived his life so far from such manufactured dreams that he was unable to tell what was plausible or implausible in them. And all of this was fed by an inflamed sense of national oppression; he felt that the least move he made to better his condition

> would be thwarted by the British who were the focal point of the organization of his hate.[5]

Despite Wright's bewilderment, those "fragments" of American culture played a significant role in the creation of new styles of dress, music, and dance. Improvements in radio and recording technology, as well as increased radio programming, brought new sounds to Accra youth and the increased presence of Western movies contributed to a growing awareness of, and an affinity for, global cultures, especially those of the United States.

Hanging around the Cinema

During the 1950s, youth flocked to Accra cinemas to see the latest Hollywood films and gain new insights into American culture. To cater to the growing numbers, new cinemas opened and by the end of 1955 there were eight cinemas in Accra. By 1958, there were 14, spurring a local entertainment writer to comment: "The rate at which cinema houses are springing up in Accra is so fast that it is not an over-statement to say that, very soon, every quarter of Accra will have its own cinema house."[6] In the mid-1950s, the average number of tickets sold each week totaled more than 42,000, representing various classes and generations of Accra society.[7] The main patrons of these cinemas were young males and the largest and youngest audiences came from over-crowded residential areas such as Bukom.[8] Some of the youth "came to escape the boredom of leisure hours with nothing to do. Some of those who came in the evenings said there was no place at home for them to sleep until the adults had gone to bed."[9] There was also a psychological attraction for young moviegoers, as a government report on youth and the cinema suggested: They "escape from their own rather monotonous lives into a world of make-believe where they can pretend to play heroic parts."[10]

Accra youth made choices about what types of films they wanted to see. They generally enjoyed films with excitement and action. The favorites of 1956 were *Superman*, *The Prisoner of Zenda*, the *Tarzan* films, and *Robin Hood*.[11] Romantic films, information films, detective stories, love stories, and most historical films attracted little attention from young moviegoers. They were generally bored by romantic films but found scenes of lovemaking amusing, and according to one onlooker, would "hoot and whistle" when they saw them.[12] Although Indian films were also growing in popularity at the time, one client recalled: "There were Indian films around but we were afraid to watch them because if we did we couldn't sleep. We were then young boys and there was too much magic in them."[13] There were also a few locally produced films, including the Gold Coast Film Unit's first feature-length film, *The Boy Kumasenu* (1952), but the majority of the shows came from the United States and rarely remained in a particular cinema for an extended stay.[14] In May 1956, for example, the Opera cinema showed seventy-three different films, sixty-eight of which were American. Of the seventy-three films, twenty-six were westerns, seventeen were musicals, and the rest consisted mainly of action films.[15]

A favorite genre of films for youth was "Cowboy" films (American westerns). These films glorified the image of cowboys killing Native Americans and the "Shot Gun Hero became their idol."[16] This was certainly not unique to Accra. In a discussion of the popularity of American westerns on the Northern Rhodesian Copperbelt in the early 1950s, Hortense Powdermaker reiterated this idea:

> The hard-fighting cowboy, moving freely on his horse in wide-open spaces, surmounting all obstacles and always winning, is indeed an attractive hero for a people intensely fearful of losing some of their wide-open spaces to Europeans, who until recently held all the power. The cowboy is white, but not European. Through identification with him, the African can fantasy [sic] unconsciously or consciously, being as white as the dominant group and always winning over them.[17]

Still, the popularity of Westerns did not have the same impact on Accra youth as it did in other parts of Africa. In Southern Africa, for example, youth enjoyed Westerns because, according to James Burns, "that was all they knew, having been fed a steady diet of Westerns since the earliest days of the cinema."[18] In Ghana, the influence of the Cowboy genre on youth was visible in Kumasi during the politically turbulent times of the mid-1950s. A reporter described how a group of youngmen displayed cowboy imagery at a political rally: "They dressed in the movie version of American cowboy costumes, black satin with white fringe, and they wore high-heeled black, Texas boots brilliantly studded with the letters NLM and the words 'King Force'."[19] At first glance, these youth would have appeared to be mimicking what they saw in films but the cowboy imagery, as Jean Allman points out, was only one ingredient in the development of a culture of resistance that combined the "old with the new."[20]

The proliferation of American movies had a profound impact on Accra youth. Wright had this to say about Ghanaian cinema: "I recalled that I'd noted many American movies being shown in the city. I'd come across the influence of Hollywood so often in the mentality of the Africans." He also remembered the physical signs of American influence, including "cheaply framed photos of Hollywood movie stars being sold on the streets."[21] The increased availability of Western movies brought images and sounds that contributed to a growing awareness of, and an affinity for, global cultures, especially that of the United

States. T.D. Baffoe, a newspaper editor, complained that, for many youth, the "life of the American films is the only kind worth living."[22] Although signs of American culture were prominent, youth acted as culture brokers, sifting through the plethora of sounds and images and selecting those they found most desirable.

Changing Modes of Dress: Zoot Suits and Youth Identity

Visible signs of American influence became more prominent as the 1950s progressed. Some groups of Accra youth first began to express outwardly their affinity for American cultural influences and against that of the elite through their styles of dress. They adopted new types of clothing that reflected their global knowledge and symbolized a rebellion against older generations and the cultural status quo. One of the most distinctive types of dress was the zoot suit, a style that came to Accra youth through its presence in films and magazines. A presentation of new attitudes by youth was underway.

In the early 1950s, the zoot culture boomed. Accra youth adopted this American-influenced fashion and its affiliated styles of music, dance, and language as a means to assert their generational image to urban dwellers. An observer described a group of young zoot suiters: "They would have nothing less than swing and jitterbug, with over-size coats flapping here and there as they caper and gesticulate. 'Good time brother,' they often remark at the end of any 'hot' piece."[23] This new youth fashion acted as a method of resistance by directly confronting and openly defying societal norms. Zoot suit wearers in Accra rebelled against the standards of culture and the subservient role established for youth by older generations and the colonial system.

During the late colonial era, the benchmarks of culture for some members of the elite remained formal British styles of dress, music, and dance. Elite culture paints a picture of the level of disparity between the classes. Robert K. Gardiner described the dress styles and cultural focus of the Ghanaian elite:

> [They wore] heavy woolen suits, tail coats and high collars and were as correctly dressed as Englishmen would be in England.... Their madams sported Victorian wardrobes complete with corsets and plumed hats. They organised local European-style cultural societies such as lodges, literary and debating clubs and held public lectures, and magic lantern shows—programmes similar to those of parish gatherings in England. There are accounts of Ladies' Clubs which imposed a fine

> on those of their members who spoke the local language or wore native dress in public.[24]

Richard Wright echoed Gardiner's sentiments on fashion but assigns these fashion statements to another group as well: "The petty bourgeois black clerks and secretaries, etc., wore heaps of woolen clothes to draw a highly visible line of social distinction between themselves and the naked, illiterate masses." A member of the former group, Wright adds, "could not afford to be seen dressed comfortably, that is, in sandals and a toga; he had to dress like the British dressed in Britain."[25] Wright emphasized, in particular, the nature of the divide in fashion between the elite and the masses, but he also exaggerated the extent of that divide, ignoring that few urban dwellers walked around naked and, rather, most could be commonly seen mixing styles of African and Western dress, as a contemporary European traveler pointed out: "Women mix the two styles freely, wearing one style one day and one the next, or wearing an African floor-length skirt with an organdie or nylon blouse from Libertys."[26]

Although generally zoot suiters of the 1950s were looked down upon by elite Ghanaians, the latter had at one time dressed in a similar manner. Augustus Bruce, a frequent contributor to *The Ghanaian*, described dress patterns by a group he called "colonial mentalists," people who saw all African things as inferior and all European things as "par excellence." These "colonial mentalists" could be identified as early as the 1920s by the tightness of their pants, often called "family pull" because they were very tight around the ankles. According to Bruce, when the breadwinner returned home from work and sat down in his chair, it was quite a scene, with "all members of his family tugging at the base of his trousers to help him undress." Late in the 1930s, baggy pants with more room around the ankles became fashionable. Now older, members of this generation were less prone to quick changes in behavior or expression than are youth. Once settled on the baggy pants, Bruce affirmed, the colonial mentalists refused to readjust their attitudes: "Now that tight pants are in vogue [again], the 'old folk' seem to be sticking like leech to baggy trousers."[27]

In the United States, Europe, and Africa, the zoot suit became associated with particular styles of leisure, as well as dance and music cultures. In the early 1940s, African American jazz musicians in the United States adopted the style and helped to spread its appeal. The most famous of these musicians was Cab Calloway who appeared in a zoot suit in *Stormy Weather* in 1943. Other racial and ethnic groups, such as Mexican Americans and whites, also wore the zoot suit as an expression of identity.[28] According to Alan Jenkins, the zoot suit was worn in London by a group of underclass youth "known as 'spivs' or 'wide boys' who lurked at street corners to offer you nylons and other goods in short supply."[29] Earlier English forms included the "Edwardian look," a style worn by "Teddy Boys" in London that included narrow pant legs and a jacket buttoned high.[30] In South Africa the zoot suit became popular in the late 1940s among the *tsotsis*, young urban "confidence men" who grew into a "well-organised counter-society of urban gangs" in the next decade. David Coplan claims that *tsotsi* was an African variation on the words zoot suit, "a symbol of urban sophistication drawn from American popular culture, with its ready money and flashy clothes."[31]

The zoot suit probably first arrived in Ghana by an individual who had traveled abroad, but the fashion became popular through its expression in films such as *Stormy Weather* and *Street with No Name*, and magazines like *Esquire* and *Ebony*.[32] The zoot suit was first mentioned in the late 1940s in Nigeria and a few years later in Ghana. A writer for *Drum* traced its appearance in the former to the arrival of Bobby Benson, a popular Nigerian musician: "This short man with a goatie beard hit town with a Coloured girl about his height and size in 1947. They brought to town a new fashion for the boys and girls—the Zoot Suit and the Cassandra hair-do."[33] By 1955, Joe Welshing, a contributor to the Accra *Sunday Mirror*, characterized the zoot as the "favourite dress of most youngmen today," and described the style worn by Ghanaian youth as "a coat of abnormal size and a pair of 'tight' pants—an incongruous mixture of the 18th century 'reach-me-down' with a 20th century *loud* American necktie."[34]

Observers believed dress to be closely related to behavior, and delinquent behavior, in turn, could be determined by the way people dressed. Zoot cultures, in general, often elicited negative opinions from other sectors of society. In the United States, for example, the zoot had multiracial appeal but highlighted generational differences. During a 1943 show in Pittsburgh, one columnist wrote that the zoot-suited crowd signaled the "revolt of callow youth against convention and authority."[35] In Ghana, too, young zoot suit wearers brought condemnation from older generations still attached to the precepts of British culture. Welshing, for example, expressed his disdain for the zoot suit: "If anything can be more grotesque or more out of keeping with 20th century civilization, it is this type of dress … an eye-sore to a decent society." Although he acknowledged that his "fore-fathers dressed in the 'Edwardian' way," Welshing wondered about the influence of the Americans:

> It is fantastic to hear our boys say they are 'going the Yankee way.' All told, our first direct contact with the Yanks was during the Second World War. These American soldiers mixed freely with our boys and girls. And our boys no doubt out of boyish fancy blindly imitated their

> slangs, dressing, and above all, their 'take-it-easy' way of life. The Yank soldier is gone leaving behind him his 'Zoot Pants.'[36]

Welshing correctly surmised that wearing the zoot had much to do with the overall changes in attitudes among these groups of Accra youth: "It seems from the way they swank about, that they feel quite big in it, more especially as it favourably catches the eye of a rather peculiar class of girls, the type who also 'go the Yank way.'"[37] Indeed, for many youth, wearing the zoot suit increased their feelings of independence and put them into the spotlight. Eliciting both positive and negative reactions, it brought them attention from all classes within Accra society. The clothes symbolized a particular style and reflected an emphasis on materialism, but they also provided an indication of youth's knowledge of, and affinity for, American popular culture forms.

Youth responded to the criticism that they received for their style of dress but they did not see it as blind imitation. Instead, they expressed their desire to "do their own thing":

> Whether the 'Zoot' is Edwardian style or Yankee style, I personally prefer it to the Georgian ones.... I cannot see the reason why those of us who choose to have our clothes cut in a particular fashion, let it be the 'Yankee' one, should be charged with phantasy. Is it because our coats are longer, our ties are brighter and the end of our trousers are not the measurement of 48 inches?

This young man closed by saying, "Some of us prefer the 'Zoot' to any other kind."[38] Another writer supplicated readers on both sides of the dress question with the simple instructions: "To the adherents of the 'Limey' fashion I say: do not look at a 'zoot' suit if the thing makes you sick. To the supporters of the 'Zoot' too I say: if the contraption tickles you, shut your eyes whenever you see a 'Limey' suit approaching."[39]

In Accra, there was no rioting by young zoot suiters as there had been in other countries, but a change in youth culture had begun. Donning the zoot was a form of rebellion against those generational and class constraints. Stuart Cosgrove saw the zoot-suited crowd in the United States as part of a "subcultural gesture that refused to concede to the manners of subservience." Shane White and Graham White saw the zoot suit itself as a form of rebellion, but "at the most basic level [it] was about youth." According to them, the suit's emergence, and the riots associated with zoot suiters, "marked the beginnings of the modern invention of 'juvenile delinquency' and of teen culture."[40] In Ghana, too, youth who began to express cultural opinions that deviated from elite ideas were considered delinquents, a common reaction by older generations to cultural expressions that they did not or could not understand.

Opposition was united, in part, because the zoot suit contrasted with the cultural strategy put forth by the new political elite. During the lead up to independence, Ghanaian leaders began to put an increased emphasis on using cultural forms such as dress to encourage the "African Personality" and develop cohesiveness within the new Ghanaian nation. Manuh Takyiwaa described the scene: "On the eve of independence VIPs dressed in *fugar* and caps and on independence day they dressed in *kente*, a sign of Asante power and nationalism, part of Nkrumah's projection of the new 'African personality.' "[41] These symbols of Asante culture did not have the same appeal to youth indigenous to the city, particularly the Ga from Old Accra, and they continued to search for other ways to express their independence from older generations, African elites, and the new class of politically active youngmen.

Changing Musical Expressions: Americanization and "Scrap Band Mania"

During the 1950s, nightlife and leisure time in Accra changed dramatically as American influences and the drive toward independence brought about new dynamics in popular culture. By 1957, there were distinct cultural scenes in Accra, including that of the elite, that of the youngmen, and that of underclass youth outside of Convention People's Party circles and without access to financial and political clout. On the surface, the cultural scene in Accra was one of great excitement during the 1950s. By 1954, according to Ioné Acquah, Accra offered "its inhabitants a full social life. Many recreational institutions cater for the varied leisure requirements of its population."[42] For underclass youth, however, many of the cultural activities that invigorated the nightlife scene were not available to them or were not desired by them. By the middle of the decade, they began to question the excitement of Accra nightlife, and by the time of independence, they moved to incorporate new types of expression into their cultural repertoire.

The increasing availability of American records and more frequent tours by American musicians influenced the attitudes of young musicians toward American culture and, hence, the development of popular music. Ghanaian musicians had shown an increased interest in American jazz music at least since the Second World War. King Bruce, for example, became attracted to American jazz, swing, and ballroom styles when he attended Achimota School during the war. After buying some of the records, he and other musicians began to incorporate some of the styles and sounds they heard on the records. King Bruce recalled listening to Louis Jordan and his "jump" music and realized almost a decade later that a band centered around singers could make inroads into the Ghanaian music scene:

> Louis Jordan was a black American musician and his records were influential when I first started working with bands in Ghana in 1950, he had records like 'Caledonia', 'You Broke Your Promise,' 'Saturday Fish Fry' and other popular jazz numbers. His was quite a small seven piece group with a front line of trumpet and C Melody saxophone which Jordan played. Up to then instrumental dexterity had been predominant amongst jazz and swing bands, but Jordan watered this down and stressed the singing.... The instrumentals only came in to provide variety, stress emphasis and to repeat choruses.[43]

When King Bruce formed the Black Beats, he and his band had yet to distinguish themselves as instrumentalists, thus the emphasis on vocal styles suited them. He remembered the contempt in which other bands in town held them at first, admitting that "We were virtually nobodies as far as instrument playing was concerned, and then we had the cheek to form a band."[44] Fortunately, for the Black Beats, they did master their instruments and their singing style became popular. By the late 1950s, it proved to be the accepted standard for highlife music. Henry Ofori, an Accra journalist and music reviewer, was impressed with their skills when he saw them in late 1956: "I heard the Black Beats at the Sea View and my conviction is that this band has got something which no band I have heard so far has. It is not easy to describe this but there is an unmistakably pleasant mellowness about the tunes they play."[45]

Although American music had slowly been making inroads in the post-war era with the influx of records, Louis Armstrong's visit to Ghana in 1956 altered the tide of musical development. From the moment he arrived, Armstrong created a stir. Ten thousand people and thirteen popular Accra bands greeted him at the airport. While in Ghana, Armstrong realized a special relationship with the region. During a concert at Achimota College, he suddenly stopped playing and said, "I'll be damned!" After some confusion, someone in the audience asked him what was wrong. He pointed to an Ewe lady who was dancing in the audience, pulled out a picture of his late mother from his wallet, and showed it to her. When the Ewe lady saw the picture, described as a "perfect match," she asked Armstrong why he had a picture of her in his wallet. Armstrong's trip culminated when a massive crowd of more than 100,000 people turned out for an afternoon concert at Black Star Square.[46]

Just as Armstrong felt a special attachment to Ghana, some Ghanaians saw in him an African American musical icon that better fit their images of modernity than did British musicians. In 1960, when a British jazz group was set to tour Ghana, Amon Akoe, a music critic for the *Sunday Mirror* expressed bewilderment:

> I don't see any reason why I should be excited over a British jazz outfit—when I have been blessed enough to see the great Louis Armstrong himself in the flesh and hear him play jazz in Accra. Louis was born where jazz was born; and he grew up with jazz. Jazz is his life. And I believe it will be sacrilege on my part to rave about any small fry when I have heard Satchmo's jazz—which is of the first water.[47]

Armstrong's presence played a role in shifting the focus of youth culture from British to American forms, as well as promoting the role of the individual in bands. Before he came, according to E.T. Mensah, Armstrong's style of jazz was not popular in Accra: "Swing was popular but Dixieland was not.... The trumpet was pitched high so that the music was light and this wasn't popular with the African audience."[48]

Satchmo's playing style had a substantial impact on the development of highlife music. Despite his praise for Louis Armstrong and his brand of jazz music, Akoe believed that Armstrong's effect on Ghanaian music was not all favorable:

> [It] did more harm than good to our music makers. He so fired their imagination with his fireworks that they began to imitate him—blindly. That was the beginning of the 'blow blow' era of our local music, when a soloist ups in the middle of a waltz for instance, and goes on purring endless intricate high-pitched phrases out of tempo and tune with the original number. It often turns out that the soloist gets entangled in his Satchmo-style ad lib—and spoils the show.[49]

In fact, the emphasis on playing solos started before Armstrong arrived, but his recordings and those of other jazz musicians may have expedited the process. In early 1955, J.O. Panford complained about the growing fascination with soloists: "Trumpets, trombones and saxophones blow sharp, shrill sounds and fanatic fans grip their tummies, jump and kick, yell and laugh, and shout and clap their hands in glee. And when the jazzmen are done with their hot, hot numbers, fans greet them: Blow, Blow, Blow."[50] Satchmo encouraged the "blow blow" style and his influence was long lasting. Armstrong brought the Dixieland style to Accra, and some of the local musicians began copying his trumpet style and singers tried to mimic his vocals. One of his standards, "Saint Louis Blues," became a popular song for E.T. Mensah's Tempos.[51]

Armstrong brought new influences into the highlife scene but some argue that he also contributed to the decline of highlife. In reality, this decline was already under way. In general, the quality of dance bands began to decline sharply even before independence. In 1956, J.H. Nketia, the eminent Ghanaian musicologist, remarked: "Innovations now take place faster, and changes are more radical than before. Our contact with Western culture has stimulated in some musicians an increased desire for adaptations and re-creation while in others the desire to imitate has been uppermost."[52] Some musicians like King Bruce incorporated outside influences to create new styles but, by the late 1950s, many bands began to imitate Western bands in what John Collins has called the era of "copyright music"—live music played as closely as possible to the original recordings of Western musicians.[53]

The quality of dance bands and live performances raised questions among urban residents as early as 1955, when many people complained about the evils of "scrap bands." Certainly, some of the resistance came from members of older generations and the elite, who regretted the demise of large orchestras playing earlier forms of highlife that resembled traditional ballroom styles. J.O Panford, for example, wrote:

> The scrap band madness has achieved one thing: The dissolution into nothingness of the light orchestras, save two. All Stars Band and City Orchestra.... Brother, let us pray for no more scrap bands. For what do we hear these days? Unmusical music and noise! ... If you ask most (if not all) of them to play you a quickstep tune ... they will invariably give you the "hey-ba-ba-re-bop" rhythm. Get me? The boogie-woogie type, I mean. And if you are an old man like me, you are sure to kiss the canvas, dancing among toughs. Ask for slow foxtrot, and you'll have blues. Yet these jazz creatures talk at their loudest, walk at their peacockest, and talk shop and music![54]

For many urban residents, the "blow blow" era, the rise of "scrap bands," and copyright music led to the decline in the overall quality and energy of the music scene. It would seem that youth, hungry for more American music, would have been the exception but there was little to attract them to Accra's nightlife. Imitations of, and even adaptations to, American music offered little consolation when the real thing was becoming more and more available on radios and records. A columnist for *Drum* magazine claimed that the press, especially Radio Ghana's "New Records program," lavished too much praise on bands: "All this flattery makes them virtually incapable of distinguishing music from noise." The changes in highlife music reflected the growing availability of global popular culture resources. It had the potential to attract lower class youth, but the continuing influx of other cultural forms carrying images and sounds of the United States intervened to move some Accra youth in a different direction.

Cultural Associations and Creativity

In the month preceding independence, young men and women flocked to the cinemas to see the spate of rock 'n' roll movies arriving in Ghana. The first, *Rock Around the Clock*, came in February 1957. This film, recognized as the first true rock and roll film, opened at the Globe Cinema. With the arrival of this film, rock 'n' roll began its ascension into the popular consciousness of Accra society. The packed cinemas for *Rock Around the Clock* prompted cinema owners to bring in a steady stream of rock 'n' roll films over the next few years.[55] When youth rushed to see the films at various Accra cinemas, they too experienced rock 'n' roll first hand. Bukom youth, in particular, were enticed by the dancing movements, dress, and language. Some of them set out to incorporate these elements into their own expressive cultures by establishing new rock 'n' roll dancing clubs such as Black Eagle and Black Star.

Rock 'n' roll swept through the Accra youth generation. By 1959, it could be found in hotels and nightclubs, on beaches and street corners, and at dances and parties. A few years later, it could also be found at Ga ceremonies such as funerals and outdoorings. While the popularity of rock 'n' roll music and dance spread throughout Accra youth society, the art and practice of performance dancing, as well as the organization of rock 'n' roll clubs, was most significant within Old Accra. Detached from the ballroom and highlife dancing that continued to play a role in the Accra music culture, and spurred on by the growing availability of new global cultural resources, youth latched onto the sounds and images of rock 'n' roll. They adapted those images as a means to establish an independent identity, separate from older generations, and as a way to express what they saw as a more progressive view of the future. In the deteriorating and increasingly isolated environs of Old Accra, youth adapted rock 'n' roll to their surroundings and hastened its transformation into a mainstream cultural phenomenon that attracted interest from all classes.

Cinema brought visual and auditory stimuli that contributed to a growing awareness of, and an affinity for, American culture. Rock 'n' roll films not only highlighted American culture in general, but rebellious youth culture in particular. They carried concrete images and sounds to which young Ghanaian men and women could relate. Youth sometimes went to the same rock 'n' roll films repeatedly and then incorporated some of these cultural traits into their own styles. They adopted a new slang to distinguish those new styles associated with rock 'n' roll from local idioms and customs. Youth began to employ words and phrases like "cool," "the hep turn," and "digging it."[56] One participant recalled: "We spoke the American slang because we loved it and American life!"[57]

The use of American slang did not first arrive with rock 'n' roll, nor was it limited to Accra alone.[58] Young Ghanaians picked up slang from American servicemen during the Second World War. Moviegoers throughout Ghana used the term "Jack" to refer to film heroes, especially those of American Westerns, throughout the post-war era. Charles Ambler shows a similar use of the term in Northern Rhodesian cinemas in the 1940s, suggesting that it may have been influenced by the actor Jack Holt. John Collins believes that, in Ghana, the name "Jack" may refer to an earlier group of "verandah boys" in the James Town and Ussher Town areas who went by the name Jack Toronto.[59] In any event, its usage moved beyond the cinema and it became a common method in central Accra of referring to friends within rock 'n' roll circles by the late 1950s. Members of rock 'n' roll clubs also adopted specific nicknames, names that most of them continued to use forty years later. They chose their names based on music they had heard or films they had seen. The names did not all represent rock 'n' roll personalities, but they were all drawn from some aspect of American popular culture, including jazz music, rock 'n' roll, and films. Andrews Kortei Attuquaye-Fio, for example, selected the nickname, Frankie Laine, from the classic western of the 1950s, *High Noon*, which included a soundtrack with a performance by his namesake. Other rock 'n' roll dancers went by the names of Count Basie, Cab Calloway, Julie London, Joe Loss, Chris Turner, Betty Coloured, Frank Sinatra, Elvis Jordan, and Leo Turner, to mention a few.

It is not uncommon for underclass urban youth to take nicknames. Living in a densely populated and overcrowded community, there were generally others in the neighborhood with the same given name, and monikers served as a means to identify individuals more easily. They also usually related to an aspect of individual identity. Ghanaian boxers and soccer players, for example, adopted nicknames such as "Bazooka," "Bukom Banku," and "Pele." Rock 'n' roll youth adopted nicknames that identified them with American culture and distinguished them as rock 'n' roll dancers. After adopting their nicknames, their original names were rarely mentioned. Chris Turner, a female dancer in Black Star, remarked: "Our real names disappeared at that time because very often our nicknames were used to address us."[60] For rock 'n' roll club members, the use of American slang and the adoption of Western names was also an attempt to portray what they perceived as a more progressive view of modern culture.

Dress was also an important identifier of individual status and membership in a particular rock 'n' roll club. Each group had a unique style of dress, sometimes consisting of a club t-shirt with its logo imprinted on the front, "dungarees" (jeans, often with a wide bell-bottom), and *cambu* (white, leather-bottom shoes) for performances, or white tennis shoes for practices and general usage. Youth modeled their style from Americans they had seen in films and magazines. Unlike (and in opposition to) the Western-style ballroom dancers who always wore black shoes, rock 'n' roll dancers usually wore white shoes when they were dancing so that people watching could see the movement of their feet without missing anything. Simpson's Book Service on Lutterodt Street, near Kyekyeku, stocked the items but they were not cheap.[61] The dancers described the dress:

> Because of our love for rock 'n' roll, we saved 3 pounds 10s, which was quite a large amount for us then, to purchase t-shirts.... Some people also changed their dress and wore shorts and 'Kennedy' socks.... We also wore boom boom shoes, which were like boxing shoes but shorter. These were the shoes we wore for dancing. The girls wore nice dresses which were short. They also wore some beautiful underwear under their skirts which became exposed when we threw them in the air and their skirts flew up.[62]

Although traditional sanctions on dress were less strict in the urban areas, gender differences were profound. There was very little public outcry about young men dressing in blue jeans and t-shirts, clothing that many people in Accra associated with rogues. The same clothing worn by young women, however, was seen as shameful and always elicited negative comments from outsiders who did not think women should wear pants, much less blue jeans. One observer was offended "by girls in tight jeans doing rock 'n' roll" and remarked: "There seems always to be a threat that something dramatic is going to happen to the seams of these pants, which have become a new craze."[63] Women donned various styles of dresses and skirts for performances, reflecting those seen in films and magazines. These outside influences were held accountable for changes in fashion among the youth. According to a contributor to the *Sunday Mirror*, "It is unfortunate that questionable attitudes towards dress are copied from film shows, foreign catalogues, and magazines.... The fact that other people's ideas are being introduced to us does not imply that we should adopt them blindly."[64] For young men and women, jeans, dresses, and t-shirts became much more than articles of clothing; they wore these items to symbolize their knowledge of Western youth culture and as a means to express this knowledge and their changing identities to society.[65]

As a result of their attitudes toward dress, their dancing styles, and their willingness to contest traditional gender norms, the behavior of young female dancers did not sit well with members of older generations who often associated such conduct with drinking and smoking. An Accra scoutmaster expressed his opinion clearly: "The behavior of some girls at dances these days is becoming unbearable. It is the habit of some girls to ask for a drink immediately after each dance. It is the function of the man to lead a girl while dancing, but it would appear that the girls now want to lead the men. This leads to some confusion." A female observer expressed a similar view: "The impression has been created that present-day girls cannot become good mothers in future, owing to the high rate of drinking and smoking."[66] The negative comments regarding young women in particular are not surprising, especially considering the age and living arrangements of many of the female dancers who still lived with their parents in Old Accra. Some of the younger women, such as Chris Turner, had to sneak away for practice: "I was under strict parentage. I had to run from my parents for the rehearsals.... [They] did not actually know what I was doing because I was with a few friends and we would sneak out after 4:00 p.m. to dance. By 6:30 p.m. we were back home." When asked if her parents would have approved of her dancing, Turner responded confidently: "No, they would not have. They associated it with ruffians."[67]

Many government officials and elders expressed their opposition to rock 'n' roll music and dance. They continued to associate it with the underbelly of society and regarded the young men and women who danced it as representative of declining moral values and increased hedonism. Rock 'n' roll dancing did not fit with the ideas of cultural nationalism put forth by the newly independent government. Nkrumah believed that economic, political, and social development would come only with accompanying cultural development. His cultural policies emphasized the "African personality," a "cluster of humanist principles which underlie the traditional African society."[68] The pursuit of culture as a political and a nationalist tool promoted a particular type of culture in Ghana, and rock 'n' roll was most definitely not part of that plan.

The aversion to rock 'n' roll from older generations was certainly not a surprise. Popular music and dance served as a focal point of generational conflict all over Africa during this era. Middle and upper-class urban Africans, those who generally have the strongest public voice, attacked contemporary popular music forms, in large part, because of their appeal amongst lower-class youth. The most salient young fans of popular music, according to John Storm Roberts, are those who garner the most animosity from older generations:

> [They are the] excessive types like the teenage fans the Zaireans call ngembo—bats—because they hang from trees to catch sight of their idols; the secondary school pupils and working-class teenagers of 1960s Lagos, whose 'beat clubs' outraged both the 'respectable' and older musicians; [and] the kids of Nakuru, Kenya, whose Saturday afternoon 'boogies' were banned in 1971.[69]

In Ghana, during the first months of 1959, reporters from the *Sunday Mirror* sought out responses from readers to the questions "Is it good? Is it a menace? Does it throw you into ecstasy? Does it do more harm than good?"[70] The responses varied, but in general, most stated that rock 'n' roll was having a negative effect on youth. While the youth saw ballroom and highlife music and dance as too "colo" and rock 'n' roll as a new, progressive movement away from colonial attitudes, others decried the lack of traditional dancing and pleaded to the government for more of these forms. The latter saw rock 'n' roll as a sign of youth moving away from traditional values. These same people often focused on the need to reclaim African culture in the face of Western onslaught:

> Cultural imperialism has fast been taking hold of the youth of Africa today. It is for us to free ourselves from the fangs of that ugly monster. Truly imperialist culture is fast dominating our own culture. In fact, the youth of Africa today are aware that twist and rock n' roll have no place in our culture. Some call themselves rock n' roll dancers and are proud of it. It is a colonial mentality we must get rid of.[71]

For youth, however, rock 'n' roll dancing did not mean the globalization of African culture nor did it represent cultural imperialism. Youth actively selected aspects of it that reflected their increasing level of independence from the generation of their parents but rock 'n' roll also represented a form of expression that allowed them to establish their own identities within the rapidly changing urban environment.

Modernizing Tradition

Throughout the 1950s, a growing sector of Accra youth latched onto the increasing availability of global cultural resources, especially those coming out of the United States. For them, such adaptations did not represent cultural imperialism; they served as a means to set themselves apart from older generations and elites and establish an identity niche of their own. On the surface, opponents looked at youth choices in films, fashion, music, and dance and saw a dismissal of traditional identity. Most youth, however, chose what they wanted to incorporate into their cultural repertoire but they also did not caste aside indigenous cultures.

Although youth maintained the rock 'n' roll clubs throughout the 1960s and into the 1970s, Bukom youth also sought out new forms of cultural expression. They did this by adapting rock 'n' roll dance steps into *kpanlogo*. This new genre of drumming and dancing incorporated elements of previous Ga drumming and dancing styles, such as *oge* and *kolomashie* and updated them to reflect changing ideas of youth identity.[72] The development of *kpanlogo* revealed the influence of imported forms, such as rock 'n' roll, as well as acculturated styles like highlife. One of its many founders, Otoo Lincoln, called *kpanlogo*, "my own form of highlife."[73] John Chernoff echoed this relationship with older styles: "The early *Kpanlogo* groups organised themselves by saying, 'Hey, let's play highlife on our drums!' Rather, *Kpanlogo* is an old beat with a new name."[74] Annie Hayes, one of the top female dancers from the Bukom area, called it "a dance that was brought from abroad," while another dancer, Fuzzy Lee, referred to it as "*kpanlogo* rock 'n' roll."[75] Although viewed by many as a traditional style today, it is evident that the originators of the *kpanlogo* style saw it as both a global and a local form.

Indeed, the dance movements of *kpanlogo* reflected the highly energized elements of rock 'n' roll dancing. Fuzzy Lee explained: "Rock 'n' roll became popular when we added the drums to it and performed it live [i.e., *kpanlogo*]."[76] The *kpanlogo* dance steps drew heavily from rock 'n' roll, especially Elvis's pelvic shakes and, later, the motions associated with Chubby Checker's "Twist." *Kpanlogo*, then, represents the Westernization of traditional culture forms and the Africanization of imported Western cultural traits. It symbolizes the modernization of tradition, the modernization of highlife, and the Africanization of rock 'n' roll, processes that resulted in the creation of a progressive genre that better suited the contemporary milieu of underclass youth culture and ideologies.

Too often, scholars discussing the trans-Atlantic flow of cultural resources do so in terms of influences flowing *out* of Africa into areas of the African diaspora where they are transformed by people searching for identity constructs to link them with the African past. However, it is equally important to recognize that the reverse process—global cultural influences carried *into* Africa—have also had a significant impact on the development of many new and different popular cultures throughout the continent. Too often we identify these outside influences as hegemonic forces of Western cultures. Too often, too, resistance to these hegemonic forces is based not on any idea of progressive change for African societies but on the question of how can "African Culture" be preserved. The problems with this are obvious, not least of which there can be no such thing as a singular definition of African culture that is resistant to change. A continent so vast and varied cannot possibly have one single culture to define itself. Imagine an African who returns home, after a visit to New Orleans and tells his friend, "All Americans eat red beans on Monday". Surely, overhearing this conversation, any American would be compelled to correct this misunderstanding clarifying that "*some* Americans eat red beans on Mondays." On a continent almost four times as big as the United States and with a vast array of cultures, classes, and generations, to portray all outside influences as hegemonic may suggest a desire to lock Africa into an idealized and mythologized past that is already exaggerated in Western forms of media and popular culture. Lastly, to suggest that all Western forms of culture entering into Africa are hegemonic removes the capacity for African agency and assigns Africans to roles as passive consumers, blindly adopting and mimicking outside cultures without thought.

Bibliography

Acquah, Ioné. *Accra Survey* (1958) revised. Accra: Ghana Universities Press, 1972.

Akyeampong, Emmanuel and Charles Ambler eds. Special edition of The *International* Journal of African Historical Studies, 35, 1 (2002).

Allman, Jean Marie. *The Quills of the Porcupine: Asante Nationalism in an Emergent Ghana*. Madison: University of Wisconsin Press, 1993.

Alvarez, Luis. "The Power of the Zoot: Race, Community, and Resistance in American Youth Culture, 1940–1945," Ph.D. diss., The University of Texas at Austin (2001).

Ambler, Charles. "Popular Films and Colonial Audiences: The Movies in Northern Rhodesia, *American Historical Review*, 106, 1 (2001), 81–105.

Brake, Michael. *Comparative Youth Culture: The Sociology of Youth Subcultures in America, Britain and Canada*. London: Routledge & Kegan Paul, 1985. In Stuart Hall and Tony Jefferson eds. *Resistance Through Rituals: Youth Subcultures in Post-War Britain*. London: Harper Collins Academic, 1976, 58–82.

Burns, James. "John Wayne on the Zambezi: Cinema, Empire, and the American Western in British Central Africa," *International Journal of African Historical Studies*, 35, 1 (2002), 103–117.

Chernoff, John Miller. "Africa Come Back: The Popular Music of West Africa." In Haydon, Geoffrey and Dennis Marks eds. *Repercussions: A Celebration of African-American Music*. London: Century Publishing, 1985, 152–178.

Chibnall, Bruce. "Whistle and Zoot: The Changing Meaning of a Suit of Clothes." *History Workshop Journal*, 20 (1985), 56–81.

Clarkson, M.L. "A Report on an Enquiry into Cinema Going among Juveniles Undertaken by the Department of Social Welfare and Community Development in Accra and Kumasi." Accra: Dept. of Social Welfare and Community Development (1954). Reprinted as "Children and the Cinema," Advance, No. 39, July (1963).

Clarkson, M.L. "Juveniles in Drinking Bars and Night Clubs: A Report on Conditions Observed in Accra, Kumasi and Takoradi." Department of Social Welfare (1955).

Collins, John. "The Young are Reviving Ghana's Music." *West Africa*, 19/26 December (1983), 2943.

Collins, John. "The Ghanaian Concert Party: African Popular Entertainment at the Cross Roads." Ph.D. diss., State University of New York at Buffalo (1994).

Collins, John. *Highlife Time*. Accra: Anansesem Publications, 1994.

Collins, John and Fleming Harrev. *King of the Black Beat*. London: Off the Records Press, 1993.

Coplan, David. *In Township Tonight! South Africa's Black City Music and Theatre*. London: Longman, 1986.

Cosgrove, Stuart. "The Zoot-Suit and Style Warfare." *History Workshop Journal*, 18 (1984), 77–78.

Department of Social Welfare and Community Development. "Report on the Enquiry into Begging and Destitution in the Gold Coast, 1954." Accra: Government Printing Dept. (1955).

Department of Social Welfare and Community Development. "Citizens in the Making: A Report on Juvenile Delinquency in the Gold Coast in 1951." In Report of the Department of Social Welfare and Community Development, 1946–1951, Accra: Government Printing Dept. (1953), 11–36.

Department of Social Welfare and Community Development. "Delinquency Services in Ghana." *Advance*, No. 39, July (1963).

Department of Social Welfare and Community Development. *Problem Children of the Gold Coast*. Accra: Government Printing Dept. (1955).

Gardiner, Robert K.A. "The Role of Educated Persons in Ghana Society." Paper presented as part of the J.B. Danquah Memorial Lecture Series, Accra, February (1970).

Gilbert, James B. *A Cycle of Outrage: America's Reaction to the Juvenile Delinquent in the 1950s*. New York: Oxford University Press, 1986.

Graebner, William. "The 'Containment' of Juvenile Delinquency: Social Engineering and American Youth Culture in the Postwar Era." *American Studies*, 27, 1 (1986), 81–97.

Graebner, William. *Coming of Age in Buffalo: Youth and Authority in the Post-war Era.* Philadelphia: Temple University Press, 1990.

Hayford, Aba. "Development and Democracy in the Mass Media: The Hero in the Media and US—A Search." Unpublished paper, IAS Legon (1981).

Hebdige, Dick. *Subcultures: The Meaning of Style.* London: Routledge, 1979.

Howe, Russell Warren. *Black Star Rising: A Journey through West Africa in Transition.* London: Herbert Jenkins, 1958.

Jenkins, Alan. *The Forties.* New York: Universe Books, 1977.

Kelley, Robin. *Race Rebels: Culture, Politics, and the Black Working Class.* New York: Free Press, 1994.

Kendrick, A. "Growing Up to Be a Nation." *New Republic,* 23 April (1956), 15–16.

Larkin, Brian. "Indian Films and Nigerian Lovers: Media and the Creation of Parallel Modernities." *Africa,* 67, 1 (1997), 406–440.

Lury, Celia. *Consumer Culture.* New Brunswick, NJ: Rutgers University Press, 1996.

Mazón, Mauricio. *The Zoot-Suit Riots: The Psychology of Symbolic Annihilation.* Austin: University of Texas Press, 1984.

Nketia, J.H. "The Gramophone and Contemporary African Music in the Gold Coast." Proceedings of the West African Institute of Social and Economic Research, Fourth Annual Conference, Ibadan (1956), 191–201.

Nkrumah, Kwame. *Consciencism.* London: Heinemann, 1964.

Ofori, Henry. "Twelve Months of Entertainment." In Moses Danquah ed. *Ghana: One Year Old.* Accra: Publicity Promotions 1958.

Pearson, Geoffrey. *Hooligans: A History of Respectable Fears.* London: Macmillan 1983.

Powdermaker, Hortense. *Copper Town, Changing Africa: The Human Situation on the Rhodesian Copperbelt.* New York: 1962.

Roberts, John Storm. "Introducing African Pop." *Africa Report,* 20, 1, Jan.–Feb. (1975), 42–45.

Salm, Steven J. "'Rain or Shine we Gonna' Rock': Dance Subcultures and Identity construction in Accra, Ghana." In Toyin Falola and Christian Jennings eds. *Sources and Methods in African History: Spoken, Written, Unearthed.* Rochester: University of Rochester Press, 2003, 361–375.

Salm, Steven J. "The 'Bukom Boys': Subcultures and Identity Transformation in Accra, Ghana." Ph.D. dissertation, University of Texas at Austin (2003).

Takyiwaa, Manuh. "Diasporas, Unities, and the Marketplace: Tracing Change in Ghanaian Fashion." *Journal of African Studies,* 16, 1 (1988), 13–20.

White, Bob W. "Modernity's Trickster: 'Dipping' and 'Throwing' in Congolese Popular Dance Music." *Research in African Literatures,* 30, 4 (1999), 156–175.

White, Shane and Graham White. *Stylin': African American Expressive Culture from Its Beginnings to the Zoot Suit.* Ithaca: Cornell University Press, 1998.

Wicke, Peter. *Rock Music: Culture, Aesthetics and Sociology.* Cambridge: Cambridge University Press, 1987.
Wright, Richard. *Black Power: A Record of Reactions in a Land of Pathos.* First pub. 1954. Westport, CT: Greenwood Press, 1974.
Zeleza, Paul Tiyambe and Cassandra Rachel Veney eds. *Leisure in Urban Africa.* Trenton, NJ: Africa World Press, 2003.

Chapter 10

The Centralization of Africa and the Intellectualization of Blackness

Toyin Falola

Introduction

Without question, the production of knowledge on race, slavery, colonization and all forms of Western domination has been one of the most critical links between Africans and African Americans. Of course, the movement of people from and to Africa provided the foundation for this mutual intellectual engagement and dialogue. The forced movement that was produced by slavery created the origins of African American identity. Voluntary migrations have followed, with substantial increases since the 1980s, creating today a large number of blacks in the United States whose ancestors had no connections whatsoever with American slavery. For over two hundred years African Americans have been going to Africa as part of a mission of permanent settlements, semi-permanent habitations, temporary visits, and heritage trips. The concept of Blacks as a race, and as a social, cultural and political group has emerged concomitantly. African and African American scholars and the academy have recognized the concept of a black community as distinctive and have thus organized scholarly research and academic courses around it.

This chapter is about how knowledge has been generated around the black community. I will be dealing with how knowledge is constituted around the black experience (epistemology), how this knowledge is gathered and presented (methodology), and how it is put to use (activism). Aspects of this knowledge constitute a political manifesto—the use of knowledge to ensure the survival of the race, its emancipation from all forms of domination, and the generation of a proud future. We can identify a history to all these issues (process of knowledge production), a focus on the historical specificity of the black experience (focalization), as well as attacks on studies around blackness (hegemonic opposition).

The insistence of our scholars (amateurs and professionals) has been to restore that which has been devalued, to elevate a continent that has been ignored, and to promote knowledge that has been suppressed or underused. The knowledge process relates to power: how the long enduring structures of domination, racism, exploitation and marginalization have defined the black experience; how the legacy of this experience shapes responses and actions in different eras; and how the psychology of Blacks has been affected by the experience, producing multiple reactions to the reality of their contemporary experience.

The famous poem written in 1930 by Countee Cullen provides a window to the crux of my discussion. To cite a few lines:

> What is Africa to me:
> Copper sun or scarlet sea,
> Jungle star or jungle track,
> Strong bronzed men, or regal black
> Women from whose loins I sprang
> When the birds of Eden sang?
> One three centuries removed
> From the scenes his fathers loved,
> Spicy grove, cinnamon tree,
> What is Africa to me?

The question, "What is Africa to me?," is both an intellectual and a practical one. With regard to the latter, we see various activities around the back-to-Africa movement whereby a number of African Americans saw emigration as an option.[1] Even to those who did not emigrate, Africa had a relevant place in their discussions, dreams, and negotiations in relation to American society. W. E. B. Du Bois, our hero for all time, all eras, tries to answer the question as a conclusion to a major essay on race:

> What is Africa to me? Once I should have answered the question simply: I should have said "fatherland" or perhaps better "motherland"....[2]

But the "fatherland" and "motherland" created, as Du Bois explains, a sense of "being a problem, that is being an American of African descent":

> The negro is a sort of seventh son, born with a veil, and gifted with second-sight, in this American world—a world which yields him no true self-consciousness, but only lets him see himself through the revelation of the other world. It is a peculiar sensation, this double-consciousness, this sense of always looking at one's self through the eyes of others, of measuring one's soul by the tape of a world that looks on it in amused contempt and pity. One ever feels his twoness—an American, a Negro; two souls, two thoughts, two unreconciled strivings; two warring ideals in one dark body, whose dogged strength alone keeps it from being torn asunder.[3]

We also see issues around identity. To be sure, we cannot talk of identity in the singular since location does affect the contents and practices of identity, but we can see the various elements in the bonding. Ronald W. Walters has articulated the persistence of identity when he closes his book on this subject:

> ... Africans in the Diaspora are not a part of the daily particularities of African history and so cannot possess the identity which flows from these experiences. However, they do share certain aspects of this history, and the basis upon which they do so is (1) their affirmation of an African heritage; (2) their participation in the Diasporic aspects of pan African political struggles; (3) their continuing concern with the status of Africa and their efforts to improve it; and (4) their relationship to other hyphenated Africans in the Diaspora.[4]

What Walters itemized above has led to many practical cultural projects and cultural affirmation, including the practice of African religions and the emergence of an African American holiday of Kwanzaa.[5] There was also the construction of the Pan-Africanist movement, an idea that sought to create a universe of black politics and consciousness with Africa as the homeland, the organizing principle to build political connections in all continents.[6]

The practical projects—whether political, economic or cultural—have been undergirded by intellectual ideas around a set of interrelated issues: the generation of knowledge (utilitarian knowledge to be sure), the building of institutions to spread knowledge, the ideology to organize the facts and opinions, and the structures to use the knowledge. Both in Africa and the United States, the intellectualization of the black experience is one of the most successful academic achievements of the twentieth century. Indeed, the practical projects have also led to vigorous debates on a variety of options to emancipate black people.

In advancing this intellectual project, Africa forms the center of discourse. This is what I mean by the centralization of Africa, which is to say that Africa—as a continent, a people, a homeland—is put at the center of how ideas have been formulated, challenged and packaged. The heritage of those whom we are dealing with is African, whether they live in New York or Dakar. The location of those who formulated the ideas does not necessarily matter as they still have to deal with this centralization, a continent constructed as their genesis. "What is Africa to me?" to go back to the poem, is a statement that looks at the past, the present, and the future framed within an enduring notion of the centralization of Africa.

The transatlantic slave trade and the European colonization of Africa resulted in the fragmentation of identities. Nationalities have multiplied so that we have Nigerians, Sudanese and Americans even if their color remains the same. However, encounters with the West, the slave trade, and the march of modernity have all created the need to talk about race. In talking about race, there is a linkage with conquest, domination, and exploitation, all of which represent a common experience for the black race. This experience has generated knowledge about blackness in Africa and its various Diasporas.

The intellectualization of blackness is very much connected with the centralization of Africa. The creation of an epistemology on blackness derives from the African experience of encounters with the Western world. Thus, most studies deal with these experiences and their consequences for those in Africa and the Western hemisphere. The analyses focus on the African/Black conditions which cover the manifestations of living, struggle, and survival. As to be expected, the humanities and social sciences provide the lead since it is much easier for them to "Africanize" the fields than those in the sciences, and also to respond to the pathologization of Africa with a set of both observable data and research, and those based on deconstructing western triumphalist and white supremacist discourses.

There is equally a strong desire on the part of African and African American scholars to conclude their discussions with a set of solutions to the challenges facing black people. Indeed, scholarship acquires relevance when it is able to articulate a set of ideas to solve specific problems. Advocacy theories become an integral part of talking about the black experience. A terminology of "activists" or "engaged scholars" has been coined to describe those who take strategic theories of change more seriously. In African studies, they are often labeled as "radicals." In the era before the fall of the Soviet Union, they could even be described as Socialists or Marxists even if they were only marginally Leftists. In the United States, many were described as communists in order to justify the encroachment on their privacy by the FBI and to silence them. Thus, we see strong connections between the history of the black experience and those who reflect on its future. Black scholars respond to the historical reality of their black experience, to longstanding issues around race and freedom. While mindful of responding to the theories and canons in their disciplines, they seek relevance in the connections which these have with the black experience, and with their own socialization within it.

Organic Intellectuals

The journey to reach our present point began not with scholars based in the universities but with community leaders, enlightened citizens, and engaged amateur analysts who generated a substantial body of knowledge to understand our race. Oral narratives developed in virtually all black communities, together with the ability to transmit them from one generation to another. Similarly, slave narratives emerged when there were facilities and opportunities to write, and they constitute a distinct genre of their own.[7] In general, the ability to read and write was converted into an opportunity to record history and to reflect on the black experience.

In the United States, many began to talk about Africa, their conditions and the necessity of overcoming their marginalization. Their location in the United States created ambiguities in identity and relevance in a highly racialized society. After the American Civil War, blacks faced a crisis of adjustment and emancipation, leading to vigorous debates on whether or not to stay in the United States. Martin Delany championed the cause of emigration, regarding it as an appropriate response to a policy of "political degradation" of the black population.[8] Frederick Douglass, the most famous intellectual of his era, was opposed to Delany's view on emigration, although not to his characterization of the brutality of the system. Thus, irrespective of the position African Americans took during the nineteenth century, the centralization of Africa was dominant—to promote a return was to talk about Africa; to oppose emigration was to talk about Africa. Liberia and Sierra Leone became tied to the expressions of faith and fate among African Americans of this era. The majority chose to stay, leading to yet another set of vigorous debates on how to seek insertion into politics and negotiate issues around citizenship. The literature on black conditions in the United States reveals profound agonies and depression.[9]

The field of history served as the pioneer, as freed blacks spoke about their past, about Africa the homeland, and about their complicated contemporary conditions. History enabled them to situate their lives and conditions within and beyond the restrictions of race and slavery so that they could talk about a past when their people were free and a future that would bring freedom.

Black narratives of the nineteenth century and scholarly writings were emphatic about the celebration of blackness and of Africa. George Washington Williams celebrated black achievements in the United States in a well-received book published in 1883.[10] Williams and his contemporaries mounted evidence to show that blacks, wherever they were in the world, were great achievers. Alexander Crummell, one of the intellectual leaders of the time, was devoted to writing about black civilization. In 1897, he provided leadership for the establishment of the American Negro Academy, which asserted a new historical interpretation on blackness.

As we entered the twentieth century, we began to see a greater formalization of black knowledge. Carter G. Woodson, now known as the "Father of Black History," created a permanent legacy in the creation of the Association for the Study of African-American Life and History. In 1915, Woodson founded the Woodson's Association for the Study of Afro-American Life and History and, a year later, the Journal of Negro History. His objectives were to save the records relating to the black experience and to announce ideas and philosophies associated with black thinkers. Going beyond the intellectual dimension, he went into public activism in 1926 when he established Black History Week (now Black History Month). Woodson and his contemporaries had to react to issues of racial segregation and the marginalization of the black experience in schools and colleges. Woodson and his associations denounced the ideas that represented the black race as primitive and degenerate. Calling for the rejection of the characterization of black people by whites, he deliberately sought to use history and culture to promote black pride.[11] Woodson's 1933 publication, *Mis-Education of the Negro*, created an enduring legacy for the totality of his ideas and scholarship.[12] This work, which is reprinted till this day, dismissed the studies and teaching of the black experience by whites as no more than an attempt at a wrong presentation and mis-definition of his people. He also dismissed the education that blacks received, saying that it was of no service to themselves and others.

W.E.B. Du Bois stands in a class of his own, and his ideas remain relevant till today. A liberal idealist with tremendous intellectual energy, his aims were to expand the democratic space and for blacks to have a share of economic power. A pan-Africanist, his ideas crossed the Atlantic through activities that energized anti-colonial leaders. The works of Du Bois and his contemporaries reveal the multiple tensions that they had to face. All recognized the relevance of Africa to their practical and intellectual projects. They rejected the academic presentations of blackness in their day, preferring instead to create new knowledge. Indeed, Du Bois almost advocated an autonomy for black scholarship by providing revolutionary interpretations of the past and sociologizing the present. In a dense historical sociology, Du Bois presented the analysis of a fundamentally unequal and grossly unjust society, how the West profited from Africa, and how colonial domination must be ended.[13]

It is difficult to capture, in such a limited space as this, the various strands and elements in the discourses on how to uplift the black race. Suffice it to say that there were significant disagreements among them, which reveals and reaffirms the notion that scholarship and politics can never be homogenous. Marcus Garvey, Du Bois, Kwame Nkrumah, Martin Luther King Jr., to mention a few examples, theorized about race issues and offered suggestions about emancipation, but they were not articulating the same positions. Labels and categorizations may exaggerate the orientations, but it is possible to see views that seek to reconcile with the system or to promote assimilation. In Africa, whether for survival or self-interest, there were those who collaborated with Europeans to make possible the conquest of their own people. And there were those who collaborated with the colonial officers to ensure the success of the colonial administration. In the United States, an accommodationist view is associated with Booker T. Washington who called for black entrepreneurship, education and industrialism, while being disengaged from politics and the aggressive violent demand for civil rights. And there were the radicals, such as Marcus Garvey, who opted for black self-determination and sought the separation of races.[14] For Garvey, Africa should be at the very center of political and economic power for Blacks. Similar views have persisted, some pronounced by Islamic groups that turn to religion to organize a cultural separation. There is a difference in strategies as well—for instance, Martin Luther King, Jr. was an advocate of non-violence ("meeting physical force with soul force") while others like Malcolm X were in support of self-defense and violence when necessary.[15] Many of the strategies and arguments about black liberation advanced by African American leaders and intellectuals have their equivalences in South Africa where Africans also had to deal with racism, apartheid and white domination.[16]

In Africa, organic intellectuals capitalized on their access to European languages and their own indigenous ones to write books, essays, almanacs and features in the newspapers. There was no topic that they did not touch upon, from origin stories to the coming of the Europeans, all in order to announce and empower their identities, open new libraries on their people and histories, and affirm cultural glories. They generated a large body of work on origins, myths, beliefs, religions, customs and various other aspects of life.[17] Anticipating the work of Diop and others, J. Africanus B. Horton saw Africa as the "nursery of science and literature" from which others borrowed.[18] Edward Wilmot Blyden was an encyclopedic figure, a major representative of nineteenth century intellectuals, writing extensively on Islam, Christianity, economy, politics, and the future of Africa.[19] His vision of a great Africa inspired a generation of other writers. Three historical works from the period—written by Samuel Johnson, Christian Reindorf and Appollo Kagwa—have endured to this day, as classics to enjoy, as texts to understand the nineteenth century, and as sources to reconstruct histories.[20]

Creative and literary minds used ideas to create and connect a black universe. There were the apostles of Negritude, notably, Aimé Césaire and Léopold Sédar Senghor, whose words, in powerful poetry, echo black pride and resistance. Césaire celebrated African cultures, extolled their virtues, and pointed attention to African contributions to the Western world.

> We, vomited from slaveships.
> We, hunted by the Calebars.
> What? Stop on our ears?
> We, sotted to death from being rolled, mocked, jeered at,
> Stifled with fog![21]

Senghor, now named as one of the "Immortals" by the Académie Française, was always pushing the frontiers of culture, with a mix of socialism, to create a new beginning for Africa.[22] Senghor enjoins us to be the bearers of a "unique message" powerful enough to create a universal civilization. A cast of highly talented creative writers were to follow (e.g., James Baldwin, C.L.R. James, etc.), creating distinguished writings that reflect a spirit of compassion and freedom, as well as a sense of urgency to fight for liberation.

The challenges that organic intellectuals faced were not those of building careers or pressuring universities to recognize their works and validate their scholarship. The challenges they faced were living in the shadows of the trans-Atlantic slave trade, colonial domination, slavery, and racism. These challenges were not imaginary ones. As individuals and as a collective, the black race has been presented as inferior, pathologically lazy, mentally deficient, criminally oriented, and obsessed with women and drinks. The ultimate goals of the organic intellectuals were to prevent the death of the past by recovering evidence and data and analyzing them; to use this evidence to liberate the mind; and to motivate their generation to seek a better future. They sincerely believed that it was possible to infuse the knowledge of Africa and the black experience into homes (to train children) and into schools (to train people). The promotion of African values would enhance the worth of Africa, provide alternative reference points for African Americans, and build pride. They were quick to reject the notion of "universality" that privileged Western knowledge, offering instead a variety of new knowledge(s). As they offered something new, they questioned the notion of objectivity in mainstream studies that spoke about Africa and its diaspora. Organic intellectuals also articulated visions of leadership, since they recognized the need to have power in order to translate knowledge into action.[23]

African Studies/Black Studies: The Academic Connections

The insertion of the black experience into the academy has advanced the agenda of organic intellectuals. Indeed, in many ways, organic intellectuals have written the prefaces to what we now do.[24] Our inheritances include their passion and enthusiasm, their epistemologies, their attention to the centrality of Africa, even their debates and differences. We have consolidated teaching and research in colleges and schools, and we have, as a community of scholars, ensured the survival of many disciplines. We have also inserted ourselves into many mainstream departments, courses and curricular. Our collective achievements since the middle of the twentieth century should be celebrated. Our failures are clear to see, but they are sources of energy rather than of despair.

African Studies came into being in many parts of Africa after the Second World War.[25] It was a propitious moment, when the continent was undergoing the process of decolonization. Thus, the creation of all Africa-related disciplines was infused with nationalism. The humanities, to take an example, became decidedly anti-colonial and succeeded in ensuring that all negative comments about Africa were corrected, that colonially-derived syllabi were jettisoned, and that condescending attitudes about blacks formed in the colonial milieu were ended. Africanists went beyond the archives of the colonial governments to tap into older sources—local, Arabic, foreign derived (such as those of explorers, missionaries, and traders)—to reinterpret the past, thereby restoring history to Africans and Africa to history. Africanists knew that they must promote a multi-disciplinary perspective and approach (which explains the interactions between the various disciplines), they must redefine the field and take initiatives (which explains the subjects on which they chose to write), and they must validate non-written sources (which explains the stress on oral traditions). If the colonialists had credited themselves for bringing about the major changes to Africa, Africanists questioned this and pointed to evidence of the iron revolution, kingship, agriculture, and other developments to point to indigenous innovations.[26] In addition, Africanists demolished the ideas of ethnocentrism, obsessive interest in so-called exotic and erotic societies, and an approach that treated societies as static.[27] Regional historiographies grew and reflected nationalist opinions. In North Africa, Maghrebian historians rejected the characterization of their people by the French as uncivilized and revealed new understanding about Islamic and pastoral lives and societies. In South Africa, revisions and corrections had to await the dismantling of apartheid in the 1990s. Before then, Blacks were regarded as disposable items, a non-population without a place in the historical record. In West and East Africa, so successful were the historical projects that nationalist schools emerged, known as Ibadan, Legon and Makarere, with regard to the kind of ideas they generated, the students they trained, and the ideological orientation (called "schools") they established. The schools are associated with the works of notables such as K. O. Dike, Jacob Ade Ajayi, Adu Boahen, and Beth Ogot.[28]

In the United States, the creation of African American Studies took place at the same time. Before and after the Second World War, the context was that of Blacks moving into cities and urbanizing themselves, the growing influence of socialist ideas, and the beginning of the Civil Rights movement. Irrespective of the label, Africana Studies, Afro-American and African Studies, Black Studies, African-American Studies, etc., they all intend a similar focus.[29] The Historically Black Colleges and Universities (HBCUs) were enthusiastic in creating courses on the black experience, as in the case of such concentrations at Fisk and Howard Universities. The spread of such concentrations came in the 1950s and began to expand further in the 1960s after the death of Dr. Martin King Jr. and the various protests and demands that followed it. Many black students became activists and demanded the creation of Black Studies programs in their colleges. White universities joined, and by the late 1990s, there were about sixty African American Studies departments and four hundred African American Studies programs. New visions began to be espoused on race relations, and it became possible to earn degrees to the Ph.D. level.

African Studies in Africa and Black Studies in the United States are united by a set of theoretical and ideological questions on approaches, methodologies and strategies. Essentially, the aim is to create a counter-discourse to what has been regarded as anti-black knowledge and school curricula. To approach African and Black Studies, many think of alternative ways to expose the brutalities and continuing dangers of slavery and racism, economic exploitation, and Western domination.[30] Also, the approach focuses on the achievements of black peoples in all aspects of civilization. The pedagogy is infused with a notion of nationalism, an orientation that links scholarship of liberation, emancipation and progress. In Africa, the knowledge generated by colonial powers was regarded as one-sided and demeaning.[31] In the United States, the knowledge generated by the mainstream on blacks is regarded as flawed.[32] There is a constant claim that hegemonic knowledge is elitist and racist. The assumptions that have guided the works of many black scholars, irrespective of their locations, are that the acquired knowledge received from traditional sources excludes the black experience, undermines the achievements of Blacks, and erases key elements in the development of a global economy that can equitably include black people. Similarly, the belief is that this knowledge is not objective simply because its methodology is flawed: it excludes black people; when it does include them, its sources are limited and badly collected; and its analysis is racist. African scholars successfully demonstrate the limitation of a discipline like anthropology in truly representing their people, and of history in distorting the African past. African American scholars make related claims, arguing that racism is not always factored into scholarly analyses and that many conclusions from the traditional disciplines merely support capitalist interests and hegemonic power.

Black scholars have had to formulate the methodologies to study the black experience. Those who pioneered the field were trained in methods that did not necessarily pay adequate attention to the black experience. The supervision of their theses was done by teachers without the requisite experience. Many had to rise to the challenges of reinventing themselves and the new Africana discipline. There is a consensus that all forms of non-written sources have to be validated and put to use. Oral traditions and oral histories became accepted as sources to counter the idea that people without written sources have no history. There is also a focus on history from below, looking at the theme of resistance, insurgency and nationalism. Sociologists have made contributions in the areas of families, poverty and inequalities.[33]

Studies on the black experience have acquired a professional intensity for over sixty years.[34] In the United States, most of the activities have taken place in the context of African American Studies programs.[35] In this arrangement, faculty can belong to different departments. Students, too, are recruited by departments and they take courses in those programs. This approach enables an interdisciplinary approach and gives students the opportunity to major in single subjects, or to double and triple major. Where universities have created departments, these tend to have survived much longer than programs. In a number of universities, resources in funding and faculty have enabled African American Studies to grow in visibility. Today, many have built successful careers in African-American Studies and have written major books.[36] Superstars have even emerged, including public intellectuals such as Molefi Asante, bell hooks, Henry Louis Gates, and Cornel West who command significant attention.

The study of Africa and the black experience remains an arena of struggle and contestation. In Africa, the concern is the difficulty of connecting many degrees to the market. Most governments discouraged degrees and research in humanities, preferring instead the sciences and technologies. In the United States, internal struggles on campuses remain a never ending problem. Recruitment of additional faculty with expertise in Black Studies can generate tensions, especially where the concerns of traditional departments clash with those of the programs. The structuring of electives is not always easy with battles over the content and relevance of courses.

The intellectual challenges offered by blackness to mainstream education have never been fully accepted. Indeed, many still question the legitimacy of the counter-discourses on the black experience. In recent years, some have called for the abolition of what they call area studies programs. Some have urged the creation of transnational history to replace courses on Africa and the African diaspora.

Africanist Perspective and Afrocentrism

The ideological underpinnings of the study of Africans and African Americans have merged in two concepts that are very similar. In Africa, the label is that of an "Africanist perspective," and in the United States that of "Afrocentrism" or "Afrocentricity." There is no consensus on the full meanings of these terms, as each scholar has imposed a different definition on them. However, there is a consensus on the mission: the promotion of ideas relating to Africa and the black experience; and the shift in the analysis of this experience from the periphery of scholarship to its very center. Irrespective of definition, the centralization of Africa in both ideologies challenges mainstream scholarship, the dominance of the West, and the mono-causal explanation of world events as solely derived from the actions and activities of one dominant race. By refusing to accept some of the established canons, both ideologies create alternative ways of looking at the black experience and historical realities.

In Africa, the African perspective is simply dealing with the reality of Western domination and how it has been used to demean its past. Historians worked hard after 1940 to question Eurocentric arguments, stereotypes and images that have invalidated African history, misconstrued its philosophy and worldview, and deformed its entire universe. They demonstrated the antiquity of Africa, dating it back to the very beginning of humankind and providing a series of creation narratives. African kingdoms were analyzed, and North Africa, most notably Egypt, was brought into the orbit of African history—hitherto, it had been disconnected and lumped with the Middle East.[37] The totality of the historiography shows the development of Africa before the encounter with the West, the destruction of the continent by the West, and the possibilities of restoration following the end of European rule.[38]

An often repeated idea is that there is a cultural basis to sustain Africa's unity and development.[39] Various aspects of culture have been isolated for discussion in a way to affirm that, irrespective of location, Africans have many things they share in common. Thus, John Mbiti analyzed the universe of African religions and philosophy, an approach that many others have duplicated.[40] William E. Abraham of Ghana attempted the same for psychology.[41] To those who seek endogenous development, they call for a return to traditional cultural foundations. This suggestion has further enhanced the centralization of Africa as there are Blacks in different parts of the world who see Africa as the source of culture, the primordial place. They point to an authentic Africa with ideas, institutions and values so pristine that they could constitute the basis of a renaissance and revival. Regarded as anti-capitalist and anti-imperialism, the belief is that Africa's humanity is so transparent and so real that it should be cultivated as a model of living. The stress on humanity is a clever way to expose all the elements that are "backward" and "primitive" in Western civilization, most especially alienation and acquisitive tendencies.

In the United States, Afrocentricity has to contend with what those in Africa deal with, but adding other issues, the most persistent being the relationship of race to the black experience. Race matters, as the title of a book by Cornel West proclaims loudly and clearly.[42] Cornel West elaborates on the consequences of a color-coded society, following a long line of writers who have exposed the logic and atavism of a racially divided society. Molefi Asante celebrates black contributions to civilization and sees ideas drawn from ancient Egypt as necessary to transform black lives and behaviors.[43] To Asante and his ever-growing number of disciples the starting point of scholarship is ancient Egypt. Borrowing from the work of his mentor, Cheikh Anta Diop, Asante accepts the claim that Egyptian civilization was created by black people. He then goes on to argue that the core ideas in Western civilization were taken from Egypt. To him, the Afro-Asiatic origins of Western civilization in religion, art, music, sciences and philosophy have been deliberately suppressed in order to deny black creativity.

Others have followed in Asante's fashion to create black authenticity in culture and other aspects of society. Many have analyzed the age-long structures of domination in order to seek freedom, emancipation and liberation. Like African scholars, African American scholars reject the scholarly attempts to marginalize black people and the organization of courses and instructions that exclude them.

Both ideologies among Africans and African Americans have utilitarian goals as well. One is where to tap the sources of intellectual power and development. To Asante, there is no need to look to the West. To him, Blacks have the resources to use as their own model. They must seek the core of the knowledge generated by Egypt, center themselves as Africans and promote indigenous religions and values in order to reclaim what they worship and honor as their own. Asante has generated a host of criticisms from several quarters, some misplaced to be sure because they are making a case for their own constituencies instead of advancing the black agenda.

Against the background of modern conflicts and wars, following the European colonization of Africa, there are those who call for a return to the politics and society of old in such places as Ethiopia and Kush. The aggressive competition for power in the modern age is contrasted with the past to highlight institutions of cohesion and stability. In painting Africa's past as permanently peaceful (in spite of contrary evidence of wars and state formation) the idea is to show the damage of the colonial encounter and the brutal legacies of European rule.

In Africa, the insertion of African history, languages and literature into all levels of the education system has been successful. This was a long-standing goal made possible by independence. In the United States, it has been a constant struggle, although significant successes have been recorded in revising World history textbooks and in introducing black-related courses even in high schools.

No race or group of people can be entirely united by a single set of beliefs. We do have black Muslims, black Christians, and black neo-traditionalists to mention a few. In addition, we have Blacks who are assimilated to Western cultures. There are multiple identities among Blacks. This diversity of blackness is also reflected in a diversity of opinions. In Africa, there are those who have accepted the identities of the imposed colonial nations and boundaries, and those who have opted for identities derived from the precolonial nations. While all these various identities still regard Africa as the basis of their cultural existence, they do not necessarily seek a complete disconnection from other cultural contents or Western influences. They do respect the creation of black constituencies and black political communities, but they do not necessarily think that borrowing from the cultures of the past, as with Egypt, is necessary. There are also those who advocate assimilation, or those who seek integration into global cultures. They do complain about the marginalization of black people and the undermining of the collective interests of Blacks, but they see no solution in a return to Africa's past. And there are black Afro-pessimists who see very little that is good or promising about the future of Africa. When we cluster all these non-Afrocentric views, it is hard to say that they hate Africa or their own race. They simply offer an integrationist model of existence, seeing Blacks as more of porridge in a melting pot. They can read about or visit Africa, but they are saying that others can do the same, that non-blacks are free to join in the discussion, that ideas of old are hard to reproduce. There are those who misread the post-independence instability, wars and conflicts in Africa to mean the failure of Africans, even to praise themselves for being descendants of slaves, now privileged African Americans.[44] As they write to celebrate themselves, they omit one compelling fact: Africa's problems, like African American problems, are located within the structures of economic and political domination.

Conclusion

African and African American scholars have traveled a long way towards creating an established intellectual foundation and practices that have elevated the scholarship of blackness and enhanced political agendas. Various new facts have been presented and published, facts that would never have been known about Africa and African Americans. These facts have been put to good use in creating new courses that reject the claims of objectivity put forth by those who have studied black issues from their own lenses. Facts and visions have combined to produce an autonomous reality about black issues connecting accurate representation of a race and its achievements with collective social and political aspirations. Within the academy, the insertion of new and different voices has facilitated the building of diversity programs, the cultivation of multidisciplinarity and multiculturalism as ideals, and the broadening of knowledge and epistemologies beyond the Eurocentric. Indeed, the totality and complexity of our contributions to the contents and orientations of education can be described as revolutionary.

We shall always face challenges, even temporary crises that can set us back. In the United States, programs are not necessarily durable. Many have been abolished. Some programs struggle with internal politics, facing the bitter attacks by traditional fields who dominate the recruitment of faculty and students. Many programs are not even allowed to hire full-time faculty. The organization of courses makes programs dependent on elective enrollments. As those enrollments fall or become harder to sustain, the programs can be eliminated or reduced.

Thus, our first task is to sustain the durability of these programs, to make their courses and roles enduring and influential. Building, sustaining and reinventing institutional structures call for hard work and maturity. We have compelling reasons to be anchored by the necessity of diversity and multiculturalism, as well as the benefits of interdisciplinary approaches to students. Perhaps, it may be wiser to convert more programs into departments since, historically, departments have endured much longer than programs. Cases of mergers and the abolition of departments have occurred, but they tend to be fewer in numbers. Departments have permanent lines and tenure power. Programs, on the other hand, rely on irregular funding, unpredictable staff funding, and the lack of a core faculty that can keep fighting.

The second task is to generate the enthusiasm of students. We must recognize that the power of the pressure by students led to the creation of many of the programs and departments in the first place. Students are the best allies in the struggle to maintain the survival and credibility of courses on Africa and the black experience. Ground is being lost in elementary, middle and high schools. In Africa, we do have a generation of students who cannot speak or use indigenous languages with any degree of competence. In the United States we have students who cannot recognize the photographs of Martin Luther King, Jr. or talk about the civil rights movement. The ideals and visions of pan-Africanists such as Marcus Garvey and Du Bois have been compromised. Instead of building connections and speaking about a pan-Africanist global vision, we are consumed with useless discussions on the tensions between African Americans and Africans. While students have a share of the blame, the bulk of the responsibility has to be transferred to parents, the society at large, and the representation of the issues in the media. In the United States, the insertion of the black experience into the curriculum is often presented as a rude intervention. When the concept of Afrocentrism left college campuses, the worry was how its possible spread to high schools would be received. Popular culture has not always played a beneficial role. In Africa, globalization has brought a variety of popular cultures that have undermined indigenous languages and knowledge.

Our third task is to seek an agenda that promotes diversity on campuses. The politics of Afrocentrism and that of multiculturalism are not the same and should not be confused. The politics of multiculturalism blend very well with the aspirations of hegemonic power and traditional disciplines. Multiculturalism has its ideas to pursue.[45] Many of us do not have problems with the ideas and ideals of multiculturalism. What is more difficult to handle is the politics of Afrocentrism since certain segments of the public and universities are frightened by rhetoric they associate with radicalism. Some even see Afrocentricity as culture and race wars, a battle that is not limited to campuses but fought in the pages of newspaper, courts and congress. Those in power seek the knowledge that reinforces power; those at the margins of power seek the knowledge for inclusion and centering. Multi-culturalism, on the other hand, is not necessarily critical of hegemonic systems. Defined in a friendly manner, multiculturalism simply offers a tool to understand others so that the rules of engagement can be more clearly controlled. We have to continue to seek the truth about ourselves, and use the truth to create a patrimony of collective interests.

Our fourth task is to return to the vision of the founding fathers of pan-Africanism which was to fuse the ideas of African and African American intellectual and political leaders into a powerful political project. The fragmentation of that vision from the 1960s has been one of the greatest mistakes made by black intellectuals. The challenge of our age is to restore this unity in order to generate strength in numbers. To be able to do this, we cannot shy away from the label of activist-scholar. Traditional departments use the notion of objectivity to take away activism from scholarship. Yet, the objectivity they claim is no more than the defense of capitalism, race domination, and Western hegemonic power. Their so-called objectivity is activist scholarship in favor of capitalism, capitalist extension, and white supremacy. Our own activism is in defense of freedom, a far nobler goal. We also have to promote a notion of community, an amalgamation of scholars and community activists, that is, the cooperation and alliance of academic and organic intellectuals. The community has to be large since I am suggesting diasporic connections between Africans in Africa, Africans in the United States, and African Americans. This is a powerful collective that is global and huge, but manageable.

Finally, irrespective of our ideological positions, we must, on a permanent and consistent basis, seek the means to harvest from our rich traditional values and histories. As we do, we shall see great wisdom in the activities and actions of our pioneers to centralize Africa, to create a diasporic network of ideas, and to come up with a global vision of responding to collective issues around racism and domination. We have discovered the past; now let us change the future.

Bibliography

Abraham, Kinfe. *Politics of Black Nationalism: From Harlem to Soweto.* Trenton, NJ: Africa World Press, 1991.

Abraham, William E. *The Mind of Africa.* Chicago: The University of Chicago Press, 1962.

Adams, Russell L. "African-American Studies and the State of the Art." In Azevedo, Mario (ed.). *Africana Studies: A Survey of Africa and the African Diaspora.* Durham, NC: Carolina Academic Press, 1998.

Adams, Russell L. "Intellectual Questions and Imperatives in the Development of Afro-American Studies." *Journal of Negro Education*, vol. 53. 3 (Summer, 1984): 210–225.

Ajala, Adekunle. *Pan-Africanism: Evolution, Progress and Prospects.* London: Andre Deutsch, 1973.

Alkalamat, Abdul et al. *Introduction to Afro-American Studies: A People's College Primer.* Chicago, IL.: Peoples College Press, 1986.

Aptheker, Herbert. *A Documentary History of the Negro People in the United States.* New York: The Citadel Press, 1951.

Aptheker, Herbert (ed.). *One Continual Cry: David Walker's Appeal, Its Setting and Its Meaning.* New York: Published for A.I.M.S. by Humanities Press, 1965.

Asante, Molefi. *Kemet, Afrocentricity and Knowledge.* Trenton, NJ: Africa World Press, 1990.

BaNikongo, Nikongo (ed.). *Leading Issues in African-American Studies.* Durham, NC: Carolina Academic Press, 1997.

Banks, William M. *Black Intellectuals: Race and Responsibility in American Life.* New York: W. W. Norton & Company, 1996.

Baraka, Amiri (ed.). *African Congress: A Documentary of the First Modern Pan-African Congress.* New York: Willaim Morrow, 1972.

Blyden, Edward Wilmot. *Christianity, Islam and the Negro Race.* London: W. B. Whittingham, 1887.

Bracey, John; Meier, August; and Rudwick, Elliot (eds.). *The Black Sociologists: The First Half Century.* Belmont, CA: The Wadsworth Publishing Co., 1971.

Campbell, James T. *Middle Passages: African American Journeys to Africa, 1787–2005.* New York: The Penguin Press, 2006.

Césaire, Aimé. "Notes on a Return to the Native Land." In *Collected Poetry.* University of California Press, 1983.

Cooper, Anna Julia. *A Voice from the South, by a Black Woman of the South.* Xenia,OH: Aldine Printing House, 1892.

Cross Jr., William E. *Shades of Black: Diversity in African-American Identity.* Philadelphia, PA: Temple University Press, 1991.

Cruse, Harold. *The Crisis of the Negro Intellectual: A Historical Analysis of the Failure of Black Leadership.* New York: Quill, 1967.

Delany, Martin. *The Condition, Elevation, Emigration, and Destiny of the Colored People of the United States.* Originally printed in Philadelphia, by the author, in 1852. A reprint with an Introduction by Toyin Falola was published by Humanity Book (New York) in 2004.

Diop, Cheikh Anta. *The African Origin of Civilization: Myth or Reality.* Westport, CT.: Lawrence Hill & Co., 1974.

Diop, Cheikh Anta. *The Cultural Unity of Black Africa.* Chicago: Third World Press, 1978.

Du Bois, W. E. B. *Dusk of Dawn: An Essay Toward an Autobiography of a Race Concept*. New York: Harcourt Brace and Co., 1940.

Du Bois, W. E. B. *The Souls of Black Folk: Essays and Sketches*. 1903; New York: Fawcett, 1961.

Du Bois, W. E. B. *The World and Africa*. International Publishers, 1975.

Equiano, Olaudah. *The Interesting Narrative of Olaudah Equiano, or Gustavus Vasa, the African*. 2 vols. London, 1789.

Esedebe, P. Olisanwuche. *Pan-Africanism: The Idea and the Movement, 1776–1963*. Washington, D.C.: Howard University Press, 1982.

Falola, Toyin. *Nationalism and African Intellectuals. Rochester:* University of Rochester Press, 2001.

Falola, Toyin (ed.). *African Historiography: Essays in Honor of J. F. Ade Ajayi*. London: Longman, 1993.

Falola, Toyin (ed.). *Dark Webs: Perspectives on Colonialism in Africa*. Durham: Carolina Academic Press, 2003.

Falola, Toyin and Jennings, Christian (eds.). *Africanizing Knowledge: African Studies Across the Disciplines* (co-edited), (New Brunswick and London: Transaction, 2002.

Falola, Toyin and Jennings, Christian (eds.). *Sources and Methods in African History: Spoken, Written, Unearthed* (co-edited). Rochester, NY: University of Rochester Press, 2002.

Foster, Francis Smith (ed.). A Brighter Coming Day: A Frances Ellen Watkins Harper Reader. New York: The Feminist Press of the City of University of New York, 1990.

Franklin, John Hope and Moss Jr., Alfred A. *From Slavery to Freedom: A History of the African Americans*. 7th edition. New York: McGraw-Hill, Inc., 1994.

Frazier, E. Franklin. *The Negro in the United States*. Rev. ed. New York: Macmillan, 1957.

Fredrickson, George M. *Black Liberation: A Comparative History of Black Ideologies in the United States and South Africa*. New York: Oxford University Press, 1995.

Hayford, J. Caseley. Gold Coast Native Institutions with Thoughts upon a Healthy Policy for the Gold Coast and Ashanti. London: Frank Cass, 1970.

Holt, Thomas. *Black Over White: Negro Political Leadership in South Carolina During Reconstruction*. Chicago: University of Illinois Press, 1979.

Horton, J. A. *West African Countries and Peoples and A Vindication of the African Race* London: W. J. Johnson, 1868.

Jewsiewicki, B. and Newbury, D. (eds.). *African Historiographies: What History for Which Africa?* Beverly Hills, CA: Sage Publications, 1986.

Johnson, Samuel. *The History of the Yorubas*. (1897).

Joseph, Peniel E. *Waiting 'Til The Midnight Hour: A Narrative History of Black Power in America*. New York: Henry Holt and Co., 2006.

Kagwa, Appollo. *The Kings of Buganda*. (1901).

Karenga, Maulana. *The African American Holiday of Kwanzaa: A Celebration of Family, Community, and Culture*. Los Angeles: University of Sankore Press, 1989.

Lewis, Rupert and Bryan, Patrick (eds.). *Garvey: His Work and Impact*. Trenton, NJ: Africa World Press, 1991.

Mbiti, John. *African Religions and Philosophy*. London: Heinemann Publishers, 1969.

McCartney, John T. *Black Power Ideologies: An Essay in African-American Political Thought*. Philadelphia: Temple University Press, 1992.

Mensah, Sarbah, *Fanti National Constitution: A Short Treatise on the Constitution and Government of the Fanti, Ashanti, and Other Akan Tribes of West Africa, Together with an Account of the Discovery of the Gold Coast by Portuguese Navigators, a Short Narration of Early English Voyages, and Study of the Rise of British Gold Coast Jurisdiction by John Mensha Sarbah*. London: William Clowes, 1906.

Norment Jr., Nathaniel (ed.). *The African American Studies Reader*. Durham, NC: Carolina Academic Press, 2001.

Oliver, R. *In the Realms of Gold: Pioneering in African History*. Madison: University of Wisconsin Press, 1997.

Reidorf, Carl. *A History of the Gold Coast and Asante*. (1895).

Richburg, Keith B. *Out of America: A Black Man Confronts Africa*. New York: Basic Books, 1997.

Robinson, Cedric J. *Black Movements in America*. New York: Routledge, 1997.

Rodney, Walter. *How Europe Underdeveloped Africa*. Washington DC: Howard University Press, 1972.

Senghor, Léopold Sédar. *The Collected Poetry*, translated and with an introduction by Melvin Dixon. Charlottesville: University Press of Virginia, 1991.

Thompson, Daniel C. *Sociology of the Black Experience*. Westport, CT: Greenwood Press, 1974.

Thompson, Mildred (ed.). *Ida B. Wells-Barnett: An Exploratory Study of an American Black Woman, 1893–1930*. Brooklyn, NY: Carlson Publishers, 1990.

Thompson, Vincent B. *Africans of the Diaspora: The Evolution of African Consciousness and Leadership in the Americas (From Slavery to the 1920s)*. Trenton, NJ: Africa World Press, 2000.

Thorpe, Earl E. *The Central Theme of Black History*. Westport, CT: Greenwood Press, 1960.

Trotman, C. James (ed.). *Multiculturalism: Roots and Realities*. Bloomington & Indianapolis: Indiana University Press, 2002.

Turner, James (ed.). *The Next Decade: Theoretical and Research Issues in African Studies: Selected Papers from the Africana Studies and Research Center's Tenth Anniversary Conference*, Ithaca, NY: Cornel University, 1984.

Turner, Nat. *Confessions of Nat Turner*. Virginia: Southampton Institute, 1831.

Walters, Ronald W. *Pan Africanism in the African Diaspora: An Analysis of Modern Afrocentric Political Movements*. Detroit: Wayne State University Press, 1993.

West, Cornel. *Race Matters*. New York: Vintage, 1994.

Williams, George Washington. *History of the Negro Race in America*. New York: G.P. Putnam's Sons, 1883).

Woodson, C. G. *The African Background Outlined*. New York: Negro University Press, 1958.

Woodson, Carter G. *The Mis-Education of the Negro*. Washington, DC: Associate Publishers, DC, 1933.

Notes

Introduction

1. Jim Hite, "Land Use Conflicts on the Urban Fringe: Causes and Potential Resolution," Paper Presented at the Strom Thurmond Institute of Clemson University, SC (1998), 2.

2. George Soros, quoted in Peter Schwab and Adamantia Polis, "Globalization's Impact on Human Rights," in A. Polis and P. Schwab, eds., *Human Rights: New Perspectives, New Realities* (Boulder, CO: Lynne Rienner, 2000) 210.

3. Peter Schwab, *Africa: A Continent Self-Destructs*,(New York: Palgrave, 2001) 123.

4. Ibid., 123–24.

5. Gary Teeple, *Globalization and the Decline of Social Reform: Into the Twenty-First Century*, 2nd Edition (Ontario: Garamond Press, 2000), 1–5.

6. Birgit Schaebler and Leif Stenberg eds., *Globalization and the Muslim World: Culture, Religion, and Modernity*, First Edition (New York: Syracuse University Press, 2004), xv–xvi.

7. Stanley Fischer, "The Challenge of Globalization in Africa," (Remarks Presented at the France-Africa Summit, Yaoundé, Cameroon, January 19, 2001), 1. Stanley Fischer held the post of First Deputy Managing Director of the International Monetary Fund.

8. Ibid., 1.

9. James L. Maruba, ed., *Globalization and Africa* (New York: Nova Science Publishers, 2008).

10. George Klay Kieh Jr., ed., *Africa and the New Globalization* (Surrey, London: Ashgate Publishers, 2008).

11. Paul Tiyambe Zeleza, *Rethinking Africa's Globalization* (Trenton, NJ: Africa World Press, 2003).

12. Pádraig Carmody, *Globalization in Africa: Re-colonization or Renaissance?* (Boulder, CO: Lynne Rienner, 2010).

13. Malinda Smith, *Globalizing Africa* (Trenton, NJ: Africa World Press, 2010).

14. Frederick Cooper, *Africa Since 1940: the Past and the Present* (Cambridge: Cambridge University Press, 2002).

15. Paul Nugent, *Africa Since Independence: A Comprehensive History* (Hampshire: Palgrave, 2004).

16. Toyin Falola, ed., *Africa, Vol. 5* (Durham, NC: Carolina Academic Press, 2003).

17. Martin Meredith, *The Fate of Africa: A History of Fifty Years of Independence* (New York: Public Affairs, 2005).

18. Howard Handelman, *Challenges of Third World Development, 6th Edition* (New York, N.Y.: Longman, 2011), 16.

Chapter 1

1. Theodore Vrettos, *Alexandria: City of the Western Mind* (New York: Free Press, 2001), 3.
2. Adda B. Bozeman, *Conflict in Africa: Concepts and Realities* (Surrey: Princeton University Press, 1976), 118–119.
3. Toyin Falola, "Intergroup Relations," in *Africa: African cultures and Societies Before 1885*, Vol. 2, Toyin Falola ed., (Durham, NC: Carolina Academic Press, 2000), 19.
4. Kieh Jr. ed., *Africa and the New Globalization.*
5. Quoted in E. W. Bovill, *The Golden Trade of the Moors: West African Kingdoms in the Fourteenth Century*, 2nd Edition (Princeton, NJ: Markus Wiener Publishers, 1995), 121.
6. Herbert S. Klein, *The Atlantic Slave Trade* (Cambridge: Cambridge University Press, 1999), 2.
7. Ibid., 8.
8. Bernard Lewis, *Race and Slavery in the Middle East* (Oxford: Oxford University Press, 1990), 51.
9. Bernard Lewis, *The Arabs in History* (Oxford: Oxford University Press, first published 1950 reprinted 1993), 92.
10. E. Harris, *The African Presence in Asia: Consequences of the East African Slave Trade* (Evanston, IL: Northwestern University Press, 1971), 112.
11. Klein, *The Atlantic Slave Trade*, 9.
12. Klein, *The Atlantic Slave Trade*, 79.
13. Walter Rodney, *How Europe Underdeveloped Africa* (Washington, D.C.: Howard University Press, 1982), 83.
14. M. John Hawkins, "The Third Troublesome Voyage ... to the Parts of Guinea, and the West Indies, in the Yeeres 1567 and 1568," in Richard Hakluyt, The Principal Navigations, Voyages, Traffiques and Discoveries of the English Nation, New York: 1928, 53–55, cited in David Northrup, ed. *The Atlantic Slave Trade* (Boston: Houghton Mifflin Company, 2002), 102–103.
15. Gustav Ungerer, "Portia and the Prince of Morocco," *Shakespeare Studies*, January 1, (2003). Online version, goliath.ecnext.com/coms2/gi_0199-3181225/Portia-and-the-Prince-of.html (accessed April 14, 2010).
16. Eric Williams, *Capitalism and Slavery* (Chapel Hill, NC: The University of North Carolina Press, 1944).
17. Franklin D. Roosevelt and Samuel I. Roseman, *The Public Papers and Addresses of Franklin D. Roosevelt*, Vol. 10 (New York: The Harper Brothers, 1950), 314.
18. J. Gus Liebenow, *African Politics: Crises and Challenges* (Bloomington, IN: Indiana University Press, 1986), 1.
19. Apollos O. Nwauwa, "The Legacies of Colonialism and the Politics of the Cold War," in Toyin Falola, ed., *Africa: Contemporary Africa*, Vol. 5 (Durham, NC: Carolina Academic Press, 2003), 18.
20. Ibid., 22.
21. Claude Ake, *A Political Economy of Africa* (Ibadan, Nigeria: Longman, 1981), 59.

22. Ibid.

23. United Nations Industrial Development Organization, *Industrialization in Africa: Principles and Guidelines for Co-operation and Development*, Second Conference of Ministers of Industries, Cairo, 1973.

24. Roshen Hendrickson elaborates more on the difficulties between African states, the IMF, and the World Bank in Chapter Two of this book.

25. Charles W. Corey, "Africa Is New Frontier of Global Economy," www.america.gov/st/econ ... /20081010111004WCyeroC0.1286432.html, October 10, 2008 (accessed April 9, 2010).

Chapter 2

1. David Held, Global Covenant: The Social Democratic Alternative to the Washington Consensus (Cambridge: Polity Press, 2004), 1.

2. For a systematic analysis of historical transformation in politics, economics and culture, see David Held, Anthony McGrew, David Goldblatt and Jonathan Perraton, Global Transformations: Politics, Economics and Culture (Stanford: Stanford University Press, 1999).

3. Figures are of Purchasing Power Parity in 2005, from the World Bank's 2008 World Development Indicators.

4. Shaohua Chen and Martin Ravallion, "The Developing World Is Poorer Than We Thought, But No Less Successful in the Fight against Poverty," Policy Research Working Paper 4703 (August 2008).

5. Peter Duignan and Lewis Gann, The United States and Africa: A History (New York: Cambridge University Press, 1984), 58–79.

6. Nathan Nunn, "The Historical Origins of Africa's Underdevelopment," Nov 8, 2007, http://www.voxeu.org/index.php?q=node/779.

7. Duignan and Gann, United States and Africa, 133–136.

8. Crawford Young, The African Colonial State in Comparative Perspective (New Haven: Yale University Press, 1994).

9. Critics such as Shatz focus on the failure of the policies, while De Walle focuses on the failure of the implementation. Sayre Shatz, "Structural Adjustment," in in George C. Bond and Nigel C. Gibson, eds., Contested Terrains and Constructed Categories: Contemporary Africa in Focus (Boulder, CO: Westview Press, 2002); Nicolas van de Walle, African Economies and the Politics of Permanent Crisis, 1979–1999 (Cambridge: Cambridge University Press, 2001).

10. International Monetary Fund, "World Economic and Financial Surveys: Regional Economic Outlook: Sub-Saharan Africa," (October 2011), httpA://www.imf.org.

11. For example, Julius E. Nyang'oro and Timothy M. Shaw, "The African State in the Global Economic Context," in *The African State at a Critical Juncture: Between Disintegration and Reconfiguration* (Boulder, CO: Lynne Rienner, 1997); "Africa and the World Economy," in Naomi Chazan, Peter Lewis, Robert Mortimer and Donald Rothchild, eds. *Politics and Society in Contemporary Africa* (Boulder, CO: Lynne Rienner, 1992).

12. Giovanni Arrighi, "The African Crisis," *New Left Review* 15 (2002).

13. Economic Commission for Africa, "Economic Report on Africa 2004: Unlocking Africa's Trade Potential," (2004), http://www.uneca.org/era2004/.

14. United Nations Conference on Trade and Development, "Economic Development in Africa: Export Performance following Trade Liberalization: Some Patterns and Policy Perspectives," (July 29, 2008), http://www.unctad.org.

15. Claire Melamed, "Briefing: Wrong Questions, Wrong Answers—Trade, Trade Talks and Africa," *African Affairs* 105/420 (2006), 451–460.

16. International Monetary Fund, "World Economic and Financial Surveys: Regional Economic Outlook: Sub-Saharan Africa," (October 2011), httpA://www.imf.org.

17. Ibid.

18. Richard Gibb, "Post-Lomé: the European Union and the South," *Third World Quarterly*, Vol. 21, No 3 (2000), 463.

19. Gorm Rye Olsen, "The European Union: 'European interests', bureaucratic interests and international options" in *Africa and the North: Between Globalization and Marginalization*, ed. Ulf Engel and Gorm Rye Olsen (New York: Routledge, 2005), 129.

20. Stephen R. Hurt, "The European Union's external relations with Africa after the Cold War: Aspects of Continuity and Change," in Ian Taylor and Paul Williams, eds. *Africa in International Politics: External Involvement on the Continent* (New York: Routledge, 2005).

21. United States Department of Commerce International Trade Administration, "U.S.-African Trade Profile," USDC Market Access and Compliance Office of Africa (July 2010).

22. United States Department of Commerce International Trade Administration, "U.S.-African Trade Profile," USDC Market Access and Compliance Office of Africa (July 2010).

23. Eckart Naumann, "AGOA at nine: some reflections on the Act's impact on Africa-US trade," January 2009, http://www.agoa.info/?view=about&story=details.

24. Melamed, "Briefing: Wrong Questions, Wrong Answers," 457.

25. "Cotton Producers celebrate WTO ruling against US subsidies," www.irinnews.org, October 16, 2007.

26. Martin Khor, "Trade: Africans played pivotal role at turning point of WTO talks," *Third World Network Info Service on Trade and WTO Issues* (Aug 08/06), http://www.twnside.org.sg/title2/wto.info/twninfo20080806.htm.

27. Melamed, "Briefing: Wrong Questions, Wrong Answers," 457.

28. Katherine Vyborny, "What Could the Doha Round Mean for Africa?" *Carnegie Endowment for International Peace* Web Commentary, June 12, 2007, http://www.carnegieendowment.org/files/vyborny_wc1.pdf.

29. ECA, 2004.

30. A.U. Santos-Paulino and A.P. Thirlwall, "The Effects of trade liberalization on imports in selected developing countries" *The Economic Journal* 114 (2004).

31. For example, Melamed, "Briefing: Wrong Questions, Wrong Answers," 458; the International Trade Union Confederation; Oxfam International.

32. Corinne Delechat, Arto Kovanen, and John Wakeman-Linn, "Sub-Saharan Africa: Private Capital Fueling Growth" *IMF Survey Magazine*, (May 22, 2008), http://www.imf.org.

33. United States Department of Commerce International Trade Administration, "U.S.-African Trade Profile," USDC Market Access and Compliance Office of Africa (March 2003).

34. United States Department of Commerce International Trade Administration, "U.S.-African Trade Profile," USDC Market Access and Compliance Office of Africa (July 2009).

35. United Nations Conference on Trade and Development. "World Investment Report 2011." http://www.unctad.org.

36. IMF, 2008, 6.

37. Dilip Ratha, Sanket Mohapatra and Zhimei Xu1, "Outlook for Remittance Flows 2008–2010: Growth expected to moderate significantly, but flows to remain resilient," *Migration and Development Brief* 8 (The world Bank, November 11, 2008), http://siteresources.worldbank.org/INTPROSPECTS/Resources/334934-1110315015165/MD_Brief8.pdf.

38. Todd Moss, *Adventure Capitalism: Globalization and the Political Economy of Stock Markets in Africa* (New York: Palgrave Macmillan, 2003), 22.

39. Percy S. Mistry, "Reasons for Sub-Saharan Africa's Development Deficit that the Commission for Africa Did Not Consider" African Affairs, 104/417 (2005)

40. Eric Helleiner, *States and the Reemergence of Global Finance: From Bretton Woods to the 1990s* (Ithaca: Cornell University Press, 1994).

41. Caroline Thomas, "The International Financial Institutions' relations with Africa: Insights from the issue of representation and voice," in *African in International Politics: external involvement on the continent,* ed. Ian Taylor and Paul Williams (New York: Routledge, 2005).

42. Thomas M. Callaghy, "Networks and governance in Africa: innovation in the debt regime" in *Intervention and transnationalism in Africa: global-local networks of* power, ed. Thomas M. Callaghy, Robert Latham, Ronald Kassimir (Cambridge, 2001), 122.

43. Ibid.

44. USTR, 2008, 35

45. Ibid.

46. Moyo Dambisa, "Why Foreign Aid Is Hurting Africa," *Wall Street Journal*, April 16, 2009.

47. United Nations, "Millennium Development Goal 8: Delivering on Global Partnership for Achieving the Millennium Development Goals" MDG Gap Task Force Report 2008, http://www.un.org/esa/policy/mdggap/mdg8report_engw.pdf.

48. Carol Lancaster and Ann Van Dusen, *Organizing U.S. Foreign Aid: Confronting the Challenges of the Twenty-first Century* (Washington D.C.: Brookings, 2005), 10–13.

49. UN, 2008.

50. DATA, "The DATA Report 2009: Monitoring the G8 Promise to Africa Executive Summary," http://www.one.org/international/datareport2009/.

51. Jeffrey Sachs, *The End of Poverty: Economic Possibilities for Our Time* (Penguin, 2006).

52. William Easterly, *The White Man's Burden: Why the West's Efforts to Aid the Rest Have Done so Much Ill and So Little Good* (Penguin, 2007).

53. Douglas Rimmer, "Learning About Economic Development From Africa," *African Affairs* 102 (2003), 469–491.

54. Dambisa Moyo, *Dead Aid: Why Aid is Not Working and How There is a better way for Africa* (New York: Farrar, Straus and Giroux, 2009).

55. Paul Kagame, "Africa has to find its own road to prosperity," *Financial Times*, May 7, 2009.

56. Firoze Manji and Carl O'Coill, "The missionary position: NGOs and development in Africa," *International Affairs* 78 3 (2002) 567–83.

57. Rasna Warah, "The Development Myth," May 12, 2009, http://www.zmag.org/znet/viewArticle/21438.

58. OECD, "Private Equity: An Eye for Investment under African Skies?" *Policy Insights* #60 (April 2008), www.oecd.org/dev/insights.

59. Moss, 2003; Kathryn C. Lavelle, "Architecture of Equity Markets: The Abidjan Regional Bourse," *International Organization* 55,3 (Summer 2001).

60. ECA, 2008

61. Robert Wade, "Choking the South," *New Left Review* 38 (2006).

62. "Investors' enthusiasm grows for the new frontiers," *Financial Times,* November 20, 2007; "In for the long haul? Why a boom is under way in emerging markets," *Financial Times,* October 18, 2007.

63. Ernest Harsch, "Africa braces for global shockwaves," *Africa Renewal* 22 4 (2009). http://www.un.org/ecosocdev/geninfo/afrec/vol22no4/224-shockwaves.html.

64. Helmut Reisen, "The Fallout form the Financial Crisis: Emerging Markets under Stress," *Policy Insights* #83 (December 2008), www.oecd.org/dev/insights.

65. Harsch, 2009.

66. International Monetary Fund, "World Economic and Financial Surveys: Regional Economic Outlook: Sub-Saharan Africa," (October 2011), httpA://www.imf.org.

67. "Accra Declaration," July 2007. http://www.pambazuka.org/aumonitor/images/uploads/ACCRAJuly2007AUSummitDECLARATION.pdf.

68. "Civil Society Gains Strength at African Union ECOSOCC Meeting," Africafiles, 9-10-2008, http://www.africafiles.org/article.asp?ID=18975.

69. "Africa: Trade Unions Speak Out on Trade," *AfricaFocus Bulletin* (070317), Mar 17, 2007 www.AfricaFocus.org.

70. Pharmaceutical and biomedical issues are discussed in more detail in Chapter 7 of this book.

71. Oxfam, "Oxfam Celebrates Win-Win Outcome for Ethiopian Coffee Farmers and Starbucks," June 20, 2007, www.oxfam.org.

72. Michael Barratt Brown, "'Fair Trade' with Africa," *Review of African Political Economy* 112 (2007), 267–277.

73. E. Osei Kwadwo Prempeh, *Against Global Capitalism: African Social Movements Confront Neoliberal Globalization* (Surrey: Ashgate, 2006), 91–105; Patrick Bond, "Strategies for Social Movements from Southern Africa to the United States" *Foreign Policy in Focus,* (January 20, 2005).

74. Bretton Woods Project, "Civil Society letter on IMF review of lending instruments, facilities and policies," September 30, 2008, www.brettonwoodsproject.org.

75. Thomas, "The International Financial Institutions' Relations with Africa," 180.

76. Claude Ake, *Democracy and Development in Africa* (Washington D.C: Brookings, 1996).

77. Claude Ake, *Democracy and Development in Africa* (Washington D.C: Brookings, 1996).

78. Alliance for a Green Revolution in Africa, "Concrete Actions to Accelerate Africa's Green Revolution," Sept 7, 2010, http://allafrica.com/stories/201009120003.html.

79. Richard Jonasse, "Africans Face Competing Visions of Agricultural Development at a Critical Juncture," May 20, 2010, www.foodfirst.org.

Chapter 3

1. See H. Jon Rosenbaum and William G. Tyler, "South-South Relations: The Economic and Political Content of Interactions among Developing Countries," *International Organization,* 29, 1 (1975) 243–274; and Yves Sabolo, "Trade between Developing Countries, Technology Transfers and Employment," *International Labor Review,* vol. 122, no.5 (1983).

2. See Wiswa Warnapala, "Bandung Conference of 1955 and the Resurgence of Asia and Africa" in *Daily News,* Sri Lanka (1955 [2005]) http://www.dailynews.lk/2005/04/21/fea01.htm.

3. See Jerker Hellström, "China's Emerging Role in Africa: A Strategic Overview," *FOI Studies in African Security* (2009) www.foi.security/africa; and Nazli Choucri, "The Nonalignment of Afro-Asian States: Policy, Perception, and Behavior," *Canadian Journal of Political Science*, Vol. 2, No. 1 (1969) 1–17.

4. See Hamilton Russell Cowie, *Australia and Asia: A Changing Relationship* (South Melbourne: Thomas Nelson, 1993).

5. Fidel Castro, speech to UN as NAM Chairman, October 12, 1979.

6. See Cedric Grant, "Equity in Third World Relations: A Third World Perspective," *International Affairs*, vol. 71, no. 3 (1995) 567–587.

7. See http://www.unctad.org/.

8. See http://www.g77.org/doc/index.html#aim.

9. Jarle Møen, "Trade and Development: Is South-South Co-operation a Feasible Strategy?" *Forum for Development Studies*, 2 (1998) 245–270.

10. Ibid.

11. Ibid., 252.

12. Adam Sneyd, "South Commission/South Center." Globalization and Autonomy Online Compendium, 2005. http://www.globalautonomy.ca/global1/glossary_entry.jsp?id=OR.0045.

13. South Commission, *The Challenge to the South* (Oxford: Oxford University Press, 1990).

14. Adam Sneyd, "South Commission/South Center," Globalization and Autonomy Online Compendium (2005) http://www.globalautonomy.ca/global1/glossary_entry.jsp?id=OR.0045.

15. Ibid.

16. Gumisai Mutume, "Africa Opposes New Round of Trade Talks," Africa Recovery, United Nations, vol. 15, no. 3 (2001)

17. Quoted in ibid., 7.

18. Ibid.

19. Carlos G. Aguilar, "South-South Relations in the New International Geopolitics," *Global Studies Review*, vol. 6, no. 3 (2010).

20. Gumisai Mutume, "Hope Seen in the Ashes of Cancún: WTO trade talks collapse, as Africa and allies stand firm," *Africa Recovery*, Vol. 17, 3 (2003) 7.

21. Global Envision, "South-South Cooperation Defies the North," (2006) http://www.globalenvision.org/library/3/1371.

22. See Ibid., Møen, "Trade and Development: Is South-South Co-operation a Feasible Strategy?," 252–53, and Sabolo, "Trade between Developing Countries, Technology Transfers and Employment."

23. UNCTAD, "The New Geography of International Economic Relations," Background Paper No.1, Doha High Level Forum for Trade and Investment (December 5–6, 2004).

24. Ibid., 1.

25. Ibid., Global Envision; and Oscar Agliatello, "Is South-South Trade the Answer to Bringing the Poor into the Export Process?" in *International Trade Centre Executive Forum*, Berlin (Sept. 27–30, 2006).

26. UNCTAD, "The New Geography of International Economic Relations," 2.

27. United Nations, *Africa's Cooperation with New and Emerging Development Partners: Options for Africa's Development* (New York: Office of the Special Advisor on Africa, 2010), 5.

28. Ibid., 6.

29. Trade Law Center of Southern Africa, "African Trading Relationship with Brazil," (2007), http://www.tralac.org/unique/tralac/pdf/20071023.

30. Trade Law Center of Southern Africa. "African Trading Relationship with India," (2007) http://www.tralac.org/cgi-bin/giga.cgi?cmd=cause_dir_news&cat=1044&cause_id=1694#india.

31. See *The Standard*, Nairobi, December 9, 2010.

32. Jian-Ye Wang and Abdoulaye Bio-Tchané, "Africa's Burgeoning Ties with China," *Finance and Development*, Quarterly Magazine of the IMF, vol. 45, no. 1 (2008) 44–47.

33. Ibid., 44.

34. Ibid., 44.

35. Denis M. Tull, "China's Engagement in Africa: Scope, Significance and Consequences," *Journal of Modern African Studies*, vol. 44, no. 33 (2006) 463.

36. Wang and Bio-Tchané, "Africa's Burgeoning Ties with China," 45.

37. Tull, "China's Engagement in Africa: Scope, Significance and Consequences," 463.

38. Ibid., 463.

39. Leslie Feinberg, "China Cancels Africa's Debt" (2005) http://www.odiousdebts.org/odiousdebts/index.cfm?DSP=content&ContentID=9341.

40. Ibid.

41. Tull, "China's Engagement in Africa," *China Daily*, November 26, 2004.

42. Global Envision, "South-South Cooperation Defies the North."

43. Aguilar, "South-South Relations in the New International Geopolitics."

44. Ibid.

45. See *The Economist*. "Africa is One of the World's Fastest-Growing Regions" (January 6, 2011) http://www.economist.com/node/17853324.

46. Ibid.

Chapter 4

1. Eric M. Edi, *Globalization and Politics in the Economic Community of West African States* (Durham, NC: Carolina Academic Press, 2007), 49–51.

2. Edi, *Globalization and Politics in the Economic Community of West African States*, 52.

3. George Klay Kieh, Jr., "The New Globalization: Scope, Nature and Dimensions," in George Klay Kieh, Jr., (ed.), *Africa and the New Globalization* (Surrey, England: Ashgate Publishing Limited, 2009), 13.

4. Ali A. Mazrui, "Numerical Strength and Nuclear Status in the Politics of the Third World," in Seifudein Adem and Abdul S. Bemath, (eds.), *The Politics of War and the Culture of Violence: North-South-Essays by Ali A. Mazrui* (Trenton, NJ: Africa World Press, Inc., 2008), 181–83.

5. George Klay Kieh, Jr., "Introduction: From The Old to the New Globalization," in Kieh, Jr., (ed.), *Africa and the New Globalization*, 4. See also Jeffrey Herbst, "Africa and the Challenge of Globalization," Paper Presented at the Conference on Globalization and Economic Success: Policy Options for Africa," (Singapore, November 7–8, 2005), 1.

6. Erik Gilbert and Jonathan T. Reynolds, *Africa in World History: From Prehistory to the Present* (Upper Saddle River, NJ: Pearson Education, Inc., 2004), 167.

7. See A. Adu Boahen, *African Perspectives on Colonialism* (Baltimore, MD: The Johns Hopkins University Press, 1987), 34–57.

8. Jeffrey S. Lantis, "Weapons Proliferation and Conflict," in Michael T. Snarr and D. Neil Snarr, (eds.), *Introducing Global Issues*, Fourth Edition (Boulder, Co.: Lynne Rienner Publishers, 2008), 15–18.

9. I. William Zartman, *Ripe for Resolution: Conflict and Intervention in Africa* (New York, Oxford: Oxford University Press, 1985), 15.
10. Olatunde J. C. B. Ojo; D. K. Orwa; C. M. B. Utete, *African International Relations* (London, New York, Lagos: Longman Group Ltd., 1985), 137.
11. Ojo et al, *African International Relations*, 138.
12. Ali A. Mazrui, "The Barrel of the Gun and the Barrel of Oil in North-South Equation," in Seifudein Adem and Abdul S. Bemath, (eds.), *The Politics of War and the Culture of Violence*, 219.
13. Kieh, Jr., "Introduction: From The Old to the New Globalization," 24.
14. Edi, "Globalization and Politics in the Economic Community of West African States," 51.
15. Edi, *Globalization and Politics in the Economic Community of West African States*, 51–2.
16. Ojo et al, *African International Relations*, 130–31.
17. Ibid., 131.
18. Ojo et al, *African International Relations*, 131–2.
19. Ibid., 132.
20. Ojo et al, *African International Relations*, 136.
21. Richard Joseph, "Democratization in Africa after 1989: Comparative and Theoretical Perspectives," in *Comparative Politics*, Vol. 29, No. 3, *Transitions to Democracy: A Special Issue in Memory of Dankwart A.* Rustow, (April 1997), 365–372.
22. Peter Schwab, *Africa: A Continent Self-Destructs* (New York: Palgrave, 2001), 41–44.
23. Schwab, *Africa: A Continent Self-Destructs*, 37.
24. Ibid., 37–38.
25. Ibid., 38–39.
26. Judy Duncker, "Globalization and Its Impact on the War on Terror," in John Davis (ed.), *Africa and the War on Terrorism* (Burlington, VT: Ashgate Publishing Company, 2007), 66.
27. Ibid., 66–7.
28. Ibid., 63.
29. Ibid., 63–4.
30. Ibid., 63 and 75.
31. Ibid., 64.
32. Ali A. Mazrui, "Between Global Governance and Global War: Africa before and after September 11," in Seifudein Adem and Abdul S. Bemath, (eds.), *The Politics of War and the Culture of Violence*, 269–70.
33. Simon Katzenellenbogen, "It Didn't Happen at Berlin: Politics, Economics and Ignorance in the Setting of Africa's Colonial Boundaries," in Paul Nugent and A. I. Asiwaju, (eds.), *African Boundaries: Barriers, Conduits and Opportunities* (Edinburgh: Center of African Studies, University of Edinburgh, 1996), 21.
34. John Reader, *Africa: A Biography of the Continent* (New York: Alfred A. Knopf, Inc., 1997), 575.
35. Quoted in Paul Nugent and A. I. Asiwaju, "The Paradox of African Boundaries," in Paul Nugent and A. I. Asiwaju, (eds.), *African Boundaries: Barriers, Conduits and Opportunities* (Edinburgh: Center of African Studies, University of Edinburgh, 1996), 2.
36. Reader, *Africa: A Biography of the Continent*, 569, 575, and 576.
37. Paul Nugent, "Arbitrary Lines and the People's Minds: A Dissenting View on Colonial Boundaries in West Africa," in Paul Nugent and A. I. Asiwaju, (eds.), *African Boundaries: Barriers, Conduits and Opportunities*, 35.

38. Ieuan Griffiths, "Permeable Boundaries in Africa," in Paul Nugent and A. I. Asiwaju, (eds.), *African Boundaries: Barriers, Conduits and Opportunities*, 76.

39. Ojo et al, *African International Relations*, 137. Also see Emmanuel M. Mbah, *Land/Boundary Conflict in Africa: The Case of Former British Colonial Bamenda, Present-Day North-West Province of the Republic of Cameroon, 1916–1996* (Lewiston: The Edwin Mellen Press, 2008), 44–51.

40. Anthony Allot, "Boundaries and the Law in Africa," in Carl Gosta Widstrand, (ed.), *African Boundary Problems* (Uppsala: Scandinavian Institute of African Studies, 1969), 18.

41. Jos van Beurden, "Eritrea vs Ethiopia: A Devastating War Between Former Friends," in Mekenkamp, et al (eds.), *Searching for Peace in Africa: An Overview of Conflict Prevention and Management Activities* (Utrecht, the Netherlands: European Platform for Conflict Prevention and Transformation, 1999), 132–134.

42. Beurden, "Eritrea vs Ethiopia," 134.

43. Ibid., 134.

44. Schwab, *Africa: A Continent Self-Destructs*, 46. See this source for a brief but vivid discussion on the history of both countries before 1997.

45. Bolande Akande Adetoun, "The role and function of research in a divided society: A case study of the Niger-Delta region of Nigeria," in Elizabeth Porter, Gillian Robinson, Marie Smyth, Albrecht Schnabel and Eghosa Osaghae (eds.), *Researching Conflict in Africa: Insights and Experiences* (New York: United Nations University Press, 2005), 47–49.

46. Schwab, *Africa: A Continent Self-Destructs*, 120–21. The chaos in Zimbabwe has also resulted in a decline in tourism both for Zimbabwe and its neighbors such as the Republic of South Africa, but especially Botswana where it has been partly responsible for a slow-down in Gross Domestic Product, and in Malawi where it has resulted in a decline in both import and export trade.

47. Ibid., 122. The same applies to Nigeria where despite internal disputes and those against western oil corporations, capital has continued to be invested for drilling.

Chapter 5

1. NGOs are sometimes known as non-profit or private voluntary or charity or philanthropic organizations or holistically as the Third Sector, the first sector being the governments and the private sector being the second. Civil societies are grassroots groups that largely depend on mass mobilization and voluntarism for their operations. They are usually interested in improving the lives of people, and operate in political, social, economic, cultural and environmental realms. They engage in provision of services or protection of their environment. Some civil societies engage in lobbying or advocacy work, while others engage in activism. Community-based organizations (CBOs) are the best examples of civil societies or organizations or associations. For more information on typologies see Maurice Amutabi, *The NGO Factor in Africa: The Case of Arrested Development in Kenya* (New York/London: 2006).

2. Under public service contracting, NGOs are given funds by donors to implement development projects in the South; these are functions previously performed by Southern governments and private companies. This is increasingly becoming popular in the South. Through this process, NGOs often compete for tenders with private companies and government ministries to supervise development projects or provide consultancy services.

3. In some of the interviews, I do not use real names of my informants and respondents. This is to protect their identity. However, I provide real names of informants and respondents who did not request that their identity not be disclosed and who assured me that they would not suffer in anyway if their identity were known.

4. Judith Tendler, *Turning Private Voluntary Organizations into Development Agencies: Questions for Evaluation,* AID Program Evaluation Discussion Paper No. 12. Washington DC: USAID, 1982.

5. Robert Jackson and Carl G. Rosberg, "Why Africa's Weak States Persist: The Empirical and the Juridical in Statehood," *World Politics* 35 (1): 1–24, 1982; and Joel Migdal, *Strong Societies and Weak States: State-Society Relations and State Capabilities in the Third World*, Princeton (Princeton, N.J.: Princeton University Press, 1988). See also Robert Jackson and Carl Rosberg, *Personal Rule in Black Africa: Prince, Autocrat, Tyrant* (Berkeley: University of California Press, 1982) and Joel Migdal, *Strong Societies and Weak States: State-Society Relations and State Capabilities in the Third World* (Princeton, N.J.: Princeton University Press, 1988).

6. See Dambisa Moyo, *Dead Aid: Why Aid Is Not Working and How There Is a Better Way for Africa* (London; Allen Lane: Penguin Books, 2009).

7. See Samir Amin, *Accumulation on a World Scale* (New York: Monthly Review Press, 1974); Samir Amin, *Unequal Development: An Essay on the Social Formations of Peripheral Capitalism* (New York: Monthly Review Press, 1976); Immanuel Wallerstein, "Dependence in an Interdependent World." *African Studies Review* 17 (April 1974): 1–26; Andre Gunder Frank, "The Development of Underdevelopment." Monthly Review, 18 (September 1966): 17–31; Andre Gunder Frank, *Capitalism and Underdevelopment in Latin America: Historical Studies of Chile and Brazil* (New York: Monthly Review Press, 1969); Andre Gunder Frank, *Latin America: Underdevelopment or Revolution* (New York: Monthly Review Press, 1969); Walter Rodney, *How Europe Underdeveloped Africa* (Washington DC: Howard University Press, 1980); and Kema Irogbe, "Globalization and the Development of Underdevelopment of the Third World," *Journal of Third World Studies,* Spring (2005), Vol. 22 Issue 1, 41–68.

8. See John Clark, *Democratizing Development: The Role of Voluntary Organizations* (London: Earthscan Publications, 1991); John Clark, *The State and the Voluntary Sector,* Human Resources and Operations Policy Working Paper No. 12. Washington: World Bank, October (1993); David Hulme and Michael Edwards (eds), *Making a Difference? NGOs and Development in a Changing World* (London: Earthscan, 1992); Rajesh Tandon, *The Relationship between NGOs and Government.* Mimeo paper presented to the Conference on the Promotion of Autonomous Development. New Delhi: PRIA, 1987; Rajesh Tandon, *NGO Government Relations: A Source of Life or a Kiss of Death* (New Delhi, India: Society for Participatory Research in Asia, 1991); Rajesh Tandon, *NGOs and Civil Society* (Boston: Institute for Development Research, 1992); and Yash Tandon, "Foreign NGOs, Uses and Abuses: An African Perspective." In *IFDA Dossier* 81, April/June (1992).

9. The twentieth century saw five major famines in Kenya, in 1913–1914, 1943–1945, 1968–1974, 1982–1984 and 1994–1998. Drought, the prolonged absence of rain, is a recurring feature in northern Kenya. Famine is however, a severe economic, political and social dislocation when people do not have adequate food and face massive starvation. While drought does not always lead to famine, drought and famine are often intimately and intricately intertwined in northern Kenya. See Maurice Amutabi, *The NGO Factor in Africa: The Case of Arrested Development in Kenya* (New York/London: 2006), 23–34.

10. Oxfam, *Annual Report,* (Oxford: Oxfam, 2005).

11. Interviews, Saku Mulume, Garbatula Isiolo, Kenya 15 November 2003; Charfarno Issa, NGO Beneficiary 28, Merti, Isiolo, Kenya. 17 October 2003. See also C. Toulmin, "Tracking through Drought: Options for Destocking and Restocking", in I. Scoones (ed.) *Living with Uncertainty: New Directions in Pastoral Development in Africa* (London: Intermediate Technology Publications, 1994).

12. Julia Adan, interview with the author, Isiolo, October 11, 2003.

13. R. Behnke C. Kerven, "Redesigning for Risk: Tracking and Buffering Environmental Variability in Africa's Rangelands," *Natural Resource Perspectives*, No.1, (1994).

14. S.E Nicholson, "The Method of Historical Climate Reconstruction and its Application to Africa," *Journal of African History*, 20, (1979): 31–49.

15. Fred Malwa, interview with the author, Nairobi, August 19, 2003.

16. R. Behnke and C. Kerven, "Redesigning for Risk."

17. Ibid.

18. Salim Falana, interview with the author, Isiolo, October 14, 2003.

19. Chafano Tari, interview with the author, Merti, Kenya, October 28, 2003.

20. James Ngatia, interview with the author, Nairobi, Kenya, August 17, 2003; Agnes Sirwa, interview with the author, Nairobi, August 19, 2003; Salome Yatar, interview with the author, Kalokol, Turkana, Kenya, November 16, 2003.

21. Rehema Hirsi, interview with the author, Merti, Kenya. October 28, 2003.

22. Many ordinary respondents to my interviews around Oxfam projects pointed out the many advantages that they have derived from Oxfam, materially, such as receiving fresh herds. Others pointed out that Oxfam had given them "hope and desire to live".

23. Oxfam, *Annual Report* (Nairobi: Oxfam, 2002).

24. Beatrice Ndeto, interview with the author, Nairobi, August 19, 2003.

25. Tom Mukonambi, interview with the author, Nairobi, November 3 2003.

26. Josephine Ndemo, interview with the author, Isiolo, October 13, 2003.

27. Ibid.

28. KNA/BV/104/43—Oxfam: Katumani Maize Seed Project.

29. R. Behnke and C. Kerven, "Redesigning for Risk."

30. Grace Mchula, interview with the author, Lodwar, Turkana, November 5, 2003.

31. Lekilan Sokuro, interview with the author, Maralal, Samburu. October 28, 2003.

32. Soki Patel, interview with the author, Samburu, Kenya. October 29, 2003.

33. Rose Lewashina, interview with the author, Kisima, Samburu, Turkana. October 29, 2003.

34. Ariaal Fratkin, *Pastoralists of Kenya: Surviving Drought and Development in Africa's Arid Lands* (Boston: Allyn and Bacon, 1998).

35. M. Duffield, "The Emergence of Two-Tier Welfare in Africa: Marginalization or an Opportunity for Reform?" *Public Administration and Development*, 2, (1992): 139–154.

36. M. Duffield, "The Emergence of two-tier Welfare in Africa", 139–154.

37. *Daily Nation* Newspaper (Nairobi), 17 February 2000, 1.

38. M. Duffield, "The Emergence of Two-Tier Welfare in Africa", 147.

39. J. Clark, *For Richer for Poorer: An Oxfam Report on Western Connection with World Hunger* (Oxford: OXFAM, 1986).

40. Sam Nyikal, interview with the author, Nairobi, August 19, 2003.

41. Charles Elliot, "Some Aspects of Relations Between the North and the South in the NGO Sector," *World Development*, 15, supplement (Autumn), 1987, 59.

42. M. Duffield, "The Emergence of two-tier Welfare in Africa", 149.

43. Ariaal Fratkin, *Pastoralists of Kenya,* 23–24.
44. Mercy Lemum, interview with the author, Kalokol, Turkana, Kenya. 15 September 2003.

Chapter 6

1. See Pádraig Carmody, *Globalization in Africa: Recolonization or Renaissance?* (Boulder, CO: Lynne Rienner, 2010); John Mukum Mbaku and Suresh Chandra Sexana, *Africa at the Crossroads: Between Regionalism and Globalization* (Westport, CT: Praeger, 2004); George Kieh, Jr., (ed.), *Africa and the New Globalization* (Hampshire, Burlington: Ashgate, 2008); For studies on globalization and gender, see Mary Johnson Osirim, *Enterprising Women in Urban Zimbabwe: Gender, Microbusiness, and Globalization* (Bloomington and Indianapolis: Indiana University Press); Christopher Chase-Dunn, *Global Formation: Structures of the World Economy* (Lanham, MD: Rowman and Littlefield, 1998); and Valentine Moghadam, *Globalizing Women: Transnational Feminist Networks* (Baltimore: Johns Hopkins University Press, 2005).
2. Martin Meredith, *The Fate of Africa: A History of Fifty Years of Independence* (Cambridge, MA: Public Affairs, 2006).
3. Madam Esther Teboh, Deputy-Mayor Batibo, 2002–2008, Interview by author, December 29, 2010, Batibo, NWP, Cameroon.
4. Mbaku and Sexana, *Africa at the Crossroads*, 102.
5. Kieh, Jr. (ed.), *Africa and the New Globalization*, 34.
6. David Held, Anthony McGrew, David Goldblatt and Jonathan Perraton, *Global Transformations: Politics, Economics and Culture* (Stanford: Stanford University Press, 1999).
7. See, Frederick Cooper, "What is the Concept of Globalization Good For?" *African Affairs* 100: 399 (2001), 189–213. 2001 and Osirim, *Enterprising Women,* 2.
8. See the introduction of, Randall E. Stross, *Technology and Society in Twentieth Century America: An Anthology* (Richard D. Irwin, Inc., 1989), 1–4. See also Manfred B. Steger, *Globalization: A Very Short Introduction* (Oxford: Oxford University Press), 28–29; and Bridget Teboh, "Science, Technology and the African Woman during (British) Colonization: 1916–1960: the Case of Bamenda Province," in Toyin Falola and Emily Brownell, (eds.), *Landscape and Environment in Colonial and Post Colonial Africa* (London and New York: Routledge, 2011).
9. Toyin Falola, *Britain and Nigeria: Exploitation or Development?* (London: Zed Books Press, 1987); See also Vincent B. Khapoya, *The African Experience: An Introduction*, 2nd Edition (Upper Saddle River, NJ.: Prentice Hall, 1998).
10. Bridget Teboh, "Historicizing 'The Moghamo-Bali *ibit* /Conflict: German Encounters with 'Rebellious Vassals,'" in Toyin Falola and Raphael Chijioke Njoku, (eds.), *Wars and Peace in Africa: History, Nationalism and the State* (Durham, NC: Carolina Academic Press, 2010), 143–187.
11. Khapoya, *The African Experience*, 140. See also Crawford Young, *The African Colonial State in Comparative Perspective* (New Haven: Yale University Press, 1994).
12. Khapoya, *The African Experience*, 141; See also, Falola, ed., *Britain and Nigeria*; Steven J. Salm and Toyin Falola (eds.), *African Urban Spaces in Historical Perspective* (New York: University of Rochester Press, 2005) and Frederick Cooper, *Africa Since 1940: the Past of the Present.*

13. A. Mama, "Women's Studies and the Studies of Women in Africa during the 1990s," Working Paper Series 5/96, Dakar, Senegal: CODESRIA, 1996, 28–29.

14. Walker, *Women and Gender*, 13.

15. K. Jayawardena, *The White Woman's 'Other' Burden: Western Women in South Asia during British Rule* (New York: Routledge, 1995); N. Chaudhuri and M. Strobel, eds., *Western Women and Imperialism: Complexity and Resistance* (Bloomington: Indiana University Press,1992); M. Strobel, *European Women and the Second British Empire* (Bloomington: Indiana University Press, 1991); H. Callaway, Gender, *Culture, and Empire: European Women in Colonial Nigeria* (Urbana and Chicago: University of Illinois Press, 1987). See also A. Tripp, "A New Look at Colonial Women British Teachers and Activists in Uganda, 1898–1962," *Canadian Journal of African Studies* 38, no. 1, (2004); N. Boyd, *Emissaries The Overseas Work of the American YWCA 1895–1970* (New York: The Women's Press, 1986).

16. M. Adams, "Colonial Policies and Women's Participation in Public Life: The Case of British Southern Cameroons." *African Studies Quarterly*, 8, no.3 [online] URL: http://web.africa.ufl.edu/asq/v8/v8i3a1.htm. See also, Special Issue on "Indigenous Women and Colonial Cultures," *Journal of Colonialism and Colonial History*, 6, no. 3 (2005); Special Issue on "Revising the Experiences of Colonized Women: Beyond Binaries," *Journal of Women's History*, 14, no. 4 (2003); Special Issue on "Gendered Colonialism and African History," *Gender and History*, 8, no. 3 (1996); and A. Tripp, A. "A New Look at Colonial Women British Teachers and Activists in Uganda, 1898–1962." *Canadian Journal of African Studies* 38, no. 1, (2004).

17. For more on colonial legacies of independent African nations see, Paul Nugent, *Africa Since Independence: A Comparative History* (New York: Palgrave, 2004); See also Cooper, *Africa Since 1940*, (2002); Toyin Falola, (ed.), *Africa*, Vol. 5 (CAP, 2003).

18. Osirim, *Enterprising Women*, 22. For more works on gendered nature of segmentation within globalization, see, Valentine Moghadam, *Gender and Globalization: Female Labor and Women's Mobilization*, Occasional Paper, 11. Normal: Women's Studies Program, Illinois State University, (2000); Valentine Moghadam, "Gender and Globalization: Female labor and Women's mobilizations," *Journal of World Systems Research* 5, no. 2: (1999), 367–88.

19. Joni Seager, *The State of Women in the World Atlas*, New 2nd Edition (New York: Penguin Group, 1997), 62–3.

20. Seager, *Atlas*, 108.

21. These conferences include Mexico 1975, Copenhagen 1980, Nairobi 1985, Beijing 1995, Beijing+5, 2000, etc. For a thorough reading of the nature and increasing interest, number of delegates to, and impact of the UN Conferences worldwide, see Seager, *The Atlas*, 13.

22. Margarita Papandreau, UN spokesperson/Director of Committee for Women, Nairobi, Kenya, July 1985.

23. UN Millennium Declaration and Millennium Development Goals (MDGs), 2000, New York.

24. UN Treaties Office, December 1996.

25. Seager, *The Atlas*, 104; UN, UN Treaties Office, December 1996; See also, *The UN and the Advancement of Women, 1945–1995*, NY: UN, 1995.

26. Seager, *The Atlas*, 104. Tripp, "A New Look at Colonial Women British Teachers and Activists in Uganda, 1898–1962," 153.

27. United Nations 1996, 17.

28. Decree N°97/205 of 07 December 1997 split the former Ministry of Social and Women's Affairs into two full and separate ministries: the Ministry of Social Affairs, and the Ministry of Women's Affairs. When that happened, most people especially women were

hopeful as they thought women's issues could better be addressed, and problems resolved faster by more female headed ministries. They were wrong.

29. For MINCOF's lack of funding and authority see, Melinda Adams, "Appropriating Global Discourses for Domestic Aims: National Machinery for the Advancement of Women." In *Annual Meeting of the American Political Science Association.* 2004a, 12.

30. Sports, especially football (soccer) has always been a better unifying factor in Cameroon where Anglophone and Francophone issues tend to, and continue to create tensions in society.

31. UN Secretary-General Kofi Annan, 2006.

32. Seager, *The Atlas,* 104, especially "Gains and Losses."

33. See UNDP, Human Dev Report, 1995, 1996, NY: OUP, 1995, 1996; also see UNICEF, The progress of Nations 1996, NU: UNICEF, 1996.

34. Maxine Baca Zinn, Pierrette Hondagneu-Sotelo and Micheal A. Messner, eds., *Gender through the Prism of Difference* (Oxford and New York: Oxford University Press, 2005), 4.

35. Catherine Coquery-Vidrovitch, *African Women: A Modern History* (Boulder, CO: Westview Press, 1997), 63.

36. These are very low figures already used by the World Bank in a 2008 study. See, Shaohua Chen and Martin Ravallion, "The Developing World Is Poorer Than We Thought, But No Less Successful in the Fight against Poverty," *Policy Research Working Paper* 4703 (August 2008).

37. Seager, *The Atlas,* 122.

38. *Njanggis* or money-go-rounds are indigenous Cameroonian rotating savings and credit clubs or associations. They are found all over Africa, especially West Africa and known by various local names.

39. For more on reproducing African communities in the United States see, Bridget Teboh, "Reproducing African Communities in the US: Settlement Patterns, Reproduction and Social Organizations," in Emmanuel Yewah and Dimeji Togunde, (eds.), *Across the Atlantic: African Immigrants in the United States Diaspora,* (Champaign, IL: University of Illinois Press, November 2010), 75–93.

40. Graham Jr., Otis L., "Tracing Liberal Woes to '65 Immigration Act," in *Christian Science Monitor,* 88: 23, (1995) 19–23.

41. This act, a product from the struggle of the Civil rights movements, dramatically changed the way immigrants were granted residence and work in the United States because it abolished national-origin quotas. Previously, such quotas had hindered migration from the developing world according to Kutler and Stanley 2003; David 1985.

42. Seager, *The Atlas,* 81.

43. Ibid., 81–2.

44. Bridget Teboh, "African Women's Survival 101: Tontines, *Njanggis,* Money-Go-Rounds as Alternatives to Failed 'Capitalist' Economies," at the SASE Conference on *Capitalism in Crisis: What Next? Economic Regulation and Social Solidarity after the Fall of Finance Capitalism,* Paris, France, July 16–18, 2009.

45. Bridget Teboh, "*Money-Go-Rounds*: Navigating a Hostile Gendered Economic Environment in the Grassfields [Cameroon]. "Gendering African History: In Honor of E.A. Alpers and Christopher Ehret" paper presented at African Studies Association (ASA)'s 50th Annual Meeting, on *21st Century Africa: Evolving Conceptions of Human Rights* at The Sheraton Hotel and Towers, New York, NY, October 18–21, 2007.

46. In Francophone West Africa they are known as *tontines,* and in Ghana and Sierra Leone *Osusu.* Bridget Teboh, 1995, "Women and the *Njanggi* Phenomenon in Cameroon." Paper

presented at the (AAA), African Activist Association, 3rd Annual Young Scholars Conference at UCLA, April 7–8, 1995.

47. Shirley Ardener, 1964.

48. Shirley Ardener and Sandra Burman, eds., *Money-Go-Rounds: The Importance of ROSCAs for Women* (Berg: Oxford/Washington, DC., 1995).

49. Beatrice G., student and single mother, interview by author, July 08, 2008, Boston, USA.

50. Bridget Teboh, "Reproducing African Communities in the US," in Yewah and Togunde, eds. *Across the Atlantic: African Immigrants in the United States Diaspora*, 89.

51. Bridget Teboh, "Women and the Njanggi Phenomenon in Cameroon," Unpublished Paper.

52. Ngwa Bernadetta, Retired teacher, interview by author, July 10, 2008, Boston, MA, USA.

53. Bridget Teboh, "Reproducing African Communities in the US," 75–93.

54. Orozco, 43, cited in E. Yewah and Togunde, "Towards a Fresh Perspective in Understanding African Migration to the United States Diaspora," in Yewah and Togunde (eds.), *Across the Atlantic*, 2–3.

55. E. Yewah and Togunde, "Towards a Fresh Perspective in Understanding African Migration to the United States Diaspora," in Yewah and Togunde (eds.), *Across the Atlantic*, 3.

56. Tripp, A. "A New Look at Colonial Women British Teachers and Activists in Uganda, 1898–1962." *Canadian Journal of African Studies* 38, no. 1, (2004).

57. Yoweri Museveni, recent interview, Kampala, Uganda, 1994.

58. Beatrice Kiraso, newly elected Member of Parliament, Uganda, 1996.

59. Aili Mari Tripp, Isabel Casimiro, Joy Kwesiga, and Alice Mungwa, *African Women's Movements: Changing Political Landscapes* (Cambridge and New York: Cambridge University Press, 2009), 153.

60. See, Margaret Krome of Madison's semimonthly column for *The Capital Times*. E-mail: mkrome@inxpress.net (Published: January 18, 2006).

61. afrol News/Africa Recovery, 10 May.

62. The Inter-Parliamentary Union (IPU) is a Geneva-based organization representing 138 parliaments worldwide. IPU President Anders Johnsson, commenting in 2004 on the Rwandan success story said European Nordic countries had an established history of women's participation in decision-making, but that Rwanda has beaten the long-time leader, Sweden, where women constitute 45 percent of parliamentarians.

63. Executive Director Noeleen Heyzer, UN Development Fund for Women (UNIFEM). UNIFEM participated in post-genocide reconstruction in Rwanda, helping women to prepare for political office.

64. In the US, France and Japan for instance, women hold only slightly more than 10 per cent of parliamentary seats. See Tripp et al, *African Women's Movements*, 2009; Inter-Parliamentary Union (IPU), *Women in Parliament, 1945–1995*; and UNIFEM, Progress of the World's Women 2002 Report.

65. For more on gender quotas see, Aili Mari Tripp and Alice Kang, 2008. "The Global impact of Quotas: On the Fast Track to Increased Female Legislative Representation." *Comparative Political Studies* 41 (3): 338–61.

66. Uganda, Kenya, South Africa, Malawi, Namibia, Senegal, Zambia, Tanzania and Sierra Leone have all embraced the 50-50 campaigns. Only a few countries in Europe, Bulgaria and Slovenia have these 50-50 movements. For more details see, Tripp et al., *African Women's Movements*, 152.

67. Steady, *Women and Collective Action in Africa*, 56.

68. African Union, *Solemn Declaration on Gender Equality in Africa*, 2004. Cited in SOAWR, "Policy Briefing"3.

69. SOAWR, Solidarity for African Women's Rights Coalition, is a coalition of 30 civil society organizations across Africa working to make sure that The Protocol stays on policy-makers' agendas always, and to also urge African leaders to safeguard women's rights through the ratification and implementation of The Protocol. For more details on SOAWR go to www.soawr.org.

70. SOAWR, Policy Briefing, 3.

71. Decision on the African Women's Decade, Assembly/AU/Dec. 229 (XII).

72. These 13 Recommendations are divided into two groups: short-term (2010–2011) and medium-term (2012–2020). Some of them are drawn from the Communiqué of the *"Stakeholders Meeting on Domestication and Implementation of the Protocol to the African Charter on Human and Peoples' Rights on the Rights of Women in Africa,"* 16–18 July 2009, Kigali, Rwanda organized by SOAWR, UNIFEM and the AU Gender Directorate, and the Communiqué of the SOAWR Annual Review and Agenda-Setting Workshop, Theme: *"Spreading Our Wings: A Multi-Sectoral Approach to Women's Rights"* 5–7 October 2009, Panafric Hotel, Nairobi, Kenya.

73. President Obama, Interview with AllAfrica's Charles Cobb, Jr., Reed Kramer and Tami Hultman, Blue Room, the White House, 2008 on the eve of his first visit as US President to Ghana.

Chapter 7

1. Case in point, the 1985 Daima Dam on the Senegalese River, built by the governments of Mauritania, Senegal and Mali, led to the irrigation of 10,000 hectares of desert soil. While a few individuals became millionaires, the dam also brought infectious diseases. The dam prevented the flow of salt water to the area that had checked the snail population, resulting in the spread of schistosomiasis. By 1990, 60 percent of the population in the region showed signs of infection. See R. Robbins, *Global Problems and the Culture of Capitalism* (Boston: Allyn and Bacon, 2002), 235–36.

2. "Food Security in Africa: the impact of Agricultural Development: A hearing before the subcommittee on Africa and Global Health of the committee on foreign affairs House of Representatives," July 18, 2007, submitted by Dr. Hess, 9. While the percentage of persons going hungry decreased, the actual numbers increased from 169 million to 206 million between the years 1990 and 2006. Evidence presented by Dr. Calestous Juma, "Food Security," 35.

3. Kofi Annan, Speech: "The Green Revolution—Africa to Feed itself," May 05, 2010.

4. This was not the case for North Africa, especially Egypt, which was hard hit. J. Abu-Lughod, *Before European Hegemony: The World System AD1250–1350* (Oxford: Oxford University Press, 1991).

5. Eugenia Herbert, "Smallpox inoculation in Africa," *Journal of African History*, vol. 16, 4 (1975), 539–59. While direct connections can be made to "Arab" traders, Herbert contends that it is also possible that knowledge of inoculation could also have been independently innovated in parts of Africa.

6. K. Kipple, *The Cambridge World History of Human Diseases* (Cambridge: Cambridge University Press).

7. Walter Rodney makes the most comprehensive arguments regarding the impact of the slave trade on the over-all impact of African health. W. Rodney, *How Europe Under-*

developed Africa (London: Bogle-L'ouverture, 1972). Lisa Lindsay summarizes Manning's simulation models, that are available at http://www.worldhistorynetwork.org/migrationsim/afrsim/atlanticafr.html. L. Lindsay, *Captives as Commodities* (Upper Saddle River, NJ: Pearson, 2008), 74–75. While other forms of slavery took place in Africa such as domestic slavery and the Red Sea and Indian Ocean slave trade, their impact was different. While in many cases mortality rates were just as high during the transit of slaves, the demographic impact was lessened by the fact that domestic slaves stayed in Africa and thus contributed to production of food, and other slave trades tended to be on a smaller scale and over a longer period.

8. G. Hartwig and D. Patterson, *Disease in African History* (Durham, N.C.: Duke University Press, 1978), 3–21.

9. See G. Waite, "Public Health in Precolonial East-Central Africa," in Feierman and Janzen eds., *Social Basis of Health and Healing* (Berkeley: University of California Press, 1992), 227–31. K. Flint, *Healing Traditions: African Medicine, Cultural Exchange, and Competition in South Africa, 1820–1948* (Athens: Ohio University Press, 2008).

10. G. Prins, "But What Was the Disease? The Present State of Health and Healing in African Studies," *Past and Present,* No. 124 (Aug 1989), 170–71.

11. D. Cordell, J. Gregory, and V. Piche, "The Demographic Reproduction of Health and Disease: Colonial Central African Republic and Contemporary Burkina Faso," in Feierman and Janzen (eds.), *Social Basis of Health and Healing* (Berkeley: University of California Press, 1992), 52–54.

12. See R. Packard's work, *White Plague, Black Labor: The Political Economy of Health and Diseases in South Africa* (Berkeley: University of California Press, 1989). Also look at Mike Davis work on famine, *Late Victorian Holocausts: El Niño Famines and the Making of the Third World* (London, New York: Verso, 2002).

13. "Food Security in Africa: the impact of Agricultural Development: A hearing before the subcommittee on Africa and Global Health of the Committee on Foreign Affairs House of Representatives," July 18, 2007.

14. In the case of Tanzania the British actively promoted the sowing of maize rather than rice as a means to provide food security to the region. C. Fourshey " 'The Remedy for Hunger is Bending the Back:' Maize and British Agricultural Policy in Southwestern Tanzania, 1920–1960," *International Journal of African Historical Studies.* Vol. 41, No. 2 (2008), 93. Cassava replacing sorgum and millet—D. Cordell, J. Gregory, and V. Piche. "Demographic Reproduction of Health and Disease: Colonial Central African Republic and Contemporary Burkina Faso," In Social *Basis of Health and Healing,* 56.

15. For millet and groundnuts see R. Franke and B. Chasin, *Seeds of Famine: Ecological Destruction and the Development Dilemma in the West African Sahel* (Montclair, NJ: LandMark Studies, 1981).

16. For a historical analysis of the 1968–74 Sahel famine in West Africa and the impact of French colonial government on this region see R. Franke and B. Chasin, *Seeds of Famine.*

17. SAPs did radically restructure African economies, yet they failed to lift African nations out of poverty or debt, as intended. Between 1980 and 2000, sub-Saharan African countries paid more than $240 billion in debt service, amounting to four times their debt in 1980. African governments spent more money servicing this debt than on education or health services, both of which were sorely needed for building human capital and combating Africa's major health epidemics. See Demba Moussa Dembele, "The International Monetary Fund and World Bank in Africa: A 'Disastrous' Record," in Vicente Navarro, (ed.), *Neoliberalism, Globalization and Inequalities* (Amityville, NY: Baywood Publishing, 2007), 369–77.

18. The links between poor health and individual and national poverty are outlined by the World Bank and World Health Organization in *Dying for Change? Poor People's experience of Health and Poor Health*. Washington, DC, 2002.

19. See P. Nugent, *Africa Since Independence*, 341.

20. P. Bond and G. Dor, "Uneven Health Outcomes and Political Resistance Under Residual Neoliberalism in Africa," in Vicente Navarro ed., *Neoliberalism, Globalization and Inequalities* (Amityville, NY: Baywood Publishing, 2007), 359. 2001 statistics from New York Times Almanac 2002.

21. D. Grady, "Where Life's Start is a Deadly Risk," *New York Times*. 5/23/09.

22. P. Bond and G. Dor, "Uneven Health Outcomes and Political Resistance Under Residual Neoliberalism in Africa," 354. Compare this to 26 physicians per 10,000 in the US or 23 per 10,000 in the UK (World Health Statistics 2009).

23. Rainer Chr. Hennig "IMF forces African countries to privatise water" http://www.africaaction.org/docs01/wat0103.htm, last accessed July 15, 2009.

24. "Food Security in Africa," 9.

25. D. Bryceson. *Food Insecurity and the Social Division of Labor in Tanzania, 1919-1988.* (London: MacMillan,1990)

26. During the colonial period the British had encouraged the growing of cotton, particularly in the Gezira scheme which was irrigated and serviced by seasonal wage labor. J. O'Brien and E. Gruenbaum, "A Social History of Food, Famine, and Gender in Twentieth Century Sudan," in R.E. Downs, D. Kerner, and S. Reyna eds., *The Political Economy of African Famine* (Amsterdam: Gordon and Breach Science Publishers, 1991), 177-85.

27. Christophe Dongmo, "Green Revolution and Food Self-Sufficiency: Cameroon's Land Theory of Economic Development." CL-Experts : 24.06.2008, (http://www.CamerounLink-Experts.com/docs01/.htm,) [last accessed on December 05, 2010].

28. L. Timberlake, *Africa in Crisis* (Earthscan: Philadelphia, 1986), 71

29. R. Patel. *Stuffed and Starved: The Hidden Battle for the World Food System.* (Brooklyn: Melville House, 2007), 149

30. "Food Security in Africa," 35

31. G. Andrae and B. Beckman; *The Wheat Trap: Bread and Underdevelopment in Nigeria* (London: Zed Books, 2008)

32. D. Wright, *The World and a Very Small Place in Africa* (New York: M. E. Sharpe, 2004), 217-20.

33. O'Brien and Gruenbaum, "A Social History of Food," 183-4.

34. Ibid., 185.

35. Obrien and Gruenbaum, 183-84.

36. Dembele, 372.

37. O'Brien, "Sowing the Seeds of Famine: the political economy of food deficits in Sudan," in *World Recession*, 193.

38. Bond and Dor, 359. R. Patel, 150-151

39. "Food Security in Africa," 22.

40. Compare this to the $50 billion a year it spends on developmental assistance to developing nations. James Wolfensoln, President of World Bank, quoted in the film *The Trade Trap*, Bullfrog Films, 2003.

41. From 2006, "Food Security in Africa," 2.

42. D. Wright, *The World and a Very Small Place in Africa*, 217-18.

43. SODERIM, SODERIM Report, May 1997. In Yagoua, Mbo Plains (Mungo), Nanga Eboko, and Doumé (East), companies likethe Société d'expansion et de Modernisation de la Riziculture de Yagoua (SEMRY), and the Société de Développement de la Riziculture dans la Plaine Mbo expanded rice cultivation.

44. Mark DeLancey, *Historical Dictionary of the Republic of Cameroon,* 232. See also, Mark DeLancey, *Cameroon: Dependence and Independence* (Boulder: Westview Press, 1989).

45. DeLancey, *Historical Dictionary of the Republic of Cameroon*, 6, 221.

46. Ibid., 238.

47. Ibid., 338-39.

48. These were the Regional Colleges of Agriculture (Bamenda, and Ebolowa), Institute of Agricultural Research (IRA-Nkolbisson), National School of Waters and Forests (Mbalmayo), Agricultural Technical Colleges (ETA), Institute for Agricultural Research and Development (IRAD), the Nature Conservation School (Garoua), the Agricultural Science Institute (ITA), Advanced National School of Agronomy (ENSA), and the National Institute for Rural Development (INADER).

49. Dongmo, "Green Revolution," 24.06.2008.

50. These include, the National Fund for Rural Development (FONADER, 1969); National Produce Marketing Board (NPMB, September 1972); Cameroon Chamber of Commerce, Industry and Mine (March 1986); Nkam Development Corporation (SODENKAM); and Hevea Cameroon (HEVECAM), created in Dizangue in 1975 to counter growing rubber prices on the international market.

51. DeLancey, 193.

52. Dongmo, "Green Revolution," 24.06.2008.

53. A. Ahidjo, Anthologies des Discours, 1957-1979, 4 Volumes, Dakar: NEA, 1980.

54. Bridget Teboh, "Reproducing African Communities in the US: Settlement Patterns and Social Organizations," in Emmanuel Yewah and Dimeji Togunde eds., *Across the Atlantic: African Immigrants in the United States Diaspora* (Champaign, Illinois: The University Press/Common Ground, 2010), 79.

55. DeLancey, 191.

56. Institutions such as the West African International Bank Cameroon (BIAOC), Meridien Bank, BIAO-Meridien Bank Cameroon (BMBC), Paribas Cameroon, Societé Camerounaise de Banque (SCB), Cameroon Bank, Cameroun Development Bank (CDB), Bank of Credit and Commerce Cameroon (BCCC), and International Bank for Commerce and Industry Cameroon (BICIC) all filed for bankruptcy.

57. Jacques Doo Bell, "Impunité: Voici les Barons qui ont Pillé nos Banques," *Le Messager*, July 27, 2006.

58. F. Mousseau and A. Mittal, *Sahel: A Prisoner of Starvation*, 21.

59. "Mali: No famine, but a perennial problem of poverty" from IRIN, **humanitarian news and analysis,** a project of the UN Office for the Coordination of Humanitarian Affairs. http://www.irinnews.org/report.aspx?ReportId=55852, [last accessed July 24, 2009].

60. "USDA News Release: International Assistance Announcement for 2007 and 2009" USDA website. Given that 65 percent of food aid is spent on transportation and business costs, and that these costs had increased dramatically in the past years (causing aid delivered in the early 2000s to fall by 52 percent), purchase of local food aid would not only enable an increased amount of food but would presumably help African farmers. Testimony of Mr. Hess, "Food Security in Africa," 22.

61. Oakland Institute is a think tank focused on issues of global food security, has out-

lined the negative implications of such a "Green Revolution."

62. In typical irony, the US shipped $147 million of emergency food relief, but offered only $53 million to help Malawi grow its own food. Celia Dugger, "Ending Famine, Simply by Ignoring the Experts," *New York Times,* 12/2/07. Also see film "A Perfect Famine," 2002 by Television Trust for the Environment.

63. G. Ashton, "Bill Gates' support of GM crops is wrong approach for Africa." *The Seattle Times.* Feb 27, 2012.

64. R. Robbins, *Global Problems and the Culture of Capitalism*, 223-224.

65. *Mail and Guardian*, Sept 2009.

66. Wellings et al, "Sexual Behaviour in Context: a global perspective," *The Lancet*, 11 November 2006, 368, 9548, 1706–28.

67. Of course much of this is related to internal factors, though Mbeki did surf the web for reasons not to believe that HIV contributed to AIDS.

68. H. Bradford, "'Her Body, Her Life': 150 Years of Abortion in South Africa," in Meade, T. and Walker, M. (eds.), *Science, Medicine, and Cultural Imperialism* (New York: Palgrave MacMillan, 1991), 14.

69. For information on this apartheid program see H, Bradford, "'Her Body, Her Life'" and B. Klugman, "The Politics of contraception in South Africa," *Women's Studies International Forum*, Vol. 13, No. 3, (1990), 261–271. H. Rees, "The Abortion Debate in South Africa," *Critical Health,* 34 (June 1991), 20–26.

70. C. Burns raises this same point for the earlier period of fertility control in South Africa in "Sex Lessons from the Past."

Chapter 8

1. James Harf and Mark Lombardi, (ed.), *Taking Sides: Clashing Views on Globalization 5th Edition* (New York, NY: McGraw Hill, 2009), 255–256.

2. Stephen Marglin, "Development as Poison: Rethinking the Western Model of Modernity" in *Annual Editions, Developing World 10/11* (New York, NY: McGraw Hill, 2010), 25.

3. Mary Williams, *Culture Wars: Opposing Viewpoints* (Farmington Hill, MI: Greenhaven Press, 2003), 10.

4. M. Elliot, "The China Century" *Time:* January 11, (2007), 3.

5. Amy Chua, *Day of Empire: How Hyperpowers Rise to Global Dominance and Why They Fall* (New York, NY: Doubleday 2007), 292.

6. Lucian Pye, "Erratic State, Frustrated Society," *Foreign Affairs,* Vol. 69, (1990), 58.

7. Gary Wederspahn, *Intercultural Services: A Worldwide Buyer's Guide and Sourcebook* (Houston, Texas: Gulf Publishing Company, 2000), 5.

8. Robert Kohls, *Survival Kit for Overseas Living: For Americans Planning to Live and Work Abroad, Fourth Edition* (Yarmouth, Main: Intercultural Press, Inc., 2001), 25.

9. Bruce Trigger, *A History of Archaeological Thought, Second Edition* (New York, NY: Cambridge University Press, 2007), 232–23.

10. Edward Tylor, *Primitive Cultures* (London: John Murray, 1871), 1.

11. Iris Marion Young, *Justice and the Politics of Difference* (Princeton, NJ: Princeton University Press, 1990), 86.

12. Seth N. Asumah, "The Nation State and Policy Making in Africa: Reconsidering the

Effects of Structural Variables and Systemic Dynamics," in S.N. Asumah and I. Johnston-Anumonwo, *Issues in Africa and the African Diaspora in the 21st Century* (Binghamton, NY: Global Publications Inc., 2001), 8.

13. Richard Fredland, *Understanding Africa: A Political Economy Perspective* (Chicago: Burnham Press, 2001), 39.

14. Ibid., 41.

15. Kwame Gyekye, *Tradition and Modernity: Philosophical Reflections on the African Experience* (New York, NY: Oxford University Press, 1997), vii.

16. Ibid.

17. Handelman, *The Challenges of Third World Development*, 16.

18. Franz Boas, "Museums of Ethnology and their Classification," *Science*, 9, (1887): 589.

19. M. Spiro, "Cultural Relativism and the Future of Anthropology," *Cultural Anthropology*, 1:3 (1986): 259–286.

20. Marion Levy, "Social Patterns (Structures) and Problems of Modernization," in Wilbert Moore and Robert Cooke (eds.), *Readings on Social Change* (Upper Saddle River, NJ: Prentice Hall, 1967), 207.

21. Handelman, *The Challenges of Third World Development*, 14.

22. T. Friedman, "The World is Ten Years Old: The New Era of Globalization," in C. Kegley, and E. Wittkopf, (eds.), *The Global Agenda: Issues and Perspectives* (New York, NY: McGraw Hill, 2001), 302.

23. D. Held, A. McGrew, D. Goldblatt,. and J. Parraton, "Managing the Challenge of Globalization and Institutionalizing Cooperation Through Global Governance," in C. Kegley, and E. Wittkopf, (eds.), *The Global Agenda: Issues and Perspectives* (New York, NY: McGraw Hill, 2001), 134.

24. Ali Mazrui, "Africans and African Americans in the Changing World Trends: Globalizing the

Black Experience," in Asumah and Johnston-Anumonwo, *Issues in Africa and the African Diaspora in the 21st Century*, 3.

25. William Nester, *International Relations: Politics and Economics in the 21st Century* (Belmont, CA: Wordsworth, 2001), 519.

26. Immanuel Kant, "Essay on Perpetual Peace," in P. Gay, (ed.), *The Enlightenment* (New York: Simon and Schuster, 1974), 790–92.

27. William Nester, *International Relations: Politics and Economics in the 21st Century*, 519.

28. P. Henriot, "Globalization: Implications for Africa," (2001) http://www.sedos.org/english/global.html.

29. S. Booker and W. Minter, "Global Apartheid," *The Nation* (July 9, 2000).

30. Frances Stewart, "Globalization, Liberalization, and Inequality: Real Causes, Expectations, and Experience," (January, 2000), 2. http://www.findarticles.com/cf_0/m1093/1_43/59480145/print.jhtml.

31. Ibid.

32. Ibid.

33. N. Birdsal, "Managing Inequality in the Developing World," in Griffiths, R. (Ed.) *Annual Editions: Developing World. 01, 02* (Guilford, CT: McGraw Hill/Dushkin, 2001) 43.

34. J. Naisbits, *Global Paradox: The Bigger the World Economy, the More Powerful it's Smallest Players* (London: Brealey, 1994), 14.

35. W. Mwangi, "Who Gains and Who Loses from Globalization and Liberalization,"

EcoNews Africa, 5, (January 1996), 1.

36. United Nations Development Program, *Human Development Report Index*, 1999.

37. V. Sundarum, "Impact of Globalization on Indian Culture," *Perspective* www.boloji.com/perspective/233.htm (2006), 1.

38. T. Cowen, "Globalization and Culture," *Policy Forum: Cato Policy Report* (July, 2003), 8.

39. Held et al, "Managing the Challenge of Globalization and Institutionalizing Cooperation Through Global Governance," 143.

40. United Nations, *United Nations Least Developed Countries Report 2009.*

41. Henriot, Globalization: Implications for Africa, 4.

42. Booker and Minter, "Global Apartheid," 15.

Chapter 9

1. See Steven J. Salm, "'Rain or Shine we Gonna' Rock': Dance Subcultures and Identity construction in Accra, Ghana," in Toyin Falola and Christian Jennings (eds.), *Sources and Methods in African History: Spoken, Written, Unearthed* (Rochester: University of Rochester Press, 2003), 361–375 and "The 'Bukom Boys': Subcultures and Identity Transformation in Accra, Ghana," Ph.D. dissertation, University of Texas at Austin (2003), especially chapters 5 and 6.

2. For government-sponsored studies, see M.L., Clarkson, "Children and the Cinema," Accra: Department of Social Welfare (1954); M.L., Clarkson, "Juveniles in Drinking Bars and Night Clubs: A Report on Conditions Observed in Accra, Kumasi and Takoradi," Department of Social Welfare (1955); Department of Social Welfare and Community Development, "Citizens in the Making: A Report on Juvenile Delinquency in the Gold Coast in 1951," in *Report of the Department of Social Welfare and Community Development, 1946–1951* (Accra: Government Printing Dept., 1953), 11–36; Department of Social Welfare and Community Development, "Report on the Enquiry into Begging and Destitution in the Gold Coast, 1954," (Accra: Government Printing Dept., 1955); Department of Social Welfare and Community Development, *Problem Children of the Gold Coast* (Accra: Government Printing Dept., 1955); and Department of Social Welfare and Community Development, "Delinquency Services in Ghana," *Advance*, No. 39, July (1963).

3. Geoffrey Pearson looks at the history of "hooligans," a term used to describe "gangs of rowdy youths," as a subcultural group during the early twentieth century in London. See Geoffrey Pearson, *Hooligans: A History of Respectable Fears* (London: Macmillan, 1983).

4. Richard Wright, *Black Power: A Record of Reactions in a Land of Pathos* (first pub. 1954), (Westport, CT: Greenwood Press, 1974), 70–72.

5. Ibid., 73.

6. Henry Ofori, Twelve Months of Entertainment," in Moses Danquah (ed.) *Ghana: One Year Old* (Accra: Publicity Promotions, 1958), 20.

7. Ioné Acquah, *Accra Survey* (1958) revised (Accra: Ghana Universities Press, 1972), 153–154.

8. The government report noted the complete absence of girls at some shows. See M.L. Clarkson, "A Report on an Enquiry into Cinema Going among Juveniles Undertaken by the Department of Social Welfare and Community Development in Accra and Kumasi," (Accra: Dept. of Social Welfare and Community Development, 1954). Reprinted as "Children and

the Cinema," *Advance*, No. 39, July (1963), 3.

9. Clarkson, "Children and the Cinema," 3.

10. Ibid., 5.

11. On one occasion, children came to Central Accra in special trucks from Lagos Town (later New Town) and Nima to see *Superman* and more than two hundred were unable to gain admission. See Clarkson, "Children and the Cinema," 4–5.

12. Clarkson, "Children and the Cinema," 5. Richard Wright also noted that "it was clear that the African was convinced that movies ought to move." See *Black Power*, 173.

13. Interview with Count Basie, Accra, 29 May 2002. Indian films, however, did become more popular by the 1980s in many parts of English speaking West Africa. See Brian Larkin, "Indian Films and Nigerian Lovers: Media and the Creation of Parallel Modernities," *Africa*, 67, 1 (1997), 406–440.

14. Some of the films listed in the *Daily Graphic* entertainment section on 7 January 1954 included *Son of Ali Baba*, *The Black Castle*, *The Brat*, and *O! What a Girl*. The caption of the latter announcement attracted viewers with the promise that the film contained "plenty of hot music by the best American Negro Bands." The following night, the films shown included *Flying Disc Man from Mars*, episodes 7–12, and *The Lone Rider Crosses the Rio*. See *Daily Graphic*, 7 January (1954), 12, and 8 January 1(954), 12.

15. See the "Entertainment" section in the *Daily Graphic* of May (1956).

16. Aba Hayford, "Development and Democracy in the Mass Media: The Hero in the Media and US—A Search," unpublished paper, IAS Legon (1981). 12. See also, interview with Kwesi Podi, Accra, 1 April 2000.

17. Hortense Powdermaker, *Copper Town, Changing Africa: The Human Situation on the Rhodesian Copperbelt* (New York: 1962), 254. See also Charles Ambler, "Popular Film and Colonial Audiences: the Movies in Northern Rhodesia," *American Historical Review*, 106, 1 (2001), 81–105; and James Burns, "John Wayne on the Zambezi: Cinema, Empire, and the American Western in British Central Africa, *International Journal of African Historical Studies*, 35, 1 (2002), 103–117.

18. James Burns, "John Wayne on the Zambezi," 116.

19. A. Kendrick, "Growing Up to Be a Nation," *New Republic*, 23 April (1956), 15–16.

20. Jean Marie Allman, *The Quills of the Porcupine: Asante Nationalism in an Emergent Ghana* (Madison: University of Wisconsin Press, 1993), 102.

21. Wright, *Black Power*, 172.

22. Quoted in "A *Drum* Enquiry: Should We Knock the Rock?" *Drum* (Ghana ed.), April (1961), 27–28.

23. W.S. Johnson, "Night Life in Christiansborg," *Sunday Mirror*, 1 November (1953), 11.

24. Robert K.A Gardiner, "The Role of Educated Persons in Ghana Society," paper presented as part of the J.B. Danquah Memorial Lecture Series, Accra, February (1970), 7.

25. Wright, *Black Power*, 206.

26. Russell Warren Howe, *Black Star Rising: A Journey through West Africa in Transition* (London: Herbert Jenkins, 1958), 233–234.

27. Augustus Bruce, "Colonial Mentality," *The Ghanaian*, April, 6, 4 (1963), 9 & 27.

28. The zoot suit and its associated cultural expressions have been the subject of numerous studies, and the event that has received the most analysis is the "zoot-suit riots" of 1943, a series of conflicts that took place in Los Angeles, Detroit, and Harlem between zoot suiters and armed servicemen. See Luis Alvarez, "The Power of the Zoot: Race, Community, and Resistance in American Youth Culture, 1940–1945," Ph.D. diss., The University

of Texas at Austin (2001); Robin Kelley, *Race Rebels: Culture, Politics, and the Black Working Class* (New York: Free Press, 1994); and Mauricio Mazón, *The Zoot-Suit Riots: The Psychology of Symbolic Annihilation* (Austin: University of Texas Press, 1984).

29. Alan Jenkins, *The Forties*, (New York: Universe Books, 1977), 103. For more information on the zoot suit in Europe, see Bruce Chibnall, "Whistle and Zoot: The Changing Meaning of a Suit of Clothes," *History Workshop Journal*, 20 (1985), 56–81.

30. See Michael Brake, *Comparative Youth Culture: The Sociology of Youth Subcultures in America, Britain and Canada* (London: Routledge & Kegan Paul, 1985), 58–82; Stuart Hall and Tony Jefferson (eds.), *Resistance Through Rituals: Youth Subcultures in Post-War Britain* (London: Harper Collins Academic, 1976); and Dick Hebdige, *Subcultures: The Meaning of Style* (London: Routledge, 1979).

31. See David Coplan, *In Township Tonight! South Africa's Black City Music and Theatre* (London: Longman, 1986), 162–163. On gangs in 1950s South Africa, see "The Americans," *Drum* (West African ed.), December (1954), 14–16; and "Kort Boy," *Drum* (West African ed.), December (1954), 18, 20. 22. For a 1980s version of the *tsotsis*, see the South African film *Mapantsula* (1988), directed by Oliver Schmitz.

32. For a discussion of popular contemporary pant styles in Ghana, see "Watch Those Pants, Man!" *Drum* (Ghana ed.), September (1962), 46–47.

33. "Hot Showman!" *Drum* (Ghana ed.), No. 78, October (1957), 9.

34. Joe Welshing, "Kill This 'Zoot' Fashion!" *Sunday Mirror*, 24 July (1955), 3.

35. J.A. Rogers, *Pittsburgh Courier*, 26 June (1943). Quoted in Shane White and Graham White, *Stylin': African American Expressive Culture from Its Beginnings to the Zoot Suit* (Ithaca: Cornell University Press, 1998), 260. For another study on dress, behavior, and juvenile delinquency see William Graebner, "The 'Containment' of Juvenile Delinquency: Social Engineering and American Youth Culture in the Postwar Era," *American Studies*, 27, 1 (1986), 81–97.

36. Joe Welshing, "Kill This 'Zoot' Fashion!" *Sunday Mirror*, 24 July (1955), 3.

37. Ibid.

38. Seth Kumah, "Leave the Choice to US," *Sunday Mirror*, 7 August (1955), 3.

39. Bob Bay, "If the 'Zoot' Makes you Sick Don't Look at It," *Sunday Mirror*, 7 August (1955), 53.

40. Stuart Cosgrove, "The Zoot-Suit and Style Warfare," *History Workshop Journal*, 18 (1984), 77–78. For similar views, see James B. Gilbert, *A Cycle of Outrage: America's Reaction to the Juvenile Delinquent in the 1950s* (New York: Oxford University Press, 1986); Celia Lury, *Consumer Culture* (New Brunswick, NJ: Rutgers University Press, 1996), 192–225; and Shane White and Graham White, *Stylin': African American Expressive Culture from Its Beginnings to the Zoot Suit* (Ithaca: Cornell University Press, 1998), 259. In his study of Buffalo, William Graebner questions the use of the term juvenile delinquency because it "implies motivation and subsumes analysis," but, he adds, youth culture "might be best defined as an educated version of 'juvenile delinquency'" because both terms assume that whatever acts or culture they generate are simply a function of being young. See William Graebner, *Coming of Age in Buffalo: Youth and Authority in the Postwar Era* (Philadelphia: Temple University Press, 1990), 127–128.

41. Manuh Takyiwaa, "Diasporas, Unities, and the Marketplace: Tracing Change in Ghanaian Fashion," *Journal of African Studies*, 16, 1 (1988), 17.

42. Acquah, *Accra Survey*, 29. For more on the history of African leisure activities, see Emmanuel Akyeampong and Charles Ambler (eds.), special edition of *The International Journal of African Historical Studies*, 35, 1 (2002); and Paul Tiyambe Zeleza and Cassandra

Rachel Veney (eds.), *Leisure in Urban Africa* (Trenton, NJ: Africa World Press, 2003).

43. King Bruce, quoted in John Collins and Fleming Harrev, *King of the Black Beat* (London: Off the Records Press, 1993), 21.

44. Ibid.

45. Henry Ofori, "Music in the Making: A Very Busy Season," *Daily Graphic*, 5 January (1957), 10.

46. Interview with A.M. Opoku, Accra, 4 April 2000. This story is also mentioned in "Satch wants to be Back," *Sunday Mirror*, 27 October (1963), 1. While in Ghana, a film crew shot footage for a film, *Satchmo the Great*, but it was never released by United Artists. There is, however, an album of the same name. Armstrong traveled through West Africa again in 1961. See Daniel Ofori, "Satchmo in West Africa," *Drum* (Ghana ed.), February (1961), 24–27.

47. "Amon Okoe Discusses Discs," *Sunday Mirror*, 17 January (1960), 2. Accra youth expressed a similar preference for American over British rock 'n' roll in the early 1960s.

48. Quoted in John Collins, *Highlife Time* (Accra: Anansesem Publications, 1994), 18.

49. Amon Okoe, "Amon Okoe Discusses Discs: This Beat Singer is Beaten with an Oldie," *Sunday Mirror*, 9 October (1960), 10.

50. J.O. Panford, "Scrap Band Mania," *Sunday Mirror*, 13 February (1955), 3.

51. See John Collins, "The Ghanaian Concert Party: African Popular Entertainment at the Cross Roads," Ph.D. diss., State University of New York at Buffalo (1994), 342–343.

52. J.H. Nketia, "The Gramophone and Contemporary African Music in the Gold Coast," *Proceedings of the West African Institute of Social and Economic Research, Fourth Annual Conference*, Ibadan (1956), 192.

53. John Collins, "The Young are Reviving Ghana's Music," *West Africa*, 19/26 December (1983), 2943.

54. J.O. Panford, "Scrap Band Mania," *Sunday Mirror*, 13 February (1955), 3.

55. Some of these included: *Shake, Rattle and Rock*, with Fats Domino and Lisa Gaye (1957); *Rock, Rock, Rock*, with Alan Freed, the disc jockey who coined the term "rock 'n' roll" (1958); *Disc Jockey Jamboree*, featuring more than twenty rock 'n' roll artists (1959); and much later, *Twist Around the Clock*, with Chubby Checker (1964). See *Daily Graphic*, 23 August (1957), 12; 3 May (1958), 16; and 7 February (1964), 8.

56. "Rock 'N Roll Comes to Ghana," *Sunday Mirror*, 22 June (1958), 1; "Amon Okoe Discusses Discs: GBS Must let Peter Dig 'Rock' Now," *Sunday Mirror*, 17 January (1960), 2; and "It's Music," *Sunday Mirror*, 23 August (1959), 11.

57. Interview with Count Basie, Accra, 29 May 2002.

58. In Kumasi, youth referred to Charles Asinor, a popular disc jockey on Radio Ghana, as *Akoayi oye tough* (this guy is tough!). A columnist for a popular magazine noted: "The term 'oye tough' is the highest compliment one could enjoy." See "Radio Personalities," *The Ghanaian*, April/May, 5, 4 & 5 (1962), 22.

59. See Charles Ambler, "Popular Films and Colonial Audiences: The Movies in Northern Rhodesia, *American Historical Review*, 106, 1 (2001), 81, 162; and personal correspondence with John Collins, 18 May 2001.

60. Interview with Chris Turner, Accra, 26 April 2000.

61. Interview with Count Basie, Accra, 28 April 2000. See also advertisement for Simpson Book Service, *Drum* (Ghana ed.), August (1963), 35.

62. Kennedy' socks were argyle socks pulled up over the calf. Interview with Frankie Laine, Accra, 29 June 2002. See also, interview with Count Basie, Accra, 29 May 2002.

63. "West Africa Whispers," *Drum* (Ghana ed.), January (1958), 15.

64. Mirror Forum, "Present Types of Fashion: Are They Proper for Ghanaians?" *Sunday Mirror*, 6 October (1963), 12.

65. For a discussion of the cultural contexts of dress and rock 'n' roll, see Peter Wicke, *Rock Music: Culture, Aesthetics and Sociology* (Cambridge: Cambridge University Press, 1987).

66. Elizabeth Fosu, "Some Dos and Don'ts at Dances," *Sunday Mirror*, 16 November (1958), 5.

67. Interview with Chris Turner, Accra, 26 April 2000.

68. Kwame Nkrumah, *Consciencism* (London: Heinemann, 1964), 79.

69. John Storm Roberts, "Introducing African Pop," *Africa Report*, 20, 1, Jan.–Feb. (1975), 42–43. See also Bob W. White, "Modernity's Trickster: 'Dipping' and 'Throwing' in Congolese Popular Dance Music," *Research in African Literatures*, 30, 4 (1999), 156–175.

70. "Is This Crazy?" *Sunday Mirror*, 1 March (1959), 1.

71. Abbey Okai, "Nkrumaism and Africa's Youth," *The Ghanaian*, 7 July, 7 (1964), 35.

72. *Oge* originated from Liberia and was style of percussion music that was popular amongst the Ga during the 1950s, and *kolomashie*, a form of Ga street music or processional music, was created by fishermen. It became popular in the 1940s and was used in the nationalist struggle during the 1950s.

73. Interview with Otoo Lincoln, Accra, 16 November 1999.

74. John Miller Chernoff, "Africa Come Back: The Popular Music of West Africa," in Haydon, Geoffrey and Dennis Marks (eds.), *Repercussions: A Celebration of African-American Music* (London: Century Publishing, 1985), 163–164.

75. Interview with Annie Hayes, Accra, 12 June 2002; and interview with Fuzzy Lee, Accra, 21 May 2000.

76. Interview with Fuzzy Lee, Accra, 21 May 2000.

Chapter 10

1. James T. Campbell, *Middle Passages: African American Journeys to Africa, 1787–2005* (New York: The Penguin Press, 2006).

2. W. E. B. Du Bois, *Dusk of Dawn: An Essay Toward an Autobiography of a Race Concept* (New York: Harcourt Brace and Co., 1940).

3. W. E. B. Du Bois, *The Souls of Black Folk: Essays and Sketches* (1903), New York: Fawcett, 1961), 17.

4. Ronald W. Walters, *Pan Africanism in the African Diaspora: An Analysis of Modern Afrocentric Political Movements* (Detroit: Wayne State University Press, 1993), 385.

5. Maulana Karenga, *The African American Holiday of Kwanzaa: A Celebration of Family, Community, and Culture* (Los Angeles: University of Sankore Press, 1989).

6. On Pan-Africanism, see Adekunle Ajala, *Pan-Africanism: Evolution, Progress and Prospects* (London: Andre Deutsch, 1973); Amiri Baraka, ed., *African Congress: A Documentary of the First Modern Pan-African Congress* (New York: Willaim Morrow, 1972); and P. Olisanwuche, Esedebe, *Pan-Africanism: The Idea and the Movement, 1776–1963* (Washington, D.C.: Howard University Press, 1982).

7. Among others, see Olaudah Equiano, *The Interesting Narrative of Olaudah Equiano, or Gustavus Vasa, the African* (2 vols, London, 1789); Nat Turner, *Confessions of Nat Turner* (Virginia: Southampton Institute, 1831); and Herbert Aptheker, ed., *One Continual Cry: David*

Walker's Appeal, Its Setting and Its Meaning (New York: Published for A.I.M.S. by Humanities Press, 1965).

8. Martin Delany, *The Condition, Elevation, Emigration, and Destiny of the Colored People of the United States.* Originally printed in Philadelphia, by the author, in 1852. A reprint with an Introduction by Toyin Falola was published by Humanity Books (New York) in 2004.

9. See, for instance, Francis Smith Foster, ed., *A Brighter Coming Day: A Frances Ellen Watkins Harper Reader* (New York: The Feminist Press of the City of University of New York, 1990); Anna Julia Cooper, *A Voice from the South, by a Black Woman of the South* (Xenia, OH: Aldine Printing House, 1892); Mildred Thompson, ed., *Ida B. Wells-Barnett: An Exploratory Study of an American Black Woman, 1893–1930* (Brooklyn, NY: Carlson Publishers, 1990).

10. *History of the Negro Race in America* (1883).

11. C. G. Woodson, *The African Background Outlined* (New York: Negro University Press, 1958).

12. Carter G. Woodson, *The Mis-Education of the Negro* (Washington, DC: Associated Publishers, DC, 1933).

13. W.E.B. Du Bois, *The World and Africa* (International Publishers, 1975).

14. Rupert Lewis and Patrick Bryan, eds., *Garvey: His Work and Impact* (Trenton, NJ: Africa World Press, 1991).

15. An analysis of political strategies can be found in John T. McCartney, *Black Power Ideologies: An Essay in African-American Political Thought* (Philadelphia: Temple University Press, 1992); William M. Banks, *Black Intellectuals: Race and Responsibility in American Life* (New York: W. W. Norton & Company, 1996); and Cedric J. Robinson, *Black Movements in America* (New York: Routledge, 1997).

16. See, for instance, George M. Fredrickson, *Black Liberation: A Comparative History of Black Ideologies in the United States and South Africa* (New York: Oxford University Press, 1995); and Kinfe Abraham, *Politics of Black Nationalism: From Harlem to Soweto* (Trenton, NJ: Africa World Press, 1991).

17. See, for instance, Mensah Sarbah, *Fanti National Constitution: A Short Treatise on the Constitution and Government of the Fanti, Ashanti, and Other Akan Tribes of West Africa, Together with an Account of the Discovery of the Gold Coast by Portuguese Navigators, a Short Narration of Early English Voyages, and Study of the Rise of British Gold Coast Jurisdiction by John Mensha Sarbah* (London: William Clowes, 1906); J. Caseley Hayford, *Gold Coast Native Institutions with Thoughts upon a Healthy Policy for the Gold Coast and Ashanti* (London: Frank Cass, 1970).

18. J. A. Horton, *West African Countries and Peoples and A Vindication of the African Race* (London: W. J. Johnson, 1868).

19. Edward Wilmot Blyden, *Christianity, Islam and the Negro Race* (London: W. B. Whittingham, 1887).

20. Samuel Johnson, *The History of the Yorubas* (1897); Carl Reidorf, *A History of the Gold Coast and Asante* (1895); and Appollo Kagwa, *The Kings of Buganda* (1901).

21. Aimé Césaire, "Notes on a Return to the Native Land" in *Collected Poetry* (University of California Press, 1983).

22. Léopold Sédar Senghor, *The Collected Poetry,* translated and with an introduction by Melvin Dixon (Charlottesville: University Press of Virginia, 1991).

23. On the nature of black leadership over time, see, for instance, Vincent B. Thompson, *Africans of the Diaspora: The Evolution of African Consciousness and Leadership in the Americas (From Slavery to the 1920s).* (Trenton, NJ. Africa World Press, 2000); and Harold

Cruse, *The Crisis of the Negro Intellectual: A Historical Analysis of the Failure of Black Leadership* (New York: Quill, 1967).

24. The connections are clear to see in the essays in Herbert Aptheker, *A Documentary History of the Negro People in the United States* (New York: The Citadel Press, 1951).

25. B. Jewsiewicki and D. Newbury, eds., *African Historiographies: What History for Which Africa?* (Beverly Hills, CA: Sage Publications, 1986); and R. Oliver, *In the Realms of Gold: Pioneering in African History* (Madison: University of Wisconsin Press, 1997).

26. Toyin Falola, ed., *Dark Webs: Perspectives on Colonialism in Africa* (Durham: Carolina Academic Press, 2003).

27. Toyin Falola and Christian Jennings, eds., *Africanizing Knowledge: African Studies Across the Disciplines* (co-edited), (New Brunswick and London: Transaction, 2002); and Toyin Falola and Christian Jennings, eds., *Sources and Methods in African History: Spoken, Written, Unearthed* (co-edited) (Rochester, NY: University of Rochester Press, 2002).

28. Toyin Falola, ed., *African Historiography: Essays in Honor of J. F. Ade Ajayi* (London: Longman, 1993).

29. Abdul Alkalamat et al., *Introduction to Afro-American Studies: A People's College Primer* (Chicago, IL.: Peoples College Press, 1986); Russell L. Adams, "Intellectual Questions and Imperatives in the Development of Afro-American Studies," *Journal of Negro Education*, vol. 53. 3 (Summer, 1984): 210–225.

30. Among others, see E. Franklin Frazier, *The Negro in the United States* rev. ed. (New York: Macmillan, 1957).

31. Toyin Falola, *Nationalism and African Intellectuals* (University of Rochester Press, 2001).

32. Nikongo BaNikongo, ed., *Leading Issues in African-American Studies* (Durham, NC: Carolina Academic Press, 1997); and Nathaniel Norment, Jr., ed., *The African American Studies Reader* (Durham, NC: Carolina Academic Press, 2001).

33. John Bracey, August Meier and Elliot Rudwick, eds., *The Black Sociologists: The First Half Century* (Belmont, CA: The Wadsworth Publishing Co., 1971); William E. Cross, Jr., *Shades of Black: Diversity in African-American Identity* (Philadelphia, PA: Temple University Press, 1991).

34. See, for instance, James Turner, ed., *The Next Decade: Theoretical and Research Issues in African Studies* (1984); Earl E. Thorpe, *The Central Theme of Black History* (Westport, CT: Greenwood Press, 1960); and Daniel C. Thompson, *Sociology of the Black Experience* (Westport, CT: Greenwood Press, 1974).

35. Russell L. Adams, "African-American Studies and the State of the Art," in Mario Azevedo, ed., *Africana Studies: A Survey of Africa and the African Diaspora* (Durham, NC: Carolina Academic Press, 1998), 31–49.

36. The list is rather extensive. For its range, see the issues and bibliographies in John Hope Franklin & Alfred A. Moss, Jr., *From Slavery to Freedom: A History of the African Americans*, 7th edition (New York: McGraw-Hill, Inc., 1994); Thomas Holt, *Black Over White: Negro Political Leadership in South Carolina During Reconstruction* (1990); and Peniel E. Joseph, *Waiting 'Til The Midnight Hour: A Narrative History of Black Power in America* (New York: Henry Holt and Co., 2006).

37. Cheikh Anta Diop, *The African Origin of Civilization: Myth or Reality* (Westport, CT.: Lawrence Hill & Co., 1974).

38. The best read work on this is that of the famous Guyanese historian, Walter Rodney, *How Europe Underdeveloped Africa* (Washington DC: Howard University Press, 1972).

39. Cheikh Anta Diop, *The Cultural Unity of Black Africa* (Chicago: Third World Press, 1978).

40. John Mbiti, *African Religions and Philosophy* (London: Heinemann Publishers, 1969).

41. William E. Abraham, *The Mind of Africa* (Chicago: The University of Chicago Press, 1962).

42. Cornel West, *Race Matters* (New York: Vintage, 1994).

43. Molefi Asante, *Kemet, Afrocentricity and Knowledge* (Trenton, NJ: Africa World Press, 1990).

44. Keith B. Richburg, *Out of America: A Black Man Confronts Africa* (New York: Basic Books, 1997).

45. See, for instance, C. James Trotman, ed., *Multiculturalism: Roots and Realities* (Bloomington & Indianapolis, In.: Indiana University Press, 2002).

Index